The Real Deal

The Real Deal

The History and Future of Social Security

Sylvester J. Schieber *&* John B. Shoven

Yale University Press ▾ *New Haven and London*

Designed by Charles Ellertson.
Set in Cycles and Arepo types by Tseng Information Systems.
Printed in the United States of America by Vail-Ballou Press,
Binghamton, New York.

Library of Congress Cataloging-in-Publication Data
Schieber, Sylvester J.
The real deal : the history and future of social security /
Sylvester J. Schieber and John B. Shoven.
p.   cm.
Includes bibliographical references and index.
ISBN 0-300-08148-0 (cloth). — ISBN 0-300-08149-9 (pbk.)
1. Social security—United States—History.   2. Social security—
United States—Finance.   I. Shoven, John B.   II. Title.
HD7125.S328   1999
368.4'3'00973—dc21   99-25243
                                                    CIP

A catalogue record for this book is available from the British Library.

⊛ The paper in this book meets the guidelines for permanence
and durability of the Committee on Production Guidelines
for Book Longevity of the Council on Library Resources.

10   9   8   7   6   5   4   3   2   1

We dedicate this book to

Sean J. Schieber
born February 20, 1976

James B. Shoven
born July 7, 1986

and all the other workers
of the Third Millennium

Contents

Figures

Tables

Acknowledgments

*T*he two of us have worked together on Social Security and retirement issues for roughly twenty years. Ours is one of those magical partnerships where the whole is more than the sum of the parts.

This book would have been impossible for us to develop without the able help and unbelievable commitment of Brian Harrigan, a history teacher at Gonzaga College High School in Washington, D.C. During the summers of 1997 and 1998, he spent untold hours in the National Archives, the historical library and files of the Social Security Administration, and other libraries and research facilities to develop background materials that are essential elements of the story told here.

In his archival work Brian Harrigan was aided by the staff at the National Archives and at the library archives at the University of Wisconsin. Larry DeWitt, the historian at the Social Security Administration, was particularly helpful. He was extremely generous in sharing basic research materials that we used. Tim Kelley at the Social Security Administration was also extremely helpful in providing transcripts of the meetings of the 1994–1996 Advisory Council on Social Security and other transcripts and papers from the earlier history of the program.

Gordon Goodfellow at Watson Wyatt Worldwide helped with many of the technical computations throughout the story presented here. Marjorie Kulash, also of Watson Wyatt Worldwide, helped us organize and present materials in a way that significantly enhanced the story. Clemens Sialm provided research assistance at Stanford. Stephen Goss in the Office of the Actuary of the Social Security Administration indirectly provided significant support through his generous sharing of cost estimates and other information that had been developed on various provisions and proposals for reforming Social Security.

Throughout this volume we quote the work of Martha Derthick, who in the late 1970s wrote a superb, if not the superlative, history of Social Security policy development in America. While we were trying to piece together an extremely important set of facts related to Social Security policy development in the early 1970s, she was willing to dig through her research files to help us.

We want to especially thank the anonymous reviewers who read the draft manuscript and offered us many useful suggestions. Because of the widespread interest in this topic and the reviewers' fascination with the story we have told here, we have come to know some but not all of these reviewers. Several of their names appear in the following list, although not all the people listed here were among the reviewers. We must thank Henry Aaron, Joel Dickson, Martin Feldstein, William Gale, Don Lamm, Tom MaCurdy, Olivia Mitchell, Bob Shiller, Kent Smetters, Spencer Thompson, David Wise, and Steve Zeldes for helpful comments on earlier drafts of this book or on related articles we have written. Spencer Thompson not only gave us lots of ideas to chew on and much feedback on our drafts but also was a generous financial sponsor of our research.

We want especially to thank Nina Droubay at Watson Wyatt Worldwide. For at least ten years now she has provided the coordinating assistance that has allowed us to work together. Over most of this period our shared research has been a secondary element in our respective careers. We could never have accomplished what we have together if Nina had not been able and willing to create order out of our peripatetic lives, hectic schedules, and independent efforts. She has served as scheduler, reader, production coordinator, and director as needed. She is the binding that allows the joining of our efforts.

We must also remark on Yale University Press's commitment to the publication of this volume on an extremely compressed production schedule. We have benefited tremendously from the editorial support of Susan Abel from the Press. The quality of her work significantly enhanced the telling of our story. Rosannah Reeves (NBER) and Susan Farris (Watson Wyatt Worldwide) also helped us control quality while still producing this book at a rapid pace.

Finally, we would like to thank our wives, Vicki Schieber and Katie Shoven, for understanding, or at least tolerating, our obsession with this topic and the book. Without their carrying more than their share of our families' burdens, we could not have written *The Real Deal*.

In Memory of Shannon J. Schieber

Shannon J. Schieber was born on August 8, 1974. She was an extremely bright, outgoing, lovely girl who was the president of the student body during her senior year in high school and president of her freshman class at Duke University. Shannon graduated from Duke in three years with a triple major in economics, mathematics, and philosophy and a 3.6 grade point average. In addition to being an academic superstar, she was the co-captain of the equestrian team while she was at Duke. Shannon worked for two years after graduating from college. She returned to school in the fall of 1997 on a full academic scholarship at the Wharton School, University of Pennsylvania, to pursue a doctorate in finance and insurance. She worked with the Junior Achievement Program, while maintaining her own demanding academic schedule. Early on the morning of May 7, 1998, while she was studying for the last final exam of her first year of graduate school, someone broke into her apartment and murdered her. The day she was killed, a group of inner-city high school seniors in Philadelphia had scheduled a party for her to thank her for teaching them economics on a volunteer, unpaid basis.

Just days before her death, Shannon had written to her father about some research they were going to pursue together during the summer and about her growing interest in the subject of retirement saving and behavior. In her e-mail, she wrote:

> The Pension Research Council Symposiums bring together so many amazing practitioners and academics, and the papers presented uncover and detail so many interesting anomalies and empirical facts. The econometric and statistical methods employed are voluminous. Still, there is something lacking.
>
> Look at the broader world of investing—you find models such as Arbitrage Pricing Theory (Ross) and CAPM (Markowitz, Sharpe, Lintner, Black) that, while beaten down in so many frameworks, keep

popping back up again because they possess this, albeit flawed, wonderfully intuitive ability to explain what's going on. Look at Asset Pricing—the work of Merton in 1973 and Black-Scholes shortly thereafter developed an entirely new branch of finance overnight. Again, many criticize their assumptions and find fault with Black-Scholes' option pricing model, but there is no model which consistently beats it empirically! Similarly, look at the topics of capital structure and the role of debt in Corporate Finance. In 1958, virtually no one understood, relative to today, what was going on when firms made financing decisions, and along come Modigliani-Miller to revolutionize the financial world.

As we have discussed, much of academia, particularly those in academia with a theoretical bent, are off in the clouds looking at problems and creating models which are so far removed from everyday economics as to be virtually meaningless. Of course models are supposed to abstract away from the dirty details of daily transactions so as to explain actions, decisions, preferences, etc., in a broader context, but once you start looking at a single representative agent economy you've lost virtually all of the interesting items in pension issues.

What every single paper in the paragraph before last had in common is this: all were groundbreaking papers in areas that many practitioners thought that they already understood. Every paper forced people to look at common practices in finance in a new light. Each model spawned a flurry of empirical work.

In the area of pensions and retirement savings, we currently have the opposite: many great contributions of an empirical nature which statistically examine patterns of investment but offer little explanation as to why we are seeing these patterns. Obviously there is no one model that will encompass all of these different anomalies, but why aren't more academics looking at these sorts of things? [Douglas] Bernheim has come up with some pretty neat stuff in the way of creative models, but is this something that is too big to tackle? What about Peter Diamond? or Jim Poterba? or Zvi Bodie? Why is it that so many people still have to cite Yaari's 1965 Life-Cycle paper? Have there been no meaningful contributions to this theory since then?

It may be that I am just unaware of what is out there, but I do think that there is a theory waiting to be developed for some of these issues. I would be interested in starting with this shift from Defined Benefit to Defined Contribution plans. I don't know that much about the numbers, but it seems that it should be fairly straightforward to model consumer preferences with regard to these sorts of plans. Is this area a benchmark for changes that will be made in the Social Security system?

To the extent that personal accounts lose the benefit of the government's unique ability to diversify risk intertemporally, what sort of added costs are individuals facing in privatized plans? What sort of assumptions are needed in equilibrium to guarantee that they can expect to be at least as well off and to what extent do these assumptions depend on equity returns?

As you see, I have tons of widely varying questions, and I really ought to get back to my Finance 912 studying. Still . . . I think that there are a lot of exciting things that could be examined in the wonderful world of pensions.

Shannon was studying for her Finance 912 exam when the intruder broke in and murdered her. At her funeral, we decided to write this book in her memory. It is undoubtedly a poor substitute for what her research contributions would have been in the area of retirement research or other economic issues. But it addresses an issue that she was becoming increasingly interested in understanding from the perspective of a young person concerned about the future of her generation and the ones to follow.

The Real Deal

Chapter 1

Social Security: Avoiding
the Downstream Catastrophe

*F*or more than twenty years, the movie *To Fly* has been shown several times each day at the Air and Space Museum of the Smithsonian Institution in Washington, D.C. The beginning of the movie is set in 1876. In an early scene a balloonist is seen floating over a very peaceful river, where he notices a trapper paddling in a canoe. After a bit, from his high perch the balloonist sees some dangerous white water and waterfalls downriver. The balloonist, seeing that the trapper has no inkling of the impending danger, screams down to the trapper that there is white water downriver and he must get to shore for his own safety. In the movie, the trapper paddles safely toward shore. This scene is a good analogy for the nature and scope of the financing problem now facing Social Security.

The Nature and Scope of the
Social Security Financing Problem

During 1998, Social Security collected approximately $52 billion more in tax revenues than it incurred in expenses through the Old-Age and Survivors Insurance and Disability Insurance (OASDI) programs. In addition, it earned an estimated $49 billion in interest on the bonds held in the trust funds. Trust fund balances in the combined programs were approximately $760 billion at the end of 1998.[1] Like the peaceful image of the fellow paddling down the river in *To Fly*, Social Security's current funding flows and trust fund balances might encourage us to be sanguine about the downstream prospects. No other government program here, or indeed in the world, is going to register $100 billion more in total annual revenues than in outgo for the next several years. But there's turbulence downstream.

1

Social Security's actuaries and trustees have been telling us for some time that the OASDI program is significantly underfunded for future generations of retirees. The most recent Trustees' Report suggests that the payroll tax would have to be about 2.19 percentage points higher than it is today to provide promised benefits over the next seventy-five years.[2] But surely, you might think, we can't really believe that a 2 percent problem is such a big deal. If you took 2 percent of the authors' combined accumulated wealth today, you wouldn't be talking about big money. If you took 2 percent of the wealth of Microsoft's Bill Gates, you would be talking about a great deal more. In the case of Social Security's need for added funds, we are talking about 2.19 percent of $140 trillion ($140,000,000,000,000).

What the 2.19 says is that if our Social Security trust funds today held about $3.8 trillion, the current payroll tax of 12.4 percent of covered pay supporting Social Security should be enough to get us through the next seventy-five years of the program's operations as specified in current law. The 12.4 percent includes both the workers' and the employers' side of the payroll tax financing Social Security but does not include the part of the payroll tax supporting Medicare. To understand what the 2.19 means in practical terms, we have to look at how we might adjust current law to bring the system back into balance.

One option, of course, is simply to cut benefits to bring the system back into line. If we cut them immediately, the cut would have to be about 15 percent across the board. That is not only a 15 percent cut in benefits for somebody who is retiring next month or next decade; that is a 15 percent cut for everyone getting benefits today. For the average retiree today getting around $800 per month, that would mean an immediate reduction in benefits to $680. That grandmother or older aunt of yours receiving benefits by herself now that her husband is gone would be more likely to go from around $600 per month to not much more than $500. With the surpluses we are running and $760 billion in the bank, immediate benefit reductions are an unlikely prospect. If we wait to do the fixing until the year 2030—roughly when the actuaries tell us the trust fund will go broke—then we would have to cut benefits by at least 25 percent. To put that in a current context, the average benefit for everybody retired today would drop from $800 to $600 per month. The older widow scraping by on $600 per month would receive only $450. The cuts in benefits that would be required to bring this system back into balance immediately would seem quite austere to the people affected.

Well then, why don't we just raise the payroll tax by 2.19 percentage points? It really can't be that big a deal, can it? To make up what actuaries call the actuarial imbalance through a tax increase would require an

18 percent increase in the cost of Social Security over the next seventy-five years. Such an increase in the tax that has become the largest federal tax for many workers is no trivial matter. If the increase were imposed in 1999, it would amount to $78 billion and it would grow at the compound rate of average wage growth in the future. When we were looking at benefit cuts, we considered putting them off until 2030, and we could do the same for the payroll tax. If we did so, the payroll tax would have to increase by nearly 45 percent just to pay the benefits provided under current law that year. To put that into the current context, an increase in the payroll tax of that magnitude in 1999 would be $195 billion.

President Clinton has been looking into this issue; he sized up the challenge that we are facing fairly succinctly in a speech to Georgetown University students.

> This fiscal crisis in Social Security affects every generation. We now know that the Social Security trust fund is fine for another few decades. But if it gets in trouble and we don't deal with it, then it not only affects the generation of the baby boomers and whether they will have enough to live on when they retire, it raises the question of whether they will have enough to live on by unfairly burdening their children and, therefore, unfairly burdening their children's ability to raise their grandchildren. That would be unconscionable, especially since, if you move now, we can do less and have a bigger impact. . . .
>
> It's very important you understand this. . . . If you don't do anything, one of two things will happen—either it will go broke and you won't ever get it; or if we wait too long to fix it, the burden on society of taking care of our [the baby boom] generation's Social Security obligations will lower your income and lower your ability to take care of your children to a degree most of us who are your parents think would be horribly wrong and unfair to you and unfair to the future prospects of the United States. . . .
>
> Today, we're actually taking in a lot more money from Social Security taxes enacted in 1983 than we're spending out. Because we've run deficits, none of that money has been saved for Social Security. . . .
>
> And if nothing is done by 2029, there will be a deficit in the Social Security trust fund, which will either require—if you just wait until then—a huge tax increase in the payroll tax, or just about a 25 percent cut in Social Security benefits.[3]

There is actually a great deal more to the president's statement than meets the eye. Let's begin with the opening sentence about the "fiscal crisis" now facing Social Security. In immediate terms, Social Security is no more

Table 1.1   Trust Fund Accumulations, Projected Balances,
Depletion Dates, and Unfunded Obligations, by Year of Estimate

Year of estimate	Projected Maximum Trust Fund Balance ($ billions)	Projected Actuarial Balance as Percent of Payroll	Year Trust Fund Projected to Be Depleted	Present Value of Tax Income *plus* Current Fund *Minus* Obligations ($ billions)
1983	$ 20,750	0.02	2063	$ 148.3
1984	18,393	−0.06	2059	37.4
1985	11,955	−0.41	2049	−268.8
1986	12,739	−0.44	2051	−342.6
1987	12,411	−0.62	2051	−377.6
1988	11,838	−0.58	2048	−664.0
1989	11,930	−0.70	2046	−849.5
1990	9,233	−0.91	2045	−1,242.7
1991	8,020	−1.08	2041	−1,185.1
1992	5,535	−1.46	2036	−1,772.6
1993	4,923	−1.46	2036	−1,863.7
1994	2,976	−2.13	2029	−2,841.9
1995	3,275	−2.17	2030	−2,832.7
1996	2,829	−2.19	2029	−3,094.2
1997	2,834	−2.23	2029	−2,922.1
1998	3,777	−2.19	2032	−3,073.3

Sources: Annual Report of the Board of Trustees of the Federal Old-Age and Survivors Insurance and Disability Insurance Trust Funds for 1983 to 1997 (Washington, D.C.: Social Security Administration) and the Office of the Actuary, Social Security Administration.

in "crisis" today than the man in the canoe described earlier. The program's actuaries, however, have warned us several times that there is a significant problem downstream. Not only have they warned us repeatedly of Social Security's actuarial imbalance, but their estimates of the magnitude of the imbalance have consistently worsened over the last fifteen years, as reflected in Table 1.1. By every measure—including projected maximum trust fund balances, year of depletion, and projected underfunding, each subsequent valuation shows a situation worse than the one before.

From the president's perspective, if we don't do something about Social Security soon, we are going to have a much larger problem to deal with than if we do something now. The numbers we set forth earlier give this general statement more specific context. President Clinton clearly states that the prospects of delay come at the risk of significant additional costs.

His assessment that such potential cost increases would be "horribly wrong and unfair" to the youth of our society or those not yet born is one that is shared by many people who have looked carefully at Social Security's financial situation. Not everyone shares that perspective. It is not uncommon to hear some engaged in the debate about Social Security say there is no crisis facing the program today. This is clearly a view not shared by the president. The dichotomy in the two views is one of perspective. The man on the tranquil river in the canoe sees no danger. The man in the balloon high above the river's surface sees potential catastrophe. Those who see no crisis in Social Security are enjoying the perspective of the accumulating trust fund and its balance. Those who foresee crisis are listening to the actuaries who see large financing problems downstream.

The third paragraph in the quotation taken from President Clinton's speech raises another issue that is important to the debate over how to deal with Social Security's financing problems. That is how the money deposited in the trust funds is being used. The point the president alludes to is the accumulation in the trust funds that has occurred since the passage of the 1983 Amendments to the Social Security Act and how those funds have been used. One of the potential results of the 1983 Amendments was to partially prefund the baby boomers' retirement benefits by having the trust funds accumulate substantially larger balances than they have held historically. Since 1983, the OASDI trust funds have grown from virtually zero until they held a balance of $760 billion at the end of 1998. When Social Security collects more money through the payroll tax than it pays out in benefits, it hands over the excess cash to the Treasury Department and is issued special government bonds. These bonds earn interest at the same rate as other long-term bonds issued by the government.

The issue that the president raises is whether the accumulation in the Social Security trust fund since the 1983 Social Security Amendments represents accumulated savings backing future benefits. The point he makes is that the rest of the federal government has run substantial deficits since 1983 and has effectively used the accumulating Social Security trust funds to mask the effects of these deficit operations on the larger economy. What the president is saying is that the accumulation of $760 billion has not been saved but has been used to support other government operations—defense, road programs, farm programs, food stamps, and the like.

After the experience of the ballooning federal debt in conjunction with the trust fund accumulations of the last fifteen years, questions have arisen about the government's ability to convert added payroll tax collections into national savings. The question whether we can really accumulate a substantial pool of financial wealth through a government mechanism like the Social Security trust funds has actually been at the center of policy debate for more than sixty years. But it is central to much of the discussion that will unfold around Social Security policy considerations as we attempt to deal with the financing problems the system now faces.

The estimate that an additional 2.19 percent of future covered payroll would be sufficient to resolve Social Security's current underfunding for the next seventy-five years is based on an underlying assumption that we could increase the payroll tax by that amount today—or rather that we could actually have done so at the beginning of 1998—and could have "saved" the money. If we could save the money and accumulate the returns on it over time, it would lessen the payroll tax burden on future workers or reduce the prospective cuts to future beneficiaries. But our ability actually to save the money is the crucial factor in this strategy. If our current trust fund devices are merely a mechanism to hide other government deficit operations, we may be forced to find alternative ways of saving.

Until now we have been focusing on the estimated underfunding of the system over the seventy-five-year projection period the actuaries use in monitoring Social Security's financing. The problem with this fixed assessment is that the seventy-five-year period used to assess the system will be different next year from the one used this year. We lose the current year in next year's assessment and add a year at the end of the assessment period. The problem arises because we are actually enjoying very good Social Security financing years now but expect future years to be much more costly than current ones. Stephen Goss, the senior Social Security actuary with lead responsibility for the program's long-range cost projections, has estimated that the underfunding of the system is 4.7 percent of covered payroll if we wish to solve the financing problem in perpetuity.[4] This suggests the system is underfunded by $6.6 trillion and that the tax increases or benefit cuts to bring the system back into balance would have to be more than twice those discussed earlier.

Whether we characterize Social Security's current financing prospects as a crisis or not is beside the point. Public policymakers must change Social Security's course in order to assure the retirement security of most of today's workers. In Washington our elected officials have a tendency to focus on downstream issues within the context of two-year election cycles. The problem with this focus is that the serious problems in Social Security's future are not going to reveal themselves clearly as immediate problems for at least another ten to fifteen years. As President Clinton has said, we can wait to deal with this issue, but the potential result would be "horribly wrong and unfair" to our children and "to the future prospects of the United States."

The financial stakes are important, but they are not the only consideration that must guide our resolve to act sooner rather than later. It is important that Congress deal with Social Security's financing imbalance soon, because the program's underfunded status damages the public's perception about the long-term viability of the program. It is said that the majority of workers under age fifty believe they will not get the full benefits now provided by Social Security when they retire. Some people dismiss such reports as an example of the public cynicism that pervades our society today. While most people do not understand the arcane nuances of Social Security financing, many of them do catch the yearly news reports telling of the annual release of the Trustees' Report. The headlines generated last year by the annual Trustees' Report indicated that Social Security would run out of money in 2032. It just so happens that 2032 is within the normal life expectancy of virtually all workers under age fifty today. Is it cynicism on their part to believe that their benefits are not secure when the program's own trustees report that Social Security will run out of money in their lifetimes? More likely, it is simply common sense that leads many people to conclude they cannot expect to receive what Social Security is currently promising them.

The Need for an Informed Electorate

In his State of the Union Address to Congress on January 27, 1998, President Clinton declared that it was time for the nation to begin a dialogue on the "necessary measures to strengthen the Social Security system for the twenty-first century." He went on to say that "all the American people should be invited to join in this discussion, facing these issues squarely, and forming a true consensus on how we should proceed."[5] In his address, the president announced that a series of public policy forums would be held around the country, and then a White House Conference on Social Security would be held in December 1998. He indicated that early in 1999 he would convene the leaders of Congress to craft historic legislation that would re-create "a Social Security system that is strong in the twenty-first century."[6] During the remainder of the year, a number of public policy forums were held around the United States. The White House conference that the president announced at his State of the Union message was held on December 8, 1998.

The fundamental basis for our system of government is individual rights.

Our citizens' rights are the central framework of political dialogue, the entitlements over which we bargain, the collateral of the social contract.[7] As the national discussion about Social Security—the need for change and ways the system might change—unfolds, many claims will be made about individual rights, group rights, social contracts, and the like. There is a considerable mythology surrounding Social Security in this country, and out of this mythology come many people's views about their rights and those of others within the context of the program. The perception of rights arises when people talk about the funding of the program—and the sense that someone has stolen the payroll taxes that we have sent to Washington, or at least misappropriated them. The perception of rights arises when people say, "I've paid for my benefits," with the implication that any adjustment to benefits would be unfair. The perception of rights arises when people say that "they've just changed the program from what it was originally intended to be, and if we just went back to the original plan . . . ," everything would be okay.

Many of the myths surrounding Social Security were created and have been perpetuated by the people who founded and ran the program over the years. Indeed, Franklin Roosevelt insisted that the program was to be financed with a payroll tax so that workers would conclude that they had paid for their benefits and "so no damn politician can ever scrap my social security program."[8] The use of the terminology of insurance and contributions is intended to skirt the perception that people are being "taxed" to finance benefits and to mask the huge welfare payments being made to many participants in the program, even those in the middle and upper classes. The participants have been led from the outset to believe they have only gotten what they paid for from Social Security. It didn't make any difference that Ida May Fuller, the first retiree to be paid Social Security benefits, had paid in an accumulated total of $24.75 in taxes and received a first monthly benefit of $22.54 and a grand total of $22,888.92 in benefits over the course of her retirement.[9] The myth that people are only getting what they have paid for has stuck in the public mind; the practical arithmetic proving that they have gotten enormous unwarranted benefits to the tune of $11.4 trillion has been easily brushed aside.

As with most mythology, when you begin to dig into the preconceptions relating to Social Security, the story turns out to be a good one rather than a true one. But the stakes of Social Security are tremendous and the facts are important. For many older people today, Social Security is their only source of income, or at least their biggest income source by far. While that is probably not the way it should be, it is the fact of life as we approach the end of the twentieth century and the sixty-fifth birthday of the program. Social Security is also the biggest investment that many workers will make in their lives. Often the nature and size of that investment are forgotten when we think about the program, but they should not be.

Few people received as good a deal as Ida May Fuller in relative terms, but the generations of retirees until now have received generous benefits relative to their contributions. But the future is not so bright. There is a growing sense of insecurity about what benefits will be there in the future for young workers. In some regards it is part mythology that they won't, but it is no myth that future beneficiaries cannot expect the good deal that their predecessors received from the program.

Added to the growing concern, on the part of an expanding segment of the workforce, about Social Security's soundness is the increasing awareness that there are other ways to finance retirement security. The prevalence of 401(k) plans and employees' widespread participation in them gives many workers a sense of control of their own destiny that they cannot possibly perceive as money from payroll taxes disappears from their paychecks. When workers get a quarterly statement with their 401(k) balance, they know that the money is theirs and protected by law. When, or if, they get a statement from Social Security, it is a promise of a benefit that Congress has specifically reserved the right to modify at any time it pleases. And there is a lot of discussion in Washington these days about modifying benefits—not in an upward direction, either.

What the Debate Is About

The current discussion about Social Security is in technical terms about how we fund our retirement system. It is about how benefits are earned and how they are provided. There is more than one approach to these matters. For some people, the current way of doing business is the only way. The approach that we took to organizing our Social Security program in 1935 was commonly used in other countries around the world at the time. But times change, and so do the institutions that we create. Certainly no one who has looked seriously at Social Security disputes that our system will be different for our grandchildren than it was for our grandparents. The question is how it will be different.

In other countries around the world, including several with systems much older than our own, people have looked at their social security institutions in recent years and in some cases have changed them significantly. Countries like Australia and Sweden have undertaken social security reforms in the last few years that encompass the kinds of alternatives for "privatization" of Social Security that are being suggested by some policy analysts in the United States. Australia has moved to a system of private mandatory individual accounts as its form of retirement saving and the system has been widely supported by both organized labor and employers. Australian workers' accounts are organized through business and unions in the way our 401(k) system is. Sweden has converted its system to individual accounts as well. While most of the Swedish retirement program is still run by the government, it allows workers to redirect 2.5 percent of their covered payroll to accounts managed by financial brokers.

The most ardent advocates of the existing Social Security system argue with religious fervor in defending current approaches. They often attempt to discredit people who do not share their perception of how to do things, as being motivated by heathen ideas or mercenary intentions. Their sense that decisions related to Social Security are based on higher motivations has been nurtured from the very beginning of the program. Arthur Altmeyer, the first true senior manager of Social Security, described Social Security's training program as one of indoctrination, where they kept new staff, from clerks to senior managers, in training at headquarters for months before they let them go into the field. They did it "so they just had religion. They had it complete." [10] One of his associates, Wilbur Cohen, who had come to Washington as a young man in 1934 to work on the development of the Social Security Act and would spend the remainder of his career as a prominent architect of the program, virtually did make the system his religion. When his mother wrote to him that one of his friends would find work because God is merciful, Cohen wrote back, "There is no God that is not made by man. There is no hope that is not made by man. We must have faith in men that they will so reorganize the social system that all of us can live intelligent, significant lives." [11] This sense of higher mission that permeated the development of Social Security policy from the outset remains part of the culture of the system yet today. Those who believe in it suggest that anyone who wants to go another way intends to abandon community values to pursue individual gain.

We caution you to be wary of the rhetoric around the debate on Social Security reform and the assertions about the motivations of people who suggest significant changes to the system. Keep in mind that the president of the United States, the leader of the political party of Franklin Roosevelt, has said that this program has the potential to be "horribly wrong and unfair" unless it is reformed. When countries like Australia and Sweden adopt social security reforms of the sort they have, it does not mean that the people of those countries have fundamentally abandoned their basic concerns for their fellow citizens.

Here in the United States the debate is about whether we should "fund" our retirement system to a greater extent than we have in the past and, if so, how we would actually go about doing that. The way our system has been organized until now, it uses most of the payroll taxes collected in any one year to pay benefits in that same year. Some people are convinced that that is not an efficient way to organize a retirement system. If we should decide to accumulate larger funds in the future than we have in the past, the question is how we can make sure those funds are actually saved. President Clinton in the remarks quoted earlier asserted the conclusion, already reached by many, that since 1983 the current accumulation in our trust funds has not represented actual savings, because of the massive deficits we ran elsewhere in the federal budget. Some people look at this assertion and a long history of similar developments and conclude that Social Security, as a large government entity, will never be an accumulator of the kind of wealth implied by a decision to fund benefits more heavily than we have in the past. Others, primarily those dedicated to the current benefit financing structure and approach, believe we can. Thus, two sets of proposals are being considered. One set simply would have the government accumulate a larger trust fund and invest it in the stock market. The other would go more in the direction that Australia or Sweden has gone.

The issues that are under discussion are extremely important not only to retirees' income security but to the very fairness and security of our whole society. Some of the policy scenarios that flow out of the debate now getting under way could burden our children and grandchildren with significantly higher taxes, which we would reject out of hand. Some of the alternative scenarios portend benefit cuts that we would judge harsh if we were to consider them for current beneficiaries.

As the options for reforming Social Security are brought to the table, some people want to quell consideration of some of them. This is especially true for those with a "religious" (in the context in which Altmeyer used the term) or ideological rationale for their particular approach to fixing Social Security. It is extremely important that you understand, as you consider alternative approaches, what specific proposals recommend before you pass judgment on them. Some of the Social Security policy discussants label certain proposals radical, in the hope that they will not be considered in the context of the larger debate. While these proposals may be radical from the perspective of people who only want to do things the way we have always done them, they are not at all radical within the context of what is going on in other developed countries around the world. Our admonition here is to focus on content, not code words, as you assess any of the Social Security reform proposals under consideration. The stakes are too high to do otherwise. As we said in the beginning, we are talking about trillions of dollars in the aggregate, but then, that is a concept that most of us cannot really grasp. For most of us, these issues ultimately turn out to be personal. At this level the stakes are also significant.

It's Real Money We're Talking About

Assume for the sake of discussion that a young woman (we will call her Annette) graduated from college in December 1998. Assume that she started work at a starting salary of $30,000 per year in January 1999, just as she turned twenty-two. Assume that over her career, her wages will go up at the rate of inflation plus 1 percent. This rate of increase in wages reflects what Social Security's actuaries think will happen to average wages in the United States over Annette's working lifetime. Assume that Annette works until the age at which she can get full Social Security benefits under current law—that is, age sixty-seven—and then retires. The total amount of her payroll taxes plus those her employer contributed to finance Social Security retirement benefits would be equal to slightly more than $210,000 in 1998 dollars. The value of her lifetime payroll taxes, if she could let them accumulate at a rate of interest 4 percentage points over inflation, would be slightly more than $540,000 in today's dollars. If Annette's wages grew more rapidly than average, so that she reached the maximum level of earnings subject to the payroll tax after working for twenty years and then earned at or above the maximum for the remainder of her career, her contributions plus interest would be worth nearly $1 million. For many Annettes, Janes, Johns, Petes, and so forth, who will begin to work this year, Social Security is likely to be the biggest single investment of their lives. For today's workers, Ida May Fuller's deal is no longer on the table. The Annettes of this world can expect to get back considerably less than the value of their Social Security contributions plus a reasonable rate of interest on them.

How we fix Social Security has important implications for the generations of people now getting benefits, those well along in their careers, those just embarking on a working life, those only now preparing to do so, and those not yet born. Wherever you might be in that spectrum, you should consider those in the other age groups. One way we might rebalance the system would be to reduce benefits significantly for Annette's grandmother who is now widowed and in her seventies, and for Annette's parents, who are in their mid-fifties and hoping to retire in the next five to ten years. Annette's grandmother has little flexibility in how she will deal with the changes to the system, although we should leave open that her benefits might be cut as part of a legislative fix. Annette's parents have somewhat more flexibility—to work a little longer than they planned or to save a bit more over the coming decade than they have been doing, to make up for benefit reductions.

One way we could solve the current Social Security problem is to raise Annette's payroll tax by about 20 percent, bank the extra money to earn interest on it, and, if we are lucky, squeak through. If Annette is your daughter or granddaughter, though, you may wonder whether Annette isn't already committed to paying about enough for her elders' current or future retirement. Annette has her own goals of getting married, raising a family, and leaving them a better world than she herself inherited. At some point, every dollar we take out of Annette's paycheck is a dollar that comes out of her family's budget for food or clothing or out of its education fund. If we are going to ask Annette's generation to put more money into the pot, we'd better make pretty sure that Annette is part of the discussion. We'd also better make sure that we fix the system this time in a way to guarantee that ten or fifteen years down the line we are not back at her door asking her, her husband, and their children for yet more money.

When we passed the major amendments in 1977 fixing Social Security we declared to the American people that we had fixed its financing. Just six years later we were back trying to "save" Social Security once again. After the 1983 Amendments we told the American people we had at least fixed it through virtually all the baby boomers' retirement years. Now we concede that it can't make full payments at the time the last of the baby boomers are first going to be eligible for unreduced benefits. Given all the generations with an interest in not only their own welfare but that of their forebears and descendants, this is a complicated problem. It deserves our careful attention. But the need for care should not be confused for an excuse to delay. As President Clinton makes so clear, moving sooner rather than later is vitally important. It is time to sort out the issues and get on with the changes needed to our retirement system. The remaining pages of this book provide background and context for sorting through the complicated issues in the Social Security reform debate.

What This Book Is About

This book is written to enable you to strip away much of the mythology surrounding Social Security. It is divided into three parts. The first part develops the early history of the program up through 1972. The first chapters in Part 1 tell what the initial architects wanted Social Security to be and what we ended up getting. It tells why the program grew to be so wildly popular with the American public. We believe understanding this history is important because it was during this period that many of the myths about Social Security developed. We also believe that understanding this history is important because we accept the proposition that those who ignore history are inevitably condemned to repeat it. The second part of the story deals with the troubled times since 1972—and tries to explain why the wheels fell off a program that had been perceived as wildly successful. The third part of the story identifies the options for reform that we must now consider and evaluates them and their implications. The discussion includes a proposal of our own.

Part I

Social Security in America:
From Conception to Maturity

Chapter 2

The Context for the Passage
of the Social Security Act in 1935

T he passage of the Social Security Act in 1935 was the culmination of a movement that had been under way in the United States for several decades. This was a movement to adopt a wide-ranging package of federal "social insurance" protections for workers. Our national inclination toward and glorification of rugged individualism made us naturally reluctant to undertake the kind of programs inherent in the Social Security Act. A variety of forces that came together in the 1930s, however, overcame enough of our resistance to such endeavors for us to start an experiment that had been in process elsewhere in the world for decades and within various states of the Union for years.

The Roots of Social Insurance

The "national" social insurance movement started in Germany, which inaugurated sickness and maternity benefits for industrial workers in 1883. In 1884, Germany set up a workers' compensation program. And in 1889, Otto von Bismarck expanded the program to cover invalidity, old-age, and death benefits.[1] In 1911, Germany added survivor benefits to its system. Germany was in the vanguard of this movement for several reasons. One reason for Germany's early sponsorship of social insurance programs was its rapid industrialization during the latter half of the nineteenth century in comparison to other European economies. Another reason is the perception of the role of the state in providing for the general welfare, a perception which is attributed to writings by German philosophers and economists of the period. The final reason is the early development of organized labor in Germany under the auspices of the "socialist" movement.[2] Across Europe, rising cries for socialism were seen as a threat to the established political and economic order. Part of Bismarck's goal in instituting the social insurance programs he sponsored was to stem the tide of socialism.

Once under way, the social insurance movement spread far and wide. By the mid-1930s, Argentina, Australia, Austria, Belgium, Bolivia, Brazil, Bulgaria, Canada, Chile, China, Colombia, Costa Rica, Cuba, Czechoslovakia, Denmark, Ecuador, Estonia, Finland, France, Germany, Great Britain, Greece, Greenland, Hungary, Iceland, India, Ireland, Italy, Japan, Latvia, Lithuania, Luxembourg, Mexico, the Netherlands, Newfoundland, New Zealand, Nicaragua, Norway, Panama, Paraguay, Peru, Poland, Portugal, Romania, Russia, El Salvador, South Africa, Spain, Sweden, Switzerland, Turkey, Uruguay, Venezuela, and Yugoslavia had some form of social insurance programs in operation. While no national program had sprung up in the United States prior to 1935, forty-four states had some form of workers' compensation programs, forty-six provided "pensions" for widowed mothers, and twenty-four had an "old-age pension" system.[3] Pensions in this context were public assistance benefits provided to those who could demonstrate financial hardship.

Our willingness to finally go the route of so many other countries in adopting a national social insurance program in 1935 was the result of three major forces. The first was the increased dependence on wage income that had arisen over the preceding half-century as the country had industrialized. This dependence on wage income made workers and their dependents vulnerable to losing their means of sustenance because of economic downturns, disabling injuries, illness, death of a spouse, and old age. The second force was the terrible economic environment caused by the Great Depression. And the third was a complicated set of political movements raising fundamental questions about economic and political structures we had adopted.

Changing Economic and Social Structures

The economy in the United States during the early part of the nineteenth century was predominantly rural or craft-oriented. In 1880, more than half the labor force was still engaged in the agricultural sector of the economy. By 1910, agricultural employment had declined to 31.4 percent of the labor force. By the mid-1930s, less than one in five workers found employment in agriculture. It was largely the movement of younger workers into urban jobs that accomplished the shift to an industrial economy.[4]

In the pre-industrial economy the primary source of income for most families was a farm or small craft business, either of which tended to be a family-owned and -run operation. Within the typical small business unit, every member of a family was part of the production process. As age, disability, or other problems limited one's abilities, daily tasks could be allocated so that less demanding tasks could be performed by the older family members.

Agricultural employment levels have always been less sensitive to recessions and depressions than nonfarm employment. Growing urbanization of the workforce increased the degree to which employment levels responded to the overall performance of the economy. Through the first three decades of the twentieth century, unemployment rates among nonfarm workers were consistently more than double the rates in the agricultural sector. As nonfarm employment became a larger and larger share of total employment, general unemployment tended to track the volatility of nonfarm unemployment more closely. And volatile it was. In the years from 1905 to 1909, the annual nonfarm unemployment rate ranged from a low of 3.9 percent to high of 16.4 percent. In the period from 1920 to 1924, the range of variation was from 4.1 to 19.5 percent of available workers.[5]

In addition to providing a basis for employment, the business structure of early nineteenth-century America also provided older family members with significant control over the family's financial assets, the largest of which was generally the farm or business itself. Steven Sass points out that throughout the nineteenth century, "the over-65 age cohort controlled more wealth than any other group. They could even command an income after transferring title to their offspring; nineteenth century documents record numerous cases of parents passing property to their children in return for guarantees of financial support."[6] Industrialization changed the status of older workers and limited their opportunities for gradual retirement. The increasing mechanization of production required vigorous and competitive workers. The aged who had held the reins of economic power in the agrarian economy were at a distinct disadvantage in the industrialized world.

Just as the elderly were becoming economically vulnerable to industrialization, their relative numbers in society were expanding steadily. In 1870, just after the Civil War, 3 percent of the total population was over the age of sixty-five. By 1900, the share of the population over this age had grown to 4.1 percent, and by 1930 it was up to 5.4 percent.[7] According to actuarial estimates in 1935, the portion of the population over sixty-five would roughly double, to make up 11.3 percent of the total by 1980.[8] Forty-five years later, this projection proved to be almost precisely correct.

While industrialization posed new threats to older people, large industrial firms were not totally insensitive to the economic problems of the elderly. The history of employer-sponsored retirement plans tells us that these plans originated because employers were concerned about continued employment of "superannuated" workers—that is, older workers who could no longer perform their assigned tasks at a level that justified the wages they were being paid. In the United States, employer-sponsored retirement plans first arose in the rail industry in the 1870s.

During the late nineteenth and early twentieth centuries, the railroads had problems with the continued employment of very old workers for two reasons: concern for public safety and risks to capital stock. The railroads discovered early on that superannuated workers posed a significant risk of accidents. Often rail accidents resulted in the death of passengers and in significant loss of capital stock. Such accidents garnered adverse press coverage, dampened the public's enthusiasm for using the rail services of the company involved, and diminished the efficiency of financial operations.

When the superannuated worker problem arose, the railroads initially reassigned such workers to positions as night watchmen or to other jobs that minimized their risk to the companies' rolling stock and the public safety. Often such reassignments were coupled with a reduction in pay to match the reduced responsibilities of the new position. As the industry matured, however, there were limits to the extent such jobs could absorb the flow of superannuated workers from maturing workforces. Historian William Graebner tells us that by the end of the nineteenth century, the railroads had become "holding institutions" for old workers.[9]

The fundamental reasons that railroads set up the first retirement programs in the late 1800s were directly related to their business and human resource strategies as they dealt with the phenomenon of an aging workforce. During the second decade of the century, retirement benefits were offered by a new range of firms, including employers in the higher education, banking, utility, and insurance industries. About a dozen private pension plans were in operation in 1900; the number grew to about 60 by 1910, 270 by 1920, and 420 by 1930.[10] While the pension system was growing during the early part of the twentieth century, the provision of benefits was limited to only the largest firms. The overwhelming majority of older workers had no hope of ever getting such a benefit from their employer. They were increasingly vulnerable to the volatile job market of the industrial economy in which they worked. Their vulnerability was exacerbated by economic downturns, and the worst of these ever experienced in the United States descended upon them in the early 1930s.

The Economic Environment in the Early 1930s

The stock market crash in 1929 and the depression that set in at the beginning of the 1930s were not unprecedented events in American history. The difference in this case was in the order of magnitude of the economic dislocations that resulted from the Great Depression. These dislocations affected virtually every sector of the economy and every segment of society.

Between 1924 and 1931, the price of wheat paid to farmers dropped from an average of $1.30 to 44 cents per bushel, a drop of two-thirds. Over the same period, the price of cotton dropped from $113 to $29 per bale, a decline of three-fourths.[11] Adding insult to injury, the Dust Bowl across the Great Plains and the boll weevil in the South were devastating to farm yields for these crops. In 1919, total farm sales of crops, cattle, and other produce equaled $16.00 billion. By 1929, total farm sales had dropped to $11.95 billion. In 1932, farm sales were $5.24 billion, down 67 percent from 1919, and 56 percent from 1929.[12] Farm land and buildings lost 28 percent of their value between 1920 and 1930.[13] While both incomes and value of assets were falling, farm mortgages were rising. Between 1910 and 1930, farm mortgages rose from $3.3 billion to $9.2 billion.[14]

In 1930, 1,345 banks holding $864 million in deposits closed their doors. In 1931, another 2,298 banks with deposits of $1,692 million suspended operations. In these two years, the deposits involved in bank closures exceeded by more than $200 million the deposits of all banks that had failed in the preceding twenty-nine years.[15] In the case of savings and loan institutions, 37 had failed between 1921 and 1925, with total losses of $800,000. Between 1926 and 1929, 82 failed, with losses of $2.5 million. In 1931 alone, 159 failed, with losses of $2.3 million, and in 1932, another 190 failed with losses amounting to $24.7 million.[16] The devastation that hit banks and savings institutions was equally hard on other elements of the financial markets.

The market value of all stocks listed on the New York Stock Exchange was $89.7 billion on September 1, 1929. At the end of the year, the market value of these stocks had fallen to $64.7 billion. By the end of 1931, the value of these stocks stood at $26.7 billion. Another six months later, they had fallen to $15.6 billion. In thirty-four months, the stocks on the New York Stock Exchange had lost 83 percent of their value. The value of all bond issues listed on the New York Stock Exchange fell from $49.3 billion at the end of August 1930, to $36.9 billion at the end of May 1932, a drop of 25 percent.[17]

In the labor market, unemployment peaked in 1932 at 25.2 percent of the total workforce. Among the nonfarm workforce, it reached a high of nearly 38 percent. While workers across all segments of the workforce were hit hard by unemployment, the elderly were particularly ravaged. By 1930, 54 percent of the men over age sixty-five were out of work and looking for a job, and another quarter still had jobs but were temporarily laid off without pay.[18] Not only did the Depression eliminate many employment opportunities for older workers, but the stock market crash and rash of failures among financial institutions wiped out the limited resources that many older workers had accumulated. Furthermore, many of those who had pension protection lost it when businesses collapsed during the economic devastation. Andrew Achenbaum reports that "forty-five plans, covering one hundred thousand employees, were discontinued between 1929 and 1932; other plans, lacking an adequate fiscal base, curtailed benefits."[19]

Political Stirrings in the Face of Economic Chaos

The collapse of economic markets during the Great Depression in the United States and elsewhere around the world had led to a fundamental questioning of the capitalist system. British historian Arnold Toynbee commented that 1931 was different from earlier years in "one outstanding feature. In 1931, men and women all over the world were seriously contemplating and frankly discussing the possibility that the Western system of Society might break down and cease to work."[20] This was a time when people did not have to look very far back in history to see what could happen in countries like Russia when the economic and social orders broke down. There was palpable fear that something radical could happen even in countries like the United States unless the economic bloodletting of the Great Depression was somehow stanched.

The economic misery that overtook the country during the Depression was at the center of the political dialogue and national campaigns of 1932. During that campaign, Franklin Roosevelt had coined the phrase "New Deal" during his run for the presidency. Frances Perkins, who served as his secretary of labor, tells us that the phrase was not a specific set of programs meant to deal with the economic chaos that had beset the country and victimized so many people.[21] The New Deal that FDR had campaigned on was a general concept meant to be psychologically soothing to people who were victims of the crashing economic markets. It "was an idea that all the political and practical forces of the community should and could be directed to making life better for ordinary people."[22] It was out of this "idea" that the range of programs, including Social Security, evolved as a set of specific responses to the problems faced by various segments of the public.

Although the "New Deal" that Roosevelt campaigned on was not a set of specific proposals, it was intended to respond to the public perception that traditional economic structures were not operating appropriately. There was a widely held sentiment that wealth in the country had become increasingly concentrated in the hands of a smaller and smaller number of corporations and individuals. Opinion held that the concentration of wealth had led to an overexpansion of industrial capacity, on the one hand, and deficient purchasing power on the part of the general public, on the other. As one pundit wrote, the enemy of prosperity was that "American shoe factories are equipped to turn out almost 900,000,000 pairs of shoes a year. At present, we buy about 300,000,000 pairs. . . . American oil wells are capable of producing 5,950,000 barrels a day, against a market demand of 4,000,000 barrels."[23] Two economics professors looking at the role of capital and labor in the production of goods had found that total capital invested in the economy had quadrupled between 1899 and 1922 and that labor had increased only 61 percent. Output had grown by only 140 percent.[24]

At the extreme, the perceived failure of the capitalist system led some elements to suggest that we should pursue the communist or socialist approaches to government and economic organization that were being adopted elsewhere in the world. A more moderate set of proposals to deal with the overinvestment in excess industrial capacity was to divert "surplus funds" going for such purposes as governmental expenditure programs that would increase the purchasing power of the masses. This could be achieved by taxing high incomes and inheritances and setting up social insurance programs. The taxation of the well-off would keep funds from being invested in useless capital. The distribution of money to those who would spend it on consumption of goods and services would stimulate the demand for these and revive production.[25] The result of expanding production, of course, would be that the unemployed would be called back to jobs. In this fertile environment, a host of proposals arose. At least two of them posed potential problems for FDR as he was figuring out the specifics of what the New Deal was going to be.

In 1934, Francis E. Townsend, a retired California doctor, proposed that every citizen over sixty years of age who was not employed or a felon be entitled to receive $200 per month, on the condition that the recipient spend the benefit within thirty days of its receipt. This proposal was aimed at simultaneously providing for the elderly, who were particularly vulnerable to the Depression's effects, while stimulating the demand for goods and services. The program was to be financed by a 2 percent tax on all transactions.

Townsend organized a whole movement around his plan, and the elderly responded with enthusiasm. As many as twenty-five million people signed petitions in support of the Townsend Plan.[26] For many of the people over age sixty who would be eligible for a benefit, the Townsend Plan held out the prospect of a higher income for not working than they had ever earned in their working lives. To put the generosity into context, the $200 per month promised by the proposal in 1934 would be roughly equivalent to $3,900 per month in 1998 dollars. By comparison, the average monthly benefit for a retired worker receiving Social Security in 1998 was around $800 per month.

The estimated annual cost of the Townsend Plan in 1934 would have been $24 billion if ten million people had taken advantage of it. The total domestic output of the United States that year was $61 billion. Townsend argued that the virtuous circle of added demand resulting from putting this money into the hands of the elderly and requiring that they spend it each month would significantly increase demand for goods and services and thus increase employment. As more people got jobs, they would expand their own consumption, thereby further stimulating both the demand for goods and services and output and employment levels. Most serious analysts at the time did not believe that the heightened demand the plan was expected to spur would expand the economy nearly enough for the 2 percent transactions tax to adequately finance the promised benefits. The popularity of the plan, however, made it impossible to dismiss on the political front. At the same time, its overall generosity and costs made it politically impractical.

As the Townsend proposal was gaining popularity, Senator Huey Long of Louisiana was beginning a run for the presidency. Long had supported Roosevelt during the 1932 Democratic convention, delivering the Louisiana and Mississippi delegates for Roosevelt's nomination. By the middle of 1933, the end of FDR's "first hundred days," Long and Roosevelt had parted company. Roosevelt felt strongly that certain social changes had to be made, but that they should be made peacefully within the system. Long was also committed to change, but he was willing to use other means to achieve it. While governor of Louisiana, Long had used strong-arm tactics to terrorize the legislature, intimidate the courts, and dominate the state bureaucracy so totally that even the lowest level of government employees served only at his pleasure. He had his bodyguards maul hecklers and burn the printing presses of his opponents. He had a tax levied on large-circulation newspapers (which was ultimately overturned by the Supreme Court) because the press in New Orleans had opposed many of his activities. The New Dealers looked at Long as being little different from Hitler or Mussolini. Roosevelt considered him to be one of the most dangerous men in the country.[27]

To advance his own cause and status with the national electorate, Long had written a book, *Every Man a King,* advocating massive redistribution of wealth. Among other things, he proposed offering a free college education to everyone, a homestead worth $5,000 for every family, veterans' bonuses, and old-age pensions for anyone over age sixty with less than $10,000 in cash. To take advantage of the public sense that it was the wealthy who were really to blame for the Depression, Long proposed that the financing of his plan would come from a tax levied on millionaires.

As FDR considered the proposals that were being put on the table, he had two sets of concerns. One had to do with the political issues that he faced. The Depression had created an environment that made social change possible. Political unrest and activist agitation made social change imperative. The popularity of the Townsend and Long plans required some kind of a response. The Townsend Plan was becoming popular enough in some congressional districts that it was the chief political issue and candidates who supported it were getting elected.[28] Huey Long was gaining popularity with his "chicken in every pot" and "soak the rich" campaign, and FDR and his political people were afraid that Long could siphon off 10 percent of the Democratic vote in the 1936 presidential election.[29] They were afraid that this marginal loss of Democratic votes might allow the Republicans to take back the White House.

Roosevelt's other set of concerns centered on the practical public policy issues that providing an old-age retirement program would create. The type of plans Townsend and Long were proposing went against the grain of FDR's own fiscal conservatism. This was not merely a matter of the level of benefits being offered. His more fundamental problem was that both those plans would be financed in a way that would create significant liabilities for the federal government in the future. He felt that it was "dishonest"[30] or "immoral"[31] to set up a program that would create such burdens for future Congresses and presidential administrations to deal with.

Roosevelt concluded that the economic, social, and political dynamics required him to include an old-age retirement proposal as part of his New Deal package. His characterization of what he intended to do addressed the issues being raised by the other would-be policymakers. He said, "I am fighting Communism . . . Townsendism. . . . I want to save our system, the capitalistic system; to save it is to give some heed to world thought of today. I want to equalize the distribution of wealth."[32] Bearing all of this in mind, he set in motion the process for developing a legislative proposal that culminated in the passage of the Social Security Act.

Chapter 3

Developing the Social Security Act of 1935

*T*he Social Security Act was signed into law on August 14, 1935. The programs that have evolved out of this legislation are what many consider the essence of Franklin D. Roosevelt's New Deal. It is this act and succeeding amendments that many people think of when they refer to FDR's creation of the welfare state in the United States and its continuation into the twenty-first century. While many people would suggest Social Security was FDR's crowning achievement in social welfare legislation, the programs we think of as Social Security today are significantly different from what he espoused and signed into law in 1935. To fully understand and appreciate this divergence, one must begin with the evolution of the Social Security Act during the early part of FDR's first term.

The Social Security Act has from its inception comprised a number of titles, each with major provisions defining benefit programs or their financing. The act has included unemployment insurance, means-tested welfare assistance for the elderly and the blind, means-tested welfare assistance for families with dependent children, and "old-age insurance" for workers retiring at sixty-five or older. The story here focuses primarily on the set of programs which pay cash benefits that are generally thought of as Social Security today and are formally known as the Old-Age and Survivors Insurance and Disability Insurance (OASDI) programs. To the extent that other programs included under the umbrella of the Social Security Act are important in discussion of the evolution of the OASDI programs, we will cover them.

Setting the Stage

During 1934, two legislative measures were introduced in Congress that were precursors to the Social Security Act. The first of these, known as the Wagner-Lewis bill, sought to induce the states to enact unemployment insurance programs. This particular proposal had considerable support from the Roosevelt administration. It was drafted by Thomas Eliot, the assistant solicitor for the Department of Labor. Frances Perkins, the secretary of labor, strongly endorsed the bill in hearings before the House Ways and Means Committee. The president also sent a letter to the committee endorsing the measure, but it died without being brought to the full House of Representatives for consideration.[1] The second proposal, known as the Dill-Connery bill, would have authorized the appropriation of $10 billion per year to pay one-third of the costs of old-age assistance provided through state programs for needy elderly people. The Roosevelt administration took no official position on this measure. It passed in the House of Representatives but died in the Senate.[2]

While Congress was considering these measures early in 1934, several interested parties raised concerns with President Roosevelt about particular provisions in the proposals and advocated further study of the issues before Congress moved on such legislation. Also several people were suggesting to FDR that the time was ripe for more comprehensive "social insurance" legislation than these bills individually would achieve. By the late spring of 1934, the president concluded that it was desirable to delay action on both measures, with an eye toward developing comprehensive legislation that would be submitted to Congress in early 1935. On June 8, 1934, President Roosevelt submitted a message to Congress addressing broad security issues. In FDR's words, "People want some safeguard against misfortunes which cannot be wholly eliminated in this man-made world of ours."[3] He said that that safeguard related "to security against the hazards and vicissitudes of life," especially those associated with "unemployment and old age."[4] He indicated that he thought a program of "social insurance" was the way to address these problems and that he was commencing a study to formulate a comprehensive proposal on it to be submitted to Congress in the next year.

On June 29, 1934, the president issued Executive Order No. 6757 creating the cabinet-level Committee on Economic Security and the citizen Advisory Council on Economic Security. The Committee on Economic Security was to study the problems related to the economic security issues raised in his June 8 statement and to make recommendations to the president by

December 1, 1934, regarding proposals to "promote greater economic security."[5] The advisory council was to assist the committee in an advisory role
in carrying out its considerations. The committee was charged with estab-
lishing a technical board comprising qualified representatives from various
governmental agencies and departments and was also charged with appointing an executive director who would be immediately responsible for
developing the necessary studies and investigations to serve as the basis for
the legislative proposals. The executive director had authority to appoint
staff as necessary to carry out the analytical work. The executive director
and staff were to carry on their work under the direction of the technical board.

Concepts and Conflicts

By the time FDR had created the Committee on Economic Security, two
major schools of thought had evolved in the United States on how to approach the design and implementation of such programs in this country.
One of these, labeled the Ohio model, evolved from the work of Issac M.
Rubinow and his student Abraham Epstein. The other, labeled the Wisconsin model, evolved from the work of John Commons and John Andrews.

Rubinow and Epstein had both extensively studied the evolution and development of social insurance programs around the world and had formed
organizations to advocate and encourage the development of such programs in the United States. John Commons was an economics professor at
the University of Wisconsin and John Andrews headed up the American
Association for Labor Legislation (AALL).[6]

Commons and Andrews' thinking on social insurance had evolved over
the years along the lines of a relatively pure insurance model. With this approach, one insures against a specified risk by accumulating a contingency
fund that can be used to cover the expense when the contingency insured
against actually occurs. This underlying approach was at the heart of the design of the Wisconsin unemployment insurance program that was adopted
in 1932. Under this plan the benefits were financed through a state tax accumulated in individual employer accounts subject to specified reserve limits.
Each employer account covered only that employer's workers. So the employer who experienced little or no unemployment would not have to make
contributions once the reserve limit was achieved. Those who experienced
frequent unemployment would have to make constant contributions.

This approach to social insurance was quite individualistic. It was considered "social" insurance because it was mandated by the government and provided protections that would not arise naturally in a free market environment. This approach was thought to discourage unemployment because it penalized employers for laying off workers, in that employers experiencing unemployment claims had to make larger contributions than those who did not. Because benefits were being financed at the individual employer level, cost considerations kept benefit levels low. This latter feature meant that the "adequacy" of benefits under this approach was downplayed.[7]

Rubinow and Epstein dismissed the concept of using social insurance as a preventive tool. In the case of unemployment insurance, they argued that the forces that created unemployment were beyond the control of individual employers. They maintained that the purpose of such a program was to provide "adequate" financial support for the unemployed. In their model, reserves would be pooled, not accumulated at the level of the individual employer. This approach to social insurance called for government subsidy in addition to individual premiums, for two reasons. The first was that such subsidies were necessary to provide "adequate" benefits to meet unemployed workers' needs.[8] The second was that this insurance covered social ills caused by dysfunctions within the economy; these were beyond the control of individuals, and thus the financing of the insurance should not be borne by the covered individuals alone. This approach to social insurance tended to be redistributional in character. It called for all insured to pay premiums at equivalent rates but paid a disproportional share of benefits to those actually experiencing the problem being insured against.

Each approach to social insurance was vigorously supported by its advocates, and the alternative was aggressively criticized by the opposing camp. In the context of developing the Social Security Act, the important distinguishing feature between the approaches was the different redistributional characteristics in the two. The Wisconsin model, following a relatively pure insurance approach, did not favor income redistribution or supplemental governmental financing. This model was characterized by relatively low benefit levels, especially at the outset. The Ohio model, on the other hand, favored social adequacy over principles of individual equity and called for government subsidization. If a retirement system were designed according to these alternative approaches, the system that followed the Ohio model would provide benefits thought to be "socially adequate" more quickly than a system formulated along the lines of the Wisconsin approach.

Developing the Social Security Act

The members of the Committee on Economic Security agreed that Secretary of Labor Frances Perkins, the committee chair, should take the lead in getting the work of the committee under way. In doing so, she relied heavily on her assistant secretary, Arthur Altmeyer. Altmeyer had a doctorate in economics from the University of Wisconsin, where he had been a student of John Commons and associate of Edwin Witte. Witte had played a leading staff role in the development of the Wisconsin unemployment compensation legislation that had been adopted in 1932. On July 24, 1934, Altmeyer called Witte and asked him if he would serve as executive director of the Committee on Economic Security. Witte accepted the position and reported for duty in Washington on July 26.[9] He brought Wilbur Cohen, one of his students, to serve as his assistant. On August 13, the Committee on Economic Security named Altmeyer chairman of the technical board. Thus the leadership of both the committee's staff and the technical board came from the Wisconsin school of social insurance. Witte and Altmeyer were in control of virtually all aspects of proposal development.

Witte's expertise in social insurance had been largely concentrated in the area of unemployment insurance before his appointment as executive director. While he oversaw the work of all of the staff, his own professional contribution on the development of the social security legislation was largely in the unemployment area. Three others were largely responsible for the development of the proposals that would benefit the elderly. Those three were Barbara Armstrong, a professor of economics and law from the University of California at Berkeley, J. Douglas Brown, a professor of economics from Princeton University, and Murray Latimer, the head of the Railroad Retirement Board and a pension expert who had written extensively on the development of the employer-based pension movement in the United States. They were supported by a small group of analysts and actuaries, including a young actuary named Robert J. Myers.

The Players

Perkins and Roosevelt's vision of what Social Security could become was achieved through the work of a set of highly educated and committed people. They were largely of two stripes. Witte and Altmeyer were practical men. Barbara Armstrong and J. Douglas Brown, the chief drafters of the old-age insurance provisions of the act, were academics, students of social insurance, and headstrong theoreticians. The two sets of players had a common goal of devising a significant new body of federal social insurance legislation.

Witte's biographer would write of him that "he could treat limited, immediate problems and subjects incisively and lucidly, but he did not conceptualize in a grand manner." Witte was a social engineer who directed his energies "towards working out the technical details of new legal and institutional structures, rather than in conceiving radical new designs for social order. As he designed institutions, he used blueprints that were compatible with what he understood to be prevailing American political and economic concepts." More a builder than an architect, he played a crucial role. Frances Perkins would say that he "drove a team of wild horses" to develop the Social Security Act in a miraculously short time.[10] When he finished his work on the Committee on Economic Security, he went back to Wisconsin. Witte was often referred to as the Father of Social Security but he saw himself simply as a pragmatist who sought to make the world a better place in which to live.

Arthur Altmeyer came to be known as Mr. Social Security for his shepherding the organization through much of its first two decades of operation. As the chairman of the Social Security Board and then the first Social Security commissioner, Altmeyer saw himself as a behind-the-scenes administrator. For him, the organization took precedence over the individual. He believed that "if you have any desire to be a public character, you're not likely to be interested in administration as such. I think anonymity is desirable so that you don't get the public involved in making decisions based on personality rather than accomplishments. . . . So I have said many times that a successful administrator ought to be about as interesting as spinach—cold spinach at that."[11]

Where Witte and Altmeyer were driven by practical considerations and were willing to accommodate differences of opinion in the interest of making progress, Barbara Armstrong and J. Douglas Brown were headstrong academics, among the "wild horses" that Perkins talked of Witte's having to control during 1935. An air of intellectual superiority or haughtiness seeps through the oral histories left by Armstrong and Brown. Armstrong found the accommodation to practicality particularly disagreeable and was not enamored of those who were willing to engage in it. She referred to Witte as being a "half Witte" and Altmeyer as a "quarter Witte."[12] While Brown was not so harsh, he also made it clear that the "academics" who worked on the Committee on Economic Security were not bound by the practical considerations that concerned Witte and Altmeyer. After the committee's package was submitted to Congress, Armstrong went back to California and resumed her career as a law professor. Brown, who had worked from Princeton on the development of the old-age insurance proposals, stayed there. But he continued to be involved in the development of Social Security policy for many years to come.

Building the Plan

Much of the story about the development of the provisions covering the elderly in the original legislation submitted to Congress comes from the observations of the major players. Edwin Witte kept a detailed diary, posthumously published in book form in 1962, of the course of the legislation.[13] The respective roles of Armstrong, Brown, and Latimer are captured in a set of oral history interviews of prominent people involved in the Social Security program. The interviews were done many years after the work on the original proposal. The consistency in the recollections of the architects of the original retirement plan is remarkable, however, and there are clear indications that all three cited notes and other historical documents in their oral history interviews.

The oral history interviews reveal strong differences of opinion about the specific provisions that were to be included in the retirement legislation. This was less the case for Armstrong, Brown, and Latimer than between the three of them and Witte and Altmeyer. Armstrong is clearly the most outspoken in this regard, and she appears to have had a particularly contentious relationship with Witte regarding the elements of the legislation. She, along with Rubinow and Epstein, were the most prominent researchers and writers in the area of social insurance in the United States. Armstrong had published a study analyzing social insurance programs around the world in 1932,[14] and many of her observations and conclusions about how such programs should be structured aligned her much more closely with the Ohio approach to social insurance than with the Wisconsin model. Philosophically, Armstrong was clearly at odds with both Witte and Altmeyer.

Frances Perkins would later observe that the "university people—teachers and professors" presented an obstacle to getting the legislative package and supporting materials together. She said that she and her colleagues soon discovered that they had assembled a "team of very high-strung people" to do the necessary work. The staff was possessed of "great pride of opinion" and was "quite vocal."[15] Her characterization of the staff was consistent with the oral history observations of Barbara Armstrong and J. Douglas Brown. They both made it quite clear that they considered themselves academics interested in good social policy and not bound by the kinds of practical considerations that Perkins, Altmeyer, and Witte must have been obsessed with in their work on the legislation.

Witte had come to town thinking of a retirement program run at the state level; Armstrong clearly thought that it had to be national. Witte thought about a system that would be financed purely through employer and employee contributions; Armstrong thought it should be subsidized by government contributions. Witte thought the constitutional hurdles to a contributory system might be too great; Armstrong thought such hurdles could be surmounted.

Providing Retirement Income Security for the Elderly

There was relatively universal agreement that the ultimate goal of any program covering the needs of the elderly for income security should include employer and employee contributions. The reason for this consensus across the various schools of thought was that a noncontributory plan would almost certainly include means-testing provisions. Virtually all students of social insurance thought that means tests were demeaning. People who qualified for means-tested benefits were generally considered to be personal failures by the rest of society. The proponents of old-age social insurance saw the problem of inadequate income security in old age as largely the fault of industrialization and economic organization rather than of personal failure. Virtually all social insurance advocates felt strongly that solutions for a systemic economic problem—income insecurity due to age— should not stigmatize those affected. If the benefits provided to the elderly were to be financed by worker contributions, then the benefits would be an earned right with no stigma attached.

While a contributory retirement plan was the ultimate goal of all social insurance advocates, they faced pressing practical issues about how to provide income security for elderly people who were already retired or out of work and whose resources were inadequate. A contributory plan would not help these people because they had no earnings from which to contribute. Thus, it was important to craft a plan that would make some provision for those needy elderly for whom a contributory plan would not work. Under the Ohio model of social insurance, subsidized benefits for early beneficiaries could be financed out of general revenue contributions. Under the Wisconsin approach, that is, in a plan based on traditional insurance principles, such financing would not be available.

In the ultimate legislative recommendations by the Committee on Economic Security, Title I of their proposal would establish a means-tested old-age assistance program operated at the state level but partially financed by federal matches of state expenditures on benefits. Title II of their proposal called for old-age insurance benefits that would be based on wages on which contributions were made. The title actually covering these contributions was separate from that outlining the benefits because there was considerable concern that if the two were combined, the Supreme Court would find the bill unconstitutional, as it had the Railroad Retirement Act that had been passed earlier.

In mid-November 1934, a meeting of outside experts was organized in Washington to discuss the evolution of the analysis and recommendations under the auspices of the Committee on Economic Security. The president addressed the group on November 14 and laid out certain tenets regarding the evolving legislation. He indicated that unemployment insurance would definitely be part of the program. He said that it should be a cooperative federal-state program, with the federal government managing the funds, but that administration of insurance benefits would be carried out by the states. He clearly indicated that the program should encourage employment based on sound insurance principles and avoid the commingling of insurance and relief elements.[16]

In the area of providing security for the elderly, Roosevelt was more equivocal. He noted that in recommending and signing the Old-Age Pension Act while governor of New York, he had expressed the "opinion that full solution" to the old-age income security problem could be achieved only on the basis of "insurance principles. It takes so very much money to provide even a moderate pension for everybody, that when the funds are raised from taxation only a 'means test' must necessarily be made a condition of the grant of pensions."[17] Roosevelt equivocated on whether the initial social insurance legislative proposals would cover the elderly: "I do not know whether this is the time for any Federal legislation on old-age security."[18]

This last statement sent the advocates of provisions for old-age benefits into a rage. Barbara Armstrong was virtually certain that Witte had drafted the president's statement and was setting the stage to exclude old-age insurance provisions from the package of legislative recommendations that was being pulled together. She was convinced that neither Witte nor Altmeyer supported the old-age provisions that she and Brown and Latimer were developing. To bring attention to the matter, she and Brown leaked a copy of the president's statement to the press.[19] A public uproar followed the press coverage. Internally, a certain amount of finger pointing took place about who had put this phraseology into the president's speech. It was clear the president did not much care for the controversy, and he quickly established that he was fully committed to developing a program to cover the elderly and that it would be part of the initial recommendations from the Committee on Economic Security.

Once it was clear that there was a full-blown commitment to social insurance benefits for the elderly, the staff pressed on with the old-age provisions for the legislative package. Roosevelt's November statement that the solution had to be based on "insurance principles" was an indication that he expected the plan to be contributory. Given his earlier position on the potential costs of a government-financed old-age assistance program, it is likely that he also wanted a system that would be self-financing. In the development of the proposal, however, a conflict arose that harked back to the differences in the two schools of thought on social insurance.

The proposal on old-age insurance, as conceived by Armstrong, Brown, and Latimer, called for the initial contributions to be made in 1937. Since it would take some time for earned benefits to become worthwhile, initial benefits would not be payable until 1942. Benefits were to be indirectly based on contributions and linked to covered earnings on which contributions were made. Over time, workers who had made larger contributions by virtue of higher earnings or longer periods of paying taxes would receive higher benefits. Financing a program purely on the basis of contributions based on workers' earnings, however, meant that benefits would be extremely small during the early years of the program. Providing benefits that would be considered "adequate" to meet retirees' income needs would require outside subsidies. The architects of the proposal resolved the conflict through several plan features. Although the proposal was based on the "insurance principles" of paying retirees on the basis of their contributions, the initial proposal called for two forms of benefit subsidization. The first of these provided that workers with low levels of earnings would get somewhat higher benefits relative to their preretirement level of earnings than would workers with high earnings. The second proposed subsidy was to provide higher benefits for retirees in the early years than would be economically warranted purely on the basis of contributions made in their behalf.

The retirement plan put together by the committee's staff envisioned that initially private-sector workers on hourly wage or salary who earned less than $3,000 per year would be covered under the system. This would include about 55 percent of the total workforce at the time. Initial benefits were to only be paid to those who were at least sixty-five in 1942 and who had contributed to the system in each of the five years from 1937 through 1941. In 1942, the number of beneficiaries was expected to be a relatively minuscule portion of the total population over the age of sixty-five. Subsidization of early retirees' benefits under the committee's proposal was to be achieved by tapping the contributions of current workers. The excess contributions were to accumulate in the form of government bonds.

In a commercial retirement plan operated through an insurance company, workers' contributions are accumulated with interest throughout their working lives and then are paid out during their retirement period. If a plan of this sort is to be self-sustaining, subsidies of one group of workers have to come at the expense of benefits to another group. In the case of the proposal developed for the Committee on Economic Security, its architects did not want the subsidization of early retirees' benefits to come at the expense of employees retiring later. Thus, the framers proposed that after the plan matured, starting in the 1960s, the government would make a contribution to make up for the fact that some of the initial contributions to the system were used to subsidize the benefits of early beneficiaries.

By Christmas Eve of 1934, there was general agreement among the members of the Committee on Economic Security on the recommendations to be included in the package to be sent to Congress. Final sign-off on the report and the accompanying legislative recommendations by all the members of the committee was not achieved until mid-January 1935. The report was to be submitted to Congress on January 17, and the press materials announcing the proposal had already been distributed. On the afternoon of January 16, President Roosevelt was reviewing the final package when he discovered a table in the report showing that the old-age insurance program would be running significant deficits after 1965[20] that would require a government contribution sometime later, around 1980.[21] He immediately suspected an error in the report and summoned Secretary Perkins and then Edwin Witte to help sort out the matter. Upon being informed that this was an element of the package as designed, FDR insisted that it had to be changed.

The secretary of Treasury, Henry Morgenthau, Jr., had raised an objection about this very same matter as the members of the committee were deliberating over the final form of the report, but Secretary Perkins had prevailed upon him to sign the report without qualification.[22] Barbara Armstrong was convinced that it was Morgenthau who had brought this matter to Roosevelt's attention,[23] although Perkins suggested that FDR found the issue on his own.[24] Perkins quotes FDR as saying, about the prospect that the old-age insurance program would require government subsidies in the future, "This is the same old dole under another name. It is almost dishonest to build up an accumulated deficit for the Congress of the United States to meet in 1980. We can't do that. We can't sell the United States short in 1980 any more than in 1935."[25] This statement ties in directly and consistently with FDR's feelings at the time he signed the old-age assistance law in New York while serving as governor. At that time he said the full solution to the old-age problem could be achieved only through a program based on "insurance principles." It also follows from his statement to the advisory council the preceding November, when he said that the old-age retirement system had to be based on such principles. Roosevelt clearly envisaged and intended to develop a plan that was contributory and self-supporting.

After this meeting at the White House on the afternoon of January 16, the report was withdrawn from the president. Secretary Perkins set about polling the members of the Committee on Economic Security, and all agreed that the president's wishes on the funding matter were to be addressed.[26] At the president's insistence, the offending table was taken out of the report and the package was modified to indicate that the schedules of tax rates and benefits included were merely one approach to providing old-age benefits that Congress might consider. The report was not filed with the president in final form until the morning of January 17, although it still bore the date of January 15.[27]

The staff members who had worked on the old-age insurance provisions came up with a new set of provisions and cost estimates to go along with it. J. Douglas Brown identifies the projections around the new plan as the "M 9 tabulation" which he translates as Robert Myers' "ninth shot at it."[28] The modified plan and the projected financing suggested that the old-age insurance element of the program would be self-supporting, as Roosevelt clearly intended. His demand that the proposal be modified to comply with his wishes so late in the game is an indication of how strongly he felt about the matter. The modified plan was not introduced until congressional hearings on the package were under way. It was presented by Secretary of Treasury Henry Morgenthau and came to be known as the Morgenthau amendment.

Congressional Deliberations and Passage of the Act

On January 17, 1935, President Roosevelt transmitted the report of the Committee on Economic Security and a message to both the House of Representatives and the Senate recommending legislation on economic security. On January 21 and 22 the House Ways and Means Committee and the Senate Finance Committee, respectively, began hearings on the proposed legislation. Witte's diary indicates that both committees focused on the old-age assistance provisions in the act covered in Title I. In the Ways and Means Committee the old-age insurance provisions in Title II proved to be controversial and were nearly stricken at one point. Ultimately, the Ways and Means Committee completely redrafted the legislation, making several substantive changes to the provisions. The committee also changed the name of the bill from the Economic Security Act to the Social Security Act. The Ways and Means Committee reported out the bill on April 5 and the House began its consideration on April 11. Roughly fifty amendments to the committee bill were offered but none were adopted. On April 19, 1935, the House of Representatives adopted the Social Security Act by a vote of 371 to 33.[29]

The strongest opposition to the legislation arose in the considerations by the Senate Finance Committee. Witte indicates that it was the adroit management of the chairman, Senator Pat Harrison of Mississippi, that salvaged the old-age insurance provisions included in Title II. The most contentious matter in the Finance Committee's deliberations was an amendment sponsored by Senator Bennett Clark from Missouri. This amendment would have exempted employers with pension programs from participation in the old-age insurance program. President Roosevelt and other supporters of the legislation opposed the Clark amendment because of the concern it raised over "adverse selection." The concern was that employers with relatively highly paid workers would opt out of the system. Given the redistributional nature of benefits, this would have left the program holding the most expensive beneficiaries, without the benefit of the contributions from better-off workers. Thus, better-off workers would be able to escape their expected redistributional contributions if the Clark amendment were to pass. In the Finance Committee this amendment was defeated in a tie vote. The legislation was reported out of committee on May 20, without the Clark proposal. On June 19, the full Senate adopted the Clark amendment in a vote of 51 to 32. Then the Senate passed the full bill by a vote of 77 to 6.

As with all measures of this sort, the initial bills adopted by the House and Senate had a number of inconsistencies that had to be reconciled in a conference committee that then submitted its reconciled bill back to both chambers for final passage. The conference committee did not begin deliberations until the end of June. With the exception of the Clark amendment, which had not been included in the House version of the legislation, all the differences between the House and Senate versions were worked out by July 16. Both the Senate and House accepted the changes in this conference report on July 17, but each chamber instructed its conferees to hold firm to their respective positions on the Clark amendment.

The conference committee then undertook to redraft the Clark amendment in a fashion that would be acceptable to both chambers. When it became clear that the task was going to extend beyond the end of the congressional session, the conferees recommended that the Social Security Act be adopted without the Clark amendment, with the understanding that a joint committee would be formed to prepare such legislation for the next session of Congress. The conference report was adopted by the House on August 8 and by the Senate on August 9. Interestingly, the Clark amendment never came back up in the next session of Congress or subsequently.

Names and Games

There is some disagreement over the origins of the name Social Security and its later adaptation. The term clearly did not originate with Franklin Roosevelt. In a speech that Frances Perkins delivered at the Social Security headquarters in Baltimore in 1962, she described the Cabinet-level discussions leading up to the formation of the Committee on Economic Security. She had been advocating the implementation of a social insurance program for some time prior to June 1934, when the committee was formed. When the president finally agreed to move forward on the study of social insurance, Perkins indicates, he intentionally called the study group the Committee on Economic Security because he did not "like the word 'social.' That meant dole." Perkins made it clear that Roosevelt was adamant that he did not "believe in the dole." [30]

Arthur Altmeyer in his later writings would suggest that Simón Bolívar, the South American liberator, may have coined the term equivalent to "social security" in 1819. In a speech at that time he said, "The system of government most perfect is that which produces the greatest amount of happiness possible, the greatest amount of social security, and the greatest amount of political stability." [31]

As a concept, social security was meant to be more encompassing than that of social insurance with its connotations of contributing. Indeed, the Social Security Act with its provisions for Old-Age Assistance (OAA), Aid to Families with Dependent Children (AFDC), and so forth, went well beyond the range of pure "social insurance" as it was thought of at the time.[32] Most authors credit Abraham Epstein with inventing the name. He had founded an organization, the American Association for Old Age Security, in 1927 but had changed its name to the American Association of Social

Security in 1933. The purpose of the organization was to push for the adoption of programs along the lines of his and I. M. Rubinow's philosophies that were behind the Ohio model of social insurance discussed earlier. As part of the organization he sponsored, Epstein also published a magazine under the title *Social Security*.[33] His organization's prominence in the field at the time the Social Security Act was being considered would seem to make him a more likely source for the name.

In the development of the Social Security Act and the analysis behind it, both Rubinow and Epstein were largely left out of the process. Witte makes a case that they were consulted and that they provided input. They had participated in a conference held in New York in October 1934 on the recommendations to be made on old-age security. Epstein had also participated in the national Conference on Economic Security sponsored by the advisory council in November 1934 in Washington. After FDR had objected to the financing provisions in the original committee package submitted to him, Witte and Murray Latimer consulted with Epstein on the matter.[34] However, the consultation occurred after the inclusion in the package of the adjustment to the proposal, intended to remedy the deficit financing problem.

Barbara Armstrong presents a somewhat different picture of the role that Rubinow and Epstein played in the process. She laments that Rubinow was not accorded the respect due his longtime contributions in the field. She and J. Douglas Brown had gone to visit with Rubinow at one juncture in the evolution of their work for the Committee on Economic Security. However, Rubinow was seriously ill at the time (he was to die in 1936), so it is not clear that he could have made a significant contribution in any event. Epstein, on the other hand, was not only able to contribute but also apparently interested in being part of the process. Armstrong observes that Epstein was an extremely difficult man to work with and that his cantankerous nature may have been the motivation for not including him directly on the staff when the legislative package was in the works.[35] At the same time, the prominent role played by Altmeyer and Witte and their association with the Wisconsin model may have been equally important.

Epstein ultimately became extremely critical of the Committee on Economic Security and the package that its members submitted to Congress. His own explanation for his critical view of their work was that they had turned his concept of "social security" on its head. He opposed the adoption of pure contributory "social insurance" of the sort that Bismarck had implemented in Germany, but he wanted a plan that included some provision for governmental contributions. Of course, the old-age insurance plan finally submitted to the Congress was to be self-supporting, with no governmental contribution.

Final Retiree Provisions in the Original Act

The final provisions in the Social Security Act adopted in 1935 called for a schedule of payroll taxes to begin at a rate of 1 percent apiece for both workers and their employers on the first $3,000 of annual earnings. The initial payroll tax rate for workers and their employers was to increase in half-percentage-point increments every three years until it reached 3 percent of covered wages in 1949. The contributory funding was projected to be adequate, so that no added government contribution would be required to finance the old-age insurance benefits. The original act, however, did not provide for tax revenues to go directly into a separate accumulating trust fund to finance the benefits. The architects of the Social Security Act were concerned that if there were a direct link between the taxes financing benefits and the benefits themselves, the law might be found unconstitutional. The plan designers believed that keeping the tax and the benefit provisions completely separate would ensure that the scope of the law fell well within the government's powers to tax incomes and spend the money on federal programs. The original act called for Congress to make an annual appropriation to a trust fund that would finance old-age benefits. It was expected that this appropriation would be equal to annual tax collections plus a fixed interest rate of 3 percent on the accumulating fund.

Hourly wage earners and salaried workers in private businesses were covered under the original Social Security Act, except railroad workers, who were left out because they were to be covered in their own separate federally mandated retirement system. People over the age of sixty-five who quit working would be eligible for benefits. To receive one of the retirement annuities that were slated to commence in 1942, a worker would be required to have had covered earnings for the preceding five years. Workers attaining age sixty-five prior to 1942 would have their contributions returned with interest. Estates of workers who died before receiving an annuity would also benefit from a return of the employee's contributions with interest.

The original act anticipated that workers with low earnings would receive more heavily subsidized benefits than would employees with higher earnings. In addition, it provided that the initial beneficiaries of retirement annuities would receive subsidized benefits. These subsidized early benefits were to be financed through the payroll tax schedule adopted in the law. The tax rates set in the law were projected to be somewhat higher in the long term than the cost of benefits that would be paid to workers once the system had fully matured. In other words, future beneficiaries would receive benefits of slightly lesser value than the contributions in their behalf would warrant in order to meet concerns about the adequacy of benefit levels for initial retirees.

The Signing

President Roosevelt signed the Social Security Act into law on August 14, 1935. His statement at the signing was brief but made a number of extremely important points. He referred to the changing organization of industry over the preceding century and the economic insecurity that it posed for workers. He noted that the historic act that he was signing would help to alleviate that insecurity. But he stated quite definitively that we "can never insure one hundred percent of the population against one hundred percent of the hazards and vicissitudes of life." He was prophetic in his affirmation that the Social Security Act that he was signing that day represented "a cornerstone in a structure which is being built but is by no means complete." Given his fiscally conservative nature and the strong position he had taken on the funding of the *social insurance* provisions in the act, he saw this legislation "as a protection to future Administrations against the necessity of going deeply into debt to furnish relief to the needy." Summarizing these themes, FDR saw the Social Security Act of 1935 as "a law that will take care of human needs and at the same time provide the United States an economic structure of vastly greater soundness." [36]

Chapter 4

Starting Up and Starting Over

*W*hen Franklin Roosevelt signed the Social Security Act into law, there was absolutely no administrative infrastructure to put the old-age insurance program into operation. Between August 1935, and January 1, 1937, mechanisms had to be developed to collect taxes and track the earnings of workers for determination of benefits. The initial estimates suggested that between twenty-five and thirty million workers would be covered in 1937, but there was no record system available for administering the requirements of the law. Computers for processing data and devices for storing it in electronic form had not been invented yet. To complicate matters, Senator Huey Long engaged in a Senate filibuster as the clock wound down to the end of the congressional session, with the result that Congress recessed in the fall of 1935 without appropriating funds for Social Security operations.[1]

The law itself came under immediate scrutiny, criticism, and legal challenge. Everyone knew from the outset that the constitutionality of this sweeping legislation would be tested. The crafters of the legislation were preoccupied with this concern and developed a structure to stand the test, but the earlier fight between FDR and the Supreme Court on New Deal legislation meant that all bets were off on how the court would rule. However, the Committee on Economic Security had input from the highest judicial levels on how to avoid constitutional problems. While the act was being developed, the secretary of labor, Frances Perkins, had attended a tea at the home of Supreme Court Justice Harlan Stone. In response to Justice Stone's question about how things were going, Secretary Perkins indicated that the committee was having a tough time working through the constitutional issues. In response, she said, "He looked around to see if anyone was listening," and cupping his mouth, he confided, "The taxing power, my dear, the taxing power. You can do anything under the taxing power."[2]

In addition to the legal challenge, many people in the policy community were not happy with the character of a retirement plan that followed strict insurance principles. Here the challenges would come from two directions. The liberal advocates of social insurance wanted a program that would provide more generous benefits to more people. The conservative critics of old-age insurance worried about the implications of the funding proposed in the law.

Getting Started

Each of the programs created under the Social Security Act faced several practical problems. The benefits to be provided for workers in the contributory retirement program were to be based on workers' covered earnings. This meant that a system of records for individual earnings had to be created. The board's statisticians estimated that some 26 million records would have to be established initially and that another 2.5 million records would be added each subsequent year during the early stages of the program. Individual identification was going to be a challenge. They expected 294,000 Smiths, 227,000 Johnsons, 165,000 Browns, and so forth, to be included in the initial enrollment. The staff concluded that fingerprinting was the best method of identification. But "unfortunately, the method has for so long been associated with tracing of criminals that there seemed little likelihood of the American people's accepting it as an aid in social security identification."[3] Instead they devised the employee account number system that is still in use today.

While your Social Security identification number may seem a random grouping of numbers to you, its various elements have specific meaning to Social Security. The first three digits in the number, the "area number," indicate the general area of the country in which the account number is assigned. For the most part, each state has a unique set of area numbers. For example, if you applied for your number while in California, the first three digits of your Social Security number will be from 545 to 573. If you received your number in Florida, it would be somewhere between 261 and 267. The next two numbers indicate subareas within the larger general area of assignment. The last four numbers are serial numbers within the group area. The system has the capacity to track up to a billion individual records. A similar set of identifiers was established for employers.[4]

After the system was devised, the next challenge was to assign numbers to covered workers and employers. After considering the U.S. Employment Service and their own fledgling field office operations, the board decided to use the Post Office Department with its 45,000 post offices and 350,000 employees to handle the enrollment. Employer registration forms were mailed to three million employers in mid-November with a return filing deadline of November 21, 1936. On November 24, 1936, the Post Office distributed to all known employers a number of employee application forms based on the number of employees as reported in the employers' own filings. The employees could return their forms through their employer, union, or postman, or by sending it back to any post office. When the employee applications were returned to a local post office, they were forwarded to a "typing center" for processing. The typing center assigned a number to each worker, issued a card to be sent to the worker and a form to set up an individual account in the records office of the Social Security Board. This registration drive, run through the Post Office Department, continued through June 30, 1937, when it was taken over by Social Security. By December 22, 1936, twenty-eight days after the initial distribution of employee applications, the Post Office reported receiving 22 million completed applications. By August 31, 1937, 33.5 million applications had been filed.[5] The enrollment process was accompanied by a significant campaign to raise public awareness. It included brief film clips that were shown before feature movies in theaters, pamphlets and posters directed at workers, and public service radio spots.

After account numbers had been assigned, additional challenges had to be met. These included setting up actual accounts and posting wage records for covered earnings. In this case, consideration was given to a stamp system like that used in Britain and elsewhere. Employers would buy stamps and issue them to workers on the basis of their covered earnings and taxes. Workers would paste the stamps in their earnings record books and periodically send them to Social Security. This option was rejected partly because the system offered too much opportunity for counterfeiting and other abuses. More important, however, was the opposition of the Bureau of Internal Revenue, which did not want to share the responsibility with the Post Office Department for collecting taxes, although the IRS indicated a willingness to turn over sole responsibility to the Social Security Board itself. The Internal Revenue Service took on the task, which is handled in largely the same fashion today as was the system devised and implemented in the 1930s.[6]

Setting up individual accounts, capturing and posting earnings entries, and providing information about the earnings record as needed for determining benefits were problems that no one had faced before. The magnitude of the task was a significant impetus to the development of electronic record keeping. The initial system for maintaining records relied on data being captured on Hollerith punch cards that were sorted, duplicated, tabulated and summarized, and printed as needed in administering the program. Computers would not be invented for another ten years and electronic data storage for another twenty. Retrospectively, it is amazing that a system of this sort could be put in place in such a remarkably short period of time.

In his memoir, Altmeyer acknowledges that not everything went flawlessly. The senior officials in the Bureau of Old-Age Benefits did not work well together in the initial stages because the board could not come to a consensus on selection of a person to run the bureau.[7] In the longer term, however, Altmeyer attributed the successful operation of the program to three factors: the way the operation was staffed, the training program developed for staff, and the research program that was implemented.

There was a great deal of pressure to use the staff openings of this new national program as an opportunity for patronage. Unemployment rates were still extremely high. The system would require thousands of new employees, located all across the country. In the midst of hard times, the potential security and value of a government job brought a flood of applicants willing to use whatever connection they could to land gainful employment. Despite the pressure, the board resisted hiring through patronage and sought to staff operations on the basis of ability and in accordance with Civil Service guidelines. They hired experienced professional people to fill the senior positions.[8]

The training program went beyond developing workers' skills for their particular positions in the organization. It also provided basic orientation on the historical evolution of the program and the economic and social issues that had warranted the passage of the enabling legislation. In conjunction with hiring, the training program was intended to "imbue" the employees with their "affirmative responsibility" in carrying out the provisions of the Social Security Act.[9] Over the years, historians and other observers of the Social Security Administration have often commented on the enthusiasm bordering on religious zeal that has permeated the organization. Undoubtedly, the commitment shown to the program by its staff is linked at least in part to the training indoctrination.

The Social Security Act also specified that the Social Security Board should conduct research related to the legislation. Shortly, the research unit set up by the board had the largest technical staff of any federal agency carrying on economic and social research. The staff studied the need for social insurance, the most effective means of providing it, and the policy matters related to its administration. Operational research could be carried out on some of the richest and most extensive data on workers and retirees that could ever be assembled. This research program often put the program and its administrators in a superior position to advocate program expansions and defend its operations. It was not uncommon for members of the research staff to be loaned or "detailed" to congressional committees at work on new proposals under the umbrella of the Social Security Act.

Resolving the Question of Constitutionality

In setting up the Railroad Retirement Act, Congress had established a service-based pension system for all railroads subject to the Interstate Commerce Act. It created a pension fund within the Treasury Department to pay benefits. It mandated contributions by the railroads and their workers with the employers contributing at twice the rate of the workers. It granted retroactive service credits to existing and future employees and to anyone who had been employed within one year of the date of the act's passage. For workers re-employed after the passage of the act, it granted service credits for prior railroad employment. If a railroad hired a worker who had previously been employed by another railroad, the worker was granted retroactive service credits charged to the new employer on the basis of the earlier service. In May 1935 the Supreme Court found the Railroad Retirement Act unconstitutional because it violated the due-process clause of the Fifth Amendment by "taking the property of one and giving it to another." In addition, they found that the act was unconstitutional because it did not "effect a regulation of interstate commerce within the meaning of the Constitution." [10] The Railroad Retirement Act was modified and enacted again later in a form that resolved the matters the court had found objectionable in its 1935 consideration of the program.

The Supreme Court was considering the original Railroad Retirement Act as the Committee on Economic Security was deliberating over the programs that would become the Social Security Act. In the case of the Old-Age Benefits program, the drafters were convinced that the financing of the plan could be justified under the taxing powers of Congress if the tax rates and levels were segregated from the benefits to be provided. The benefits provisions could be justified under the spending powers of Congress. In the proposed legislation and the final act, the separation was achieved by putting the benefits provisions in Title II and the tax provisions in Title VIII. The separation was so complete that the original legislation did not directly use the payroll taxes to finance the benefits to be provided under the act. The law set up a separate Old-Age Reserve Account but called for Congress to make annual appropriations to the account in accordance with its spending powers. Indeed, some pundits were concerned that Congress might not make the annual appropriations and that the promised benefits might not be paid. Thus, it was not the provisions of the act itself that were to fund the account and so the benefits, but the annual appropriation action taken by the Congress. In practical terms, the linkage between the taxes and benefits anticipated in the law was achieved through their common dependence on covered earnings. But the direct linkage between contributions and benefits in the literature on social insurance was not included in the original act itself. According to the language of social insurance, the plans are contributory. The Social Security Act of 1935 made it clear that the financing of the program was through a "tax" mechanism.

In May 1937 the Supreme Court found the old-age benefits and financing provisions of the Social Security Act constitutional. In its decision the court concluded: "Congress did not improvise a judgment when it found that the award of old age benefits would be conducive to the general welfare." It determined that the administration and the Congress had carefully considered the need for the legislation, and the court agreed that "the problem is plainly national in area and dimensions. Moreover, laws of the separate states cannot deal with it effectively." In the decision the court observed that its role was not to judge the "wisdom" of the scheme of benefits, but to judge the power of Congress to enact such a scheme.[11]

The framers of the Social Security Act were surprised that the Supreme Court's ruling on the old-age provisions was based on the Constitution's general welfare provisions. This meant that the careful separation between the tax and the benefit provisions of the act was unnecessary. It meant that the legislation could be based on the principles of social insurance, but also that the language of the legislation could be construed according to that of social insurance.

Early Policy Concerns

Some historians conclude that the Social Security Act of 1935 was the culmination of the fight between the competing schools of social insurance in the United States. The more conservative, antiredistributional model of social insurance from the Wisconsin school, as represented by John Commons and Edwin Witte, won out over the more liberal redistributional model advocated by I. M. Rubinow and Abraham Epstein and their disciples, adherents of the Ohio model.[12] But FDR had said as he signed the Social Security Act in 1935 that the legislation was the cornerstone in a structure that was by no means complete. Almost immediately after the signing of the act, critics from both ends of the political spectrum began to critique the program and to agitate for change. Interestingly, their criticisms drove the opposing groups toward a common set of recommendations.

From the Left, the critique of the Social Security Act focused on the relative levels of benefits that would be provided through the federal Old-Age Benefits program in the early years of its operations and through the state-administered old-age assistance programs. The funding provisions that President Roosevelt and his treasury secretary, Henry Morgenthau, had insisted on when the act was under development meant that the old-age insurance program was not going to pay significant benefits for many years into the future. During the early years, the noncontributory old-age assistance benefits were going to be much larger, in most cases, than the benefits paid to retirees who had contributed during their working lives. This was going to make those who had contributed look like fools by comparison with those who had not. If the provision of old-age assistance benefits had been relatively rare, this might have been a tolerable situation. But some states, such as Ohio, were implementing old-age assistance laws that were making assistance pensions widely available.

Abraham Epstein had advocated a social insurance system that was contributory but also subsidized by government revenues that would come disproportionately from people with higher incomes. He argued that "instead of seeking greater security by increasing the purchasing power of the masses, as all sound social insurance programs have done, the insurance features of our Act tend to aggravate insecurity by placing practically the entire financial burden on the poorest sectors of the population."[13] Epstein pointed out that an insured worker would have to earn $100 per month every month for twenty years to earn a pension of $32.50 per month at age sixty-five under the law. The average covered wage under Social Security in its first year of operation was less than $1,000 for the whole year. The benefits promised by the Old-Age Benefits program were going to fall short of the state assistance benefits for a long time to come. Epstein, reflecting the attitude of most social insurance advocates, argued that it was time for bold national policies "to provide more adequately for the *dependent* aged and to establish decent national standards."[14]

Even though Epstein had largely been kept outside the public policy tent

during the development of the Social Security Act, his feelings about benefit levels under the Old-Age Benefits program were shared by some of the
prominent players who had developed the act. It was no accident that the
package presented to President Roosevelt by the Committee on Economic
Security had originally called for less trust fund accumulation than anticipated under the final act. J. Douglas Brown, who had worked on developing
the Old-Age Benefits proposal for the Committee on Economic Security,
had testified in 1935 against the trust fund accumulations that FDR and
Treasury Secretary Morgenthau had insisted upon. Brown later acknowledged that one mechanism that might have kept the funds from accumulating at the rate projected under the original act would have been to provide
greater benefits than were provided for under the 1935 law.[15] Barbara Armstrong later indicated that although she opposed the trust fund provisions
in the 1935 package, she had gone along with them because she saw that as
the only way to get the bill approved. She had favored an expanded package
of benefits that could have been financed from taxes as they accumulated
in the trust fund.[16]

The conservative critics of the Social Security Act of 1935 focused their
arguments first on the projected build-up in the trust fund. By doing so,
they ultimately came to the same conclusion as their liberal counterparts
had: that initial benefits were too low. Under the Morgenthau amendment,
the trust fund was expected to grow to $47 billion by 1980.[17] Under the pro-
posal that had been put forward by the Roosevelt administration, the trust
fund was to invest only in government bonds. For many people the thought
of this accumulation, especially in the form of government bonds, was too
fantastic to comprehend. At the time it was being considered, the total
outstanding federal debt was only $27 billion and no one thought of the
government as running future deficits that could accommodate such accumulations. After all, the government had accumulated only a total of $27
billion in debt in its first 159 years of operations. Who would have thought
that it would accumulate another $20 billion in the succeeding 45 years?
Further, contemporary policymakers thought of paying off the debt after
getting out of the Depression, rather than of seeing it grow in the future.
There were a number of potential problems in the projected accumulation
of the Social Security fund.

One of the questions was whether, within the context that the funding
provisions suggested, such a fund could truly be maintained as savings. A
reason for accumulating the fund was to keep the cost of financing benefits
at a reasonable level across generations. The designers of the program knew
that there were limits to the level of payroll tax rates that could reasonably

be levied on workers. In the original package developed by the Committee on Economic Security, the payroll tax rate was limited to a combined 5.5 percent of payroll, split evenly between the employer and employee. Under the Morgenthau amendment the payroll tax rate was scheduled to go as high as 6 percent of covered wages, again split between the employer and employee. The problem was that benefits by 1980 were expected to cost as much as 10 percent of covered pay, a percentage that virtually everyone perceived as too high to support on the back of a regressive payroll tax, a tax that was a greater burden on low-wage earners than on those with high wages.

It was the discrepancy between the projected cost of benefits and the perceived limit on how much workers could reasonably be expected to contribute to the system that had led members of the Committee on Economic Security to propose that the government would make a regular contribution to the system when it matured. When FDR balked at that approach, the Morgenthau amendment allowed a similar result on what appeared to be a more conservative basis. With the more rapid phasing in of the payroll tax and its higher ultimate level under the revised proposal, the trust fund was projected to grow much more rapidly. The larger trust fund would generate higher levels of interest than the smaller one. Under the 1935 Social Security Act, 1980 total tax collections were projected to be $2.2 billion, compared with benefit payments of $3.5 billion. The difference was to be made up through interest on the trust fund of $1.4 billion.[18]

The issue whether the government was truly saving the accumulating trust fund can be framed by looking at the first year of payroll tax collections when Social Security took in roughly $400 million more than it spent. Theoretically, the plan was to save or bank this $400 million so that it could be used to pay benefits many years later when the workers who had earned benefits by virtue of payroll tax payments became eligible to claim them. The way the money was saved, though, was that it was used to buy government bonds. The trust fund assets were the bonds, and the government got the cash to use for other operations such as making welfare payments and paying for public works projects, military operations, and the like. When these bonds had to be cashed many years later to pay benefits, the government was going to have to raise cash to redeem them, either by collecting the money from taxpayers or by new borrowing from the public.

One pundit put this into a personal context to explain the issue. He considered a situation where a worker saves $10 per week and puts it in a box marked "Reserve." Over a period of a year the worker saves $520 but from time to time needs money and, instead of borrowing from a bank, borrows from his reserve fund and puts in an IOU equal to the amount borrowed. The IOU is a promise to return the amount borrowed in full plus 6 percent interest. The worker continues contributing to the fund and borrowing for ten years at which point he has a box full of IOUs with an accumulated value of $8,000. In this case, the analyst argues, it is clear that the worker has accumulated no savings and that the reserve is "pure fiction." [19]

The case of the individual worker was applied by extension to the Social Security trust fund. The argument was that when

> the government puts aside a billion dollars in a year . . . and then borrows that billion, substituting its promises to pay in the form of bonds, and then pays interest each year on these billions and borrows it, giving bonds in its place, what it will have at the end of forty-three years will be a box full of bonds-claims, not upon some outside assets, but upon itself, which of course, are no claims at all. It has no means of getting the funds or interest upon the funds saved by going to the very people from whom it took these funds in the first place. . . . If the government invested these billions in the bonds of some other government or some private corporations so that it could realize on the investment out of the earnings of some other entity than itself, then it might claim to have a reserve. But of course no one would suggest doing this.[20]

In addition to the concern that the funding mechanism in the Social Security Act was not really a funding mechanism at all, another concern was that it would result in the redemption of government debt on the "shoulders of the lowest income group of the country." [21] The plan was that the accumulating trust fund would be used to buy back the federal debt that was held by the general public. The average-wage worker would pay 1 percent of his wages to create the fund that would allow this to happen. The worker earning $3,000 per year would pay taxes at the same rate. But the one earning $4,000 would have to pay taxes only on the first $3,000 of earnings and would have an effective tax rate of only 0.75 percent, and the one earning $10,000 would have an average tax rate of 0.3 percent.

Conservative critics of the program also worried that the accumulating trust fund would be an excuse to increase government expenditures, spending money on projects that would not otherwise be funded with federal revenues raised through the income tax or other regular revenue sources. From the policymakers' 1935 or 1936 vantage point, the projected trust fund would exceed total federal debt by 1960. They could not begin to fathom the amount that would be added to the federal debt during World War II and later. As the story on the trust fund build-up quoted above suggests, most people never thought of investing the added money from the trust fund in the private-capital base of the economy. That suggested the government would have to create added debt just to accommodate the Social Security funding. If the government collected the money and simply held it, it would act as a tremendous drag on the economy. The only other option was to spend the excess funds as they were collected. So the Social Security trust funding mechanism had the potential to generate federal spending totally unrelated to the provision of benefits under the program.

Yet another concern voiced by the conservatives was that the burden of the tax rate in the early years, compared to the level of benefits provided, would give the false impression that benefits could be more cheaply financed than would be true once the system matured. In 1942, when the first benefits were to be paid, between 55 and 60 percent of all workers would be paying taxes into the system, but only a minuscule portion of the population over age sixty-five would be getting benefits. Their benefits could be raised without a commensurate increase in the tax rates because such a small portion of the elderly would be receiving benefits for many years. The architects of the system did not think that it would reach maturity until sometime around the mid-1960s or even later. Only then would the portion of the retiree population over age sixty-five that was receiving benefits equal the percentage of workers contributing to the system.

Alf Landon was the Republican nominee running against Franklin Roosevelt in the presidential election of 1936. In late September that year he gave a speech in Milwaukee attacking the old-age benefits program. He said that it was a "fraud on the working man. The saving it forces on our workers is a cruel hoax."[22] At this point, John Winant, the former Republican governor of New Hampshire, who had been serving as chairman of the Social Security Board, stepped down. He had been appointed as the minority member of the board and felt constrained in his ability to defend the Social Security Act against his fellow Republicans while serving on the board. His defense of the act essentially ended his promising career in the Republican Party.

Winant's defense of the Social Security retirement program notwithstanding, the Republican National Committee distributed millions of pay-envelope stuffers, posters, and related materials to employers a week before the national election. These materials announced that payroll tax withholding was to begin on the following January 1 without mentioning the provision of benefits under the plan. One pamphlet pictured "A New Deal Judge" saying, *"You're Sentenced* TO A WEEKLY PAY REDUCTION *for*

ALL OF YOUR WORKING LIFE. YOU'LL HAVE TO *SERVE THE SENTENCE* UNLESS YOU HELP TO REVERSE IT NOV. 3, ELECTION DAY."[23] The Social Security Board was prepared for the attack and immediately distributed fifty million leaflets, primarily through the cooperation of union organizations, explaining the benefits of the program. It also released explanatory films to movie theaters at the same time.[24] Roosevelt won the election in a landslide and the immediate threat to the program was averted.

By the time tax collections were getting under way at the beginning of 1937, the conservative forces were poised to fight the financing provisions of the 1935 Act in Congress. Senator Arthur Vandenberg, a conservative Republican from Michigan, and a number of his congressional colleagues set the stage. They argued that the "reserve is unnecessary in a compulsory tax-supported system; that its ultimate accumulation of a $47,000,000,000 reserve is a positive menace to free institutions and to sound finance and that it is a perpetual invitation to the maintenance of an extravagant public debt; that it will, in effect, transfer the burden of debt retirement from the shoulders of general taxpayers to the shoulders of the lowest income group of the country in the form of a gross income tax on labor; and that it involves . . . a needless postponement of earlier and more adequate benefit payments."[25]

Senator Vandenberg introduced a resolution in January 1937 calling for the abandonment of the "full-reserve" funding of Social Security that was to be accomplished by either raising benefits or cutting taxes called for in the 1935 Act. At a Senate Finance hearing on February 22, 1937, Arthur Altmeyer made the case for staying the course prescribed in the law. As the hearing was ending, Senator Vandenberg inquired of Altmeyer if he would object to the appointment of a commission to look into the fundamental question of the appropriate funding mechanisms for Social Security. Altmeyer countered that Congress should suggest people to serve on advisory committees to the Social Security Board. Out of this discourse came an agreement that the board and the chairman of the Senate Finance Committee would create an advisory group and report back to both of them on the financing issue.[26]

In May 1937, the board joined the Finance Committee's Special Committee on Social Security in appointing an advisory council made up of representatives from the employer community, labor organizations, and some actuaries and economists. The charter of the advisory council went beyond the pure questions of funding and reserves to include consideration of accelerating the date that benefits would be paid, increasing the levels of benefits to be paid, and extending coverage to groups not included in the original legislation.[27]

While Altmeyer, as chairman of the Social Security Board, had been pushed into forming the advisory council, the board and the Roosevelt administration took it as an opportunity to consider enhancement of the system. Altmeyer had Roosevelt write him a letter in April 1938, requesting that the board develop a plan for enhancing Social Security's provisions. In addition to the issues of extending coverage, accelerating payments, and increasing benefit levels for early beneficiaries included in the advisory council's charter, FDR also asked for consideration of "providing benefits for aged wives and widows, and providing benefits for young children of insured persons dying before reaching retirement age. It is my hope that the Board will be prepared to submit its recommendations before Congress reconvenes in January."[28]

The advisory council was composed of individuals who represented the full range of opinions on the funding matter. The council was chaired by J. Douglas Brown, who had helped in the development of the original Old-Age Benefits proposals. Among the most liberal members was Alvin Hansen, the noted Keynesian economist, who was concerned about the potential fiscal drag the payroll tax would place on the economy. He perceived the opportunity to use benefit expenditures as an expansionist device. On the conservative side was M. Albert Linton, president of the Provident Mutual Life Insurance Company and an ardent advocate of "pay-as-you-go" financing. He had served as an actuarial consultant to the Committee on Economic Security during the early development of the act and had consistently opposed the "reserve funding" approach adopted in 1935. He had been a consultant to Alf Landon on Social Security and was an adviser to Senator Vandenberg.[29] Edwin Witte was also a member of the council, and he remained committed to the financing provisions incorporated in the original act.

The debate within the council on the appropriate funding approach boiled down to resolving whether the system should be based on "banking or savings principles [or] social insurance principles."[30] Linton argued that relying on the former meant that adequate pensions would be deferred for many years. Moving to social insurance principles would provide larger benefits to those becoming aged over the next ten to twenty years, thus not penalizing middle-aged and older workers simply because no plan had existed for them to contribute to in their younger days. He also argued that the 1935 Act passed on overly costly benefit promises to future taxpayers.

He cited the projected benefit levels equivalent to 10 percent of pay in 1980 as the true costs taxpayers would be burdened with at that time.[31]

Alvin Hansen looked at the issue of the accumulating trust fund quite differently from Linton. The latter was concerned about the trust fund leading to deficits in the remainder of the federal budgetary operations. Hansen saw them in a unified context and worried that the government in total had raised $400 million more in 1937 than it had spent. The payroll tax that year had raised $500 million, so it was Social Security that was to blame for the contractionary nature of the government's total budget at exactly a time when it should have been exerting an expansionary influence on the economy. Higher benefits in the short term would help to ameliorate the problem.[32]

Witte responded that the projected accumulation in the trust fund under the Morgenthau amendment had been exaggerated because of faulty assumptions used in developing it. The projection was based on an assumption that average wages under the program would equal $1,100 per year, but in fact they were only $890 in 1937. The discrepancy between the assumption and actual experience on covered earnings levels meant that benefits would be higher relative to contributions than anticipated because of the redistributive plan design. In addition, the Committee on Economic Security had relied on estimates of population and life expectancy developed during the 1920s. Updated estimates from the President's Committee on Population Growth stated by 1939 that the elderly population by 1980 would be significantly larger than previously assumed. Witte estimated that the trust fund would hold considerably less than $47 billion in 1980, and probably not half that amount.[33]

On the matter of the banking versus social insurance principles, Witte clearly embraced the former, in arguing that the fund was the only way to secure the benefits that workers were contributing toward. His was an individualistic view of the program. He felt that every worker should get back at least the equivalent of his own contributions plus interest. He acknowledged that "insurance might be a better institution, if it did not include the savings element, but it does include the savings element."[34] Linton and those who thought like him viewed the risks associated with old age as risks that should be socialized and spread broadly across society. Witte viewed them as individual responsibilities that needed to be funded over time. Because workers were myopic in their understanding of the necessity to save against the risk of not being able to work to meet their needs in old age, a program mandating that they save was the way to deal with their myopia. The Social Security program with its individualistic contribution rates and benefits was the best mechanism for achieving this goal. Possibly the clearest difference in the two perspectives was articulated when Witte confronted Brown with the prospect that moving away from reserve funding to pay-as-you-go (pay-go) financing would create tremendous cost obligations for future generations. Brown responded: "We will all be dead." [35]

A philosophical shift was clearly entailed in moving toward more adequacy-oriented benefits in the 1939 Amendments at the cost of equity considerations embedded in the 1935 Act. Arthur Altmeyer and J. Douglas Brown had an interesting discussion about this philosophical shift as the Social Security advisory council considered it. In the discussion Altmeyer asked whether the Social Security Board should seek to advocate a specific philosophy or should attempt to articulate the two alternative philosophies in such a way that Congress could assess them and choose between the two. Brown was concerned that factors other than philosophical considerations might drive policy decisions if the alternatives were spelled out for policymakers. He speculated that the "people on the Hill" might not understand the reasons for choosing one approach over the other if they were given two options from which to choose. Altmeyer responded to Brown, "What you are trying to say is that the Social Security Board is really the linkage between the experts and the non-experts." [36] According to this formulation, it was the board's role to spell out the philosophical evolution of the program and to get congressional approval of their handiwork after the fact.

Advisory Council Recommendations and Social Security Amendments

The advisory council ended up recommending a significant overhaul of the Social Security program that was largely incorporated into the Social Security Act through amendments adopted in 1939. The changes significantly altered the redistributional characteristics of the program. These amendments maintained the principle that benefits should increase on the basis of the number of years of coverage, but the relationship became much less pronounced than it was in the original act. First, benefits became payable in 1940 with only three years of coverage. Second, short-term beneficiaries received higher replacement of their earnings than originally, while long-term replacement rates for single workers were reduced. [37] These changes were accomplished by moving from a formula that based benefits on lifetime, cumulative, covered earnings to one based on average monthly covered earnings.

The redesign of the program in 1939 further redistributed benefits through the provisions covering spouses. Under the modified program a sixty-five-year-old wife was entitled to 50 percent of her husband's basic benefit; this change more than doubled the replacement rates for early retirees with spouses provided for in the original act. At the same time the 1939 Amendments increased the potential long-term benefits for those workers, as well. The 1939 Amendments also established a new category of beneficiaries: survivors. Finally, the lump-sum distributions provided in the 1935 Act were eliminated, although a small, residual lump-sum benefit justified as a funeral expense allowance was maintained. The net effect of these provisions, as with benefits for dependents, was to redistribute bene-fits toward nonworkers.

In the 1935 Act, workers who reached age sixty-five before 1942 were to be provided a lump-sum benefit based on their contributions to the system prior to their reaching age sixty-five, plus interest on their contributions. If they continued to work, they would no longer be subject to the payroll tax. Under the 1939 Amendments, these rebates were eliminated and people who continued to work beyond age sixty-five accrued benefits under the modified formulas.

On the financing side, the payroll tax increase that was scheduled to take effect on January 1, 1940, was rolled back to 1942, against the rec-ommendations of the advisory council and the Social Security Board. The advisory council called for future government contributions to the trust fund but did not make specific provisions regarding when contributions would be made or how large these might be. Under the revised schedule of benefits and tax provisions in the 1939 Amendments, the trust fund in 1955 was projected to have a balance of $6.9 billion, compared with a projected balance of $22.1 billion under the original 1935 provisions.[38] Projections be-yond 1955 were not provided in the legislative record supporting the 1939 Amendments. The matter of when, how, or whether a government contri-bution might come into play was left unresolved.

Secretary of Treasury Morgenthau testified on behalf of the modified financing proposals while they were under consideration. He stated two reasons for doing so. In the original consideration of the Social Security Act, it was assumed that the coverage by the Old-Age Benefits program would be relatively limited and that general revenue financing would be unfair to the taxpayers who would never receive benefits under its provisions. As the program had begun to unfold, it appeared that coverage was going to be far wider than originally anticipated and the issue of the fairness of using general revenues was thus less significant. The second reason for his sup-port related to concerns about the fiscal drag of the payroll tax. During the second half of 1937, the U.S. economy appeared to be heading back toward full-blown Depression, and neither Morgenthau nor Roosevelt wanted to do anything that would exacerbate the economy's precarious condition.[39]

The 1939 Amendments profoundly changed the goals of the program. Instead of being heavily weighted toward individual equity (that is, benefits based on cumulative wages), albeit income-redistributive, the program after 1939 included much broader protection against hardship. Under these amendments, the program moved away from the individualistic equity goals in the 1935 Act toward the goal of providing adequate benefits. Over the years, debate has continued over the relative weight that the equity and adequacy goals of the program should receive.

The Benefit Changes in Practice

In order to explain the late 1930s debate over Social Security's funding and benefits, it is important to understand how the benefits in the plan are earned. Social Security is what people who deal with retirement plans call a defined-benefit plan. This means that a formula is used to define the benefit the plan will pay at retirement. For traditional plans of this sort, the benefit is determined on the basis of the level of earnings a worker enjoys while in the plan. In most of these plans, the benefit also depends on how long a worker has been covered by it. In the 1935 Social Security Act, both level of earnings and covered service would be important in determining benefits, although there was some blending in the formula because it called for the benefit to be based on cumulative earnings under the plan.

The blending in the 1935 formula can best be understood in the context of a simple example of three hypothetical brothers who happened to be triplets and who turned fifty-five on January 1, 1937, right when the payroll tax first went into effect. Abe earned $2,000 a year and worked in a job covered by Social Security until he turned sixty-five ten years later, when he retired. Ben earned $2,000 each remaining year of his career but at jobs covered by Social Security in only five of the years until he reached age sixty-five and retired. Chris earned $1,000 each year. His job was covered over the remainder of his career and retired at the same time as his two brothers. Abe's cumulative earnings under Social Security would have been $20,000; Ben's and Chris's would have been $10,000 in each case.

The 1935 benefit formula stipulated that a retiree's benefit would be equal to one-half of 1 percent of the first $3,000 of cumulative earnings, plus one-twelfth of 1 percent of the next $42,000, plus one-twenty-fourth of 1 percent of the next $84,000. The three brothers' benefits are shown in Table 4.1.

Table 4.1   Hypothetical Social Security Benefits
Under the 1935 Social Security Benefit Formula

	1935 Formula
	Total monthly benefit
Abe	$29.17
Ben	$20.83
Chris	$20.83

Source: Derived by the authors.

Under the 1935 formula, Abe's benefit would have been $29.17 per month. Both Ben's and Chris's benefits would have been $20.83. Abe would have a higher benefit than Chris would, a reflection of his higher level of earnings under the plan. But Ben's and Chris's benefits would have been equal, a reflection of the way that years of service covered and levels of earnings merge in the original formula. The difference in Abe's and Chris's benefits reflect the redistributive nature of the program. Whereas Abe would have paid twice as much in payroll taxes into the plan as Chris, Abe's benefit would have been only 40 percent larger than Chris's. From the outset, however, not all of Social Security's redistribution worked perfectly. Even though Abe and Ben received equal wages over the last ten years of their careers, Abe contributed twice as much to the system as Ben, because Ben worked in jobs not covered by Social Security for five of the ten years. Despite the fact that they had been equally well off while working and Abe had paid twice as much in payroll taxes as Ben, Abe's benefit would have been only 40 percent larger than Ben's. Even though Ben had been better off while working than Chris, the two would receive the same amount of gratuitous redistribution.

The 1939 formula called for determining a retiree's benefit based on average monthly wages, with a separate feature that accounted for duration under the plan. In addition, the 1939 Amendments provided benefits for workers' spouses who did not earn benefits on the basis of their own earnings histories. Thus the 1939 Amendments enhanced the benefits that were paid to the three brothers because they happened to be married. Their wives were three sisters, triplets, as coincidence would have it, who happened to have been born on exactly the same day as the brothers. The sisters, Dee, Edy, and Flo, who were typical of many women in the 1940s, had spent their whole careers as homemakers. They would not have qualified for benefits under the original Social Security Act of 1935 but were eligible for a spousal benefit under the 1939 Amendments that was half the value of their husband's benefits.

The formula provided a benefit equal to 40 percent of the first $50 of average monthly wages plus 10 percent of the next $200, all increased by 1 percent for each year of coverage in the system. When the brothers retired in 1947, all three of them had their benefits determined on the basis of their covered wages over the ten years from the time they started paying taxes. Their average monthly wage levels were calculated on the basis of 120 months, even though they did not all work in employment covered by Social Security all ten of the years from 1937 to 1947. Abe's average monthly wage was $166.67, or his cumulative wages of $20,000 divided by 120. Ben's and Chris's average monthly wages would have been $83.33, or $10,000 divided by 120. Abe's benefit under the 1939 formula, shown in Table 4.2, would have been 42 percent larger than Ben's because both his average monthly wage and years of coverage were twice Ben's. Some of the advantage that Ben realized because of the redistribution in the system was eliminated by the 1939 Amendments, but not much of it. Abe's benefit would have been larger than Chris's only because his average wage as covered by Social Security was larger. Even though Ben and Chris had equivalent average monthly wage levels, Chris's benefit would have been larger than Ben's because he had twice the number of years covered in the system. But Ben still made out relatively better than either of his brothers, all things considered. He received nearly as much of the redistribution effect as Chris, while paying only half the taxes that Abe paid. These distribution effects were further compounded by other features in the amended program.

Under the spousal provisions, Abe and Dee received a combined benefit of $52.25 per month when they retired, compared with the $29.17 per month that they would have gotten under the original design. If Abe and Dee, who turned sixty-five in 1947, lived out their normal life expectancies, Abe died when he was seventy-eight and Dee when she was eighty-one. Under the original act, Dee would have received no benefit after Abe's

Table 4.2   Hypothetical Monthly Social Security Benefits Under 1935 and 1939 Social Security Benefit Formulas

	1935 Formula	1939 Formula	
	Total monthly benefit	Worker's benefit	Worker's + spouse's benefit
Abe and Dee	$29.17	$34.83	$52.25
Ben and Edy	$20.83	$24.50	$36.75
Chris	$20.83	$25.67	$25.67

Source: Derived by the authors.

death, but under the 1939 Amendments she received $26.12 per month until she died.

Chris had been married throughout his working career. His wife Flo died the December before she and her husband would have turned sixty-five. Although Chris had essentially paid as much in payroll taxes as Ben and had actually been covered by Social Security for more years, his total benefits under the 1939 Amendments actually came out to be significantly smaller—43 percent less—than Ben's total benefits. If Chris had died instead of Flo, she would have received a survivor benefit, but it would have been only $19.25 per month.

In defined-benefit plans, benefits are determined by formula. The actual formula that is set as the basis for benefits depends on the goals behind the program. The modification in the Social Security formula from the 1935 Act to the 1939 Amendments reflects a change in the goals for the program during its initial stages. Being able to deliver the benefits implied by the formula in a plan depends on having the funds available to meet the demands for benefits when they come due. As the earlier discussion has indicated, the initial debate over the appropriate Social Security financing methods focused on two alternative means of paying retirement benefits. One of these was referred to as the full-reserve method of funding. The other was known as the pay-as-you-go method. If we ignore for a moment how Abe and Dee and their siblings' benefits were financed, the debate over how Social Security was to be funded during the deliberations leading up to the 1939 Social Security Amendments was about how their children's contributions to the system would be used.

Extending the discussion about how benefits were set in the early days of Social Security, let us consider the case of Abe and Dee's son, Greg, who spent his life in employment covered by Social Security (henceforth, "covered employment"). Under the full-reserve method of funding, contributions on Greg's covered wages would have accumulated in an account until he reached retirement. If the program had been properly financed, Greg's accumulated contributions plus the interest they earned would have been large enough by the time he retired to finance his retirement benefits over his remaining life expectancy. Under the pay-as-you-go method, Greg's contributions would have been used to pay his parents' generation their benefits. When Greg reached retirement, his benefits would then have been financed by his children's and grandchildren's contributions.

More Names and Games

The Supreme Court's ruling on the constitutionality of the Social Security Act on the basis of the welfare clause of the Constitution offered its architects a chance to align the legislative language behind the program with its philosophical underpinnings. While policymakers talked about the Old-Age Benefits program as being social insurance, the term "insurance" had been assiduously avoided in the original law. The Supreme Court's ruling was handed down in mid-May of 1937. By early summer that year, new posters and other materials had been prepared for use in field office operations that employed the phrase "Federal Old-Age Insurance." There was also active discussion about changing the name of the Bureau of Old-Age Benefits within the Social Security Board to the Bureau of Old-Age Insurance.[40]

Part of the reason for the shift to insurance terminology flowed from the general use of the word "pensions" to refer to benefits "gratuitously" provided through assistance programs in that era. According to the standard usage, the benefits provided through Title I of the Social Security Act were pensions. But there was a tendency for the word "pensions" to be applied also to the benefits provided under Title II. For example, a headline in the *Washington Post* on July 26, 1937 read, "Social Security Board Has 29,954,821 on Pension List."[41] Calling Social Security's old-age benefits pensions was not only misleading but demeaning as well. On the Social Security Board itself, the feeling was that Title II, "designed to give benefits as a right [should be] referred to as an *insurance* program in order to stress the superiority of such treatment over the relief treatment accorded in Title I."[42]

In presenting and defending the recommendations of the advisory council to Congress, J. Douglas Brown argued that there were only two practical ways to deal with old-age dependency. The first was old-age assistance, provided in Title I of the Social Security Act, and the second was old-age insurance, provided in Title II. He argued that a hybrid program with a mix of the two or "free pensions" would not work. Free pensions were the sort of benefits that the Townsend movement and others were still advocating at the end of the 1930s. Brown articulated the philosophy that contributory insurance was vital to maintain workers' self-reliance in that it "permitted" them to finance their own old-age protection. The self-reliance embedded in our contributory Social Security program paralleled our economic and political system—it was the American way. The contribution on earnings and their relationship to benefit levels left vital financial incentives intact. People who worked harder and contributed more would receive more. If this route was not followed, "mounting dependencies [would be] both an economic and political hazard."[43] Possibly the most interesting aspect of Brown's philosophical statement was the lack of a rationale for the significant expansion of the welfare elements of the Social Security program just as he and the Social Security Board began to articulate the superiority of "incentives" and "self reliance" in a contributory social insurance program over other welfare transfer approaches.

In February 1939, Title VIII of the Social Security Act, which contained the tax provisions that raised the money for the Old-Age Benefits program, was repealed. It was re-enacted as the Federal Insurance Contributions Act (FICA). Since then, the payroll tax withholdings under the Social Security Act have been collected under the FICA banner. The 1939 Amendments, which were signed into law on August 10 of that year, changed the name of the Old-Age Benefits program to the Old-Age and Survivors Insurance program. It also created the Old-Age and Survivors Insurance Trust Fund and made provisions that the payroll taxes collected under the act could be deposited directly into the fund, thus eliminating the need for annual appropriations that had existed under the original law. In keeping with the insurance terminology, it redefined the taxes that finance the system. From the outset, it was clear that terminology was important. The 1939 Amendments institutionalized the language for the Social Security program that its founders had wanted in the first place.

Reassessing the Handiwork

If the passage of the 1935 Social Security Act was considered the culmination of the battle between the Ohio and Wisconsin models of social insurance with the latter clearly winning out, the 1939 Amendments shifted significantly back toward the Ohio approach. This is best exemplified in Abraham Epstein's assessment of the revisions. "The victory which transcends every other is, of course, the complete revision of the national old age insurance program. . . . The results achieved, frankly, exceed our fondest hopes."[44]

Needless to say, Edwin Witte had a slightly different interpretation of the 1939 Amendments. He felt the really important change was the "principle that everyone who has paid taxes gets at least some benefits has been discarded."[45] On the financing side, he was critical of the "pay-as-you-go" advocates' victory on deferring the payroll tax increase scheduled for 1940. He concluded that the modified system was inadequately financed. He knew that the cost of the program in the early years was not the flow of benefit payments that had to be made, but the accruing liabilities for future payments that would have to be made for workers paying taxes during their working lives. The new model was not covering those costs by any stretch of the imagination. Witte thought that that portended long-term financing problems for the program.

Chapter 5

To Fund or Not to Fund?

*T*he political debate over Social Security from its initial passage in August 1935 until the adoption of the 1939 Amendments four years later focused especially on the funding of the system. Critics on the Left and the Right argued against the provisions in the 1935 Act, albeit for somewhat different reasons. The question of how to fund Social Security would come up again and again as the history of the program evolved. In many regards, contemporary debates over how to deal with Social Security's financing problems in anticipation of the baby boomers' future claims are simply a throwback to the debate that Edwin Witte and Arthur Altmeyer had with Albert Linton and Senator Arthur Vandenberg from 1935 through 1939. Sorting out the issues central to that debate is extremely important to understanding the historical evolution of our Social Security system and the debate over how we should change the system to meet the needs of future retirees.

The Benefits of Full-Reserve Funding

The reasons for funding a retirement plan can best be understood through an example. In order to simplify the explanation of the importance of accumulating retirement plan assets, completely ignore Social Security for the moment. Assume that a worker, Patti, is covered by a pension plan that will pay her a benefit equal to 1 percent of her final average pay over the last five years she works, multiplied by the number of years that she pays into the system. Assume Patti starts to work at age twenty-one, continues to work until age sixty-five, at which time she retires, and lives to her normal life expectancy. Assume that she earns $25,000 in her first year of employment and that her salary grows at a rate of 5 percent per year

Figure 5.1   Patti's Accumulated Pension Benefits
and Fund Balances over Time

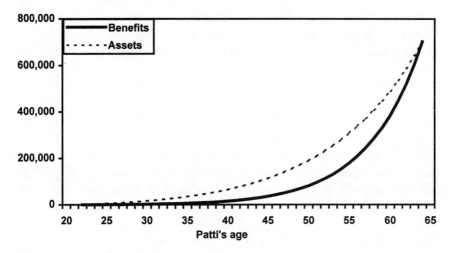

Source: Watson Wyatt Worldwide.

throughout her career. Assume that an annual contribution of 4.1 percent of her pay is made to fund Patti's pension each year, that the contribution is made to a pension fund, and that the assets in the fund earn a rate of return of 8 percent per year.

In the first year that Patti works, she earns some benefit rights, even though no actual retirement benefits will be paid to her for 45 years. The value of those benefit rights after that first year of employment are only about $90, even though contributions of slightly more than $1,000 are made to the plan under the assumptions that we have laid out here. Figure 5.1 traces the growth in the value of Patti's accumulated pension rights and the fund balances that have been put aside at each point in her career. The top line in the figure traces the accumulating assets in the plan. The bottom line in the figure traces the growing value of benefits owed to Patti. Under the assumptions, the fund balances are somewhat higher than the earned benefits right up to the point where Patti retires. The reason is that the example is structured so the annual contribution is a constant percentage of Patti's pay each year of her career. It could have been structured, alternatively, so the contribution pattern exactly matched the growth in benefit rights, but that would have meant that Patti would have had to contribute at an increasing rate as she aged. The approach used in the example is more in keeping with the spirit of the design of Social Security, at least as it was conceived in 1935.

At the end of Patti's career, under the assumptions used in developing this example, she has accumulated a pension with a lifetime value of slightly more than $700,000. At retirement, the accumulated assets in the pension fund are equal in value to the value of her pension. When we look at the total accumulated value of her pension by comparison with her contributions, the contributions only account for 21 percent of the accumulated balance. Interest on the funds makes up the rest. The value of "banking" the annual contributions in this case is that the interest on the "savings" helps to finance a significant part of Patti's retirement benefit.

In the example of Patti's pension, the value of the interest on the fund is somewhat greater than the level expected from Social Security contributions under the design of the plan established in the 1935 Act. There are several reasons for this. Under the 1935 Social Security Act, contribution rates were to be phased in over a number of years, starting at 1 percent on each employer and employee in 1937 and increasing every three years until they reached a combined total of 6 percent in 1949. In the example of Patti, the contribution starts off at the full career rate right at the beginning of her career. In addition, the original Social Security Act anticipated that early beneficiaries would receive somewhat larger benefits than they had "paid for" through their contributions. These excess benefits to early retirees would diminish the interest income to the fund during the early years. The cost of the excess benefits paid to early retirees was to be made up by a contribution rate that was somewhat higher than the long-term cost of the system when workers paid in for all their careers. In other words, workers who entered the system after it had been operating for a while would pay slightly more over their full working lives than the value of their benefits, if we consider both their own and their employers' contributions. Finally, our assumptions are not the same as those used in estimating the costs in the original system. Finding their assumptions and replicating all of them would have been a tremendous task that would not have improved the lesson presented in our example. Under the initial projections developed for the 1935 Social Security Act, interest on fund accumulations was expected to be 40 percent of the trust fund's total income by 1980.[1] While the interest on the fund was potentially very valuable in generating income for the system, the policymakers who had ultimate authority over the evolution of Social Security soon discovered that its funding structure presented them with a set of problems.

If we hark back to the earlier example of Abe, Ben, and Chris presented in Chapter 4, workers who had only a short time to participate in the plan before reaching retirement age could not accumulate a significant fund balance during their remaining working careers. A system that was designed to pay benefits to each group of workers in accordance with their accumulated contributions would pay low benefits to early beneficiaries. To offer Abe and Dee and their siblings decent benefits, the system had to be able to tap contributions from Greg's generation of workers to a much greater extent than the 1935 Act allowed. Because of this, the two ends of the political spectrum jointly opposed the funding provisions that FDR had demanded in 1935.

In addition to the desire to pay initial beneficiaries higher benefits than the 1935 Act provided, fundamental questions persisted about whether the funding in the system was really funding. In Patti's plan described above, we assumed that her annual contributions were banked and that her "savings" earned a return that contributed to the financing of her ultimate benefits. Many policymakers did not believe that that would be the case with the funding included in the original Social Security law.

When Funding Is Funding and When It Is Not

Albert Linton and Senator Vandenberg did not disagree with Edwin Witte's conceptual arguments about the relative merits of funding Social Security benefits. But, they believed that the inherent nature of the federal government in the United States would not allow the funding of Social Security in the way that Witte envisaged. In order for the funding actually to create the benefits that Witte believed would accrue to the program, it would have to result in an accumulated store of wealth or capital in the overall economy. Here Linton and Vandenberg saw several problems. First, the pooling of wealth in government hands would create the potential for the federal government to undertake a social investing program that they philosophically abhorred. Second, the trust fund accumulation would eliminate the direct public access to the federal debt that provided a valuable service to the operation of financial markets. Third, the accumulation in the fund would give the government the opportunity actually to spend money that would not otherwise be available. Fourth, the availability of the funds would be an excuse for policymakers to raise the level of Social Security benefits above what workers could finance over time.

As we noted earlier, Social Security's potential accumulation of a $47 billion trust fund by 1980 as projected under the 1935 Act was being considered in the context of a static perception of an existing federal debt of less than $30 billion. One way that Social Security funds could be "saved" in a macroeconomic context would be for them to be used in buying up the federal debt held by the public. Presumably, the holders of the federal debt are "savers" and the buying back of their federal bonds would free up assets that they could use to create other assets in the economy. However, if federal debt was only $30 billion and the Social Security trust fund was going to hold more than that, it was natural to wonder how the excess would be invested.

In his memoir, Arthur Altmeyer tells us that he and Senator Vandenberg had an off-the-record discussion about the potential investment of trust fund accumulations that were in excess of government debt levels. Altmeyer suggested that a provision could be put into the Social Security Act that would require the Treasury to invest the excess in private securities. He said that the senator responded by saying, "That would be socialism."[2] In his oral history, Altmeyer indicates that this exchange was somewhat tongue-in-cheek.[3]

Altmeyer could carry on a jocular exchange with a conservative senator about the prospect of the government's buying up private assets, but the Social Security Board was careful to plan for all reasonable contingencies and drew up general plans for investing the funds in things other than government securities. These included plans that "preference shall be given to those which are issued to finance social undertakings, such as housing. . . . With regard to the broad scope and social significance of the undertakings which would be supported by the funds, it is difficult to make any statement which would stand the test of political change and which would not be subject to varying interpretation. Low-cost housing, schools, hospitals, and the production of certain types of capital equipment could be justified from the point of view of social welfare."[4] It was exactly this kind of plan that Vandenberg feared.

The prospect of the Social Security trust funds buying up all the outstanding federal debt was also one that would create economic problems for the economy. The Federal Reserve System uses its holdings of federal debt and those of its member banks in the creation and management of the country's money supply. In addition, many investors use federal debt instruments in the overall management of their investment portfolios that would be made significantly more complicated without them.

Pay-As-You-Go Financing as an Alternative
to Full-Reserve Funding

All the other concerns notwithstanding, conservative opponents' biggest fear about the large accumulation of Social Security trust funds, as shown by the debate outlined in Chapter 4, was that the money would not be saved and would be put to other uses. In April 1937, Arthur Vandenberg wrote an article on the dangers of the projected trust fund accumulation in the *Saturday Evening Post*. First, he put the expected 1980 accumulation of $47 billion into a contemporary context. It was eight times the money supply in the whole United States at that time. It was three times the total production of all gold in the world between 1900 and 1937. It was equal to the total assessed valuation of all combined realty in thirty-nine states of the Union. It would be enough to buy all the farms in America, including buildings, and still leave nearly $14 billion to spare. And here was this treasure all in one place, convenient to congressional raiders. It would undoubtedly be used to "pay the current running expenses of the Government."[5]

Senator Vandenberg said that the alternative to full-reserve funding was to move Social Security to pay-as-you-go financing. Under this approach, the tax collections from workers were used almost immediately to pay benefits for people already retired. The system would build up only a small reserve in this case, the purpose of which was simply to tide it over during periods when the economy was not performing well and unemployment had reduced the numbers of workers and swelled the retiree group. The senator argued that this approach was as safe as or safer than full-reserve funding, that it was cheaper, and that it would release a substantial portion of the payroll taxes in the legislation for better use.[6]

In the pay-as-you-go system, often abbreviated as "pay-go," the potential to begin to use payroll taxes immediately had to look awfully attractive. It provided the potential to pay much larger benefits within a shorter time frame than reserve funding would allow. Under this system, no money is saved or invested, it is simply transferred from workers to retirees. The combination of these two features alone was almost sufficient justification to move toward the pay-go plan. After all, critics from both the Left and the Right were critical of the long wait for benefits under the 1935 Social Security Act and the relatively miserly benefits, to boot. Furthermore, many intellectuals of the period, including John Maynard Keynes, were convinced that excess saving had been one cause for the Great Depression. If people saved, that meant they were not using their income on consuming. If the money that would otherwise have been saved were spent instead on consumption, it would stimulate demand for consumer goods and services. With a higher demand for goods and services, more people would be needed in the factories and businesses that produced those. It was thought that added savings would not lead to added demand for capital goods because of the excess capacity that already existed in the industrial sector. Alvin Hansen, the Harvard economist who had argued for liberalization of benefits on the 1937–1938 Social Security advisory council, embraced Keynesian theory on these matters.

In a pay-go retirement system, the total benefits paid from year to year have to be essentially equal to the total revenues collected. Such a system does utilize a small contingency trust fund, simply because it is impossible to get benefits and revenues to be absolutely equal in any given year. In a program like our Social Security system, the amount of benefits paid is equal to the total number of people getting benefits times the average benefit paid by the system. The amount of tax revenue available to the system is equal to the payroll tax rate, including both the employer and employee portion of the tax, times the number of workers who pay the tax, times workers' average covered earnings. For the algebraically inclined, the math of such a system is shown in equation 1 in Figure 5.2.

The cost of a pay-go retirement plan is generally considered in light of the payroll tax rate that it takes to sustain it. In one such as Senator Vandenberg was advocating, two very important ratios would determine its costs. The required tax rate to support such a system is the product of the relative number of beneficiaries and workers times the ratio of average benefits to average covered earnings. For the algebraically inclined, once again, this is shown in equation 2 in Figure 5.2. People who work with retirement plans often call the ratio of beneficiaries to workers the dependency ratio—it is the number of retirees dependent on benefits relative to the number of workers supporting them. The ratio of benefits to wages in a retirement plan is often referred to as the replacement rate—it reflects how much of an average worker's earnings are replaced by the retirement benefit when he or she retires.

Jumping ahead in our story for a moment, our Social Security system today is run largely on a pay-go basis. Currently the dependency ratio is slightly more than 0.3, meaning that there is approximately one retiree for every three workers. The average replacement rate is slightly less than 0.4, meaning that the average Social Security benefit today is about 40 percent of the average level of covered earnings for workers in the economy. In rough terms, then, our system should be costing around 12 percent of

Figure 5.2   The Mathematical Operations of a Pay-Go Retirement Plan

Revenues = Expenditures

$$(1) \quad t \cdot N_W \cdot W = N_B \cdot B$$

Where:

  t = payroll tax rate paid by employers and employees

  N_W = number of covered workers employed in a year

  W = average wages of covered workers during the year

  N_B = number of retirees receiving benefits

  B = average benefits paid to retirees

and such that:

$$(2) \quad t = (N_B/N_W) \cdot (B/W)$$

Source: Developed by the authors.

covered payroll—that is, $0.3 \times 0.4 = 0.12$. Given that the actual payroll tax rate for our system today is 12.4 percent, not including Medicare, one can see the simple model does pretty well and even accounts for the moderate cash-flow surplus the system is currently running.

In a pay-go retirement system, the higher the number of Social Security recipients per payroll taxpayer, the higher will be the required tax. Also, the higher that levels of average benefits are by comparison with average covered earnings, the higher the payroll tax in a system of this sort. To jump ahead a bit once again, the simple financing model that dictates that the cost of our system is the product of the dependency ratio and the system's replacement rate are all one needs in order to understand the essence of the long-term Social Security financing problem we face today. The average replacement rate is expected to decline slightly in the future as retirement age increases in current law are implemented starting in the year 2000. But the dependency ratio is expected to increase from roughly 0.3 today to 0.5 by 2030—that means that we are expected to move from our current ratio of one retiree for every three workers to one retiree for every two workers by 2030.

A shift of 0.2 percentage points in the dependency ratio might seem small, but it suggests the necessity for a long-term tax rate approaching 20 percent to sustain our Social Security program. We will return to this part of the story later, but for now it is important to understand how the debate between those arguing for full-reserve funding and pay-go evolved. It is also important to understand how the resolution of that debate had significant implications for the evolution of the system and how it relates to the potential solutions for the future financing problems Social Security now faces.

Social Security in Frogdom

We have already introduced two of the leading protagonists in the debate over approaches to funding, M. A. Linton and Arthur Altmeyer. For these two serious men, the debate between them would take some very odd twists. In December 1937, Linton sent Altmeyer an article he had found, which he thought adequately supported the contention that the trust fund accumulations anticipated in the full-reserve funding approach in the 1935 Social Security Act would not be achieved. Linton had gotten the article, written by J. H. Van Deventer, from a friend, but the source of the publication was unknown. The article described the establishment of a national retirement system in Frogdom. The motivation for initiating it was that the frogs experienced declining ability to catch insects as they aged. The enlightened ruler of the kingdom decided to implement an old-age pension for the inhabitants. Under the plan, younger frogs were to catch one more insect per day than they needed to sustain themselves and then to contribute it to the emperor. The emperor would give the contributor

> a receipt for it together with an assurance in writing that when he could no longer earn his daily bugs through the skill of his tongue, he would be fed by the Government.
>
> Frogdom took to this plan enthusiastically. . . . [with] the somewhat naïve idea that the Government had constructed some huge warehouse in which it accumulated a surplus of dried bugs from the daily contributions made by members of the kingdom.
>
> If the truth must be known, such a thing was not happening at all. The bug contributions exacted from the subjects of Frogdom, on pain of fine and imprisonment, were not segregated at all but went into the general Royal larder from which the Emperor frog, his immediate Royal family, his henchmen, and the ruling legislators of Frogdom, drew their rations. It was a great thing for the frog legislators especially, who depended upon patronage for election and maintenance in office. For they had the privilege of shipping great quantities of bugs to their constituents . . . on the slightest pretext imaginable.
>
> Of course, the rub came many years later when a large number of contributing frogs arrived at pension age. "But when they got there,

the cupboard was bare." They had Frogdom's I.O.U.'s it is true, but they could not live on paper.

The Emperor of Frogdom, however, solved the problem very neatly. He made his subjects contribute two bugs per day thereafter instead of one, which certainly was a masterpiece of progressive statesmanship.[7]

Linton, and others like him, thought that it was impossible for our government to accumulate and store wealth. The tax revenues from workers' paychecks raised to build the trust fund would simply wind up being used for other functions. When the pool of retirees grew large and made its claim on the trust fund, the government would again go to the taxpayers to gather the funds to pay pensions. In this vision, Social Security would be a program that transferred income across generations from those who were working to those who were no longer able to do so. It was no different from Frogdom.

Altmeyer responded only two days after Linton had sent him the article, and he offered a new ending to the story:

The government of Frogdom had outstanding fly bonds calling for the future payment of flies. These bonds also bore interest at the rate of three flies for every hundred flies owed by the government to the holders of these bonds. The government therefore decided that since flies were the staff of life, it would pay off the holders of these fly bonds and place these fly bonds to the credit of the aging frogs. The result was that when the superannuated frogs reached the end of their fly-catching days, the government of Frogdom was able to give them the flies which it would otherwise have been required to give the previous holders of the fly bonds, thus enabling these worthy frog patriarchs to retire full of flies as well as honor.

It so happened that at the time the system was started Frogdom was just passing out of a depression so that the government of Frogdom instead of using all of the flies to buy fly bonds previously outstanding issued more fly bonds which it placed to the credit of contributing frogs. These flies were used to feed other frogs whose station in life was such that they would otherwise have starved but who when given sufficient fly diet became useful and productive members of Frogdom. As a matter of fact many of them were immediately placed at work by the government building fly farms where the flies might multiply ad libitum. The result was that the frogs in Frogdom for all time to come had much more plentiful supply of flies. Therefore it was possible not only for retiring frogs to have an ample fly diet but also for all frogs to have a plentiful supply of flies. So far as history shows, the frogs of Frogdom lived so happily ever after that they almost forgot to croak which is more than can be said for ornery human beings.[8]

In one regard, Altmeyer confirmed Linton's worst fears. Linton had worried that the cash accumulated through the Social Security payroll tax would be diverted to finance new government programs. It did not take a creative mind to understand that the government's building of fly farms in Frogdom would translate into investment in "social undertakings" to improve the welfare of society. Altmeyer believed that the Social Security trust fund could be an accumulator and holder of wealth that would allow workers to "bank" a portion of their earnings and reclaim them after retirement. In this vision, Social Security would be a program that allowed workers to transfer income over time, from their working career to their retirement. The different visions that Linton and Altmeyer held about how Social Security should be financed were not easily reconciled.

Chapter 6

Unresolved Issues

*T*he 1939 Amendments significantly altered the nature of Social Security from the original design of the 1935 Social Security Act. In doing so, however, they did not resolve the differences between the advocates of the original plan design and its critics. Indeed, both groups could claim that their vision of the system was embodied in the restructured program. Virtually everyone embraced the addition of benefits covering an expanded array of the "vicissitudes of life," the acceleration of the payment of first benefits, and the improvement of benefit levels for early beneficiaries. But the new benefit structure did not resolve all the concerns voiced by critics of the program about adequacy of benefit levels, and it drew questions about individual equity from both critics and supporters. The three-year delay in the increase of the payroll tax scheduled to take place in January 1940 only temporarily pacified the advocates of moving to "pay-as-you-go" financing; meanwhile, it convinced "reserve funding" advocates that government contributions would ultimately be required. The reduction in the projected accumulation of the fund at once diminished the concerns of those opposing reserve funding and heightened the concerns of those advocating it, because the new law was silent on how funding shortfalls would be accommodated. These issues would preoccupy policymakers throughout most of the 1940s.

Benefit Issues

Passage of the Social Security Act in 1935 and the amendments in 1939 did not stamp out the Townsend movement or other, similar groups advocating universal pensions for the elderly. The Townsend Plan, which proposed pensions for everyone over age sixty who would quit work and spend the money, although it was wildly outside the realm of reality in 1935, was retooled to offer a benefit of $60 per month instead of the original amount of $200 per month. Some members of Congress who had been strong Townsend Plan advocates, such as Senator Sheridan Downey, a Republican from California, naturally took an active interest in the evolution of Social Security. They particularly worried about the limited numbers of people over sixty-five who received benefits in the early years and the amassing of trust funds in the face of profound economic need among the elderly.

The Social Security benefit levels established in the 1939 Amendments persisted throughout the 1940s. Average covered earnings for workers who paid payroll taxes in 1937 were about $76 per month. A worker at this level of earnings who retired after five years of participation in the system would get a benefit of about $23 per month. In many states, the old-age assistance —that is, means-tested welfare-benefit levels for people who never contributed anything to finance them—were significantly higher than old-age insurance—that is, contributory Social Security—benefits for those who had contributed. One way of dealing with the problem of inadequate benefits during the early years of the program was to establish a universal pension system. Advocates of this approach used Great Britain as an example of how we should arrange our system. When the British implemented their old-age retirement system in 1926, they provided that benefits would be paid two years later at the same level as though retirees had contributed all their working lives. Workers in covered industries were folded into the system immediately. This system did not attempt to emulate the "banking or saving principles" underlying America's Social Security program.[1]

In addition to the concerns about the relatively small benefits that early retirees were receiving, there were persistent questions about the heavy subsidization of benefits to a selectively small segment of the elderly population. Robert Myers in the Office of the Actuary estimated that a worker who had earned $50 per month in covered employment for five years before retiring at age sixty-five under the 1939 Act would receive expected lifetime benefits equal to one hundred times the employee contributions into the system. A similar worker who had earned $150 per month would receive lifetime benefits worth fifty times his or her contributions.[2] But at the end of the 1940s, only one-fifth of the total elderly population was receiving old-age insurance benefits, and many of those receiving them were among the most affluent of the elderly. Giving some people, essentially a relatively small and well-off minority, big retirement subsidies raised fundamental questions about Social Security's fairness.

After the passage of the 1939 Amendments, there were signs that the pressure for a universal pension was affecting policy deliberations even within the Roosevelt administration. In late March 1940, Paul McNutt, the head of the Federal Security Agency, was scheduled to give a speech before the National Industrial Conference Board. At that point, FDR had not signaled that he intended to run for the presidency again that year, and McNutt aspired to the position. The Social Security Board, as part of the Federal Security Administration, was within his purview. In his speech, McNutt intended to endorse the federal government's establishment of a flat, universal, old-age pension system to be financed through a graduated income tax. This system would replace both the old-age assistance and the old-age insurance programs under the Social Security Act. Arthur Altmeyer got a copy of the speech two days before it was delivered and appealed to the president's press secretary, Stephen Early, to bring the speech to Roosevelt's attention. Early got back to Altmeyer and indicated that the president did not want McNutt delivering the speech as written and specifically did not want him advocating a flat universal pension system. Altmeyer drafted an alternative speech that was handed to McNutt to deliver just as he was about to go in front of the audience in New York City.[3]

The story of McNutt's speech is a remarkable one in at least two regards. The first is that the issue was important enough within the Roosevelt administration that the White House would intervene in a speech by one of its senior political appointees. The second is the ability of Altmeyer and the Social Security agency to command the president's attention and force the head of the parent agency to change a public statement. Altmeyer might have been McNutt's subordinate on the organizational chart, but he clearly was not subordinate in this case.

Changing McNutt's speech did not end the pressure to radically redesign Social Security. The 1940 Democratic platform called for "a minimum pension for all who have reached the age of retirement and are not gainfully employed" as soon as possible.[4] In a speech to the Teamsters Union in September that year, the president said he hoped the United States would soon "have a national system under which no needy man or woman within our borders will lack a minimum old-age pension."[5] He went on to say that he wanted to couple the minimum pension with a system allowing workers to "build up additional security for their old age."[6]

The Senate Finance Committee established the Subcommittee to Investigate the Old-Age Pension System and put Senator Downey, the Townsendite, in charge. Downey's view was that Social Security was not a "contributory plan but almost wholly a fake scheme of social dividends in which payments of public money will be disbursed in the inverse order of need; that is substantial payments to the prosperous and meager pittances to the miserable."[7] Complaints about the unfair distribution of public subsidies under Social Security were addressed directly to President Roosevelt through Downey's committee. President Roosevelt called on the Social Security Board to help him respond to them. In a memorandum to the president, Arthur Altmeyer explained that if benefits were to be "adequate" in a social insurance system, those paid to initial beneficiaries would exceed the actuarial value of benefits that could be purchased on the basis of their own contributions. The *actuarial value of benefits* is simply the amount of benefits that would be paid to a person on the basis of the accumulated value of that person's contributions plus interest paid out over his or her life expectancy as estimated by actuaries. The estimate of benefits payable is based on the life expectancy for a person with a given set of personal characteristics. Altmeyer felt that it was essential that benefits bear a relationship to preretirement wages in a retirement system of the sort we had adopted. After all, he reasoned, this was "the fundamental purpose of contributory social insurance." Senator Downey and his colleagues argued that a national noncontributory old-age pension program would resolve these problems.[8]

With pressure from the Republicans and the Democrats in Congress for something other than the existing system and similar pressure from unions and business leaders, the Social Security Board's Bureau of Research and Statistics designed a "double-decker" system as a possible alternative. The first deck would provide a flat benefit of $40 per month to any single individual over age sixty-five who did not qualify for benefits based on the covered employment during his or her working career and whose income was not more than $20 per month. For a couple, the benefit would be $60 per month for those whose income was not more than $30 per month. For those with incomes above the $20 or $30 limits, there would be a dollar-for-dollar reduction in the first-deck benefit.[9]

An individual worker who had sufficient time in covered employment to earn an "insurance benefit" would receive the first-deck benefit plus a second-deck benefit equal to 15 percent of average monthly wages in covered employment, adjusted to account for years of covered employment. If a retiree who was eligible to receive an insurance benefit had a spouse who was not eligible for such a benefit for lack of covered employment, the spouse would be eligible for a $20 first-deck benefit and 50 percent of the insured spouse's second-deck benefit. Insured benefits would not be subject to means tests but would be reduced by earnings.[10]

The practical effect of this program would have been to implement a universal pension system of the sort advocated by the Townsendites and other such groups, albeit at a level somewhat below what they advocated. The research staff at the Social Security Board estimated that the elderly receiving benefits would increase from 2.6 million in 1950 under the old-age insurance program to 9.8 million under the double-decker proposal. The cost of old-age insurance benefits and the federal share of old-age assistance benefits was expected to be $2.0 billion in 1950 and would jump to $4.4 billion under the alternative system.[11]

Concerns about Social Security's benefit structure persisted through the 1940s. At the decade's end, Representative Carl Curtis, a Republican from Nebraska, was still criticizing the greater subsidization of well-off retirees relative to those worse off under Social Security. "Primary insurance benefits which would be awarded in 1950 under the bill proposed here by the majority for a worker who has been steadily employed at an average of $250 a month are $16 a month greater than the benefits for a worker steadily employed at $100 per month. Yet, less than $2.47 differential in primary benefit amounts can be justified actuarially by the higher contributions of the $250-a-month man. In other words, the higher paid man has paid for $2.47 more in benefits but receives $16 more in benefits."[12] The double-decker plan developed by the Social Security staff would have alleviated this problem. It would have folded in all the elderly immediately. Another laudable element of the plan, according to its supporters, was that it would immediately have presented the system and taxpayers with the cost of supporting a full cohort of retirees and thus have relieved perceived pressures to increase benefits under the existing Social Security system that was being phased in gradually.

Despite the potential for quelling widespread criticism, the Social Security Board opposed the adoption of the double-decker plan developed by its own staff, because board members were worried that it would erode and eventually destroy "the rationality of a contributory social insurance system under which the benefits, contributions and wage loss were inter-related."[13] The opposition to the kind of flat benefit in the first deck of the double-decker proposals was based on a concern that beneficiaries would perceive that there was no link between contributions and ultimate benefits. The language of higher benefits for higher contributions was extremely important in opposing the double-decker approach. But such considerations were totally absent when it came to paying higher combined benefits to a retired worker with low earnings who had a dependent spouse than to a worker with higher lifetime earnings and contributions but no dependent spouse. The board stood its ground against the universal double-decker plans and managed to sustain the structure put in place in 1939, one that still defines the essence of our Social Security system today.

Funding Issues

The 1939 Amendments delayed the scheduled increase in the payroll tax that was to take effect in 1940. The benefit changes also meant that outlays in the early years of the program would increase, although outlays would be reduced in relation to the benefit schedule embedded in the 1935 Act once the program matured. The net effect of this was a much slower build-up in the trust fund in the 1939 Act compared with the earlier one.

It seemed clear that the program would require added financing in future years over what was provided in the 1939 Amendments, but the Social Security Board initially gave another impression. Arthur Altmeyer held a press conference on August 7, 1939, to announce the amendments to the Social Security Act. The question was put to him whether the changes to the law did not raise the prospect of having to use general revenues raised through the income tax to support the program. He responded that they did not, because the lower benefits in the distant future would offset the higher benefits paid in the early years of operation. He said, "If you took the total cost of the system for the 45 years, it would be the same under the new law as under the old law. . . . If the cost calculations in 1935 are correct, you will not have to have general taxation to support the system."[14]

Although the cost of the 1935 and 1939 versions of Social Security might have been projected to be the same, the projected revenue streams were quite different. Under the original act, 25 percent of the fund revenues in 1955 were expected to come from interest on accumulated assets. By 1980, this share of revenues coming from interest on the assets was expected to rise to 40 percent of total assets. Under the 1939 Amendments, only 8 percent of total system revenues would come from interest on the fund in 1955, and by 1980, it would have been even less than that. The lack of the projected trust fund accumulation almost certainly meant that general revenues would be needed later. Altmeyer must not have appreciated that as the amendments were passed, because his statement to the press would seem to have played directly into the hands of the system's critics, who had only just begun the fight on holding down payroll taxes.

The 1939 Amendments represented a step toward pay-as-you-go financing. Secretary of Treasury Morgenthau, originally a key advocate of a funded system, modified his position on the matter. Rather than full funding, in 1939 he endorsed an alternative funding goal. He recommended the adoption of an "eventual reserve amounting to not more than three times the highest prospective annual benefits in the ensuing 5 years."[15] In the context of pension-funding conventions, this rule had virtually no grounding, but in the context of strong political inclinations to keep tax rates low, the rule had tremendous appeal. Both the Ways and Means Committee and the Senate Finance Committee cited the rule in their reports on their bills that eventually became the 1939 law. A provision was inserted in the 1939 Amendments requiring that Social Security's trustees report to Congress immediately whenever the trust fund reached the level of funding laid out in the "Morgenthau rule."

After the 1939 Amendments to the Social Security Act were adopted, the first increase in the payroll tax was to take effect on January 1, 1943. But the Revenue Act of 1942 slid the date for that increase back to January 1, 1944. At the end of 1943, the increase scheduled for January 1, 1944, was moved back to March 1 of that year. The Revenue Act of 1943, which took effect at the end of February 1944 and which was passed over the president's veto, set the scheduled date for the first increase in the payroll tax back to January 1, 1945. The importance that Roosevelt placed on the funding of the system can best be considered from the perspective that he had previously vetoed only a single bill of those put to him during ten years in office. Toward the end of 1944, yet further new legislation postponed the scheduled increase in the payroll tax once again, this time to January 1, 1946. With Roosevelt now dead, the Revenue Act of 1945 moved the date for the initial increase in the payroll tax to January 1, 1948. In 1947, Public Law 379 deferred the increase to January 1, 1950.[16]

The Morgenthau rule effectively defined a contingency reserve target for running Social Security on a pay-as-you-go basis. For legislators during the 1940s who thought along the lines that Senator Vandenberg did, Morgenthau's rule served as a marker for determining the appropriateness of scheduled tax increases. Part of the explanation for the repeated delays in increasing the payroll tax can be found in looking at the peculiar economic situation that existed during the 1940s. The U.S. economy was swinging into a massive production surge just as the decade started. This meant high employment levels and good wages.

The economic circumstances of the 1940s directly affected the cost burdens that Social Security placed on the economy. In the last chapter we showed that the cost of a pay-go plan depended on two important ratios in the economy: the ratio of the number of beneficiaries (N_B) to the number of workers (N_W)—that is, (N_B/N_W)—and the ratio of average benefit levels (B) to average wages (W)—that is, (B/W). During the economic boom that occurred during World War II, the number of people who retired was retarded by the war effort. It was everyone's patriotic duty to help out, and older people incapable of combat service contributed by staying at or returning to work in wartime production. In addition, many women who would otherwise have been homemakers were called into the marketplace, a situation that created higher than normal total employment levels. The combination of the reduced number of retirees and exaggerated numbers of workers suppressed the first of the two crucial ratios that determined the pay-go cost of Social Security. The second was similarly depressed. The benefit levels adopted in the 1939 Amendments were left intact throughout the 1940s. This meant that average benefit levels remained relatively stable over the first ten years in which they were paid. But the abnormally high demand for workers meant that wages ended up growing much more than had been anticipated at the end of the 1930s. Both ratios served to depress the payroll tax rates needed from a pay-go perspective to sustain Social Security.

Despite the rollback in the payroll tax increase set for January 1, 1940, in 1941, tax collections amounted to $688 million and disbursements amounted to $91 million. The accumulated trust fund at the beginning of 1941 had been $1,745 million and the operations for the year were going to add roughly another $600 million. Anticipated total disbursements over the period from 1941 to 1945 were expected to peak at $580 million in 1945. In the first annual report filed by the Board of Trustees of the Old-Age and Survivors Insurance Trust Fund, the trustees had to report that they were already exceeding the Morgenthau rule. But they argued that this was to be expected in a program such as Social Security was during its initial phasing-in of retirees.[17]

In spite of the repeated delays in increasing the payroll tax, the revenues rolling into the trust fund continued to significantly exceed the money going out. During 1941, the payroll tax revenues were nearly eight times the total benefits for the year. This relationship narrowed over the remainder of the decade, but in 1949, revenues were still 2.6 times expenditures in the program. At the end of 1949, the trust fund accumulation stood at $11.3 billion, a gaudy seventeen times the total disbursements for the year. In the projections for the next year, the trust fund was expected to grow to $13 billion. In the original projections accompanying the 1935 Social Security Act, the trust fund was only projected to hold $14 billion by 1950. And that was on the assumption that the payroll tax rate would have risen steadily to 6 percent, split between employers and employees, rather than at the 2 percent, where it was stuck throughout the 1940s.[18]

The Morgenthau rule was the basis for opposition to payroll tax increases. In 1943, Senator Vandenberg made it clear that "the reason Congress postponed the 100 percent increased pay-roll tax in 1941 and 1942 was that the reserve at the existing 1-percent rate of current taxation did produce a trust fund which was in excess of 'three times the highest annual expenditures anticipated during that 5 fiscal-year period.' "[19] At the end of 1944, Vandenberg wrote Altmeyer telling him that he continued to "believe that the available figures recommend another 'freeze' for 1945 on the basis of the 'Morgenthau rule.' "[20] Throughout his considerations of the tax rate issue, Vandenberg consistently held to the philosophy that the measure of adequate funding was the amount of revenue collected in any given year against the expense of paying current benefits. He never gave any indication that he worried about the liabilities that were accumulating as workers contributed to the system.

The repeated onslaught of legislative repeals of scheduled increases in the payroll tax moved the program inexorably toward the pay-go approach. Not everyone was sanguine about this development. Although President Roosevelt had gone along with the 1939 Amendments' three-year delay in increasing the payroll tax, he opposed the subsequent delays. When Congress was considering the delay in the tax increase scheduled for January 1, 1943, FDR wrote to the chairmen of the Senate Finance and House Ways and Means Committees. He argued that "a failure to allow the scheduled increase in rates to take place under present favorable circumstances would cause a real and justifiable fear that adequate funds will not be accumulated to meet the heavy obligations of the future and that the claims for benefits accruing under the present law may be jeopardized."[21] President Roosevelt vetoed the Revenue Act of 1943 because it included a delay in the payroll tax increase, but the veto was overturned. At the end of 1944, in signing H.R. 5565, which delayed the increase in the payroll tax from January 1, 1945, to January 1, 1946, the president noted in his accompanying statement, "I have felt in the past and I still feel that the scheduled rate increase, which has been repeatedly postponed by Congress, should be permitted to go into effect. The long-run financial requirements of the Social Security System justified adherence to the scheduled increases."[22]

When President Roosevelt died on April 12, 1945, Social Security was well on its way to operating on the pay-go funding basis. Critics of the contemporary U.S. welfare state may have a lot to blame on FDR, but the documentary trail of historical evidence does not support their blaming him for saddling us with a pay-go Social Security system. He had condemned the immorality of running up large unfunded liabilities in the program in 1935.

With the exception of 1939, when other overriding fiscal considerations warranted it, he consistently stuck by the position that his Social Security program should be funded against the prospect of future liabilities.

When FDR first spoke out against the unacceptability of running up unfunded liabilities that would burden future Congresses, it was January 1935 and he was focusing on the situation Congress would potentially be facing in 1980. To put his concerns in contemporary perspective, we offer you a little case study. We know of a couple in which the husband was born in 1914 and his wife a couple of years later. His annual earnings over virtually all his years under the program were at or above the maximum level of earnings covered by the payroll tax. His wife was a career homemaker. They retired sometime in 1979, and both survive today, receiving combined annual benefits approaching $25,000 per year. So far, they have received benefits in today's terms with a value of roughly half a million dollars. The annual cost of these benefits is merely the tip of the iceberg of the total obligations that Social Security has faced with this couple. While they may be a bit unusual because they have outlived their joint life expectancy as assessed at the time they turned sixty-five, their situation is not so very different from the general conditions the program faces today. The annual cost of Social Security on a pay-go basis is around $350 billion per year today. But the Social Security actuaries estimate that the value of the benefits that have been earned by workers now in the system and by people now retired exceed $10 trillion. The hypothetical situation that FDR thought would be wrong to present future Congresses with has come home to roost.

Arthur Vandenberg was a crucial force in the move toward pay-go financing throughout the 1940s, but he had to receive support from both parties in Congress to postpone payroll tax increases repeatedly. The congressional override of FDR's veto of the Revenue Act of 1943 took a vote of two-thirds in both the House and the Senate. The rationale for pay-go financing was a salve for congressional consciences, no matter what the individual member's political philosophy. For conservatives, the rationale was that the move to pay-go would retard the prospect of excessive benefits in the long term. For the liberals, the rationale was that this step would offer the prospect of increasing benefits in the short term.

Edwin Witte had gone back to Wisconsin after he finished his work on the Committee on Economic Security in 1935. He wanted no part of the day-to-day rough-and-tumble of the political world in Washington. But he remained actively engaged in the discussion about the evolution of Social Security and he remained true to his belief that the system should be funded if it was to be secure. He worried that to move to pay-go was to ignore the true cost of the national retirement system he had helped craft. He was convinced that the switch would result in what he called a Santa Claus state,[23] where benefits could be expanded without the government's having to face the true cost of doing so. He worried in 1938 that the success of Vandenberg and his allies in attacking the reserve-funding approach to Social Security finance would result in their "convincing the American public that it is not necessary to pay any attention to accruing liabilities." He was concerned that if that happened, we would "give such a large increase in benefits that they cannot possibly be financed without a very great increase in taxes."[24] In 1948, after the proponents of pay-go financing had been largely successful, Witte observed that it was "a very bad practice not only to fail to meet current liabilities but to keep from the public the fact of an ever-growing debt additional to the acknowledged debt of the United States."[25]

Arthur Altmeyer's internal efforts to get Congress to adhere to payroll tax schedules paralleled Witte's external writings and speeches on the subject. Altmeyer makes it clear in his memoir that he and his staff were responsible for the drafting of the president's various statements in opposition to tax delays. In addition, he was a regular participant in the congressional hearings on the subject and routinely advocated sticking with the scheduled increases. In this setting he raised questions not only about the creation of long-term obligations that future taxpayers would be saddled with paying, but also about the long-term fairness of a pay-go system as it matured. In this regard he pointed out:

> It is a mathematical certainty that the longer the present pay-roll tax remains in effect, the higher the future pay-roll tax must be if the insurance system continues to be financed wholly by pay-roll taxes. Therefore, the indefinite continuation of the present contribution rate will eventually necessitate raising the employees' contribution rate later to a point where future beneficiaries will be obliged to pay more for their benefits than if they obtained this insurance from a private insurance company.
>
> I say it is inequitable to compel them to pay more under this system than they would have to pay to a private insurance company, and I think that Congress would be confronted with that embarrassing situation.[26]

The matter of long-term fairness was one that would come up again years later. In the short term, the fairness issue was more difficult to sort out. On the one hand, it was clear that early retirees were getting much larger benefits than their contributions had financed. On the other hand, the comparison of benefits between those on old-age assistance and those getting retirement benefits from Social Security raised a totally different set of equity questions.

Stuck Running in Place

To some observers it is surprising that the benefits established in the 1939 law persisted throughout the 1940s. The opponents of moving to pay-go financing were arguing that one of the main reasons not to do so was that it would result in the early liberalization of benefits. Yet scheduled payroll tax increases were repeatedly delayed during the 1940s and the accumulating trust fund continued to grow, all without any significant pressure to implement benefit increases. One possible explanation for why benefits did not increase over the period is the preoccupation with the war. Another is that the management at Social Security was more focused on attempting to expand the program in other ways than on increasing benefits to those already in the system.

In July 1940, Arthur Altmeyer sent Senator Robert Wagner a letter with an attachment proposing a "social security plank" for the Democratic Party's national platform for the presidential election that would be held later that year. With regard to coverage, Altmeyer proposed that the system "should be extended to all employed persons, and in addition self-employed persons such as small businessmen and farmers should also have an opportunity to participate in its benefits. . . . We pledge ourselves to the extension of the . . . system to provide protection against permanent total disability. . . . We seek to make it possible for every family to receive the health and sickness services it needs, without being crushed by heavy costs when sickness comes."[27] In early December 1942, Altmeyer wrote to President Roosevelt with proposals for "expanding protection under" the Social Security Act. Here he describes "a unified national system of contributory social insurance covering the following hazards: old age, non-industrial total disability and temporary disability, cash hospitalization benefits, maternity benefits, and unemployment benefits. The coverage of this proposed comprehensive contributory social insurance system would include practically all employees. The contribution rate for this comprehensive contributory social insurance system at the outset would be about 10 percent of payroll."[28]

He noted that the program expenditures would eventually exceed 10 percent of payroll and that the "government might well pay for the excess until eventually there would be equal tripartite distribution of the cost."[29] For the remainder of the decade there would be legislative proposals to extend these kinds of benefits under the umbrella of the Social Security Act. President Harry Truman's first major thrust on Social Security policy in 1946 called for adoption of a national health insurance program, but opposition from physicians and insurance companies defeated the proposal. There were also attempts to implement a disability insurance program that Congress had failed to adopt during the 1940s.

At the end of the 1940s, the decade-long failure to adjust benefits was threatening to trivialize the Social Security program. In 1949, more than twice as many persons were receiving old-age assistance as were getting Social Security retirement benefits. The average monthly benefit paid under old-age assistance was $42 per month, compared with an average Social Security benefit of $25 per month. While the average retirement benefit had grown by 10 percent over the first decade such payments were made, it was solely due to longer periods of coverage and higher average wages for new beneficiaries. It was also considerably less than the increase in the cost of living over the period.[30]

Finally Moving Ahead

The repeated confrontations between congressional leaders and Arthur Altmeyer led to the creation of a second advisory council in 1947. The executive director of this council was Robert Ball, who was not working for Social Security at the time he was cast into this role, although he had worked for the agency previously. The thrust of this council's study was on ways to enhance Social Security benefits. The members focused on the financing of security for the aged and the disparities between retirement benefits and old-age assistance. They particularly noted that since farmers were not covered under Social Security in either the 1935 Act or the 1939 Amendments, states that were predominantly agricultural were far more dependent on old-age welfare benefits than on contributory Social Security in providing retirement security for their elderly. They suggested that because employers and employees paid for retirement benefits and old-age assistance benefits were financed partially by state and local revenues, the poorer agricultural states were facing a disproportionate financing burden under the existing arrangement. They leveraged this argument to suggest that benefit levels under the retirement program should be increased and that coverage should be expanded to include the agricultural sector, the self-employed, and domestic workers. In order to create meaningful benefits for newly covered groups, they advocated a "new start" in determining benefits.[31] The recommendations from the 1947–1948 Advisory Council evolved into a new set of amendments to the Social Security Act adopted in 1950.

After more than a decade on hold, the 1950 Amendments made important changes to the Old-Age and Survivors Insurance program. Coverage was extended to roughly an added ten million workers, including the non-farm self-employed, other than those in selected professional groups— for example, doctors, lawyers, and engineers. Regularly employed domestic and farm workers were also included. Coverage was also extended to employees who worked for state and local governments and not covered by alternative retirement systems and to employees of nonprofit organizations. The new law increased benefits by nearly 80 percent. The average benefit paid to a retired worker in June 1950 was around $26 per month. The estimated average benefit for such a person after the implementation of the new benefit schedule was $46 per month. For those who retired after the new law took full effect, the average benefit was expected to be $50 to $55 per month. Benefits for widows and orphans were increased by similar percentages. Spousal benefits were provided for men whose wives had earned benefits. Under prior law, only women qualified for dependent spouse and survivor benefits.[32]

The 1950 Amendments did not include everything that Social Security's administrative shepherds wanted. For example, the advisory council had proposed that disability insurance be added to the "vicissitudes of life" that would be covered. The House of Representatives passed disability provisions, but the Senate refused to go along. The Truman administration had advocated that the base for covered wages be raised to $4,800 per year, but Congress only approved raising it to $3,600.

But the big issue that had plagued policymakers during the first fifteen years from the passage of the original act was finally wrestled into submission. After the 1950 Amendments passed, J. Douglas Brown observed, "The early issue between 'pay-as-you-go' and 'large reserves' seems to have faded into the background. In old-age and survivors insurance, we have let the actuaries worry about the problem of balancing income and outgo over time."[33] The inexorable march toward the pay-go goal, however, meant, finally, that the low contribution rates of the 1940s could not go on forever. Under the new benefit structure, the level premium cost of the program was estimated to be 6 percent of covered payroll. If policymakers were to wait until the reserves that had accumulated through the 1940s ran out, the payroll tax would have to triple all at once. Large tax increases invited the risk of political opposition. The leaders at Social Security knew that it was much better to phase these kinds of increases in gradually. The 1950 Amendments called for the first increase in the payroll tax rate to be levied in 1951, when it would go to 1.5 percent each on employers and employees. Thereafter, it was scheduled to go up in half-percentage-point increments until it reached 3 percent in 1965 and then finally increased to 3.25 percent in 1970.[34]

The one last change that was of considerable significance was the adoption of "new start" provisions for determining benefits under the 1950 Amendments. Under the 1939 Amendments, benefits were based on average monthly covered earnings after 1936. For newly covered workers, there were no covered earnings prior to 1951, and computing average earnings over the period stretching back to 1936 would have resulted in very small benefit levels for them. The 1950 Amendments provided an alternative that allowed computation of average wages on the basis of covered earnings after 1950—or the year the worker turned 21, if that was later. This revised computation of covered earnings was also beneficial to workers who had been covered under the program all along, because wages by the early 1950s were much higher than they had been in the late 1930s and early 1940s.[35]

The 1950 Amendments marked an accord on Social Security policymaking. For the next couple of decades the program would continue to evolve and expand, but without the contentiousness that had surrounded program considerations during the 1930s and 1940s. Gone were the debates over pay-go versus full-reserve funding. Gone were the threats from the double-decker and universal pension advocates. There were at least a couple of reasons for this more peaceful environment. One was that Social Security was widely perceived as being an extremely good deal. Another was that the senior players at the administrative and legislative levels were in substantial agreement on the direction that policy should take and had a plan for getting there.

Chapter 7

A Deal That Couldn't Be Beat

Conservative proponents of universal pensions during the Social Security funding debates of the 1930s and 1940s frequently argued that the gradual phasing-in of retirees under the system gave rise to two problems. The first was that the small number of current beneficiaries relative to workers would create an illusion for policymakers and taxpayers that benefits could be more easily financed than would prove to be true in the long term. The second was that the system provided welfare subsidies that were distributed more to the well-off than to those in society who would generally be judged to be the neediest. Neither of these conditions was deniable, and the advocates of the existing system characterized them as merely the inevitable result of phasing in a national retirement program.

For those who received the benefit of the program's early largesse, the subsidies must have been a fantastic elixir. On the one hand, the subsidies were a pure windfall—the benefit of being eligible to participate in this public program at one particular point in time. On the other, the contribution requirements of the program and the public rhetoric surrounding it meant that the free money was an "earned" right. A strong case can be made that the way Social Security was phased in resulted in a system that is larger today than it would have been if we had adopted a universal pension system in the first place. The move to pay-as-you-go funding encouraged this phenomenon. The combination of the changeover to pay-go funding and the substantial windfalls for early beneficiaries created a tremendous public demand, which would not have existed under other circumstances, for the benefits provided.

Boiling the Frog

While we have no firsthand experience, legend has it that if you put a frog into a pot of boiling water it will immediately jump out to save itself. Alternatively, if you put a frog into a pot of cool water and gradually raise the temperature until it reaches the boiling point, the frog will simply swim around until it is cooked. The implementation of the Social Security program in the United States was akin to the second alternative. The phenomenon ties in directly with the underlying arithmetic of pay-go financing discussed in Chapter 5. There we showed that the cost rate of our Social Security system—that is, the tax rate needed to finance it on a pay-go basis—was the product of two ratios. The first of these is the dependency ratio, the number of beneficiaries to the number of workers (N_B/N_W). The second is the earnings-replacement rate, the ratio of average benefits to average wages (B/W). The analogy between the implementation of Social Security and the gradual increase in heat that boils the frog hinges on the way the two ratios that define pay-go costs evolved in the early years of the program. The ratios and the water temperature both started out low and increased gradually over time.

Gradually Increasing the Dependency Ratio

In the first year the payroll tax was collected, slightly fewer than 60 percent of all workers in the United States were employed in a covered job some time during the year. This number grew gradually during the early years of the program, as shown in Figure 7.1, at least in part because of the growth in the private industrial workforce during World War II. Coverage rates fell after the war because industrial activity declined. The effects of the expanded coverage under the 1950 Amendments were clearly significant, as farm workers and domestics began to be covered. Subsequent amendments in 1954 brought in self-employed farmers and offered state and local governments, even when they had their own pension plan, the option of coverage for their employees.

By the mid-1950s, close to 90 percent of the workforce was covered. Those remaining outside the system were federal civilian employees, employees of the state and local governments that chose not to enter the system, and some employees of nonprofit organizations. These groups would all remain outside the system until the 1983 Social Security Amendments brought in employees of nonprofit organizations and federal civilians hired after 1983. State and local government employees that were outside the sys-

Figure 7.1   Percentage of Workers Covered by Social Security
and of Persons over Age Sixty-Five Receiving Benefits

Percent

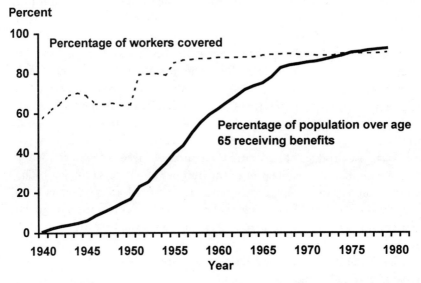

Sources: The coverage data for 1940 to 1970 are from the U.S. Bureau of Census, *Historical Statistics of the United States* (Washington, D.C.: U.S. Government Printing Office, 1975), p. 348; for 1971 to 1979, from the U.S. Bureau of Census, *Statistical Abstract of the United States, 1979* (Washington, D.C.: U.S. Government Printing Office, 1980), p. 331; for 1980, from the U.S. Bureau of Census, *Statistical Abstract of the United States, 1981* (Washington, D.C.: U.S. Government Printing Office, 1982), p. 326. Beneficiary data for 1940 to 1969 are from the U.S. Bureau of the Census, *Historical Statistics of the United States* (Washington, D.C.: U.S. Government Printing Office, 1975), p. 357; for 1970, from the *Social Security Bulletin* (March 1981), p. 73; for 1971 to 1974, from the *Social Security Bulletin* (December 1978), p. 75; for 1975 to 1979, from the *Social Security Bulletin* (March 1982), p. 66.

tem at that time and covered by their own retirement plans still remain outside it today.

Figure 7.1 shows that the percentage of the population over age sixty-five receiving Social Security benefits was phased in very slowly. In 1940, Social Security paid benefits to only 112,000 retired workers, only about 1 percent of the population over age sixty-five. Most of the elderly who had quit work prior to the first payroll tax collections in 1937 would never receive benefits. They might live for many years on old-age assistance or nothing. The gradual phasing-in of the retired population that was so bothersome to some policymakers, which is clearly visible in Figure 7.1, shows the maturing of the system.

We believe that the system reached maturity in the mid-1970s. We base

our conclusion on the picture shown in Figure 7.1. Before the 1970s, the recipient population was artificially low because of the procedures followed
in introducing the system. By the mid-1970s, virtually all the elderly who
had been denied initial coverage because they had retired before the introduction of the system had either died or been brought in on a special basis.
From then on, the percentage of the elderly population receiving benefits
would be close to the percentage of workers paying taxes.

The dependency ratio for the early years of operation of the Social Security system can be derived from the underlying numbers that define the two
lines in Figure 7.1. For any given year, the dependency ratio is defined as

$$\frac{\text{Number of beneficiaries in year X}}{\text{Number of covered workers in year X}}$$

The historical dependency ratios for the Social Security system are plotted in the left-hand panel of Figure 7.2. Comparing Figures 7.1 and 7.2, we
see that the dependency ratio grew steadily during the period when the
program was maturing. The ratio in 1953, 0.10, simply means that there
were ten workers paying taxes at that time for each person receiving bene-

Figure 7.2   Social Security Dependency Ratios
During Start-Up of the Program

Dependency Ratio   Inverse of the Dependency Ratio

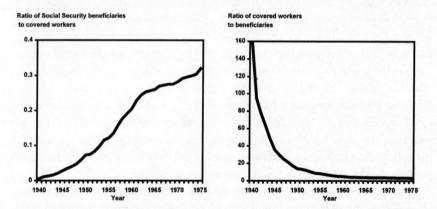

Sources: Social Security Administration, *Social Security Bulletin, Annual Statistical Supplement, 1976*
(Washington, D.C.: Social Security Administration), pp. 76, 96, and Social Security Admin-
istration, *Social Security Bulletin, Annual Statistical Supplement, 1996* (Washington, D.C.: Social
Security Administration), pp. 184, 214.

fits. By 1960, the ratio of 0.20 means that for each beneficiary, only five workers were paying taxes. In the context of the Social Security financing formula, the gradual phase-in of the program had some extremely benefi-cial effects for the early participants. It also gave the program shepherds a flexibility they would not enjoy once the system matured.

The right-hand panel shows the inverse of the dependency ratio. This is the way that many people like to think about the maturing of Social Security and the relationship between the beneficiary and working popu-lations. From this perspective, there were roughly 160 workers supporting each beneficiary in 1940. By 1950, there were only 14 workers supporting each beneficiary. By 1960, there were roughly 5 workers per beneficiary, and in 1970, approximately 3.5 workers were contributing for each beneficiary. The two panels in the graph show the same thing, but each as the inverse of the other. Both tell a remarkable story, but one that was fully anticipated by the early architects of Social Security. The gradual run-up of the Social Security dependency ratio gave its managers greater flexibility to expand benefits than they would have had under policy options that would have flattened the two lines. That is one reason Social Security's opposition to the double-decker universal plan proposals discussed in the last chapter was so strong.

Increasing Benefits Relative to Wages

The abnormally low dependency ratio in the early years of the pro-gram gave its architects inside the system and social engineers outside it an opportunity to expand benefits without the full burden of the expansion's being felt immediately by the workers paying taxes. The straightforward mathematics underlying the financing of the program had profound impli-cations for advocates of expansion. A benefit expansion in the early 1950s, when the dependency ratio was 0.10, would cost only one-third of what the same increase would cost in the early 1970s, when the dependency ratio would reach 0.30 in terms of the current tax rate needed to support the ex-pansion. The senior staff running the program during the period up to and including the early 1970s understood their opportunity quite clearly. They pushed for the expansion of benefits on two fronts.

On one front, the push made for disability insurance and health insur-ance during the 1940s continued. Ultimately, the Disability Insurance (DI) program would be passed in 1957, extending social insurance protections to cover yet another of the vicissitudes of life. The debate over a universal national health insurance system that President Truman had backed after

Figure 7.3   Average Social Security Benefit Levels in 1998 Dollars

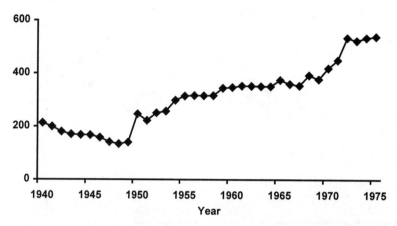

Sources: Social Security Administration, *Social Security Bulletin, Annual Statistical Supplement, 1976,* p. 96; and Social Security Administration, *Social Security Bulletin, Annual Statistical Supplement, 1996,* p. 214.

World War II culminated in the inclusion of Medicare under the Social Security Act in 1966.

The second front on the expansionists' agenda was to increase the benefit levels provided through Social Security. The results are shown in Figure 7.3. The effect of inflation on the frozen benefits during the 1940s meant that purchasing power of Social Security benefits declined over the 1940s. Between 1950 and the end of the 1960s, inflation-adjusted benefits climbed steadily, roughly doubling over the period. Then, just as the program was approaching maturity, there was a major push to increase benefits. Between 1969 and 1972, the purchasing power of average Social Security benefits increased by 41 percent. The only other increase that was larger in the whole history of the program was the 1950 increase that came at the end of a decade when the purchasing power of average benefits had declined by more than one-third. At the end of the dash for significantly higher benefits in 1972, Congress adopted new mechanisms for governing benefit increases in the future that would automatically result in further dramatic increases in benefit levels. We will return to a discussion of the implications of these changes later.

The increases in Social Security benefit levels in the early years of the program, by themselves, did not necessarily mean that the payroll tax burden to support them was increased. In the calculus of the system's financ-

Figure 7.4   Ratio of Average Social Security Benefits to Average Wages Subject to Payroll Taxes, 1940–1975

Ratio of average benefits to average wages

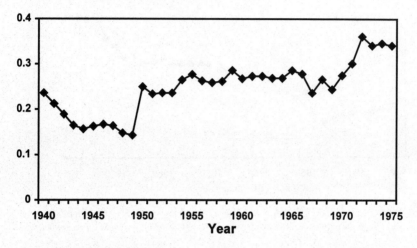

Sources: Social Security Administration, *Social Security Bulletin, Annual Statistical Supplement,* 1976, pp. 76, 96, and Social Security Administration, *Social Security Bulletin, Annual Statistical Supplement,* 1996, pp. 184, 214.

ing, it is the relation between benefits and wages that is important in determining the system's cost rate. As we discussed earlier, it is the ratio of average benefits to average wages (B/W) that must be multiplied by the dependency ratio to determine how high the payroll tax has to be to finance our Social Security system.

Figure 7.4 shows this extremely important ratio of average benefits to average taxable wages over the maturing of the Social Security system in the United States. Once again, the effects of the declining relative value of benefits during the 1940s are apparent. From 1950 until the end of the 1960s the ratio of average benefits to covered wages is relatively stable. The significant increase in benefits at the end of the 1960s and in the early 1970s, however, increased benefits relative to covered earnings quite substantially. When the ratio of average benefits to average wages rises, it drives up the cost of a pay-go plan. The increase in average benefits as compared to average wages from 1969 to 1974 reflected a 42 percent increase in this important ratio. It meant a direct increase in the payroll tax rate was needed to support the system, unless it was being offset by decreases in the dependency ratio. But the dependency ratio was also rising at this point. It rose by nearly 11 percent between 1969 and 1974. The combination of the two was multiplicative and meant an explosion in the cost of the system at that point in time.

Net Effects of Phase-In Procedures on Cost Rates

As the program matured, the tax burden to support the growing dependency ratio and the benefit-to-wage ratio drove up the cost rate. The cost rate is the payroll tax rate required to support the benefits at a given point in time. The pay-go cost rate and the actual contribution rate stated in law are shown in Figure 7.5. The difference in the pay-go rate and the statutory rate in the early days of the program reflects the "reserve" funding that existed initially. It is clear from the figure that the tax delays during the 1940s and the increases in benefits in the early 1950s essentially brought the statutory rate in the system in line with the pay-go rate. By then the program was running predominantly as a pay-go system.

As the program reached maturity, the pay-go rate reached levels that

Figure 7.5 Pay-Go Cost Rate and Statutory Payroll Tax Rates for Social Security, 1940–1975

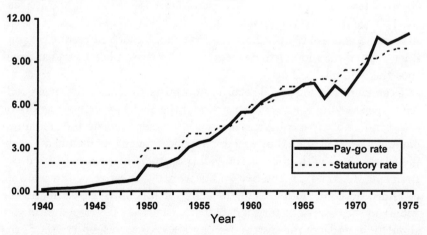

Payroll tax rate as a percent of covered payroll

Sources: Social Security Administration, *Social Security Bulletin, Annual Statistical Supplement, 1998*, p. 37. Social Security Administration, *Social Security Bulletin, Annual Statistical Supplement, 1976*, pp. 76, 96; and Social Security Administration, *Social Security Bulletin, Annual Statistical Supplement, 1996*, pp. 184, 214.

Edwin Witte and Arthur Altmeyer had worried would generate antagonism toward it. Despite the tax rates then in effect, there was remarkably little antipathy toward them. Part of the reason that workers did not resent the payroll tax was that half of it was hidden from them, in that half was paid by their employers. While most economists today agree that the employer portion of the payroll tax is borne by workers, the old adage that what you can't see won't hurt you seems to apply in this case. Another reason that workers did not resent the payroll tax was that, like the frog, workers were relatively oblivious to pain introduced gradually. The most significant reason workers willingly accepted the tax burden had to be that Social Security was an unbelievable deal for almost all participants during its phase-in period.

Is This Lotus Land, or What?

Generally the analysis of how various people have fared under Social Security is developed with regard to groups of people or to hypothetical individuals within groups. It is common to group people for such analyses by birth year. Generally, demographers refer to all the people born in a particular year as belonging to a specific birth cohort. For example, everybody born in 1940 belongs to the 1940 birth cohort. The term "cohorts," while it might bring to mind legions of soldiers for old Rome, is a convenient and compact term of art that is widely used in discussions about Social Security policy. Given the way that Social Security was phased in, the program has treated and still treats different birth cohorts quite differently. That is, it has treated the 1900 birth cohort differently than it has treated and will treat the 1960 birth cohort.

Dean Leimer at the Social Security Administration has written an excellent paper looking at rates of return under the Social Security program for a wide range of birth cohorts.[1] In essence, Leimer sums up the amount in payroll taxes contributed by each birth cohort during its members' working years, along with interest, and sums up their lifetime benefits in retirement. He compares the two and derives the effective or internal rate of return on contributions. For the early birth cohorts, he estimates the values on the basis of historical data. Later values are developed through a simulation model of the system, benchmarked to correspond to the Social Security actuaries' projections of future program operations. Since we are focusing only on the implementation of Social Security for now, we will look only at the rates of return realized by people who participated in the system in birth cohorts from 1857 up to 1915. People born in 1915

Figure 7.6 Real OASI Internal Rates of Return for Specified Birth Cohorts and Compound Real Returns on Large-Capital Stocks, 1940–1980

Real rate of return

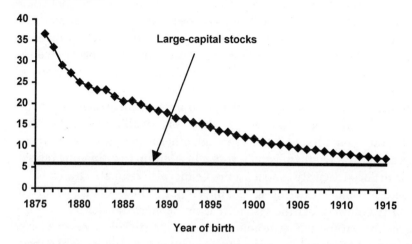

Year of birth

Sources: Dean R. Leimer, "Cohort-Specific Measures of Lifetime Net Social Security Transfers," ORS Working Paper Series, No. 59 (Washington, D.C.: Social Security Administration, February 1994), p. 16; and Ibbotson Associates, *Stocks, Bonds, Bills, and Inflation, 1996 Yearbook.*

would have turned sixty-five in 1980, about five years after Social Security reached maturity, the point where the percentage of the population over age sixty-five receiving benefits equaled the percentage of the workforce paying taxes. Today, people from those early cohorts who are still around are in their mid-eighties or older. The results of Leimer's historical calculations are shown in Figure 7.6 by the line with the declining slope.

The flat line in Figure 7.6 juxtaposes the real compound returns on large-capital stocks from the period 1940 through 1980 on the historical cohort rates of return from Social Security. We picked this period because it corresponds to the working years of people who would have turned sixty-five between 1940 and 1980. We selected corporate stocks because people might have chosen to invest their Social Security contributions in stocks if they had been required to save the amount equal to their payroll taxes but allowed to invest in something other than a government-sponsored retirement program.

While the real stock returns over the whole period from 1940 to 1980 may be somewhat lower than many people might realize, real rates of return on government bonds over this period were actually negative. From extensive research on how workers invest their retirement assets, we know that most of them invest in diversified portfolios composed partly of stocks and partly of bonds. We know that they tend to invest more heavily in stocks early in their careers and in bonds later.[2] In other words, the actual rates of return that most of these workers would have received would have been somewhat lower than the flat line in the figure. Leimer's estimates, in conjunction with the rates of return on assets otherwise widely available as Social Security was phased in, show that most early participants received rates of return that were not generally available in other preferred forms of retirement investment.

To the extent that workers from a given birth cohort received benefits from participating in Social Security that were significantly higher than benefits they could have financed through other means available to them, it was an unexpected bit of good fortune. In addition to estimating rates of return on Social Security contributions, Leimer also estimated the extent of this good fortune by calculating "net intercohort transfers" that accrued to each birth cohort under the system. The intercohort transfer for the early participants was the aggregate amount that each birth cohort received over and above what it would have received had all of the individual members' payroll taxes been invested in government bonds. These were estimates of the windfall gains that cohorts of workers realized by participating in Social Security, as opposed to investing their contributions in government bonds at the rates of return the trust funds earned. The term "windfall" literally refers to fruit blown from a tree, which a person doesn't have to go to the effort of picking. In the case of Social Security, windfall benefits for the early participants were money that the beneficiaries did not have to save and invest in order to finance their retirement income stream.

We have updated Leimer's estimates, which were stated in 1989 dollars. We report them in 1998 dollars and show the results in Figure 7.7. Birth cohorts born between 1880 and 1910 each received net transfers between $45 and $360 billion. The growth in these transfers reached its peak just as the program was coming to maturity. The cohorts born around 1910 were reaching retirement age in the mid-1970s. Beyond that point the windfall benefits provided to succeeding cohorts began to decline. But the aggregate transfers to the cohorts lucky enough to have participated in the program during the phase-in period will total roughly $7 trillion in today's dollars by the time they have all died. Later we will see that the downturn in the aggregate windfalls continued, and ultimately the windfalls would end. But that would not happen until several trillion more dollars in windfalls had

Figure 7.7   Social Security Windfall Benefits Paid
to Early Birth Cohorts of Retirees

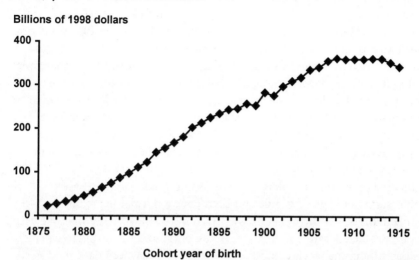

Billions of 1998 dollars

Sources: Dean R. Leimer, "Cohort-Specific Measures of Lifetime Net Social Security Transfers," ORS Working Paper Series, No. 59 (Washington, D.C.: Social Security Administration, February 1994), pp. 76–77; and calculations by the authors. Leimer used the interest rate on trust fund assets to convert current dollars into 1989 dollars. We convert the series into 1998 dollars by using corresponding interest rates between 1989 and 1997. All figures are present values as of 1998.

been provided to the first sets of cohorts to retire after the system reached maturity.

Who Got All the Free Money?

The public description of Social Security has always characterized the program as redistributive—that is, as giving relatively higher benefits to people at low earning levels than to those at higher earning levels. The income redistribution in the program, of course, stemmed from the desire to provide all retirees with *adequate* benefit levels to sustain at least a minimal standard of living. There has been very little analysis, however, of what implications the early windfall benefits have had for the distribution of benefits across the earning spectrum or across time.

To explain how the windfalls during the start-up phase of Social Security were distributed, we calculated the cumulative value of the payroll taxes that a set of prototypical workers would have paid into the system, and we compared them with the same workers' lifetime benefits. The prototypical workers are hypothetical individuals that Social Security has used historically to show how the system works and to compare the implications that alternative policies would have for various participants in the program. The workers have steady earning patterns at one of four levels, characterized as low, average, high, or at the maximum taxable earnings rate under the program. The low earner is assumed to have a steady wage equal to 40 percent of the level of average earnings for all covered workers in any given year. The high earner consistently has earnings that are 1.6 times the average level and the maximum earner has earnings each year at the maximum of the taxable wage base.

In developing our calculations, we assumed that each of these workers would survive to age sixty-five and then have a normal life expectancy for people in his or her birth cohort who lived to be at least sixty-five. We used the applicable tax rate for each year of the program's operation to calculate the payroll tax the worker and his or her employer would have paid in the worker's behalf. The cumulative payroll taxes for each of the hypothetical workers were credited each year for the annual contribution plus a rate of return equal to that realized on the trust fund assets.[3]

Benefits were calculated by using a program provided by the Social Security Administration on the Internet.[4] This program calculates a monthly benefit for a retiree at the age he or she was first eligible to receive a benefit and for any subsequent month. To compare benefits over time for people retiring at age sixty-five, we used the program to calculate monthly benefits for persons reaching age sixty-five in 1940 and every fifth year thereafter.[5] Monthly benefits were added together to give annual benefits. Annual benefits were accumulated on the basis of the present value at retirement over the normal life expectancy of each retiree.[6]

Windfall gains were calculated by subtracting the lifetime value of benefits for a particular worker from the lifetime value of payroll taxes paid. For the early workers who retired in the system, the windfalls—that is, the benefits that they received over and above the value of their own contributions, their employers' contributions in their behalf, plus interest on the combined contributions—were tremendous. This was simply free money given to the early retirees. We adjusted the estimated windfalls for each worker in each birth cohort according to the consumer price index (CPI) to report them all in 1998 dollars. We calculated the windfalls for both men and women who were single over their whole working career and for married men whose wives did not work outside the home. The results of these calculations are reported in Table 7.1.

To illustrate what is in the table and what the issue is regarding the "redistributive" character of the system, let us assume that we have two workers, Wally and Pete. Assume they were both born on January 1, 1900. They would thus have turned sixty-five on January 1, 1965. Assume further that they both married women who were also born in 1900 and that neither of their wives ever worked other than as homemakers. Finally, assume that Wally always earned a wage that was 40 percent of average covered earnings, that Pete always earned wages considerably above the Social Security taxable wage base, and that both were in covered employment from 1937 until they retired at age sixty-five. In Table 7.1 Wally would be considered a "married male worker with nonworker spouse" with "low" earnings who retired in 1965. Pete would be the same, except that he would be considered a "maximum" earner in the table.

The redistributional character of Social Security is not directly shown in Table 7.1 but underlies the calculations there. The nature of the redistribution is reflected in the ratio of the value of benefits accumulated with interest to contributions for both workers that were used to calculate the windfalls shown in the table. For Wally the ratio is 18.6 to 1. For Pete it is 10.9 to 1. That means that Wally got back 18.6 times more in Social Security benefits paid to him and his wife than the value of lifetime contributions associated with his earnings accumulated with interest at government bond rates. Pete and his wife received benefits equal to 10.9 times the value of payroll taxes paid on his wages accumulated with interest. In relative terms, Wally clearly got a better deal than Pete. In absolute terms though, Pete did much better than Wally, as Table 7.1 indicates. The table shows that Pete received total windfalls—that is, free benefits—worth $250,034 in 1998 dollars while Wally received windfalls worth $154,884. Wally did well, but Pete did much better on an absolute basis. Redistribution of this sort must have been a relatively easy sell to workers with higher earnings.

The pattern of windfalls reflected in the table does not exactly support the general notion that Social Security was as redistributional as it was marketed to be over the early years of its implementation. For the first forty to fifty birth cohorts of retirees, the program consistently paid significantly higher windfall benefits to average earners than to low earners, and to high and maximum earners than to average or low earners. The windfall benefits peaked just as Social Security was reaching maturity. For a high or maximum earner couple in which only the husband paid payroll taxes, the

Table 7.1   Average Net Social Security Windfall Benefits Paid to Retirees,
by Worker's Level of Lifetime Earnings and Year Worker Turned Sixty-Five

Year worker turned 65	Lifetime Earnings Level			
	Low	Average	High	Maximum
	Windfall benefits			
Single males				
1940	$ 28,958	$ 37,896	$ 44,731	$ 58,780
1945	30,380	33,996	39,610	48,586
1950	28,653	30,181	33,499	36,101
1955	59,035	84,447	89,799	88,666
1960	70,077	102,074	111,617	110,457
1965	77,168	112,023	120,606	119,297
1970	87,407	111,154	121,929	120,557
1975	73,780	102,097	115,156	113,693
1980	55,534	80,593	95,975	95,998
Single females				
1940	$ 34,490	$ 44,099	$ 51,561	$ 67,335
1945	36,733	40,591	46,774	56,866
1950	35,719	37,375	41,039	43,993
1955	73,607	105,828	112,977	111,843
1960	90,241	132,445	145,400	144,239
1965	99,289	145,879	157,821	156,512
1970	110,099	142,298	157,034	155,662
1975	92,076	130,094	147,835	146,373
1980	68,736	102,603	123,430	123,923
Married male worker with nonworker spouse				
1940	$ 50,461	$ 64,978	$ 76,290	$ 99,990
1945	54,222	60,550	70,332	85,897
1950	53,436	56,811	63,051	67,982
1955	111,342	161,192	172,964	171,830
1960	138,513	205,164	226,288	225,127
1965	154,884	230,975	251,343	250,034
1970	173,516	230,541	256,487	255,115
1975	147,886	216,253	248,442	246,980
1980	114,054	178,139	217,640	219,751

Source: These calculations were developed by Gordon Goodfellow of Watson Wyatt Worldwide.
He used government bond rates of return paid on the Social Security trust funds in calculating
the accrued contributions for the years during which workers were covered. He used the Social
Security benefit calculator found at *http://www.ssa.gov/OACT* to calculate monthly benefits and
used Social Security mortality tables to calculate life expectancies. He used government bond
rates of return paid on the Social Security trust funds in calculating the present values of lifetime
benefits at retirement.

windfall subsidy at the peak was worth more than a quarter-million dollars in lifetime benefits. For the single male with a lifetime of low earnings who retired at that point, the windfall subsidy was only about a third of that amount.

Social Security: A Ponzi Scheme or a Nobel Prize-Winning Concept?

The architects of the program had known that the very earliest beneficiaries under Social Security would receive extremely high Social Security payments relative to their contributions. Few probably anticipated that, for the first thirty-five years or so, almost every succeeding cohort of participants would do better than the one before and receive larger and larger windfall benefits. But giving windfall transfers that amounted to hundreds of thousands of dollars to individual middle-class workers, and even bigger ones to well-off workers, raised fundamental questions about whether the Social Security story wasn't too good to be true. As with many issues of this sort, there were two opinions.

One assessment of the Social Security system was that it was nothing more than a Ponzi scheme. This type of investment scam was named after Charles Ponzi, who ran an investment program that he started in Boston at the end of 1919.[7] He borrowed $200 to set up a storefront and offered investors 50 percent return on investments in forty-five days or 100 percent in ninety days. He managed to talk several initial investors into his investment plan, and he continued to promote it throughout the winter of 1920. When the initial investors asked for their money back with their 50 or 100 percent interest, he paid them in full. Word quickly spread about the fabulous returns Ponzi was able to generate, and more and more people lined up to invest with him.

Ponzi quickly became rich and famous, buying a huge home in historic Lexington and also acquiring a 30 percent interest in Boston's Hanover Trust Bank. The early investors in Ponzi's program cleaned up, and he continued to pay all claims in full until the Massachusetts District Attorney forced him to stop accepting money on July 26, 1920. Even then, hoping to convince the district attorney that he was on the up-and-up, Ponzi promised to pay people in full. When he was finally arrested and jailed on August 13, 1920, he had roughly $7 million in claims against him and only $2 million to meet them.

The district attorney was correct in recognizing that the scheme was ultimately bound to fail and that closing it down was the only proper course

of action. Nonetheless, if Ponzi had only been allowed to continue market-
ing his scheme and accepting new money, which was coming in at a rate
of $200,000 per day by the end, he might have been able to pay all existing
claims in full by creating new ones. As it was, several rounds of investors
did very well by Ponzi and earned returns in excess of 400 percent per year.
Payoffs to each round of investors with claims maturing under the scheme
were made by turning over money from a new round of investors. But the
final round of participants did poorly, ultimately getting back only around
25 percent of their money.

The problem with the Ponzi investment scheme is that it quickly exploded beyond the capacity of any society to keep it going. An investment
of $1,000 in this scheme requires the program manager to raise $2,000 to
pay off the initial investment 90 days later. That $2,000 requires $4,000 in
another 90 days, or 180 days from the initial investment; this investment
in turn requires $8,000 at 270 days, which requires $16,000 by the end of
the year. If you follow this path year after year, an initial investment of
$1,000 will balloon into a service obligation of more than $1 billion in just
five years. When Ponzi was shut down, he was taking in $200,000 per day,
which would convert into roughly $4 million a month. At the end of four
years, the compounding on an investment of $4 million, given the return
he was promising, would have required a new monthly investment of more
than $260 billion. The total gross domestic product of the United States in
1920 was $71 billion.

The future obligations under a system of the sort Ponzi devised simply
compound beyond the capacity of an economy and society to support it.
Edwin Witte's early concerns about the failure to fund Social Security were
based on his concern that not recognizing future obligations as workers
earned them would result in a larger commitment than future generations
of workers would be willing to support. He believed that if workers were
required to "save" a portion of their earnings each year, their appetites for
benefits would be governed at a level that would be supportable. Returns
on the savings would be paid at rates equal to the return the government
had to pay on its borrowing from the public. In a 1958 article Paul Samuelson offered an alternative perspective to Witte's that suggested a pay-go
retirement system could be sustained over time even though it had certain
Ponzi-scheme characteristics.[8]

Samuelson called the pay-go system a consumption loan model. Under
his model, when workers pay their Social Security taxes, they are surren-
dering current income that would be used for consumption if it were not
paid out as taxes. In a savings model of the sort that Witte envisaged, that

Figure 7.8   Hypothetical Population and the Operation of a Pay-Go
Retirement System

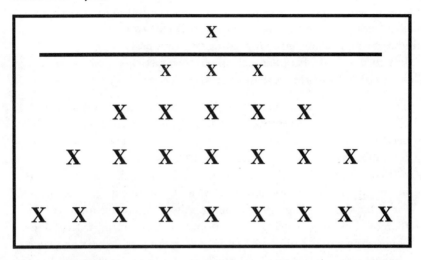

money would go into an account that would be liquidated later to finance
consumption after retirement. In the pay-go model, the consumption fore-
gone by current workers is in essence "loaned" to current retirees to finance
their retirement consumption. The loan is made, in this case, on the condition that future workers will repay it when the current generation of
workers reaches retirement.

Samuelson's model is depicted in Figure 7.8. His model has each generation of workers contributing resources to the retired generation—that is,
loaning retirees some of the workers' own current potential consumption,
which will be repaid later. In the figure each of the rows of *X*'s represents
a generation of adults in a hypothetical society. (Note that any similarity
between these hypothetical generations and the generation of people in
our society today described as Generation X is purely coincidental.) Those
above the solid line are retired; those below it are workers. At the end of
each generation, the retired population dies, the generation just below the
retirement bar ages and retires, and a new generation of workers comes
into the workforce. The contributions from the working generations are
mandatory and are a fixed fraction of earnings. In this model there are two
characteristics of the population. There are more people in each succeeding generation and they are more productive—represented in the figure by
ever-larger *X*'s—than previous generations. The increases in worker productivity result in each generation of workers' being paid a higher wage

than previous generations. With time, the aggregate size of contributions grows because of the growth in the numbers of workers and the higher wages on which their taxes—that is, their consumption loans—are levied. Each generation of retirees receives more benefits from the generations behind it than it transferred to preceding generations.

In February 1967, Paul Samuelson wrote an article for *Newsweek* magazine describing how this system worked. He wrote:

> The beauty of social insurance is that it is actuarially unsound. Everyone who reaches retirement age is given benefit privileges that far exceed anything he has paid in. And exceed his payments by more than ten times as much (or five times, counting in employer payments)!
>
> How is it possible? It stems from the fact that the national product is growing at compound interest and can be expected to do so for as far ahead as the eye cannot see. Always there are more youths than old folks in a growing population. More important, with real incomes going up at some 3 percent per year, the taxable base on which benefits rest in any period are much greater than the taxes paid historically by the generation now retired.
>
> Social security is squarely based on what has been called the eighth wonder of the world-compound interest. A growing nation is the greatest Ponzi game ever contrived.[9]

When Samuelson developed his description of the consumption loan model and wrote the article in *Newsweek*, the population structure in Figure 7.8 was very similar to the population structure in the United States as shown in Figure 7.9. The figure shows the age distribution of the population in 1965. Each of the bars represents the percentage of the total population made up by a particular age and sex group. The bars on the left show the distribution of males and the ones on the right show females in the population. The indentation in the lower center part of the distribution reflects the lower birth rates that had persisted during the Depression and World War II. Other than that, Samuelson developed his model according to a structure of the population in which there were more young than older people, and that pattern was expected to continue long into the future.

In addition to population growth, the other variable that was important to Samuelson's consumption loan model was the real rate of growth in wages, because it also helped pay successive generations of retirees higher benefits. The real rate of growth in wages is the rate at which wages grow, over and above the rate at which prices grow on goods and services that workers consume. Between the end of World War II and 1965, average

Figure 7.9   The Age Structure of the Population of the United States in 1965

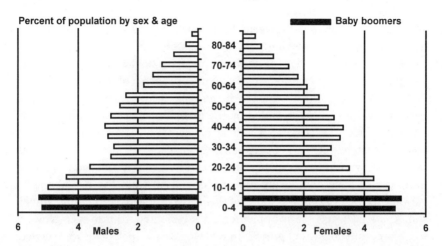

Source: The data underlying this graph can be found on the U.S. Bureau of the Census home page at *http://www.census.gov/ipc/www/idbsprd.html*.

wages grew at a compound annual rate of 2.3 percent per year over inflation, and average Social Security–covered wages grew at an annual rate of 3 percent year faster than inflation.

If It Is Too Good to Be True, It Almost Certainly Isn't

The investment program that Charles Ponzi set up and our pay-go Social Security system share the same basic structure of new contributors paying off earlier ones in the hope and expectation that future entrants will provide the funds to pay them off. One distinction between the two is that the rounds pass much more slowly. Basically, Social Security workers' contributions are made an average of twenty or more years before retirement. Then the government hands over retirement benefits over a twenty-to-thirty-year period, with each payment funded by the new contributions of current workers. Under Social Security, the promised returns were not nearly as extravagant as those Ponzi promised, and the rounds take more than a hundred times as long to play out, but the basic system is the same. Each new round of contributors or investors is paid off with the next round, which it is hoped will be even larger. If you measure the age of these kinds of systems by the number of rounds of maturing claims that have occurred, the U.S. Social Security system is only about three rounds or generations old. In fact, the Ponzi scheme had lasted at least as many rounds before the authorities brought it down.

A second difference between the two systems is that Social Security does not require a salesman with the skills of Charles Ponzi. That is because the government has the ability to make participation mandatory. But the ability of the government to mandate a program of taxes and benefits depends on the political support of the public. Public support for Social Security was undoubtedly aided by the extremely generous windfalls that were provided to early generations of participants. The system proved to be more sustainable than Ponzi's scheme because it set its abnormally high rates of return more reasonably than Ponzi had, and it reduced them over time. It also benefited during its early operation from the two necessary conditions for sustaining systems of this sort as spelled out by Paul Samuelson. As Social Security was implemented, it benefited from an ever-growing workforce and consistent growth in real wages on which taxes were levied.

Charles Ponzi's investment scheme came apart when the flow of new investors was abruptly cut off. This had to happen eventually because the system's compound growth rate was so rapid that it was bound to outstrip the total U.S. economy within just a handful of years. In the case of Social Security, the failure of the workforce or wages to grow at the compound rates Samuelson expected meant that the "greatest Ponzi scheme ever contrived" was no more a guarantee than the original Ponzi scheme had been. A lack of wage and workforce growth for a sustained period would mean a termination of the extremely good deal that Social Security promised, in the face of growth in these variables. While a stagnation in the growth of the workforce and wages would not lead to the same catastrophic collapse that the Ponzi scheme had faced, it would mean a partial termination, in that later generations of workers would not get nearly as good a deal from Social Security as earlier generations. Indeed, they would not be likely to get nearly as good a deal as they would under alternative approaches to retirement funding.

Under the sort of investment scheme that Ponzi devised or the sort of financing that our pay-go Social Security system uses, at any moment in time, some generation has contributed to the system but has not yet collected benefits. If the system is fully shut down, that generation gets a minus 100 percent return on its contribution—that is, it loses everything. In fact, if the plan is terminated at some point, the losses of the final generation exactly account for all of the gains of all of the previous generations. When the program is examined in totality, from start to finish, it is a zero-sum game, with the losers and winners exactly canceling one another out. This should not come as a big surprise. Any system that simply transfers resources from one group to another does not create added wealth.

Under a pay-go system, the failure of wages and the workforce to continue growing means that workers have to contribute an ever-larger share of their earnings to the system or that promised benefits have to be cut. This is the situation that our current Social Security system and many others around the developed world face today. It is inevitable because Paul Samuelson's dream of an ever-expanding workforce earning higher and higher wages has not been fulfilled.

The discussion of the Ponzi-like characteristics of Social Security raises a natural question: Should Social Security be shut down for the same reason that the Massachusetts district attorney put Charles Ponzi out of business? That is hard to say, but it does seem far-fetched to think that this program is going to last forever. Once we admit that it will probably be scrapped or at least changed, in the context of a partial shutdown of previous promises, then we have to recognize that we are participating in passing an enormous liability on to the generation working at the time that shutdown occurs. The longer we postpone the payment, the bigger it gets. One possibility — one that we will explore later in this book — is to unwind the system in such a way that the burden of paying for all the gains of previous generations is spread out over two or three generations.

No one has ever quarreled with the underlying logic of Paul Samuelson's model of how Social Security would work under the set of assumptions that he used to explain it. The problem was that the set of assumptions that he was looking at when he wrote his article in *Newsweek* in 1967 were historical, and those historical assumptions were not going to be a good predictor of what was going to happen in the future. His model depended on continuing growth in the workforce and real wages as far "as the eye cannot see." In less than a decade, the eye was going to get a rude awakening. But there were still several years of euphoria to enjoy before that was to happen. The opportunity was not lost on Social Security's advocates and architects.

More Is Better

In an environment where the participants in a program like Social Security were benefiting from tremendous windfall benefits, it was relatively easy to sell expansion to the public. This was especially the case where the ultimate costs of the system were not widely appreciated by the general public. And Congress was accommodating. During 1956 the Social Security Act was amended to provide monthly benefits to permanently and totally disabled workers aged fifty to sixty-four. It also provided benefits to disabled people aged eighteen or over who were children of retired or deceased workers, if disability had begun before age eighteen. Finally, provisions for women's early retirement at age sixty-two were made, primarily on the basis that wives were, on average, three years younger than their husbands. In 1960, further amendments provided disability insurance benefits to disabled workers of all ages and to their dependents. In 1961, early retirement provisions were extended to males that allowed them to retire as early as age sixty-two. The extension of this early retirement "privilege" to men in 1961 was justified on the basis of high unemployment levels that persisted during a recession then under way. In 1965, the Medicare program was created under the auspices of the Social Security Act. It would be administered as part of the program during its early years. Along the way, benefits were increased periodically to keep up with inflation, if not wage growth.

Chapter 8

The Inside Movers and Shakers

$\mathcal{P}$rograms of the size and sort that Social Security has become are the result of political decisions based on particular concepts and people and on the public constituency that supports them. Social Security grew to be our largest single commitment of federal resources today because it was widely perceived as a worthwhile endeavor. Part of the reason it was perceived as worthwhile lies in the fantastic benefits that it provided to participants during its maturing process, as discussed in Chapter 7. Another part is that it was embraced by varied interests, which would nurture it and move it along an ever-expanding evolutionary course.

Retirement programs, by their very nature, are long-term commitments. Workers often start to earn benefits in their teens and may still be drawing benefits as many as eight or nine decades later. Workers with younger spouses who qualify for benefits as dependents or survivors can stretch out the stream of benefits for additional decades. For example, one of the earliest federal pension programs that paid benefits to a relatively broad segment of the population was the system set up to benefit Civil War veterans. This system paid benefits to their spouses when the veterans passed away. One of the very last widows of a Civil War veteran died in late 1998, more than 130 years after the end of the war.

Although Social Security has not had the long history that the Civil War pension system experienced, it may be unique in the annals of retirement programs because of the enduring role that certain individuals have played in defining its character and characteristics. At the outset, Social Security was characterized by President Franklin D. Roosevelt as a "cornerstone in a structure which is being built but is by no means complete." Some sense of the designing and building has already been described in earlier chapters. But the system would never have evolved to its current state without a competent and devoted set of social engineers and builders. In several regards, this group figures as a remarkable part of the story.

Perspectives on Players and Their Motivations

Martha Derthick has written a superb history of the development of Social Security policy up through the mid-1970s.[1] Hers is a political story about the role of various people and organizations involved in the evolution of Social Security. Jerry Cates gives an alternative view of the evolving history of the program.[2] He investigates the competing social philosophies underlying it and describes the functional political forces at play in the original philosophical disputes between the Wisconsin and Ohio schools of social insurance.

Derthick's story focuses on the roles played by a number of the major characters who shepherded Social Security from its infancy to its maturity in the mid-1970s. Derthick's general framework for assessing Social Security is very useful, but our assessment of the politics of Social Security is not exactly the same as hers. Among other things, we have the added perspective of twenty years more of program operations and evolution than Derthick did in her analysis. In addition, Derthick analyzed Social Security policy from the perspective of a political scientist, whereas we are analyzing it more as an economic phenomenon.

Whereas Derthick concludes that Social Security policy was driven by people who were willing to make repeated accommodations in pursuit of ultimate goals, Cates sees conspiracy. He sees the architects of the system as so bent on making it attractive to the large middle class that they abandoned the potential to make it a truly redistributive force for alleviating the effects of the vicissitudes of life. We understand how he reached this conclusion. In the last chapter we showed that during its evolution Social Security provided tremendous windfall benefits to early retirees. But we also showed that despite the rhetoric that it was a highly redistributive program, supposedly giving disproportionately large benefits to the less well off, it actually gave significantly larger absolute windfalls to the well-off than to those with low lifetime earnings.

We cannot completely reconcile the different interpretations that Derthick and Cates give to the same set of historical facts underlying Social Security. But we do believe that the way the system was introduced and its attendant windfalls were an economic device that served the needs of many disparate interests during the maturing of the system. A convincing trail of evidence shows that various major groups involved in the evolution of Social Security policy understood the value of the start-up windfalls and used them to their advantage. Analyses developed in the Office of the Actuary over the early years of the program showed that people were getting an extremely good deal from Social Security. Often it was contended that this good deal would persist into the future, as Paul Samuelson the Nobel laureate economist believed.

Insiders at Work

Up through the mid-1970s at least, the Social Security Administration was one of the most effective and successful organizations in the history of our federal government at proactively managing the evolution of public policy for the program that it ran. Several factors account for its success. Certainly, in the early years leadership was vital. Not only did Social Security have effective leaders early on, but the original cast had remarkable tenures at developing and influencing public policy initiatives. The leadership was extremely stable, and it hit upon a formula for developing policy that proved highly effective. In addition, the leadership running the program was able to create an esprit de corps in the agency that bordered on religious fervor over taking the program to the American public. The nature of the program was such that the internal technical staff, especially the actuarial group, was often a crucial participant if not full partner with the congressional committees in developing and considering legislation. Finally, the agenda that could be taken to the American people was extremely attractive. In some regards that agenda was no more complicated than giving away money, as we discussed in the last chapter. In others, it was vastly more complicated.

Stability at the Top

During the start-up phase of Social Security, from 1935 through 1973, there were six chief executives. Of the six, Arthur Altmeyer had run the program from 1937 until 1953, and Robert Ball ran it formally from 1962 to 1973, but Ball also effectively ran the Old-Age and Survivors Insurance operations from 1953 until his departure in 1973.[3] This essentially means that from the time the first payroll taxes were collected until the system reached maturity nearly forty years later, it had only two leaders. The two were extremely different, but their respective timing and strengths played a major role in the evolution of the program. Their contributions were knit together by an extremely able staff built by Altmeyer and his early senior colleagues and reinforced by a philosophy and a set of goals that underlay the original act but then evolved further under the tutelage of Robert Ball and Wilbur Cohen. Where Altmeyer proved to be a builder of an administrative system that was crucial to Social Security's success, Ball in partnership with Cohen were the social engineers who would bring about disability protection, medical benefits, and much higher benefit levels under the program.

Wilbur Cohen, who had come to Washington as Edwin Witte's assistant in 1934, stayed on after the passage of the Social Security Act and was the first employee of the Social Security Board. Formally, he stayed in Social Security until a couple of years after Altmeyer left, when the Eisenhower administration forced him out. Even after Cohen's departure, he continued to play an extremely influential role in the development of Social Security policy. He served in senior-level political positions during the Kennedy and Johnson administrations, and as secretary of the Department of Health, Education, and Welfare (DHEW) in the latter. At that time, the Social Security Administration was within DHEW. It was during Cohen's tenure as secretary of HEW that Medicare was passed as part of the Social Security Act. He had been involved in the evolution of this legislation for more than two decades. In Martha Derthick's classification of important players in Social Security's evolution, Cohen was both a program executive and a political executive. The former tended to hold positions for a long time within the Social Security Administration itself, generally as career civil servants. The latter were senior political appointees, usually in Social Security's parent organization and in shorter-term positions.

Supporting Social Security's leaders was a talented and dedicated senior staff. Altmeyer, the good administrator, had made it a priority to recruit able leaders. Good people he attracted to the agency made careers there. In 1970, when Robert Ball was commissioner, he and his top five lieutenants (the deputy commissioner and assistant commissioners for administration, field operations, program evaluation and planning, and research and statistics) had 191 years of service inside the Social Security Administration (SSA) between them. All had come to the agency in the 1930s and had spent most of their careers there.[4]

A Vision to Pursue and a Means to Achieve It

Not only was there leadership within Social Security, there was an agenda to further build on the "cornerstone" that had been laid in 1935 and added to in 1939. At the end of June 1942, the Social Security Board, in its annual report to the president, outlined a social insurance program to provide minimum basic protection extending from cradle to grave. It called for expanding coverage by the Old-Age and Survivors Insurance program to all workers, expanding insurance protection to the temporary or permanently disabled, and expanding hospital benefits.[5] The closest this agenda came to enactment was the inclusion of some of its provisions in a bill drafted by Social Security Board officials and introduced by Senator James Murray, Senator Robert Wagner, and Congressman John Dingell in 1943.[6] While President Roosevelt never pushed specific comprehensive legislation along these lines, he claimed ownership of the concept of cradle to grave social insurance protection, which had been usurped by Sir William Beveridge when he pushed for comprehensive legislation in the United Kingdom. In his 1944 State of the Union message, the president called for a "second Bill of Rights," which included the rights "to adequate medical care . . . and to adequate protection from the economic fears of old age, sickness, accident, and unemployment."[7] The major problem with this agenda was that it was simply too large to be bitten off all at once.

Robert Ball and Wilbur Cohen would eventually find another way to achieve their ends. Instead of taking their whole agenda to Congress at one time, they would present it piece by piece over time. In 1950, they would go for a benefit increase that would put old-age insurance on a superior footing to old-age assistance. In 1951, Wilbur Cohen would curb the SSA's appetite for the national health insurance system that was the goal in 1943, in order to go after health insurance for Social Security beneficiaries. He would play on the popularity of Social Security when he launched the campaign for Medicare. The campaign would take a while, but then these champions were in the race for the long haul.[8]

Wilbur Cohen was fully committed to the concept of social insurance and saw it as superior to means-tested assistance programs. He argued that programs for the poor were always poor programs. This logic could be applied in many circumstances. It was useful in the quest for disability insurance. Disability was another of the hazards of life that people experienced, through no fault of their own in most cases. The inability to work for most disabled people meant impoverishment, often not only for themselves but for their families as well. Without a social insurance mechanism to prevent impoverishment, the victims of disability were thrown on the mercy of inferior welfare programs. Social Security had worked so well against the vicissitudes of old age that it was easy for Congress to extend it to disability in 1956. Incrementalism worked, where going for the whole ball of wax had failed. The Ball-Cohen approach demonstrated success. It also demonstrated something else. Ball supposedly reported to the Eisenhower administration in 1956. The Eisenhower administration was officially opposed to the disability provisions added to Social Security at that time. But that made little difference to Ball and Cohen.[9] The long-term Social Security agenda superseded the agenda of a sitting president.

Outsiders as Insiders

Immediately after the expansion of the program to include disability, attention turned back to Medicare. Here the beauty of the leadership structure at Social Security and its strategic pursuit of its agenda was at its finest. Edward Berkowitz recounts that the first serious medical insurance proposal leading up to the passage of Medicare was a bill put together by Cohen, I. S. Falk, Robert Ball, and Nelson Cruikshank. Cohen was by then a professor at the University of Michigan. Falk had been the original head of the research and statistics operation at Social Security, but he was by then a professor at Yale. Cruikshank had never been on the inside but was a passionate advocate of social insurance from organized labor and a confidant of George Meany, the president of the AFL-CIO.[10] It did not make any difference that Cohen and Falk were no longer at Social Security; they could still be full partners with its internal executives in developing and moving the agenda. And Cruikshank was the moral equivalent of an insider because the senior managers at Social Security used organized labor to move its agenda when they could not do so through the unenlightened political hierarchies that they found themselves reporting to from time to time. Derthick reports that "when the Eisenhower administration removed several leading program officials from their offices, the officials could not protest—but labor did. When the Eisenhower administration opposed disability insurance and health insurance, program officials could not openly campaign for them—but labor could. Always, labor had a useful role as surrogate sponsor of what in reality were proposals initiated by the SSA."[11] By the mid-1960s, Cohen was a political executive of the program and was back as Ball's boss. With the passage of Medicare in 1965, incrementalism triumphed once again, where going for the whole agenda had failed in the 1940s. Ball and Cohen were at the center of the fray.

Staying the Course Patiently

If incrementalism was the approach, steady expansion was the goal. Wilbur Cohen himself laid it out clearly. "The men and women I worked with, while they were populists, while they were progressives, while they were strong believers in social legislation, they were also strongly of the belief of the inevitableness of gradualism. In other words, they felt it was more important to take one step at a time. Or perhaps I ought to put it this way—to digest one meal at a time rather than eating breakfast, lunch, and dinner all at once and getting indigestion. This was their philosophy. I think it's the right social philosophy." [12]

Incrementalism should not be confused with timidity. The leaders at Social Security were committed to their goals in a way that was often compared, as we have mentioned, to religious fervor or even zealotry. Robert Myers, describing for a British publication the active role that SSA leaders took in the advocacy of policy, observed that "most of the American staff engaged in programme planning and policy development have had the philosophy—carried out with almost a religious zeal—that what counts above all else is the expansion of the programme." [13] It was hardly surprising that Myers should find religious zeal at the top of the organization. Altmeyer, the administrator, had built a system to assure it.

Controlling the Terms of the Discussion

One other inside element that made the SSA so effective in achieving its agenda was the role that the actuaries played in the development of policy. By their nature, retirement programs tend to be complicated. Under a funded system, someone has to figure out how much a twenty-two-year-old should save as part of a long-term program so that he or she ends up with sufficient assets to finance retirement needs some forty to seventy years later. Estimating how much needs to be saved requires a sense of how much the worker will earn each year during the career, what rate of interest that savings will earn, when the worker will retire, how long he or she will live after retiring, and a host of other contingencies. In pay-as-you-go national plans, it is important to take into account birth rates, life expectancies, the level of benefits and wages, the number of people who will work, the number who will retire, and the rate at which benefits and wages will grow, among other things.

While the typical congressional representative thinks in two-year terms and senator in six-year terms, the eighty or so years a typical person is either paying into or receiving benefits from Social Security calls for a whole different perspective. The underlying arithmetic for financing a program like Social Security is beyond many people's grasp and certainly not something most of our elected representatives can be expected to master. The actuaries are the pension mathematicians who convert all of the rules of the program and the contingencies that surround it into the two things that political leaders understand with searing clarity: the benefits that the programs they sponsor provide to their electorate, and the cost to taxpayers of providing them.

The actuaries technically work for the administration in which they serve. From the outset, however, they have been the arbiters of virtually all policy considerations within both the administrative and legislative branches of government by virtue of the fact that they develop the formal cost and benefit estimates around which all policy discussions are held. The legislative committees with oversight of Social Security policy have never had their own independent staffs capable of developing cost and benefit estimates. In the early years of the program, the system actuaries would often work directly for the committees in their consideration of policy options and in the preparation of analytical reports. With the creation of the Congressional Budget Office (CBO) in 1974, some capability for Social Security analysis had been developed within the legislative branch. But the CBO has largely focused on budgetary considerations rather than longer-term projections considered by the oversight committees in their deliberations on the sweeping goals that Social Security's leaders pursued.

Over the years, Social Security's actuaries have been a rather independent lot. The first chief actuary of the program, William Rulon Williamson, resigned in 1946 because he did not share the views of members of senior management on funding issues then under debate. The second chief actuary was Robert J. Myers. He resigned in 1970 because he did not share the expansionist goals of senior management. Myers, a lifelong Republican, was particularly upset that the Nixon administration had not wrested control of the policy-development process from Ball and his coterie of insiders. Although Ball, a Democrat, and his associates were not developing grist for specific Nixon policy proposals, they were hard at work developing such materials for the insiders outside who would push their causes on the legislative front. Since Myers resigned, there have been a number of chief actuaries. Not all of them have come away from the experience as big supporters of the program. One of them, A. Haeworth Robertson, has written two books about the future of the system.[14] The title of his second book, *The Big Lie: What Every Baby Boomer Should Know About Social Security and Medicare,* should give a not-so-subtle hint at his perspective on the program.

Regardless of what the chief actuary might have been up to at any particular point, the influence of Social Security's Office of the Actuary has been writ large on the evolution of Social Security policy. The characterization of specific policy initiatives by the Office of the Actuary plays a pivotal role in congressional consideration of them. The congressional deliberation over Social Security policy virtually always centers on the context of specific proposals. It hardly ever focuses on the accuracy of estimates from the actuaries.

A Tale of Two Bobs

At the beginning of this chapter, we made the point that Social Security was unique, in that certain individuals have had a particularly long-lasting influence on the evolution of public policy. We also made the point that the social engineers formulating the agenda for the system do not have to be inside the SSA to fulfill their role. These two points are epitomized by the historical roles of two individuals, Robert J. Myers and Robert M. Ball. Myers started his formal association with the program in 1934 and Ball in 1939.

Bob Myers was hired as a junior actuary for the Committee on Economic Security by Edwin Witte in September 1934. He worked with Barbara Armstrong, J. Douglas Brown, and Murray Latimer on the development of the old-age insurance component of the original package. Myers was the only on-staff actuary during the congressional deliberations over the Social Security Act during 1935. He was away from the program for a brief time after the passage of the act because of the lack of initial funding for operations. After short stints with the Railroad Retirement Board and in the military, Myers ended up on the actuarial staff at the Social Security Board in 1936. As noted earlier, he would go on to become chief actuary in 1946 and to resign from Social Security in 1970. During his years as an actuary at Social Security, Bob Myers established the reputation as the man with the numbers on virtually any serious policy proposal affecting the system. Even after his departure from the SSA itself, he would still be widely regarded as one of the individuals most knowledgeable about the cost implications of any proposals made to change the system.

Myers has been a prolific writer almost from the very beginning of his career. He was a central player in the consideration of virtually every piece of Social Security legislation from the beginning of the program up through his departure from the agency. He was brought back into the SSA by Ronald Reagan during his presidency, but he left to serve as the executive director of the National Commission on Social Security Reform, also known as the Greenspan commission, because it was chaired by Alan Greenspan, the current chairman of the Federal Reserve System. Up to the present day, Myers continues to write and speak publicly about Social Security policy developments. He is reported in the *Guinness Book of World Records* as having testified before congressional committees more times than anyone else in history. While always a gentleman, Myers has very strong feelings about how Social Security should be structured, administered, and evaluated.

Bob Myers is an advocate of "responsible pay-as-you-go" financing of Social Security. He believes that we can keep the system's financing burden at reasonable levels by increasing the retirement age. For example, he believes that the normal retirement age in the system should be raised at a rate of two months per year for people reaching age sixty-five in 2003 and thereafter. Increasing it at this rate, the normal retirement age would reach age seventy in 2037 and age seventy-five in 2074. Raising the retirement age helps to keep the payroll tax rate at manageable levels by reducing the level of benefits provided under the existing system for people who retire at any age. Alternatively, it can reduce the dependency ratio in the program, as higher retirement ages keep people in the workforce longer, a situation that increases the number of workers and reduces the number of retirees.

Myers believe that the program administrators at Social Security should formulate policies and recommendations in accordance with the general policies advocated by the presidential administrations in which they serve. He resigned from his position as chief actuary in 1970 because he perceived that the incumbents in the top two policymaking positions at Social Security had not and would "not faithfully and vigorously serve the Nixon Administration."[15] There is also some conjecture that Myers thought a Republican administration should have been made him commissioner, rather than keeping Ball on in that position.

Myers has always considered himself a conservative advocate of Social Security. He believes that the system should offer a "floor of protection" for workers in providing retirement security. In the initial days of the Nixon administration, he thought that Ball and Cohen and their inner circle wanted to expand the system "to be virtually monopolistic in economic security. . . . As a subsidiary matter, they would eliminate the private pension system . . . and they would completely change the system for the supply and financing of medical care."[16] Not only did Myers not like the expansionists' agenda, he didn't care for their incrementalist approach either. His view of the expansionists was that they "frequently use the 'ratchet' approach. They do not unveil their ultimate goals in their entirety. . . . They are satisfied, for the time being, when they get only a fraction of that part. They believe that there is always another day to push further forward toward their goals, and they know that once a certain expansion has been achieved, a retreat from it is virtually impossible."[17] At the time that Myers was flailing away at the inside expansionists and resigning, Bob Ball was the commissioner. He had served in the same position during the Kennedy and Johnson administrations.

Bob Ball had first come to Social Security in early 1939, shortly after he had finished college. He started as a field representative in a district office, visiting employers to get them to improve their reporting practices and visiting potential claimants who were too ill to come in to the office to file claims. He started up the management ladder in field operations but soon moved to a training position at central headquarters. Here he was responsible for helping build the "religion" and esprit de corps that Altmeyer had found so important. There is probably no better way to learn than to teach, and this position was a great opportunity for Ball to learn the history, philosophy, and foreign experience with social insurance.[18]

After a period of time in this position, Ball left Social Security to join the head of the public assistance program in Pennsylvania, Karl De Schweinitz, in setting up an institute under the auspices of the American Council on Education. Among other things, they reviewed training programs throughout Social Security. They also ran training classes for top administrators of Social Security programs around the country and held seminars on Social Security for professors who were teaching the subject. Here Ball was dealing with senior level administrators and academics who further enhanced his knowledge and grasp of fundamental issues.[19] Undoubtedly, this experience also honed Ball's skills for presentation and debate, skills that he would use many times in the future.

When the Senate Finance Committee decided to set up the second advisory council in the late 1940s, they wanted an outsider to run the study. The Republicans controlled the Senate at the time and were in the midst of an ongoing financing battle with the Democratic administration, so they wanted to make sure that the person in charge of the council's work was not an insider. Also, there weren't many people around at the time with a broad grasp of Social Security. Ball, with his knowledge of the program and his status as an outsider, was a natural candidate. He had the support of J. Douglas Brown, who had chaired the original advisory council and who was going to be on this one. Ball also had the support of Nelson Cruikshank from organized labor. And finally, Ball hit it off well with Sumner Slichter, a Harvard economist who was going to chair the second council. By Ball's assessment, being the executive director of the advisory council "was a tremendous experience that ended up with a very substantial report made in 1948 that resulted in the 1950 amendments to the Social Security Act, which, it may not be an exaggeration to say, really saved the concept of contributory social insurance in this country."[20]

In 1949, Ball returned to Social Security as the assistant director of the Bureau of Old-Age and Survivors Insurance in charge of research and legislation. His assignment could not have been a better way to prepare for his lifelong quest. Research was important because it served as the basis for justifying the expansionist proposals on the Social Security agenda. Legislation was important because it was ultimately the means for achieving expansion.

As Arthur Altmeyer was preparing to leave after Eisenhower's election at the end of 1952, he positioned Ball for his ascent to power. Up until then, the Bureau of Old-Age and Survivors Insurance had never had a deputy director. Oscar Pogge, a career civil servant, was the director of the bureau and was not going to stay in the new administration. So Altmeyer altered Ball's job description of assistant director for research and legislation, adding the phrase that he "shall also act as Deputy Director of the Bureau."[21] Within a few months after Eisenhower was sworn in, Pogge resigned and Ball became acting director of the bureau. For the time being, at least, he was now in charge of the single program set up under the Social Security Act that most people today think of as Social Security.

In moving to the head of the Bureau of Old-Age and Survivors Insurance (OASI), even if it was only temporary, Ball had managed to leap-frog long-term division directors who had been in their administrative positions for years. Altmeyer "was interested in a legacy that went more to program policy and philosophy"[22] than to administration. Altmeyer, the administrator, had not been particularly effective in moving the expansionist Social Security agenda forward. He saw in Ball the capability to do so. Altmeyer left behind a well-designed administrative system for the task at hand, a system that would serve Ball well as he focused on expansion in his remaining years on the inside.

Ball remained the acting director of OASI for a year, before the administration appointed a new bureau director, Victor Christgau. But as Charles Schottland, the commissioner during this period, observed, Ball still had a particularly predominant position under the new director. Ball himself says that Christgau gave him "wide scope . . . to act as a first-line administrator over the whole program."[23] Ball was in charge.

The internal roles that both Ball and Myers played at Social Security form an amazing story in themselves. But an even more amazing story has unfolded since their departures. For all practical purposes, neither one of them has held a significant position for any duration within the Social Security Administration since the early 1970s. Yet both of them have been at the heart of Social Security policy developments right up through the present. They are both living proof that you do not have to be on the inside to be influential.

Since his departure from Social Security, Ball has continued to be a regular member of various official commissions and councils reviewing policy issues and making program recommendations. He was a major negotiator for the package of changes to the program that were developed by the Greenspan commission in 1983 and passed by Congress later that year. He was a member of the most recent Social Security advisory council, which finished its deliberations at the end of 1996. He was a leading proponent of the faction of that council advocating that we must stand by the benefits promised under current law. He wrote a book published in 1998 on Social Security[24] and is still a frequent visitor to senior policy managers within the Clinton administration and to chief policymakers on Capitol Hill.

Bob Myers is also still actively involved in public deliberations on Social Security policy. He played a major role in the evolution of the recommendations that came out of the Greenspan commission in 1983. He served on a technical panel supporting the most recent advisory council. As recently as September 1998, he was adding to his record number of appearances before congressional committees, when he testified before the Senate Finance Committee on why we should revert to pay-go financing of Social Security.

Bob Ball and Bob Myers have been the Frick and Frack of Social Security policy development for nearly a half-century now. While there were periods during their careers when they seemed to disagree radically about policy development, their differences on the fundamental goal of a broad-based Social Security program covering all workers and their dependents were minimal. Their disagreements persist. Ball thinks that Social Security should be funded to a greater extent than under current law and that the funds should be invested in the private stock market. Myers believes we should revert to pay-go financing and that stock market investment would be dangerous. Though they may be reading from different paragraphs, they are still on the same page of a public policy bible they both helped write. They both believe fervently that the existing Social Security system should essentially be preserved and that workers should be willing to pay the higher cost of doing so. With 120 years between them of involvement in the development of the current system, this position should not be surprising.

Chapter 9

The Outside Movers, Shakers, and Takers

P. T. Barnum was a circus and carnival man who believed there was "a sucker born every minute." The implication was that he could sell people things that were worth less than their price. A favorite carnival scam has always been to entice people into games of chance by letting them accumulate winnings at the beginning of the game to get them to make bigger bets as the game evolves. Of course, the house ultimately wins, because the game of chance is structured that way. In some regards, Social Security was set up in a similar fashion. Early players were given big winnings to justify continued expansion of benefits and participation.

The success of Social Security's expansionist insiders, explored in Chapter 8, could not have been achieved without a willing public and a political process that helped it along. Among the public, there are three separate entities that we see as playing a significant role in the evolution of Social Security policy since 1935. These are organized labor, business, and organized groups of beneficiaries. In the policy world, three others sets of entities have played a significant role in Social Security developments over the years. These are the advisory councils that have been organized periodically, the academic and quasi-academic policy community, and the political policymakers who have to vote on specific legislative proposals. Understanding the roles that these groups have played is important to understanding the evolution of Social Security.

The Financial Stakeholders

Social Security is a combination of costs and benefits. The costs for the system are borne largely by workers, because the overwhelming majority of the financing comes from the payroll tax. Even though employers pay half the payroll tax, it is still part of their personnel budgets, it is a cost of hiring labor, and most economists conclude that it is part of workers' wages that is collected by the government in the form of taxes. The benefits are defined by formula, subject to a variety of conditions. For disability benefits, the beneficiary has to prove an inability to work. With survivor benefits, the insured worker must be dead and the dependents must have a family relationship with the worker, be of certain ages, and so forth. For retirement benefits, the beneficiary must be sixty-two or older and is subject to certain limitations on earnings, at least until age seventy.

The financial stakeholders in this system of costs and benefits are the workers, the employers, and the beneficiaries who participate by law. In spite of their possessing the power of the vote, individual workers, per se, have not been a major political force in the evolution of Social Security policy. Organized labor, on the other hand, has been extremely influential in the evolution of Social Security policy, as discussed in earlier chapters. It may seem contradictory to argue that the burden of payroll taxes falls on workers, but that employers are stakeholders in the system. We believe they are, because of the subsidization that has existed in the system over the years and because many employers have designed their own retirement programs around Social Security. As in the case of workers, individual beneficiaries have not been particularly effective in influencing Social Security policy, but as in the case of organized labor, collective groups of the elderly have been very vocal and effective in influencing policy developments.

Organized Labor

Martha Derthick tells us that organized labor has played a large role in Social Security policy development. "In building the social security program, organized labor was by far the most important ally of the Social Security Administration. It supported the SSA inside the advisory councils and lobbied and testified for the agency's legislative proposals. It largely conducted and financed the public campaigns for medicare. . . . Perhaps most important of all, labor was an unofficial outlet for proposals that SSA officials were not free to promote themselves because they lacked approval from political superiors."[1] But organized labor's support did not materialize immediately. At the outset, the American Federation of Labor (AFL) was concerned that Social Security might tread on its turf. Its members perceived matters such as pensions to be terms of employment that fell within their purview as a negotiator for members. Although wary, they supported the 1935 Act but were not involved in its development. They were represented on the initial advisory council, but were passive in their participation.

Arthur Altmeyer had wooed the AFL from the outset to be the advocate and supporter of Social Security. Initially, the Congress of Industrial Organizations (CIO) was considered too radical for such courtship.[2] The AFL became actively interested in Social Security in 1943 when the Wagner-Murray-Dingell bill was introduced. This was the legislation advocated by senior managers at Social Security that would have expanded Social Security's charter to include disability and health benefits. The AFL was interested in the potential extension of coverage to include disability and medical care. Since President Roosevelt would not himself support this particular legislation, its sponsors within Social Security and Congress were looking for surrogate support. Senator Wagner approached organized labor. In 1944, the AFL set up a social security department within its organizational structure.[3] It was on board for the long haul.

Labor unions exist to promote the economic and social welfare of their members. In its early days, Social Security may have seemed a threat to their reason for existence because it was an outside force that could potentially usurp unions' traditional role. Ultimately though, Social Security provided the unions with tremendous opportunity. Social Security raised the public's awareness of the plight of older workers. The industrialization of society had resulted in a drive for efficiency that rendered older workers superfluous in many cases. Social Security was a mechanism to give them hope of an alternative to a destitute old age. But it was really more a mechanism to give hope for an alternative rather than an alternative itself. Average benefits for initial beneficiaries under the original act were going to be less than $20. This benefit was not going to let workers wander off into a state of carefree retired bliss. And that is where opportunity could be found for organized labor. The unions could make pensions a benefit to negotiate for their members. The pensions, as a supplement to Social Security, had the potential to turn retirement into a truly secure phase of life.

Until the late 1940s, organized labor was generally indifferent or openly antagonistic to the pension movement. Many of the craft unions viewed employer-sponsored pensions as a paternalistic device to wean the allegiance of workers away from unions. They also feared that the provision of pensions would suppress wages for active workers. The attitudes changed, though, when the National Labor Relations Board (NLRB) ruled in 1948 that employers were bound by law to negotiate with their employees on the subject of pensions.[4] Since 1949, organized labor has been a vigorous and potent force in the expansion of the private pension movement. The organization and structure of Social Security facilitated union demands for pensions by helping make retirement possible.

When the unions negotiated with employers for pensions, they were confronted with the issue of the cost of benefits. Union members, probably more than most workers, realize the fungibility inherent in the components of pay: retirement benefits can be substituted for current pay, health benefits, and so on. Many workers may fail to realize that the provision of a pension by an employer will result in an offsetting adjustment elsewhere in the compensation package. Typically, when unions negotiate salary and benefits, these trade-offs become quite explicit. They generally negotiate a total compensation increase and then figure out how it is to be allocated among the components of compensation. For example, a total raise of twenty-five cents an hour might get allocated 60 percent to wages, 20 percent to improved retirement benefits, and 20 percent to improved health benefits.

The start-up features of Social Security gave the unions a tremendous opportunity to provide retiring members with benefits that were significantly larger than the cost that they would have to incur directly to provide them. They could offer their workers a combined package of benefits that would allow retirees to maintain their preretirement standard of living on a highly subsidized basis. In Chapter 7 we showed that the windfall benefits for long-term steady workers at average salary levels were substantial. To show how these windfalls facilitated the provision of pensions consider Figure 9.1. In the figure we show the component elements of benefits that could have been provided to workers covered by pensions in five-year intervals from 1950 to 1965. In calculating these we used average wages paid to production or nonsupervisory workers on payrolls of manufacturing firms in each of the respective years as reported by the Department of Labor. For 1950, we assumed that the combination of Social Security and the employer-sponsored retirement plan was designed to provide a total benefit to a long-career worker equal to 45 percent of the retiree's preretirement final salary. We assumed the benefit would be paid over the remainder of a normal life expectancy for someone retiring at age sixty-five in each year for which estimates were developed. For 1955, we assumed that the plan was designed to pay a benefit equal to 50 percent of final earnings in combination with Social Security. For 1960, we assumed that the combined plans would pay 55 percent, and in 1965 we assumed that they were designed to pay benefits equal to 60 percent of final earnings. We assumed

Figure 9.1 Purchasing Social Security and Pension Benefits
During Social Security's Phase-In

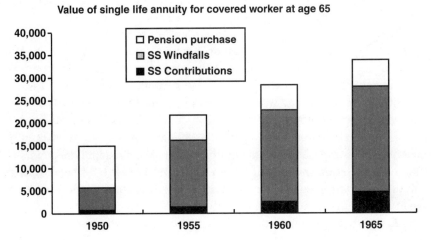

Value of single life annuity for covered worker at age 65

Source: These estimates were derived by Gordon Goodfellow of Watson Wyatt Worldwide.

increasing generosity of benefits because many employers enhanced benefits over this period and because unions, in particular, often negotiated for
benefit enhancements once they were covered under a plan.

Each of the bars in Figure 9.1 is composed of three parts. The very bottom part of the bars reflects the portion of total benefits financed by the
combined employer and employee contributions to Social Security plus
interest that were used in deriving the windfall estimates discussed in
Chapter 7. The middle part of the bar represents the Social Security windfalls for the particular workers. The top part of the bar reflects the value
of the pension that would have to be added on top of Social Security to
achieve the target benefit levels described above.

The results in the figure show that unions were in a position to negotiate for relatively moderate pension benefits that in combination with
the purchased value of Social Security and Social Security windfalls gave
their members respectable benefits in accordance with the standards of the
times. Their members had to bear the burden of the contributions toward
both Social Security and the pension, but the windfalls were essentially
free. In this context it is easy to understand why the unions were so favor-
ably disposed toward Social Security once they figured out what a good
deal it was. Each time benefits were increased or new kinds of benefits were

added in the early years of the program, the deal improved. It was simply too good to pass up.

Throughout the 1950s and 1960s, the union movement continued to press for pension improvement. After getting coverage, the next step was to negotiate for improved benefits. After getting improved benefits, the next step was to negotiate for early retirement provisions. At each step, the provisions of Social Security were the base atop which negotiations were developed. From a historical perspective, many early retirement provisions that crept into plans did so because of changing perspectives on what was a reasonable retirement age. Whether this was because of some fundamental change in worker values (that is, a labor supply factor) or because of productivity considerations (that is, a factor affecting the demand for older workers) or both is unclear. The wide acceptance of sixty-five as the traditional "normal retirement age" for retirement plans was somewhat haphazard, though more related to selection of sixty-five as the Social Security retirement age than anything else.

Social Security's early retirement age of sixty-two was established for women in 1956. The rationale for this change had nothing to do with labor market considerations; rather it was the social phenomenon that wives tended to be three years younger than their husbands on average, and the politicians thought it would be nice to let both members of working couples retire at the same time. The discussion on changing Social Security's early retirement age to sixty-two for men in 1961 focused on reducing unemployment levels. This latter reduction set the stage for reducing the retirement ages under employer-sponsored pensions.

Given the three-year cycle on major union contract negotiations, it was more than coincidence that three years after Social Security's early retirement age for men was reduced, the United Auto Workers (UAW) won retirement benefits of $400 monthly for workers at age sixty with thirty years of service. Though they were also payable to workers retiring before sixty or with fewer than thirty years of service, the benefits in that case were reduced. Under this arrangement, the normal retirement benefit was diminished to account for the early retirement, but a supplemental benefit brought the combined benefit level up to $400 per month for the thirty-year worker. These "supplements" were payable until age sixty-five as long as the retiree did not take another job. Employment income from another job reduced the pension supplement by two dollars for each dollar of earned income. Other heavily unionized industries followed the pattern set by auto industry in introducing early retirement benefits for union workers.

The early versions of the "thirty-and-out" provisions linked to age merely whetted the appetite for pure thirty-and-out provisions. This trend, coupled with the influx of the baby boom workers, made strictly service-related thirty-and-out provisions a negotiating priority by the early 1970s. During the auto negotiations on these provisions in 1973, the young workers were as committed to thirty-and-out as older workers, even though the discounted value of the additional benefits would have been relatively small for them at the time. They were not so concerned about their personal added value in retirement benefits as about clearing rungs on the position ladders that they could fill as older workers left. During the first half of the 1970s, the thirty-and-out plan became common in the steel and auto industries and then began spreading to other industries as well. Social Security made it all possible.

Employers: Interests and Reactions to Social Security

Employers' role in the evolution of Social Security is not nearly as well documented as organized labor's role. It is not clear that employers as a group have been particularly effective in influencing the structure or scope of the system. From the very beginning, the National Association of Manufacturers and the U.S. Chamber of Commerce raised concerns about the system, but that was a natural reflexive reaction of employers to government-imposed costs on employment. Although these trade groups have raised basic philosophical questions about Social Security from time to time, it is interesting that they have not been able to mobilize their members to wage an organized campaign against the program, considering its costs. We believe that business has been relatively passive about Social Security up until now because the benefits that have accrued to business have been substantially greater than the costs.

The evolution of the Clark amendment during the 1935 congressional deliberations over the Social Security Act emanated from the business community. The Clark amendment would have exempted employers who sponsored retirement plans for their own employees from having to participate in Social Security. In Chapter 3 we explained that this amendment ended up being the stickiest issue to work out between the House and Senate with regard to the final passage of the 1935 Social Security Act. Its chief advocate was Walter Forster from Philadelphia. He was a principal in a firm named Towers, Perrin, Forster & Crosby, or TPF&C for short. At the time, TPF&C was an insurance brokerage firm that was selling insurance contracts to large employers for, among other things, financing retirement benefits for their workers.

When one of the current authors (Schieber) was working on an earlier book on Social Security in 1982, he talked with principals at TPF&C about Forster's advocacy of the Clark amendment. They told him that almost immediately after the passage of the 1935 Act, Forster had recognized that his pushing for the Social Security exemption for employers with retirement programs had been a mistake. One likely reason for such a conclusion was the realization that Social Security was going to be an extremely good deal for employers who wanted to sponsor retirement plans of their own. There was ample evidence that employers were interested in setting up such plans. Retirement plans were important to business efficiency. Windfall Social Security benefits made the financing of "adequate" retirement benefits an extremely cheap proposition for employers from the 1950s through the 1970s.

If the concept of pensions was germinating among large businesses during the late nineteenth and early twentieth centuries, Social Security acted as a catalyst to speed up the process. Birchard Wyatt was the chief technical adviser to the Social Security Board during 1936 and 1937, as the board became involved in the early development of the administration systems that would be needed to put the program into operation. He had finished his doctoral dissertation at Columbia University shortly before signing on as a consultant with the board. The topic of his dissertation was private group retirement plans.[5] Steven Sass in his book *The Promise of Private Pensions* describes Birchard Wyatt as a "young and charismatic" salesman and a "remarkable leader and strategist." Wyatt's combined understanding of the potential of employer-sponsored pensions and Social Security led him to establish his own consulting firm.

When Wyatt was first organizing his business, he visualized pensions as continuing to be organized and financed through insurance mechanisms. At first, he thought he was setting up a business to compete with TPF&C in the selling of insurance contracts to companies wanting to sponsor a retirement program for their employees. But the changing regulatory environment and business opportunities turned it in another direction. George Buck, an actuary and consultant from New York, helped the Ford Motor Company set up a pension trust to fund and manage its own pension system. Being able to cut the insurance companies out of the action offered financial benefits for plan sponsors because they could cut out the commissions and loading costs charged by insurance companies on the pension annuity contracts. Wyatt quickly capitalized on the approach that Buck had laid out and opened several offices around the United States to counsel employers on setting up and running their own retirement programs.

Sass, who recognizes Wyatt's sales acumen, suggests that "Wyatt's greatest sale was selling his brand-new firm to some of the finest actuaries in the nation. In three years Wyatt recruited a cadre of first-class actuaries, including former Social Security actuary Dorrance Bronson, one of the most highly regarded figures in the profession."[6] Bronson had been a senior actuary at Social Security working for W. Rulon Williamson, the chief actuary of the system. Just before Wyatt, not yet forty years of age, died of cancer in 1946, his company was reorganized as a corporation, the Wyatt Company, and Williamson was brought in to be its first president. The knowledge of and association with Social Security was extremely important in the creation of this business.

Wyatt ended up starting a business that provided actuarial services to employers so they could set up and run their own retirement plans. In the end, his company would compete with TPF&C because the latter would change the nature of their business to provide the same services as Wyatt and his associates. Wyatt's company, Buck, TPF&C, and a host of other companies would ultimately create a multibillion dollar industry of consulting to firms on the creation and financing of their retirement programs. Virtually all of these firms were heavily staffed with actuaries who fully understood the esoteric details of retirement plan financing and the role that Social Security played in it. If the unions understood the value of Social Security in furthering their goals, it is certain these people also understood how Social Security could be used to further the interests of their business clients.

In October 1951, the U.S. Chamber of Commerce, which had had reservations about Social Security from the start, ran an article extolling the tremendous benefits that were accruing under the system. The article began: "If you got a letter in this morning's mail telling you that you had suddenly inherited $41,000 free of income and estate taxes, how would you feel?"[7] The article went on to explain the tremendous value of life insurance in the system and to assert that under the new amendments that had been recently enacted, a worker could "be entitled to $20,000 worth of pensions by paying as little as $81 in social security tax."[8] It doesn't seem that the windfall gains being provided by Social Security were a closely held secret from the business community.

Not only was there free money to be had from participating in Social Security, but it was there to serve business interests. Marion Folsom, a

Kodak executive who served on several Social Security advisory councils and who was eventually appointed the secretary of the Department of Health, Education, and Welfare, spoke directly to the issue. He told about the situation Kodak had faced after the company had been operating for about forty years. "Some of the older people had passed their peak productiveness. The management was becoming quite concerned about what they were going to do with them. They looked into it and found that some of them couldn't get along very well if retired. The company didn't have a pension plan."[9] After a while, Mr. Eastman was convinced to set one up. He set up one of the first funded plans in industrial America. Folsom indicated that many business "people were worried about what effect the government plan would have on existing pensions plans" when the original Social Security Act was under consideration. Folsom told his business counterparts that "as far as Kodak was concerned, we simply would make a reduction in our plan. Part of it would come from Social Security, part from the company plan."[10] The part coming from Social Security would be provided on a heavily subsidized basis that made the program an extremely good deal for employers in situations similar to Kodak's.

Folsom also told another story along the same lines about Charlie Wilson, the president of General Motors. In January 1950, Wilson had given a speech in Chicago, where he said:

> In a modern plant, with progressive manufacturing and conveyor assembly lines, a man who can't keep up his part of the work must be taken off that job. He can't do sixty percent of it as he gets older because that would reduce the whole production down to sixty percent. . . .
>
> The problem would seem to be how to provide pensions at a tolerable cost without destroying self-reliance, without reducing effort on the part of the individual, without tying a man to his job and without destroying the initiative of the millions on which the prosperity of our country depends. . . .
>
> Adequate Federal pensions financed on a sound basis would seem to be the real answer to the problem. . . .
>
> I do not consider that federal pensions fully paid for by employer and employee are in any sense contrary to free enterprise but amount to an extension of the principle of group insurance.[11]

Later Folsom ended up at a meeting in Hot Springs, Arkansas, where Charlie Wilson was pushing the idea that Social Security should be expanded to be more than just a floor of protection. Folsom took the other side, arguing that it was up to the companies to design supplemental plans for all their employees to supplement the "floor of protection" provided through the federal plan. At the end of Folsom's presentation, Wilson came up and told him he was sold.[12] Realizing that Social Security was not going to do the whole job, within a year or so, General Motors (GM) would set up its own pension plans as supplements to the federal plan. Dorrance Bronson, the former Social Security actuary now at the Wyatt Company, would help them do so. Both GM and its unions realized the potential value of a pension plan from their separate perspectives, and Social Security facilitated their achieving common goals.

Organizing the Beneficiary Population

In some regards, the organized interests of the potential beneficiary populations were a strong motivator behind the development of the original Social Security Act. Franklin Roosevelt and other prominent policymakers had worried about the strength of the Townsend movement and Huey Long's campaign to soak the rich. In response, they saw the sponsorship of Social Security as a conservative approach to quelling the elderly's appetite for unfunded assistance programs, derisively referred to as free pensions. The Townsend movement would continue to agitate for such free pensions at more generous levels than Social Security's benefits paid during the 1940s. But the significant increase in benefits, the expansion of coverage, and the new start provisions under the 1950 Amendments would serve to squelch organized campaigns for more.

As an organized group, the Social Security beneficiary population would remain relatively dormant until the system matured. But during the 1970s and the 1980s a number of organizations would spring up in response to threats to benefit gains achieved previously.

The Public Policy Stakeholders

Today almost every citizen has some financial stake in our Social Security system. But there are several groups of individuals involved in the development of public policy in this area which have stakes that go beyond their own personal interests in the program. We have already alluded to two of these groups in the prior discussions, the advisory councils, and the members of the House of Representatives and the Senate who actually vote on Social Security legislation. The third group includes the academics and policy analysts who do research and policy advocacy analysis in this area.

The work of the people in this third group is often sponsored by one of the other sets of players in the Social Security policy arena.

The Advisory Councils

The use of advisory councils for Social Security policy development pre-dates the program. There had been an advisory council that served as part of the development of the original law. It was to provide advice to the Committee on Economic Security, although its role was extremely limited. The first effective council was the one that Senator Arthur Vandenberg had insisted on in 1937 in the midst of his arguments with Arthur Altmeyer over the appropriate financing approach for Social Security. When Vandenberg was looking for guidance on how to move away from the reserve funding basis put in place by the 1935 Social Security Act, he simply did not trust the Social Security Board to investigate the alternatives on a fair basis.[13] Rather than let the Congress go off and study the issue on its own, Altmeyer finally conceded to the advisory council idea. Despite his reservations, Altmeyer must have been pleased with the outcome. The 1937–1938 council set the agenda for the 1939 amendments, including the provision of survivor and dependent benefits, things Altmeyer supported.

We have already described how the 1947–1948 Advisory Council on Social Security led to the important 1950 Amendments. The council's work helped set the stage for further developments. When Dwight Eisenhower became president, he appointed Oveta Culp Hobby secretary of the Department of Health, Education, and Welfare, the parent organization of the Social Security Administration. The managers at the SSA were concerned that the combination of a Republican administration and Republican-dominated Congress would spell trouble. The Republicans in Congress, after all, had fought SSA managers on funding for years and had repeatedly come back to the proposals for universal pensions. Carl Curtis was still on a universal pension campaign and advocating pay-go financing as the 1950 Amendments came under consideration.

Hobby did not put the SSA crowd at rest when she began meeting regularly with a small group of advisers on a casual basis. This group, which came to be known as the Hobby lobby, was predominantly made up of individuals from the U.S. Chamber of Commerce. The chamber was advocating universal pensions and pay-go financing. After complaints from organized labor, the lobby was expanded to twelve members, including two from organized labor and two from the agricultural sector. This group became the 1953 Advisory Council that recommended the expansions in coverage adopted in the 1954 Amendments.[14] One of Hobby's young assistants described the 1953 advisory council report as "a straight SSA report. . . . just churned up right out of Ball's boys."[15]

The 1956 Social Security Amendments included provisions requiring regular appointment of advisory councils. It specified that the Social Security commissioner would serve as the chair and that the councils would include twelve other members representing employers, employees, and the general public. For the remainder of Bob Ball's tenure inside Social Security, these councils would be strong supporters of the program and its managers' agenda. Martha Derthick observes that the history of the councils

> poses an obvious puzzle. The six advisory groups between 1937 and 1971 were strikingly different in their origins and strikingly similar in their results. The first one was inspired by Congress, even if it was technically a joint executive-legislative creature. The second was created by Congress though inspired by executives behind the scenes. The third was created by the administration acting alone. The last three were appointed by the executive (the secretary of HEW) according to statutory prescription. The second, third, fourth, and sixth councils began under Republican auspices. So did the first, if Vandenberg is regarded as its originator. Only one—the council of 1963–1965 —was unequivocally the creature of a Democratic administration. Yet they all approved the program fundamentally. None ever produced a substantial, significant critique of it. Most called for major expansion.[16]

Looking back at the advisory councils that operated during the maturing phase of Social Security, they were consistently dominated by people who were committed to the program. Early on, this came about partly because the senior policy and research staff at Social Security knew more about social insurance than anyone else. J. Douglas Brown, Arthur Altmeyer, and Edwin Witte dominated the first council that Brown chaired. Robert Ball was the executive director of the second council, and while he was considered an outsider, he was philosophically as much an insider as could have been found at the time. After the Hobby council, which was co-opted when it expanded, Ball would dominate or chair most of the remaining councils up through the beginning of the 1970s. J. Douglas Brown served on all of them, and he certainly saw the program in terms consistent with the philosophies developed by Ball and Wilbur Cohen. The seats reserved for members of organized labor were automatic votes for their approach as well. Kodak's Marion Folsom was the business representative on several of the councils. Highly respected in the business community, he was a supporter of the program and would bring other business people along to share his attitude toward it.

Besides getting the right people around each of the council tables, it was equally important to get them the right information so they could make appropriate decisions. The staffing of the various councils was carried out through the SSA except for the 1947–1948 council, when Bob Ball was in charge as an outsider. The importance of the staff's controlling the flow of information and process should not be underestimated. For example, Marion Folsom recalls that at the beginning of the 1937–1938 council the opponents of survivor benefits outnumbered the supporters by two to one. But in the end, they were all for it. "You see, we met with the social security people. They sat in on all our discussions, so everybody came out all together on the thing." [17] Through the council membership selection process and the staffing device, the outsiders became insiders, or at least partners with the insiders. To policymakers, the councils gave the appearance of outside citizens looking independently at the important issues of the day. At the conclusion of a council's deliberations, its members were often excellent candidates to appear before congressional committees and explain why specific policy measures should be considered and adopted. They helped move the agenda forward.

The Academics and Peripheral Academics

From its outset, Social Security has always been of interest to academics. Some have focused primarily on its social welfare aspects, others on its underlying economic implications for various facets of our lives. Roughly from the point that it was reaching maturity, it has been the focus of a number of historical and political science analyses. Much of the academic research that has developed around the program has emanated from people in academic institutions, but several policy research organizations have devoted special attention to the system as well. Today, this would include organizations like the Brookings Institution and the Urban Institute, which generally favor the program and its current structure, and the Cato Institute and the Heritage Foundation, which generally favor alternatives to the current system.

The social welfare researchers have on the whole concluded that more is better in the case of Social Security. They have often found reasons that the employer-based pension system is greatly inferior to Social Security and that the resources devoted to those programs would be better channeled through the national system. During the 1960s this group's influence reached its zenith. It was during this period that the Kennedy and Johnson administrations focused on poverty and dedicated significant resources toward its eradication. Social Security was perceived to be a particularly effective approach to such endeavors, because its beneficiaries did not have to bear the stigmatizing burden so often associated with other governmental welfare programs. We believe this group's focus on the good that Social Security has achieved often led it to ignore the cost burden that it implies. This was particularly true before the maturing of the system in the mid-1970s.

Economists have focused on various aspects of Social Security's role in our society and economy. While they were not generally prominent players in the discussions about the funding approach that should be followed in the early days of the program, they have expended considerable energies over the years in assessing the implications of Social Security for personal savings rates and pay-go financing for national saving. They have studied the effects of the program on behavior of the labor force at various ages, the extent to which it has helped to alleviate poverty, whether it is a good deal for its participants, and a host of other issues. Most of the attention that Social Security has received from people of this academic discipline has come since the program reached its maturity in the mid-1970s. Certainly Milton Friedman at the University of Chicago, who would later win the Nobel Prize in economics, was concerned earlier about the negative effects of Social Security on the disposition to save money. But Friedman was counterbalanced by equally prominent people like Paul Samuelson, whose analysis of the system discussed in Chapter 7 could put people at ease.

As Social Security was approaching maturity, several economists began to devote considerable attention to the program. Those like Henry Aaron and Joe Pechman at the Brookings Institution in Washington were developing analyses that would support considerable expansion of the program. For example, Aaron and Pechman, along with Michael Taussig, developed a rationale for significantly expanding benefits that served as the basis for such expansions in 1972.[18] On the other side, Martin Feldstein was beginning to publish a series of analyses suggesting that the pay-as-you-go financing underlying Social Security was having an adverse impact on the economy.[19] As the decade of the 1970s wore on, even economists within government, like Lawrence Thompson at DHEW, would become heavily involved in the analysis of Social Security policy.[20] By the middle and latter part of that decade it was increasingly apparent that economists' role was expanding.

The traditional architects of policy were wary of the economists and unhappy with the role they were assuming. Wilbur Cohen's biographer tells us that "Cohen believed that the economists simply did not understand Social Security because they had come into the policy discussions too late."[21] Bob Ball told Cohen in 1972 that they were "really going to have to work on the whole area of economic criticism" of the program.[22] Probably the most carefully articulated criticism of economists playing in the Social Security policy game during this era came from Bob Myers. He wrote an article in 1976 considering the relative roles of actuaries and economists in analyzing Social Security costs and financing. He observed that "economists in their consideration of Social Security programs, expecially [sic] ones involving long-range benefits such as OASDI, tend to lack knowledge of the fundamental nature of insurance and pension plans."[23] He went on to criticize work by Paul Samuelson, Martin Feldstein, Lawrence Thompson, and others. He concluded from these examples that "that there is no primary role" in analyzing the cost and financing of Social Security "for others than actuaries."[24]

Bob Myers' thinking notwithstanding, attention from economists has increased since the program has matured, because of its size, its intrusion into a variety of economic activities, and concerns about its potential effects. Today, we perceive that there is a growing consensus among economists on certain issues related to Social Security. For example, we believe that most economists today would agree we should be funding Social Security to a much greater extent than we have in the past. There is little consensus, however, on how that funding should be achieved.

The historians and political scientists have been major contributors to our understanding of the evolution of the system. The works by people like Andrew Achenbaum, Edward Berkowitz, Jerry Cates, Martha Derthick, Mark Leff, and others we have cited repeatedly weave a rich fabric of a story about the political evolution of Social Security in the United States and some of its most effective architects. Their work tends to be retrospective, and while it helps us understand what we have, it is less instructive about where we should go from here. Most of the people who have done research in this area are impressed with the effectiveness of Social Security in achieving universal coverage, retirement income security, and mass acceptance. They tend to conclude that we have a pretty good institution and should stick by it. We believe they fail to appreciate that Social Security was sold as a better deal than it is now turning out to be.

One group noticeably absent from *our* list of researchers is the actuarial community. The actuaries are a deferential group of old-guard professionals. The actuarial investigations of Social Security in the United States have been largely under the close control of the actuaries directly associated with the program. Bob Myers developed the estimates of the costs associated with the old-age benefits proposal for the 1935 Act. Between then and his formal departure from Social Security in 1970, he was involved in virtually all assessments of the program. He left behind a system and a philosophy that largely persist within Social Security to this day. After leaving Social Security in 1970, Myers went to work for the congressional oversight committees. He remains actively involved in policy deliberations even today. There is only one actuary in the United States who has been willing to publicly challenge the view that Bob Myers and Social Security Administration have provided to the public. That is A. Haeworth Robertson, who served as chief actuary after Myers left Social Security. Although he has written two books and given many public speeches on the subject, he has been unable to capture the public's attention with his criticism of the system's long-term financial status. He calls Social Security "one of the greatest frauds ever perpetrated on the American public." [25]

The Ultimate Arbiters

No matter what role everyone else assumes, it is the political players who ultimately own the policymaking process. This ownership lies with the politically elected leaders of the administrative and legislative branches of our federal government. The two parties are widely perceived as having traveled different roads relative to Social Security policy advocacy over the years. The Democrats have been able to convert Social Security policy into the maypole of party cohesion. For the Republicans it has been a minefield that has often exploded on them.

The maypole is a tall pole that is decorated at the top with flowers or garlands and hung with colorful ribbons that are woven into complex patterns by dancers, each of whom holds a ribbon as they all circle the pole. It is often part of the celebration of spring, part of May Day celebrations. The Democrats laid claim to the Social Security system at the outset and have consistently hailed it as FDR's greatest legacy. Especially in its start-up phase, Social Security offered the Democrats an opportunity to come back time and time again to the American electorate to expand the protections against the vicissitudes of life. Each new set of benefits was another garland in the Democratic leadership's delivery of benefits to the voting public. Higher benefits were the ribbons around which elections could be managed and won. More and bigger benefits could often be offered at a cost that seemed so trivial it was beyond belief. For those who understood that there would be future obligations, the assumption was that future generations would somehow figure out how to cope with them. As J. Douglas Brown had said to Edwin Witte when the latter was fretting about the magnitude of burdens they were creating for future generations, "We will all be dead."[26]

The Republicans began to set the stage for their experience with Social Security in the 1936 presidential campaign, when the party and Alf Landon, the Republican presidential candidate, came out in opposition to the program. His objections blew up in his face as Roosevelt was elected in a landslide. Even though the Republicans supported the program time after time, the incessant fighting with FDR and Altmeyer over the funding issue raised the specter of their opposition in principle to the whole affair. It made little difference that the move to pay-go financing allowed the system's advocates to build up benefits much more rapidly in the early years than would have been the case if Roosevelt's funding goals had been pursued. The pursuit of universal pensions for the first fifteen years of the program could be characterized as Republican opposition to the concept of soundly financed contributory social insurance. The insistence on the initial advisory councils could be seen as a threat to the able administration of the system, even though the councils repeatedly supported the agenda of the program's proponents. The active opposition to Disability Insurance and Medicare were clear proof that the Republicans had never embraced the goals of the program. Not only did they not embrace it philosophically; they did not soil their hands with its administration. It is almost unbelievable that Martha Derthick could write in 1979: "It is a remarkable fact that no active Republican has ever served as commissioner of social security."[27] John Tramburg, who served as commissioner for about a year under Eisenhower, was a registered Republican, but he was nonpolitical.

In this environment, Social Security evolved from FDR's vision of a cornerstone to an essentially completed system. It started with retirement benefits in 1935 that were to be financed on the basis of private insurance principles. It grew to include survivor and spousal benefits in 1939, and shifted much more toward the principles being advocated by social insurance theorists at the time. It inched toward pay-go financing throughout the 1940s. With significant increases in benefits in the early 1950s and coverage expansions, it moved toward universality and reached pay-go financing by the mid-1950s. In 1956, Disability Insurance was added. Finally, in the mid-1960s Medicare was provided. The structure was complete. Nearly the full scope of the vision originally held by the social engineers who had nurtured the system from infancy to maturity had been realized.

Chapter 10

The End of the Beginning

*B*y the mid-1960s, Social Security had reached its full breadth of protections against the vicissitudes of life. No new significant coverage would be added through the remainder of the century. Medicare benefits would be extended to the disabled in 1972, but that was an extension of an existing benefit to already eligible beneficiaries rather than the creation of a totally new one. Even though the system had reached the full breadth of its operation (coverage of old age, survivors, disability, and dependents), the social engineers inside the system were not finished pressing their agenda. They now shifted their attention to the second dimension of the system, its depth.

During the 1960s, Walter Cronkite was the lead news anchor for the CBS television network. Periodically on his national evening newscast he would run a piece showing that some old people in our society had to survive on diets of dog or cat food because they did not have enough resources to buy regular groceries. Officially, government statistics showed that poverty rates among the elderly were nearly three times what they were among the general population. What good was a social insurance system if it left disproportionate numbers of its beneficiaries in poverty?

Ronald Reagan had campaigned for Barry Goldwater, the 1964 Republican presidential candidate, to advocate that Social Security should be made a voluntary program. One of the Democrats' campaign television advertisements against Goldwater showed a Social Security card being burned, with the implication that the conservative Republicans would destroy the system. Lyndon Baines Johnson won the election in a landslide. The combination of Johnson's mandate and the fact that he was still pursuing President Kennedy's agenda helped create the favorable environment in which Medicare was passed in 1965. And LBJ's war on poverty set the stage for the last big policy initiative by Social Security's executives before the system would reach maturity.

Approaching Maturity but Moving On

As the program approached maturity, its underlying calculus would begin to change. No longer could benefit increases be achieved without commensurate tax increases. In order to demonstrate that, we will once again focus on the financing structure underlying the system and analyze how the underlying dynamics of pay-as-you-go funding resulted in new realities for beneficiaries and for workers. In the earlier discussion about pay-go financing we showed that two crucial ratios drove the costs of Social Security. The first of these was the dependency ratio.

The left-hand panel of Figure 10.1 shows the Social Security dependency ratio during the program's early years. As noted before, the ratio of beneficiaries to workers rose steadily over the period. This happened because the general size of the elderly population in the United States was increasing relative to that of the working-age population and because the beneficiary population had been phased in extremely slowly over a thirty-five-year period. By the mid-1970s the phase-in was over, as was the artificial growth in the dependency ratio. After that, the dependency ratio pattern would change markedly. The dependency ratio for the twenty years after the system reached maturity is shown in the right-hand panel of Figure 10.1. Once maturity was reached, the ratio became virtually static for twenty years. It is expected to remain at current levels for roughly the next ten years.

In 1965, at the completion of the campaign for passage of Medicare, Social Security executives could reasonably anticipate that the dependency ratio in the system was going to stabilize. The overwhelming majority of the people who would qualify for benefits over the next twenty years were already part of the covered population. The disability rate could not be predicted with the same accuracy as the growth in aged population, but it could be predicted closely enough to make it clear that it would not create the kind of variance in dependency ratios experienced during the start-up of the system. Most of the people who would work and pay taxes into the system over the remainder of the century were also alive in 1965. It is unlikely that Social Security executives could have anticipated the extent to which women baby boomers would enter and stay in the workforce, but that development would work in favor of the executives, not against them.

Robert Ball, the commissioner of Social Security, wrote an article in the June 1966 issue of the *Social Security Bulletin* laying out the remaining

Figure 10.1   Social Security Dependency Ratios from 1940 to 1975 and
After the Maturing of the Program from 1975 to 1995

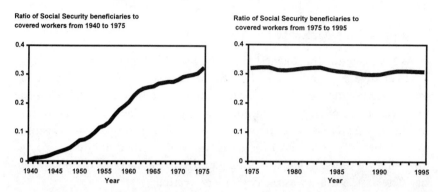

Sources: Social Security Administration, *Social Security Bulletin, Annual Statistical Supplement, 1976*
(Washington, D.C.: Social Security Administration), pp. 76, 96, and Social Security Admin-
istration, *Social Security Bulletin, Annual Statistical Supplement, 1996* (Washington, D.C.: Social
Security Administration), pp. 184, 214.

"Policy Issues in Social Security."[1] He lamented that some policy analysts
had recently been evaluating Social Security in the context of its effects on
poverty. He argued that Social Security was not just a program to reduce
poverty but a retirement system with a broader purpose. He said that

> the continued reliance on social security as the plan supplying the
> major part of retirement income has many advantages . . . over count-
> ing on private pensions to play a larger and larger role. . . .
>
> Judged as the retirement system it is, social security properly con-
> tributes to the income security of higher paid earners. . . . Any system
> of paying money to people who demonstrate they don't have enough
> money, by definition would do a better job of getting money to only
> the very poor, but why would we want to limit our economic security
> objectives to such a goal?
>
> Thus the first order of priority is an increase in benefit levels, and
> I would say that increase is needed throughout the whole range of
> covered earnings and not just for those earning minimum amounts.
> A *general* benefit increase is necessary if the program is to continue
> in its role as a useful retirement system for workers with average and
> above-average earnings as well as those at the minimum.
>
> We are concerned about the low amounts of some of the actuari-

ally reduced benefits payable under present law to those who claim benefits before age 65. More than half the men awarded retirement benefits in 1965 are getting reduced benefits because they came on the rolls before age 65, and their benefits are, on average, much lower than the benefit amounts payable to men who came on the rolls at age 65 or after.

In addition to the need for improving the adequacy of social security benefits as initially awarded, there is also the question of keeping the benefits up to date once they have been determined. . . .

Automatic adjustment of social security benefits to changes in price levels could be provided for without increases in the contribution rates that underlie the financing of the system. . . .

One possible . . . position is to relate benefits to wages before retirement . . . and then keep up to date with prices for those on the benefit rolls.[2]

Ball acknowledged that the benefit enhancements that he was proposing came with a price tag. He called for automatic increases in the earnings base subject to the payroll tax. He noted that without such increases, the share of earnings on which benefits were based would decline over time. But he went on to point out that without increases in the taxable earnings base, the ability to respond to new needs would be limited. Ball aspired to more. The general benefit increase he had in mind "could not be financed by an increase in the contribution and benefit base alone."[3] As an alternative, Ball suggested a "government contribution" was worthy of consideration.

Converting the Plan into Action

As Ball was laying out his agenda, Wilbur Cohen was an undersecretary in the Department of Health, Education, and Welfare. When Cohen went to President Johnson with a proposal for a 10 percent increase in Social Security benefits in 1966, LBJ responded: "Come on, Wilbur, you can do better than that."[4] And he did. The legislative package that the administration sent to Congress in 1967 called for increasing benefits 15 percent. But this was not going to be just another increase in benefits for those now employed. It was going to include a rebalancing of benefit distribution for workers, as shown in Table 10.1. The table shows the initial replacement rates for workers at different levels of average monthly earnings. The replacement rate, in this case, is the ratio of initial benefits to a worker's level of career earnings. The proposal called for all new beneficiaries to get

Table 10.1   Proposed Increases in Social Security
Replacement Rates for a Couple Age Sixty-Five or Over,
1965

Average monthly earnings (dollars)	Replacement Rate		Proposed Increase
	Actual	Proposed	
100	94.8%	109.1%	15.1%
200	67.5	77.6	15.0
300	56.2	64.7	15.1
400	51.0	58.6	14.9
500	47.1	54.1	14.9
650	38.8	47.8	23.2
750	33.6	45.1	34.2
900	28.0	42.0	50.0

Sources: *President's Proposals for Revisions in the Social Security System*, hearings
before the House Committee on Ways and Means, 90th Congress, 1st sess.
(Washington, D.C.: U.S. Government Printing Office, 1967), pt. 1, p. 224, as
presented in Martha Derthick, *Policymaking for Social Security*, p. 344.

higher benefits. But workers at the top of the earnings distribution would
get much bigger increases than those at the bottom.

The move to increase benefits more for workers at the top of the earnings distribution scale was in keeping with Ball's proposition that such
increases were necessary if the program was to be "a useful retirement system for workers with average and above-average earnings."[5] One possible
motivation behind the structure of benefit changes reflected in Table 10.1
may have been related to Ball's concern that "future generations of covered
workers will get protection that is worth less than the combined employer-
employee contributions with respect to their earnings."[6] Unless benefits
could be ratcheted up, Social Security was going to turn out to be a lousy
economic deal for some workers. It would be more so for high earners than
for those at the bottom of the earnings spectrum. Bob Myers concluded
that the proposal was simply the system expansionists' means of supplant-
ing employer-based plans.[7] If that was the case, it was going against the
long-held philosophy that Social Security was meant to be a "floor of protection" on which employer pensions and personal savings would build.[8]

The proposal to raise benefits in the 1967 legislative package was coupled
with recommendations for raising both the contribution base and the payroll tax rate to finance the benefit increases. For Bob Ball and Wilbur
Cohen, increasing the tax base was extremely important. As an argument
for increasing the share to be covered at any particular point, they would

often point back to the beginning of the program and note that originally a much larger share of earnings had been covered. The history of the amount covered is shown in Figure 10.2. The share of earnings covered under the system was lower in the mid-1960s than it had been previously. But other than the fact that Social Security executives wanted more revenue, there was no particular reason that any specific share of earnings should be subject to the payroll tax.

The original tax base of $3,000 that had been set in the 1935 Social Security Act came from the work done by the Committee on Economic Security. J. Douglas Brown said that the staff developing the package had used "esthetic logic" in divining that the original level should be $3,000. He described "esthetic logic" in relating how the staff had hit on age sixty-five as the appropriate retirement age stipulated in the original package. "It looked good. If you said 67 and a half, or 66, somebody would say, 'Why?' 65 somehow fits. It's like saying 50-50. It settles the argument. It's emotional, I admit. I call it 'esthetic logic.' If you said 60-40, you'd still be arguing."[9] In the case of the $3,000, Brown said, "Well most of these things are compromises, and they come out with some element of esthetic logic. $3,000 looked very good. It was $250 a month."[10] It is amazing what religious zeal can do if it's backed by a little esthetic logic.

Figure 10.2   Share of Total Earnings Subject to the Payroll Tax

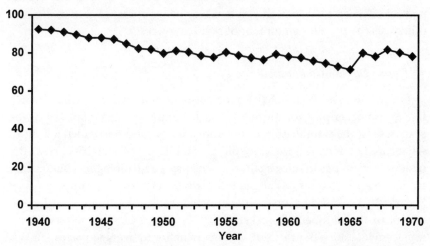

Source: Social Security Administration, *Social Security Bulletin, Annual Statistical Supplement, 1997,* p. 167.

Wilbur Cohen raised the issue of tax increases with the president in the context of their having a dampening effect on inflation as well as raising revenues.[11] LBJ was conducting his dual wars at the time, one in Vietnam and the other on poverty, and both were making significant claims on the federal purse. There were growing concerns that the high level of government expenditure was fueling the fires of inflation. Cohen had estimated that raising the taxable wage base from $6,600 to $15,000 would produce an added $4.5 billion in federal revenue.[12] Early in the development of the 1967 legislative package, Cohen also was pressing to raise the combined payroll tax from 8.8 percent to 10 percent of covered payroll. But George Meany of the AFL opposed an increase in the tax rate because of the impact it would have on union members, so Cohen backed off.[13]

In the end, Congress passed legislation that increased benefits by 13 percent, but the proposal for significant increases in benefits for high earners did not pass. The new legislation provided for the payroll tax on employers and employees to rise from 4.4 percent in 1967 to 4.8 percent in 1969. It increased covered earnings from $6,600 in 1967 to $7,800 for 1968, up from $4,800 in 1965. The new covered earnings provisions would capture roughly 82 percent of total U.S. earnings under the system.[14]

With Richard Nixon's election in 1968 and the Republicans' ascendancy in 1969, there was reason to believe that the Social Security agenda would change. It did not. Robert Ball remained commissioner at Social Security, and the next four years would result in spectacular gains in the expansionary agenda that he advocated. This would happen for a couple of crucial reasons. One was the way the system was being operated actuarially. The other was the peculiar alignment of political forces.

Tuning Up Pay-Go Financing

On the surface, Robert Ball's 1966 *Social Security Bulletin* article looked like just another play for more. It went beyond that. The maturing of the system with the stabilization of the dependency ratio portended a limit to what could be achieved with payroll tax. Stabilizing of Social Security's dependency ratio ties in once again with the pay-go financing mechanics that we laid out in Chapter 5. The payroll tax rate (t) needed to support Social Security is the product of the dependency ratio—the number of beneficiaries to the number of workers (N_B/N_W)—and the system's earnings-replacement rate—the ratio of average benefits to average wages (B/W). From now on, any increase in benefits relative to wages would result in a direct feedback effect on the necessary tax rate to finance the system. But the opposite was true as well. Even though the costs of the system were now more directly linked to benefit levels, it was being operated in a way that provided an opportunity to increase benefits substantially without having them filter through directly to the tax rate.

The actuaries' estimates of the costs of the system had always been based on the assumption that the benefit level would remain constant in the future. The benefit formula at any point in time was defined by law, and it was only changes in law that could increase benefits, so the actuaries believed that in developing their cost estimates, they were simply reflecting how the program worked. The actuaries also assumed that average wages on which taxes were levied would remain constant in the future. If they had assumed that average wages would rise over time, it would have implied that the cost rate of the program would fall as they did so. This did not seem likely, and the actuaries observed that Congress had regularly amended the benefit formula to increase benefits. Indeed if you look back to Figure 7.4, you will see that the ratio of average benefits to average wages was almost constant from 1950 through the mid-1960s.

An example will help to clarify how this worked. The dependency ratio in the late 1960s was approaching 0.3 and was not growing as rapidly as it had up through the early 1960s. For the sake of the example, assume that the dependency ratio was constant at 0.30 for a couple of years. Also assume that the ratio of benefits to wages was about 0.40, reflecting an average benefit of $8,000 per year compared to an average wage of $20,000. The tax rate that would result under this set of assumptions would be 12 percent—that is, 0.30 × 0.40 = 0.12. Now assume that wages grow by 10 percent from one year to the next. The original average wage of $20,000 would rise to $22,000 in the second year. If Social Security benefits stayed constant, the new ratio of average benefits to average wages would decline from 0.40 to 0.364—that is, $8,000/$22,000 = 0.364. If the dependency ratio remained constant and the benefit to wage ratio declined to 0.364, the resulting cost of the retirement system would now be 10.9 percent—that is, 0.30 × 0.364 = 0.109.

Under our hypothetical scenario, the Congress that was responsible for the Social Security system faced two choices. It could reduce the payroll tax to reflect the fact that the growth in wages was driving down the cost of the system. Alternatively, Congress could raise the level of benefits provided to retirees and raise the cost of the system back to the cost level it had operated at in the past. If it chose to do the latter, in our hypothetical example Congress could raise benefits exactly 10 percent and still leave the cost of the system where it had been previously. To see this, increase the

$8,000 benefit to $8,800 and follow the calculation. The new ratio of average benefits to average wages would be $8,800/$22,000 = 0.40. Multiplying that by the constant dependency ratio, the cost of the system would again be 0.12 — that is, 0.30 × 0.40 = 0.12.

The crucial variable in determining the political possibilities for raising benefits without raising Social Security's costs was the average wage level. If average wages subject to the payroll tax rose, it provided the opportunity to increase the average benefit level. That is certainly one of the reasons that Bob Ball wanted to expand the Social Security tax base. Doing so would result in subjecting more earnings of workers under the old maximum to taxes, thus increasing average taxable wages. In addition, wages for workers at lower levels of earnings would be expected to grow from one year to the next. Figure 10.3 shows average taxable wages under the U.S. Social Security system from 1940 through 1970. Average covered wages rose in every single year.

The way the Social Security system's cost rate was estimated in combination with the phenomenon of steady wage growth allowed Congress to become a public Santa Claus. It could regularly increase benefits without having to increase the payroll tax rate to do so. If Congress could act like Santa Claus, the Social Security actuaries were the elves that supplied them with gifts to distribute regularly to the voting public. It all depended on wage growth, which appeared to be as reliable as the sun's coming up in the East. Wage growth offered Congress the repeated political opportunity of giving bigger benefits to voters. And the line in Figure 10.3 gets considerably steeper after the mid-1960s than it had been previously. That simply meant that Congress was presented with the opportunity to raise benefits even more than it had in the past. In 1969, it raised benefits by 15 percent.

By the end of Richard Nixon's first year in office, Bob Myers was beside himself over the situation that was unfolding. Myers, a lifelong Republican, knew that Ball and his expansionist compatriots were Democrats. Myers had been at the SSA through the Eisenhower years, when the expansionists had not been reined in, and here he was seeing it and living through it again in the Nixon administration. As he was watching developments unfold, he began his own public and private campaign to bring the expansionists under control. He wrote a series of articles and gave several speeches decrying what was happening under the nose of the Republicans. He spoke out about senior civil servants whose loyalty extended beyond the administration in which they served and who worked to carry out the interests of the programs they ran. He noted that they would even "work with the opposition," often on a sub rosa basis, to achieve their own goals.

Figure 10.3   Average Taxable Wages Under Social Security, 1940–1970

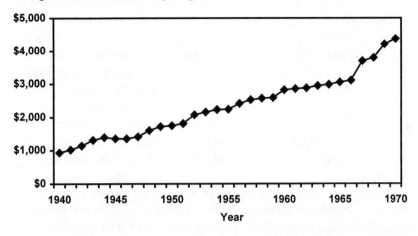

Sources: Social Security Administration, *Social Security Bulletin, Annual Statistical Supplement,* 1976, pp. 76, 96; and Social Security Administration, *Social Security Bulletin, Annual Statistical Supplement,* 1996, pp. 184, 214.

They would "spend extensive official time developing legislative proposals, drafting legislation, and writing supporting statements and speeches" for operatives who would further their agendas. Of the group of expansionists in Social Security, he said they believed that Social Security "should provide full economic security for the vast majority of the population (say, all but 5 or 10 percent). They hold the philosophy that private efforts in economic security have little likelihood of success." While Social Security had generally been considered a "floor of protection," the expansionists wanted the floor to have "a luxurious carpet laid on it through government action. . . . The expansionist school would like Social Security to be virtually monopolistic in economic security." [15]

Finally, Myers could not take it any more. He wrote to Robert Finch, the secretary of the Department of Health, Education, and Welfare:

I have previously talked with you about my strong personal beliefs and have given you much supporting factual evidence to substantiate my views—namely that certain of the top policy-making officials of the Social Security Administration (who are holdovers from the Johnson Administration) have strong beliefs in the desirability—even the necessity—of the public sector taking over virtually all economic security provisions for the entire population and thus eliminating private efforts in this area. It seems to me that this viewpoint is completely alien to that of the Nixon Administration.

Further, and equally important, it is my deeply-held conviction, as I have expressed to you a number of times in the past, that these officials of the Social Security Administration have not—and will not —faithfully and vigorously serve the Nixon Administration. Rather, they will exert their efforts to expand the Social Security program as much as possible by aiding and supporting any individuals and organizations that are of this expansionist conviction. Such anachronistic actions took place extensively during the Eisenhower Administration—against its political views. Such working at cross purposes with the Nixon Administration has occurred in the past year, and is still occurring. . . .

Evidently, no credence is placed in what I have related to you personally or in other evidence that I have furnished you on this matter, which has an important effect on the future of the Social Security program. Therefore, I must, in good conscience and personal integrity, resign. It is especially dismaying to me to have to take this action, because I had hoped to serve the Nixon Administration not only with competence and integrity—as I had tried to serve all previous Administrations—but also with great enthusiasm, since I strongly believe in its philosophy and goals.[16]

Going for the Gold

With Myers no longer on the inside at Social Security, there was even more opportunity to move ahead on the agenda for larger benefits. In 1969, another advisory council had been set up, and it was focusing on several of the issues that Bob Ball had spelled out in his 1966 *Social Security Bulletin* article quoted earlier. The advisory council submitted its final report in 1971. Its first recommendation was that Social Security benefits should be automatically increased at the rate of increase in prices and that the contribution and benefit base should be automatically increased at the rate of increase in wages. Further on, they recommended that the actuarial cost estimates for Social Security should be developed on the assumption "that earnings levels will rise, that the contribution and benefit base will be increased as earnings levels rise, and that benefit payments will be increased as prices rise."[17]

Once again, Social Security policy issues were in rare alignment, such that policymakers at both ends of the political spectrum wanted to pursue the same specific proposal to meet their own goals. Conservatives were interested in "automatic indexing" of Social Security benefits because they believed that through this method they would curtail the legislative tendency to enlarge them beyond the rate of growth of prices and wages. Liberal supporters of the program wanted automatic indexing because it secured benefits once they were attained. The stated intent of the recommendation by the advisory council was that initial benefits would grow over time at the rate of the growth of wages. Once benefits commenced, the goal was for automatic price increases to preserve the purchasing power of benefits over a retiree's lifetime.

The advisory council certified that "adequate provision has been made in the law to meet all the costs of the cash benefits program both in the short run and over the long-range future; the cash benefits program is actuarilly sound." [18] Once again they asserted the soundness of pay-go financing. Finally, they called for a change in the way that the actuaries would estimate the future costs of the system. Specifically, the council wanted the actuaries to change the assumptions that benefits and wages would remain on an even keel over the long-range valuation period for which cost estimates were developed. They noted that the method being used by the actuaries "results in a very considerable margin of safety in the financing of the program." [19] They continued: "This is true because earnings levels will in fact rise (contrary to the assumption used in the estimate), and the additional income from rising earnings is substantially greater than the benefit liability arising from the higher earnings. Thus, a long-range actuarial surplus is created each time earnings increase. As a matter of fact, if other assumptions on which the cost estimates are based turn out to be approximately correct, the additional income that develops as earnings rise will be enough to provide for benefit increases that go beyond increases in prices." [20] They went on to note their belief that the different valuation basis should be used whether or not recommendations for indexing of the system were adopted.

The recommendations for using "dynamic" assumptions that wages would grow emanated from the economics community, which was becoming increasingly interested in the program. In 1968, Joseph Pechman, Henry Aaron, and Michael Taussig, three economists at the Brookings Institution, published a far-ranging study of Social Security. They devoted a whole chapter to the assumptions used in valuing the costs and benefits of the system. They noted the contradiction in using static assumptions that benefits and wages would not grow in the future but dynamic assumptions that the demographics of the population would change. They characterized the resulting cost estimates as "a blend of static and dynamic projections" that "cannot be interpreted as forecasts of expenditures, revenues, and trust fund developments."[21]

The three Brookings Institution economists concluded that the static assumption that wages would not grow in the future resulted in the system's being perpetually overfinanced. As wages grow, both benefits and taxes increase, "but taxes increase much more than benefits because" of the redistributive structure of the benefit formula and "because benefits, which are determined in part on the basis of past, lower-earnings records, lag behind increases in earnings and payroll taxes."[22] There were two things that were extremely appealing about this analysis. First, while benefits might be subject to the actions of Congress, wages were driven by economic forces largely beyond congressional control. History did not support the assumption that wages would remain constant in the future. The simple observation that wages rose regularly, as shown earlier in Figure 10.3, seemed to mean that it would be safe to assume they would rise in the future. Second, if future wages were going to be higher than current wages, the economists at Brookings showed that it would be possible to increase benefits without a commensurate increase in the payroll tax rate.

Bob Myers opposed the move to dynamic assumptions, but on the outside he no longer had the influence he had as the internal keeper of the Social Security cost estimates. The advisory council's recommendations followed the Brookings analysis to the point of closely parallel language. Kermit Gordon, the president of the Brookings Institution, was an economist and chaired the advisory council's subcommittee on cost estimates. There were several other economists on the subcommittee, including Murray Latimer, who had worked on the original design of the system, and for them the appeal of Pechman, Aaron, and Taussig's analysis was clear. The one actuary on the subcommittee was an outsider, who did not protest the recommendation. It especially made sense within the context of the council's recommendations to index the system automatically to prices and wages.

For politicians, this was almost too good to be true. Congress was being presented with an opportunity to increase benefits even more than usual. A further pleasant by-product of moving to the new valuation methodology was that the payroll tax burden was expected to be lower for the next three or four decades than under the static valuation procedures. Table 10.2 shows the payroll tax schedule in effect in 1971 to finance Social Security benefits and the revised schedule recommended by the 1971 Advisory Council.

On March 17, 1971, two weeks before the advisory council's report was

Table 10.2   OASDI Tax Rates Under 1971 Law
and Rates Recommended by the 1968–1971
Advisory Council

Year	Tax Rate by Law	Recommended Tax Rate
1972	4.60%	4.70%
1973	5.00	4.65
1974–1975	5.00	4.45
1976–1977	5.15	4.40
1978–1979	5.15	4.35
1980–1981	5.15	4.35
1982–1986	5.15	4.20
1987–2020	5.15	4.20
2021–2045	5.15	5.50

Source: 1971 Advisory Council on Social Security, *Reports on the Old-
Age, Survivors, and Disability Insurance and Medicare Programs,* p. 96.

issued, President Nixon signed legislation which provided a 10 percent
across-the-board increase in Social Security benefits, retroactive to January 1, 1971. The tax base was raised from $7,800 to $9,000 for 1972. The
tax rate for the cash benefits programs was raised from 5 to 5.15 percent
on workers and on their employers, to take effect in 1976. The fulfillment
of the agenda to increase benefits was getting ahead of the justification for
doing so.

When Congress had reconvened at the beginning of 1971, the first bill
introduced in the House, H.R. 1, included significant Social Security legislation and also major welfare reform measures that had been passed by the
House the previous year. On June 22, 1971, H.R. 1 was passed by the House
and sent to the Senate. The Senate Finance Committee held hearings on
the bill during July and August but delayed further consideration of the bill
until February 1972. Slow progress on the combined package in H.R. 1 and
interest in providing a Social Security benefit increase before the elections
in November led to separate consideration of the Social Security legislation. In February 1972, Wilbur Mills, chairman of the House Ways and
Means Committee, introduced legislation calling for a 20 percent increase
in Social Security benefits and an increase in the maximum taxable income
to $10,200 in 1972 and $12,000 in 1973.

Mills' proposed tax rate schedule was based on the 1971 Advisory Council's recommendations. The tax schedule was endorsed by the Social Security trustees and the Nixon administration. The Mills bill also included

provisions for adjusting benefits automatically to correspond to increases in the cost of living, starting in 1975. The House Ways and Means Committee report on the Mills bill specified a change in the actuarial method of Social Security cost valuation in accordance with the advisory council's recommendations.

Toward the end of June 1972, Senator Frank Church introduced an amendment to legislation to extend the federal debt limit that embraced most of the provisions of the Mills bill. The 20 percent increase in benefits was to become effective in September 1972 instead of in June, as under the House bill. Annual taxable maximum earnings were increased to $10,800 in 1973 and $12,000 in 1974. Beyond 1974 the level of maximum earnings was to rise automatically with wages. Church's amendment also set a new tax rate schedule based on recommendations of the advisory council. This new tax rate schedule revised hospital insurance (HI) contribution rates to resolve the actuarial deficit that the program then faced.

The debt limit bill with the Social Security amendments was passed on June 30 and signed by the president on July 1, 1972, as Public Law 92-336. While the Nixon administration had opposed having a 20 percent benefit increase attached to a debt limit bill, the package was "veto-proof." Members of Congress found themselves in a happy political situation for the middle of an election year. They had provided a 20 percent increase in benefits that would show up in beneficiaries' mailboxes on November 1, a couple of days before the national election; they could further assure beneficiaries that future benefits would not be eroded by inflation. Robert M. Ball noted, "The financing recommendations of the Advisory Council made it possible to finance the existing Social Security benefits with lower contribution rates for the next 40 years than were then in the law." [23]

In the meantime, H.R. 1, including several provisions that would further modify Social Security, continued through the legislative process and finally passed as Public Law 92-603. The bill that Congress passed in June 1972 reduced the payroll tax rate from the rates that had been provided for in the 1971 Amendments. Table 10.3 shows the rates in effect prior to passage of Public Law 92-336 and the reduced rates set by the new law. Yet four months later this payroll tax reduction was completely reversed, and tax rates for all future years but three were raised, over the rates that had prevailed in 1971. The cost estimates in Public Law 92-603 were based on the new dynamic cost-estimating procedure adopted earlier in the year. This quick reversal on the payroll tax reduction was regarded as necessary to maintain the financial solvency of the program. Although this tax increase

Table 10.3   OASDI Payroll Tax Rates Established
by Legislation in 1971 and in June and October 1972

Time span	1971 Amendments	June 30, 1972 P.L. 92-336	October 30, 1972 P.L. 92-603
1973–1975	5.65%	5.50%	5.85%
1976–1977	5.85	5.50	5.85
1978–1979	5.80	5.50	6.05
1980	5.95	5.50	6.05
1981–1985	5.95	5.50	6.15
1986	5.95	5.60	6.25
1987–1992	6.05	5.60	6.25
1993–2010	6.05	5.70	6.25
2011 and later	6.05	6.55	7.30

Source: Social Security Bulletin, Annual Statistical Supplement, 1977-1979, p. 34.

was not recognizable as such at the time, it was an ominous foreshadowing of events to come.

The record of accomplishments was remarkable. In 1971 Congress raised benefits 10 percent. In 1972 it raised them 20 percent and adopted the indexing provisions that had been recommended by the advisory council. It was the shift to dynamic assumptions that allowed Congress to pass on the 20 percent increase in benefits in 1972 without throwing the plan into substantial imbalance. The dynamic assumptions simply gave Congress the opportunity to wring the conservative overfinancing out of the system. Someone who was receiving a benefit of $500 per month at the beginning of 1969 would have been getting $759 per month at the end of 1972, an increase of 52 percent. From 1968 to 1972, the span of the first Nixon administration, the cost of living as measured by the consumer price index rose by 20 percent. From 1967 to 1972, average covered wages had risen 33 percent.

Bob Ball was getting his way. When he was later asked what stood out as his major accomplishments during his tenure as commissioner, Ball would remark: "Well the 1972 Amendments (which were built on the recommendations of President Nixon), changed the nature of the program quite substantially."[24] Ball went on to note the importance of indexing and the 20 percent increase in benefits that provided a new level of protection under the system.

Not everyone was sanguine about the developments in 1972. John Byrnes was a Republican on the House Ways and Means Committee. He had advocated automatic indexing of Social Security benefits to increases in the cost of living as early as 1958.[25] But he did not support what the Congress had done in adopting the 1972 Amendments. In a floor speech when the legislation was under consideration in the House of Representatives he said: "At no point has there been a study by the Ways and Means Committee of the new method of financing that has produced the 'windfall' that now is going to be used for the 20 percent benefit increase. Not one word of testimony in public or executive session has been received on this subject. This fundamental change in the criteria by which the soundness of the social security trust fund has been measured for one-third of a century is being adopted willy-nilly by the Congress without even a cursory review."[26]

The benefit increases at the end of the 1960s and in the early 1970s significantly outstripped the cost of living or the wage base underlying the system. Martha Derthick points to the combination of an administration under the control of the Republicans and a Congress under the control of the Democrats as the mechanism that generated the significant increases in benefits. The administration would propose benefit increases to keep up with the estimated increases in the cost of living. It proposed increases of 10 percent in 1969, 6 percent in 1971, and 5 percent in 1972. The Democrats in Congress "outbid" each proposal—granting 15 percent in 1969, 10 percent in 1971, and 20 percent in 1972.[27]

After Richard Nixon was re-elected in November 1972, he demanded the resignations of all the political appointees then holding jobs in his administration. For Ball, this was the end of the line inside the Social Security Administration. Before his departure he arranged for Wilbur Cohen to receive the Arthur J. Altmeyer award at the dedication of the new Arthur Altmeyer headquarters building in Woodlawn, Maryland, a suburb of Baltimore. In his remarks, Cohen observed that there would never be another gathering of such "distinguished old-timers again."[28] It was the end of an era. The history of the next one would be remarkably different from the one that Cohen was looking back on at the end of 1972.

Part II

Overreaching and Stepping Back

Chapter 11

A Tale of Good Intentions Gone Bad

T he 1972 Amendments, including the 20 percent one-time benefit hike and the inflation indexation of the program, were in many respects the high-water mark for Social Security. In the roughly thirty-five years since inception, the program had progressed to a comprehensive old-age retirement, survivors, old-age health care, and disability program. Its generosity was such that many of the elderly could rely on it and still live in relative comfort, at least by comparison with the poorest of the elderly in the 1930s, 1940s, and 1950s. The program was so popular, in fact, that voting for increased benefits was as close as it gets to a sure bet for members of Congress. So far, each cohort of retirees had gotten far more back from Social Security than they themselves had contributed to the system, as Samuelson boasted in his 1967 *Newsweek* column,[1] and poverty among the elderly had been reduced dramatically.

Just when everything seemed to be going perfectly for Social Security and its proponents, bad news and bad times were looming ahead. Many observers, experts and laypeople alike, thought that the good times might continue for a long time, perhaps forever. Paul Samuelson was certainly in that camp and said so in his *Newsweek* column.[2] But, everything changed in 1973, and many of the socioeconomic underpinnings so important for Social Security have never been the same since. Social Security quickly went from being the star achievement of the modern welfare state in America to being one of its chronic problems. What happened to make the program so vulnerable to the new economic realities?

Unhappy Days Are Here Again

Before answering that question about Social Security itself, let's review the macroeconomic environment in which the program has operated over its entire history. Everyone knows that the 1930s were hard times and appropriately labeled the Great Depression. On the other hand, the 1940s, '50s, and '60s were good times with rising wages, significant economic growth, and relatively low rates of unemployment and inflation. The 1970s featured the worst economy since the 1930s from almost every perspective.

Arthur Okun, President Johnson's chairman of the Council of Economic Advisors, once suggested that the sum of the inflation rate and the unemployment rate could serve as a crude measure of economic discomfort.[3] Figure 11.1 shows the two most widely watched macroeconomic parameters—the unemployment rate and the inflation rate, as well as their sum, the Okun discomfort index—for the entire period from 1930 to 1997. Clearly the late 1970s and early 1980s were the worst stretch for the U.S. economy since the 1930s. The average unemployment rate was higher than it had been since the 1930s and the inflation rate was actually the highest it had been since the Civil War. The worst of the inflation began almost simultaneously with the inflation indexation of the system. This meant that Social Security payouts automatically increased with the price level. Matters were made much worse, however, because the inflation indexation adopted in 1972, to be implemented in 1975, was glaringly flawed. To add insult to injury, the high unemployment rates during the period meant that fewer workers were paying into the system than anticipated.

The Big Indexing Mistake of '72

To explain the flaws in the 1972 method of inflation-proofing the system, it is important to detail how benefits were determined under that law. In the mid-1970s, a person's benefit level at retirement was determined in two steps. First, a primary insurance amount (PIA) was calculated, and from it the actual monthly benefit was determined. The PIA is the monthly benefit that the worker would receive if he or she were single and retiring at sixty-five. Although not everyone gets the PIA, the monthly benefits for married retirees and for those retiring at any eligible age have always been determined by reference to the basic PIA.

In the early 1970s, calculating the PIA itself was a two-step process. The first step was to determine the worker's average monthly wage. At that time, this figure was, with a few possible complications, the average of the

Figure 11.1   Unemployment Rates, Inflation Rates, and the
Okun Discomfort Index, 1930–1971

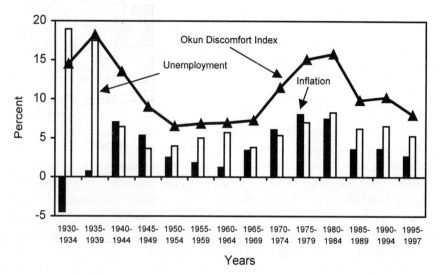

Source: Data from various issues of the *Economic Report of the President,* U.S. Government Printing
Office.

earnings subject to tax for the twenty years immediately preceding retirement. Once the average monthly wage (AMW) figure was determined, then
the potential retiree's PIA could be derived. The PIA was determined by a
multibracketed formula similar to the approach used to determine federal
income tax obligations. The PIA was equal to 119.89 percent of the first $110
of AMW plus 43.61 percent of the next $290 plus 40.75 percent of the next
$150, and so on, through four more brackets (for a total of seven brackets
in all).[4] Once the PIA was determined, calculating the monthly benefit was
simple. For instance, if you retired at sixty-two (rather than at sixty-five)
you would receive 80 percent of your PIA rather than 100 percent. If you
retired at sixty-six, you would have gotten 101 percent of your PIA.

Under the 1972 legislation on indexing the system, the PIA formula was
to be automatically adjusted whenever the consumer price index had increased by 3 percent or more since the last PIA adjustment.[5] The way in
which the formula was adjusted was simple enough. Each of the percentages in the formula converting the AMW into the PIA was increased by
a multiplication factor of one plus the cumulative inflation since the previous adjustment. For instance, the percentages in the first three brackets

in 1974 were 119.89 percent, 43.61 percent, and 40.75 percent. If there had been 10 percent inflation, the automatic adjustment would multiply each of these percentages by 1.1 to give 131.88 percent, 47.97 percent, and 44.83 percent. That was all there was to it. The dollar figures defining the brackets (that is, the first $110, the next $290, and so on) were not changed. Nothing else was changed. It seemed simple and straightforward.

It turned out that if you were trying to maintain a given level of initial real benefits or a fixed replacement ratio—that is, the ratio of initial benefits to final wage—this was not the way to do it. In fact, this method could easily lead to and, in fact, would almost inevitably lead to many individuals' having replacement ratios of greater than one. That is, eventually it would become common for people to earn more from Social Security in retirement than they had ever earned working. With enough inflation, all the percentages in the PIA formula would be increased and increased until they exceeded 100 percent. While this may sound far-fetched, if the law had been allowed to stand as it was in the mid-1970s, the average replacement rate for low-wage workers would have exceeded 100 percent sometime in the first half of the twenty-first century. Later the replacement rates for middle- and high-wage workers would also have climbed over 100 percent.

It may sound wonderful to have such generous Social Security benefits, but there was no reasonable way they could be financed. Beyond the practical issues raised by the way the benefit indexing was done in 1972, the prospect that retirees might get larger benefits for not working than they could earn for working hardly fit the way most people thought economic life in America should be organized. The early architects of Social Security had always contended that our Social Security program epitomized American values because it preserved the financial incentives in our system for people to work and reap added rewards for doing so.

The 1972 inflation indexing process worked fine for those already retired. Their AMW was fixed because they were no longer working. With each of the PIA formula percentages increasing by the amount of inflation, the PIA itself would grow by an amount reflecting inflation, and so would the monthly benefits of those already retired. The process worked like a charm. Unfortunately, it didn't work quite so well for those who were still working and who would later apply for initial benefits. Consider what happens if both wages and prices go up by 10 percent. If a worker's monthly wage goes up by 10 percent, just keeping up with the general level of wage inflation, then when he or she retires, this higher nominal earnings amount will cause the AMW to be correspondingly higher. The AMW goes up because of wage inflation; but the PIA is adjusted so it goes up at the rate of price inflation for a fixed AMW. All told, for workers still accumulating an earnings history, the system ended up being doubly indexed—wage inflation caused the AMW to go up, and price inflation caused the formula converting AMW into PIA to become more generous. Under certain conditions, real benefits and real replacement rates and the cost of the program could soar.

To show how this might work in real life, let's work through a simplified example. Assume that the Social Security benefit for a worker in the base year is equal to 100 percent of the first $500 of a worker's average monthly wage, plus 50 percent of the next $1,000 of the average monthly wage, plus 25 percent of the average monthly wage over $1,500. Let's assume that a worker, Carl, has to work only two years to earn a benefit: the base year and the next year. Assume that in the base year Carl earns an average wage of $2,000 per month and that his wage goes up by the rate of increase in average wages in the economy. We also assume that the rate of increase in wages is roughly equivalent to the rate of increase in prices, which was actually the case when the 1972 Amendments were implemented.

In the first test scenario, let's assume Carl's wage of $2,000 per month goes up by 10 percent in the second year, so he earns $2,200 per month. At the end of the second year, Carl is eligible to retire. His average monthly wage over the two years is $2,100 per month—that is, the sum of $2,000 and $2,200 divided by two. In calculating Carl's benefit, the percentage components are indexed by the rate of increase in prices, 10 percent in this case. So Carl's Social Security benefit will be 110 percent of the first $500 ($550) plus 55 percent of the next $1,000 ($550) plus 27.5 percent of the remaining $600 ($165). Carl's total benefit would be $1,265 per month, the sum of the three component elements.

In the second test scenario, let's assume that Carl's wage in the second year goes up by 30 percent, so he earns $2,600 per month. Also assume that the CPI goes up by 30 percent between years one and two. At the end of the second year, Carl's average monthly wage over the two years is $2,300 per month—that is, the sum of $2,000 and $2,600 divided by two. In calculating Carl's benefit in this case, the percentage components in the benefit formula are indexed by 30 percent. So his benefit will be 130 percent of the first $500 ($650) plus 65 percent of the next $1,000 ($650) plus 32.5 percent of the remaining $800 of his average monthly wage ($260). Carl's total benefit in this case would be $1,560 per month. Note that Carl's benefits are 23.33 percent higher in the second test scenario than the first, owing to the extra 20 percent wage and price inflation.

Sorting out what happens in these two scenarios requires that we look separately at how the increase in Carl's wages and the CPI drives both his average wage and the formula for determining his benefit. In the first case, the second year of Carl's earnings made up 52.4 percent of his total wages— that is, $2,200/$4,200. In the second case, the second year of his earnings made up 56.5 percent of his total wages—that is, $2,600/$4,600. The point here is that rapid periods of wage inflation will tend to make the years when that inflation occurs disproportionately important in determining average wages over the career. So wage inflation ends up indexing the average wage. The indexation of the percentage elements in the Social Security benefit formula by the CPI compounded the effect of wage indexation in this case. The net result was that in the first scenario, Carl would end up with a benefit that was 57.5 percent of his wage the year before he retired— that is, $1,265/$2,200. The outcome of the second scenario was that Carl would end up with a Social Security benefit that was 60 percent of his final year's earnings—that is, $1,560/$2,600. Though this example is a simplification of what actually occurred, it exactly represents what happened.

One way to look at the flaw in the 1972 inflation indexation amendments is that policymakers were trying to use a single simple formula to adjust current benefits for those already retired and future benefits for those already working. It wasn't to be quite that easy. The 1972 indexing approach created huge actuarial deficits for the system over the seventy-five-year horizon, roughly four times as great as the shortfalls we now face. It caused the benefits for initial retirees to go up faster than inflation, faster than wages, and faster than the system itself could withstand in the long run.

Who Knew What, and When?

A serious question is whether the senior executives at Social Security knew in 1972 that the formula they prevailed upon Congress to adopt could result in such significant expansion of the system. There is some evidence that they did. Our own interviews with several members of Social Security policy staff who were there, either at the time or later, gives us the impression that the potential for the 1972 Amendments to result in increased benefits relative to wages was understood by the system's senior management.

A 1970 staff paper developed by the Bureau of the Budget expressing concern that some indexing provisions could lead to increases in benefits relative to covered wages[6] suggests that staff members were paying attention to this matter. The staff paper observes: "There are two changes in the computation of Social Security currently being talked about—the implications of which are not widely appreciated. Especially if these provisions overlap, they might. . . . affect the system far beyond the intentions of the decision-makers."[7] Later on in the discussion of the cost implications, the writers observe: *"There will be no additional cost to this proposal provided that it is tied to the decoupling of benefit formula from automatic benefit increases."*[8]

Finally, a cryptic paragraph in the report of the 1971 Advisory Council on Social Security suggests concern over a possible double-indexation effect.

> The Council notes that if benefits and the contribution and benefit base are kept up to date—either automatically, as the Council recommends, or on an *ad hoc* basis—social security benefits for people retiring in the future will be substantially larger in relation to earnings just prior to retirement than they would be if the benefit provisions of present law remained in effect. This would occur because of the interaction of two factors: (1) increases in benefits to keep up with increases in the cost of living would be provided for all future beneficiaries as well as those already on the rolls when the increases took effect; and (2) increases in earnings levels . . . will be reflected in the average earnings on which benefits are based. . . . For example, under the automatic adjustment provisions . . . the median male worker retiring at age 65 in 1985 would get benefits equal to 41.1 percent of his average earnings in his 15 highest years. If the program were not kept up to date but the period for computing average earnings were shortened to 15 years, this worker's benefit would be only 35.2 percent of his high-15 average earnings.[9]

Possibly the greatest question about who knew what and when is raised by how the problem of double indexing was handled after it became openly acknowledged. The indexing provisions in the 1972 Amendments did not go into effect until 1975. These were highly inflationary times for our economy and a system of overindexing was bound to wreak havoc on the financial balance of the system. This question becomes all the more interesting when we note that the flaw was recognized before the first automatic adjustments were made in January 1975. Lawrence Thompson, who was a staff economist at the Office of Income Security Policy within the DHEW, the department overseeing Social Security, wrote about the problem with the inflation adjustments in September 1974.[10] On the cover of the paper Thompson thanks the many members of the staff of the Office of Research and Statistics in the Social Security Administration for helpful comments on an *earlier* draft.

Clearly Social Security was acutely aware of the serious flaws in the 1972 Amendments well before they became effective. This heightens the suspicion that senior managers at Social Security may have known about the double-indexation problem even before the enabling provisions were adopted in 1972. Robert Ball's 1966 manifesto in the *Social Security Bulletin*, discussed at length in Chapter 10, suggests a strong desire on the part of program executives to increase benefits under the system relative to wages. When changes were adopted to eliminate the double-indexing problem in 1977, the fix was not to take effect for people turning sixty-two until 1979. That meant that people retiring at sixty-five were not affected by the fix until 1982. The double-indexation phenomenon persisted for nearly a full decade after the time it was perceived by people monitoring the program.

Why did the system take so long to correct such a serious error? Why wasn't the law corrected even before it became effective? Could it be that some people who knew of the flaw liked the fact that benefits would be "inadvertently" increased? Unfortunately, we don't know the answer to these questions. If it was a simple mistake, it was a big one. By itself it caused one of the most important government programs to lose its financial balance. By 1977 it was determined that a payroll tax increase of approximately 8.2 percentage points would have been required to balance the system over seventy-five years. The program's seventy-five-year revenues were forecast to be only 60 percent of costs. This wasn't all owing to the botched attempt at indexing, but it was a big contributing factor.

The puzzle of why the indexing procedure was so messed up and why it was allowed to stand for so long is even more mysterious when you realize that it is not terribly hard to do it correctly. The system adopted in the 1977 Amendments works just fine and isn't much more difficult—although it is different in just about every respect—from the 1972 approach. The right way to do it, or at least a good way and the way it was done in 1977, is to treat separately those already retired and those still working. For those who are retired, simply update their benefit amounts by adjusting the monthly payment amount annually to reflect changes in the CPI. For people who are applying for initial benefits, you have to modify the calculation of the average monthly wages. Past wages have to be brought up to date by adjusting them for wage inflation between the time they were earned and a recent date.

The 1977 Amendments provided for restating past earnings through wage indexing and bringing them up to two years before the applicant became eligible for early retirement (at age sixty-two). For instance, let us take someone retiring at sixty-two in 1979. That person's earnings in 1960 would be multiplied by the ratio of the average wage level in 1977, the second year before the age of first eligibility, to the average wage level in 1960. Indexing wages to the year a person attains age sixty means that average indexed monthly earnings (AIME) do not depend on age at which one chooses to retire. Also, the lag of two years is necessary for administrative purposes. The wage index is calculated from W-2 forms, which are filed in the year following the year in which the earnings were accrued. If the average wage level in 1977 were three times that in 1960, then the workers' 1960 earnings would be tripled to give their 1960 indexed earnings. All past wages would be similarly wage-indexed. Wages earned after the indexing year go into the calculation of AIME at their nominal—that is, unindexed—values. Then the AIME would be calculated for the highest twenty years of indexed earnings (now it is for the highest thirty-five years). That is, instead of calculating the simple average of past earnings (AMW), Social Security would calculate the average of past indexed monthly earnings. Although this may sound complicated, it actually is quite easy.

The percentages in the PIA formula are not adjusted for inflation under the 1977 Amendments, but the "bend points" that define the brackets are increased by a factor reflecting wage growth. That does it. Under this system, wage growth and price inflation alone would not affect replacement rates or the generosity of the system as measured by the level of initial benefits relative to either final wage or AIME. Both the 1972 procedure and the 1977 procedures, which are still in effect, are relatively simple. But they couldn't be more different. One changes the percentages in the PIA formula (1972), and one does not; one changes the bend points (1977), and one does not; one updates past wage data for wage inflation (1977), and one does not. The bottom line, in our opinion, is that one was correct (1977) and one was not (1972).

The 1970s: A Decade of High Hopes and Dashed Dreams

One way to summarize how adverse the economic developments were in the 1970s by contrast with their assumed path is to compare the assumptions in the 1972 Trustees' Report with the actual outcomes. This information is summarized in Table 11.1 for the five years 1972–1976. No five-year forecast had ever been so far off the mark in the history of Social Security. The cumulative CPI inflation had been forecast at 14.53 percent for the five-year interval; the actual outcome was that prices rose a total of 40.6 percent. Real wages had been expected to grow by a cumulative total of 11.77 percent instead of the actual 1 percent. Finally, unemployment had been expected to average 4.2 percent per year instead of the actual 6.5 percent per year.

The combination of forecast errors wreaked havoc with the financial condition of Social Security. The problem was first acknowledged in the

Table 11.1   Comparison Between Five-Year Economic Assumptions
in the 1972 OASDI Trustees' Report and Actual Experience

Year	CPI Increases Assumed[b]	Actual	Real Wage Increases Assumed[b]	Actual	Unemployment Rate[a] Assumed[b]	Actual
1972	2.75%	3.3%	2.25%	4.00%	4.2%	5.6%
1973	2.75	6.2	2.25	0.70	4.2	4.9
1974	2.75	11.0	2.25	−3.60	4.2	5.6
1975	2.75	9.1	2.25	−2.50	4.2	8.5
1976	2.75	5.8	2.25	2.50	4.2	7.7
Cumulative	14.53	40.6	11.77	0.89	4.2	6.5

Sources: Annual Reports of the Board of Trustees of the Federal Old-Age and Survivors Insurance and Disability Insurance Trust Funds for various relevant years (Washington, D.C.: U.S. Government Printing Office), and *Economic Report of the President, 1982.*
[a] The cumulative unemployment rate shown in this table is the average rate over the period.
[b] Mid-range assumptions.

1973 Trustees' Report, but the outlook worsened with each succeeding annual evaluation. By 1975, when the first automatic indexed benefit increase occurred, the whole OASDI program was running a deficit with payouts exceeding income by $1.5 billion; in 1976 the cash flow deficit hit $3.2 billion, and the deficit in 1977 grew to $5.6 billion.[11] The trust fund, which had begun the decade with reserves of one year's outlays, was depleted to less than six months' outlays, and the situation looked bleaker, the further into the future you looked. The 1977 OASDI Trustees Report predicted ever-growing deficits and forecast that the system's costs over the seventy-five-year future would be fully 75 percent greater than the scheduled tax income.[12]

The 1975 Social Security Advisory Council called attention to the fact that the assumptions of the 1972 Amendments were not panning out. The council saw that the program faced short-term deficits that threatened the solvency of the trust funds. But the council recognized the enormous long-term financial problems of the system caused by the developing demographics (the baby boom followed by the baby bust and rapidly increasing longevity) and by the flawed overindexing in the 1972 Amendments.[13] Among other things, they called for a decoupling of the benefit structure (to allow for separate indexing of the already retired and the active workforce) to correct the flaw in the 1972 inflation-indexing procedure. The 1975 Advisory Council also advocated moving to universal compulsory coverage (in particular, bringing all federal, state, and local government employees

into the system).[14] Finally, it recognized that in the long run either benefits would have to be curtailed or payroll taxes raised. Council members
weren't alone in noticing that the good old days were over for Social Security. The Senate Finance Committee determined in 1975 that FICA taxes
would have to be increased by 20 percent by 2010 and an additional 40 percent by 2050 unless policies were changed.[15] The trustees of Social Security
announced in their 1975 annual report that "without legislation to provide
additional financing, the assets of both [retirement and disability] trust
funds will be exhausted soon after 1979."[16]

President Ford recognized Social Security's emerging financial crisis, at
least to some extent. In his 1975 State of the Union address, he proposed
that the automatic benefit increases triggered by inflation be capped at
5 percent.[17] The proposal went nowhere. In 1975, the Ford administration
apparently thought that it was premature to offer proposals to fix the indexing problem and to address the long-term insolvency of the system
identified by the trustees and the advisory council. By January 1976, however, the president had outlined his plan to overhaul the indexing debacle
and to shore up the finances of Social Security for the short run. His decoupling plan followed the path outlined by the 1975 Advisory Council.[18]
He also made a proposal to deal with the short-term solvency of the trust
funds—namely, a 0.3 percent increase in the payroll tax on both employers
and employees, effective in 1977.[19]

Previously, even-numbered years, such as 1972, were good years in which
to reform Social Security, because reform meant increasing and extending
benefits—always popular with incumbents in election years. However, by
the mid-1970s, the system was nearly mature, and the economy and demographics had turned unfavorable. From then on, Social Security reform
meant tough decisions better tackled in odd-numbered years, such as 1977
or 1983. President Ford's proposals were introduced in the House of Representatives on June 17, 1976, as the "Social Security Benefit Indexing Act of
1976," but they never made it past the Social Security Subcommittee of the
House Ways and Means Committee.[20] They did, after all, call for an election
year tax increase. One feature that the Ford administration added to try to
make the correction for inflation indexation more palatable was a ten-year
transitional guarantee. No one retiring for the next ten years would receive
lower benefits under the new benefit formulas than they would have under
the old procedures at the time of implementation of the new rules. This
can be thought of as a sweetener, but it wasn't enough for action in an election year.

Sorting It Out and Getting It Right

With the finances of the system plunging, President Carter announced his proposals on May 9, 1977. They included substantially the same new inflation indexation structure as that recommended by the 1975 Social Security Advisory Council and by the Ford administration in 1976. President Carter also proposed substantial tax increases. These encompassed complete removal of the ceiling on earnings that were subject to the employer's half of the payroll tax, an increase in the ceiling on earnings that were subject to the employee's portion of the tax, an acceleration in already scheduled increases in payroll tax rates, and a hike in the taxes on the self-employed. Perhaps owing to the rocky economy in the 1970s, President Carter also recommended that general revenues should be transferred into the Social Security trust funds to make up for payroll tax shortfalls due to unemployment rates exceeding 6 percent in the 1975–1978 period. All told, the administration's proposals were supposed to solve the short-term crisis for Social Security and reduce the long-term actuarial deficit by about 75 percent.[21]

Legislation embodying President Carter's proposals was submitted on July 11, 1977; public hearings began immediately in the Social Security Subcommittee of the House Ways and Means Committee. Despite the fact that Congress was controlled by the president's own party, the fate of Carter's proposals was anything but certain. House Ways and Means Chairman Al Ullman outlined a short-term fix for the system, which left in place the flawed inflation indexation formulas of 1972.[22] Others suggested that there wasn't time to act on the president's proposals in 1977 and that the whole matter be considered again in 1978. Eventually, the failing finances of the system, and perhaps the realization that 1978 was an election year, forced the Social Security Subcommittee, the entire Ways and Means Committee, the House, the Senate Finance Committee, the Senate, and the House-Senate conference committee to confront the tough choices that had to be made.

The Republicans on the Social Security Subcommittee successfully introduced universal coverage into the bill at that point in the process. That same provision was deleted in the House floor debate. The amount of earnings that Social Security recipients can enjoy before their monthly benefits are reduced was raised. President Carter's proposal to lift the ceiling on employer contributions completely was fought by Republicans. In the debate on the Senate floor, an amendment to provide equal increases in the wage base for the employer and the employee was defeated by a 47–46 vote with

Vice President Mondale casting the tie-breaking vote. The same amendment had generated a 9–9 tie in the Senate Finance Committee.[23] Social Security reform wasn't nearly as much fun for politicians, particularly for Democrats who thought of the program as their party's greatest accomplishment, in the late 1970s as it had been for the previous forty years.

The House-Senate conference committee had more than the usual number of differences to iron out between the actions of the two bodies. The proposal for unequal ceilings on employer and employee contributions, the use of general revenues to bail out Social Security trust funds, and the differing proposals to modify the earnings test of people collecting retirement benefits were among them. The conference was long and argumentative, but a bill was reported out on December 14, 1977, and passed in the House by the relatively close margin of 189–163 and in the Senate by a vote of 56–12 the next day, the final day of the 95th Congress. President Carter signed the Social Security Amendments of 1977 into law on December 20, 1977.[24]

The bill he signed into law was not the same one that he had introduced back in July. However, it did include the all-important decoupling provisions in the inflation-indexed benefit formulas. The new benefit formula would ultimately reduce replacement rates by 5 percent from where they were projected to be in 1979 under the old law. This 5 percent reduction was designed to offset the distortion in initial benefits caused by the overindexing in the 1972 approach. The new formula with wage indexing of previous earnings would benefit some retirees and harm others. In order to make the transition more palatable, the law guaranteed anyone reaching sixty-two before 1984 a benefit no lower than he would have received under the old law as of December 1978 on the basis of earnings through age sixty-one. While this provision reduced the effect of the new law for this group, it did not entirely protect it from the modification of the rules.

The reduction in replacement rates alone reduced the long-term actuarial deficit of the program by half. The magnitude of the change in future replacement rates from the change in the indexing formula is shown in Figure 11.2. The figure shows only the change in the replacement rates for low-wage workers retiring at age sixty-two. Table 11.2 contains the same information included in Figure 11.2, except that it shows what the 1977 Amendments did for low-, average-, and maximum-wage workers. In all cases, the dramatic growth in replacement rates under the old formula was eliminated by the 1977 Amendments. As shown in Table 11.2, only high-wage workers had their replacement rates noticeably lowered in the short run from where they had been in the late 1970s under the old law.

These benefit reductions came to be known as the benefit notch and

Figure 11.2   Replacement Rates for Workers with Low Earnings,
Before and After the 1977 Social Security Amendments

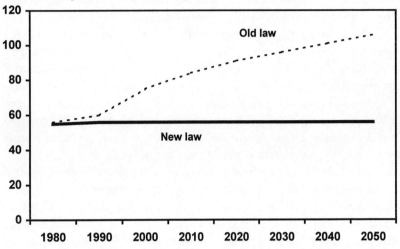

Social Security benefit as percent of preretirement earnings

Source: Taken from table 1, p. 13, in John Snee and Mary Ross, "Social Security Amendments of 1977: Legislative History and Summary of Provisions," *Social Security Bulletin*, U.S. Department of Health, Education, and Welfare, March 1978.

Table 11.2   Projected Replacement of Final Earnings Before and After
the 1977 Social Security Amendments for Workers Retiring, 1980–2050

Year	Low Earners		Average Earners		Maximum Earners	
	Old law	New law	Old law	New law	Old law	New law
1980	56%	55%	44%	43%	34%	27%
1990	60	56	48	43	35	25
2000	75	56	52	43	39	27
2010	84	56	57	43	42	29
2020	91	56	60	43	44	29
2030	96	56	63	43	46	29
2040	101	56	66	43	47	29
2050	106	56	68	43	48	29

Source: Taken from table 1, p. 13, in John Snee and Mary Ross, "Social Security Amendments of 1977: Legislative History and Summary of Provisions," *Social Security Bulletin*, U.S. Department of Health, Education, and Welfare, March 1978.

those affected by it were called the notch babies. The problem with the implementation of the 1977 Amendments was that people who were only a year or two apart in age ended up getting significantly different benefits, even though they had very similar lifetime earnings patterns and Social Security payroll tax contributions. The workers first eligible for benefits immediately after the 1977 Amendments finally took effect received smaller benefits than those who had received substantial windfalls from the double-indexing problem. When the problem was corrected, the added benefits provided to the lucky cohorts who had been affected were not adjusted. The whole flap about notch babies suggested that people born after 1917 were somehow cheated because their benefits were significantly smaller than those of the cohorts who benefited from the double indexing. The notch babies were not the ones who got cheated by the 1977 Amendments. It was the generations of taxpayers who had to support the unwarranted benefits for beneficiaries of double indexing in the 1972 Amendments who got cheated.

Table 11.3 shows the replacement of preretirement earnings under various iterations of the Social Security Act dating back to the 1939 Amendments. It shows the replacement rates for workers with low, average, and maximum earnings. In this case, the results shown are for single workers, but married couples with a single earner would have had the same pattern of replacement rates over the years. Note that the replacement rates in Table 11.3 do not correspond perfectly with those in Table 11.2. Part of the explanation for the difference is that the rates in Table 11.2 were developed on the basis of projected earnings at the time of the passage of the 1977 Amendments. The projected wages turned out to be somewhat different from those reflecting several more years of actual experience in Table 11.3, for which the numbers were calculated in 1982.

If you trace the replacement rates for workers represented in Table 11.3 at any one of the three earnings levels, it is clear that the 1972 Amendments increased replacement rates substantially; the 1975 Amendments ratcheted them up even further. The 1977 Amendments clearly reduced benefits relative to what had been in place immediately before their adoption, but they certainly did not significantly reduce benefit levels relative to traditional rates for the workers with low or average earning levels. The reason replacement rates went down for maximum earners in the table was related to increases in the level of earnings subject to the payroll tax.

The fuss about the notch babies epitomizes the history of Social Security policy over the years. On the one hand, the program architects and policymakers have often been willing to give one group of individuals sig-

Table 11.3   Replacement of Final Earnings Under Various Social
Security Amendments for Single Workers Retiring at Age Sixty-Five

	Low Earnings	Average Earnings[a]	High Earnings
1939 Amendments[b]			
Minimum coverage (3 years)	41.2%	28.8%	16.5%
Maximum coverage (43 years)	57.2	40.0	22.9
Subsequent Amendments			
1950	44.7	30.0	26.8
1952	45.2	30.3	28.3
1954	47.5	34.0	31.0
1958	46.7	34.2	31.8
1965	44.2	33.5	30.5
1967	46.9	36.3	33.5
1969	51.7	40.3	38.6
1971	53.5	43.0	39.4
1972	62.7	51.2	42.7
1975	70.2	55.9	42.6
1977[c]	52.5	41.2	27.6

Sources: Robert J. Myers, "History of Replacement Rates for Various Amendments to the Social Security Act," Memorandum No. 2 (Washington, D.C.: National Commission on Social Security Reform, 1982), p. 3; and 1994–1996 Advisory Council on Social Security background materials.
[a] The average level of annual earnings is assumed to be $1,000 for the computations under the 1939 Amendments (because wages were relatively stable in the late 1930s), and equal to average earnings in the economy for subsequent computations. The low earning level is approximately 50 percent of the average wage level, and the maximum is equal to the applicable maximum tax wage base.
[b] The minimum coverage was three years for the 1939 Amendments: the length of coverage for steady workers generally has no effect on benefits under subsequent amendments. The maximum coverage was taken as forty-three years (from age twenty-two to age sixty-five) for the 1939 Amendments (actually, forty-three years was the maximum creditable under the case showing maximum earnings under the act of 1935).
[c] Ultimate replacement rates shown. Alternative II-B assumptions used in the 1981 OASDI Trustees' Report.

nificant windfalls without spreading those windfalls to other groups with very similar characteristics. On the other hand, a benefit once given never seems to be considered for retrenchment. In looking at Table 11.3, a case can be made that the birth cohorts that received the tremendous added benefits from the double indexing introduced in 1972 should have had their benefits reduced. But they not only got to keep what they had received by the time the 1977 Amendments were implemented; they got to go right on enjoying the fruits of their overly generous benefits right up through today.

Besides the adjustments in indexation of benefits, the other provisions of the 1977 Amendments to the Social Security Act were by no means minor. Payroll taxes were raised significantly, particularly for high-income workers and future workers. The maximum amount of earnings used for calculating benefits and for assessing taxes was $16,500 for 1977 under the old law. Under the new law, this limit was raised considerably to $22,900 in 1979, $25,900 in 1980, and $29,700 in 1981. Despite all the proposals and discussion, however, the taxes on employers and employees were still subject to the same ceilings when the dust settled. After 1981 the cutoff level of earnings was to go up automatically with the rise in average wage rates. The new law accelerated and increased future payroll tax hikes, which were already in the law. The biggest increases were delayed until 1981, 1985, and 1990, however. The rate scheduled for 1990 was 6.45 percent on both employers and employees—now it would be 7.65 percent for each. The tax increases were particularly heavy for people whose earnings were above the new contribution ceilings. If we include both the employee and the employer portions, such a person paid a total of $1,930.50 in OASDHI taxes in 1977 under the old law. Under the new law, such a person was projected to owe $6,091.80 in 1987[25] for a 216 percent increase. To be fair, the old law had tax increases built into it which would have resulted in this person's having a projected 1987 liability of $4,024.80. Still, any way you look at it, the taxes on high-income workers were raised dramatically. There were many other changes. One change that was clearly overdue was altering the rhetoric and substance of the law so that it was gender neutral; all references to "wives" and "women" were replaced by mentions of "spouse" and "participants." The law no longer made any presumption that the secondary earner was female.

With the passage of the 1977 Amendments, the financial forecast for the future of Social Security improved dramatically. The intermediate or "best-guess" forecast was for surpluses at least through 2011. The estimated long-term actuarial deficit was reduced from more than 8 percent of covered payroll to less than 1.5 percent.[26] Even so, the truly long-term problem of financing the retirement of the post–World War II baby boom generation was not fully addressed. The contemporaneous estimates of the Social Security Administration were that after the amendments the system should enjoy a 0.97 percent actuarial surplus for the 1977–2001 period, followed by a 1.06 percent deficit between the years 2002 and 2026 and a still whopping 4.29 percent deficit for the 2027–2051 period.[27] What this means is that even after the amendments, the Social Security Administration could see the need to substantially cut benefits or further raise taxes in order to deal with the economy of the twenty-first century. Interestingly, the 1977 vision of the first half of the twenty-first century still looks pretty accurate now that the time of the actuarial deficits is much closer at hand.

Even though the long-term stability of the system had not been completely addressed, President Carter had much to celebrate at the signing of the bill on December 20, 1977. He described the provisions of the bill as "tremendous achievements . . . the most important social security legislation since the program was established."[28] President Carter claimed even more—he lauded Congress for taking the painful and important steps to shore up social security, and he stated: "Now this legislation will guarantee that from 1980 to the year 2030, the Social Security funds will be sound."[29] The acting commissioner of Social Security, Don Wortman, backed up his boss with the pronouncement that "we have assured the financial soundness of the program for the next 50 years."[30]

Despite the commissioner's and President Carter's proclamation that the Social Security system was secure for at least fifty years, the administration quickly recognized that the health of the system's finances was far from robust. Roughly eighteen months after the signing ceremony, Social Security Commissioner Stanford G. Ross had the following sobering thoughts about the future of Social Security: "The optimistic expansionist philosophy that underlay Social Security planning since World War II has now changed to one of guarded hope that the best of the past can be preserved while the considerable needs of the future are addressed." He added that the coming decade (the 1980s) would witness "painful adjustments in which finances and benefits [would] have to be closely scrutinized and balanced."[31] The contrast between the Carter administration's optimistic December 1977 statements and its July 1979 remarks is pretty dramatic. Unfortunately, Commissioner Ross's pessimistic assessment of the future was more accurate than Jimmy Carter's optimism at the 1977 signing ceremony.

Chapter 12

The Continued Deterioration
of the System and the Big Fix:
The 1983 Amendments

*T*he 1977 Amendments were necessary for two reasons: first, the economic assumptions behind the 1972 Amendments regarding inflation, real wage growth, and unemployment turned out to be far too optimistic, and second, the automatic indexation of benefits adopted in 1972 but effective in January 1975 was badly flawed. The 1977 Amendments were supposed to be adequate for at least twenty-five years, but Congress made that less likely by postponing most of the tax increase medicine until 1981 and later. This deferral of painful changes would become a pattern for policymakers, one that greatly harms the system to this very day.

Unrelenting Economic Problems

Despite the fact that the 1977 Amendments were needed at least in part because of the overly optimistic assumptions adopted in 1972, the 1977 economic assumptions didn't turn out to be much better. The assumptions embedded in the 1977 forecasts were substantially rosier than the consensus forecasts of independent economists at the time[1] and far more favorable than what actually transpired. With hindsight, we judge that Congress and the White House were too anxious to declare that they had repaired the system, when in fact it was still extremely vulnerable to the evolution of the economy. Table 12.1 shows a comparison between the 1977 forecasts for the key economic indicators for 1977–1981 and their actual evolution. With the inflation indexation for new beneficiaries corrected in the 1977 Amendments, the system was less vulnerable to unanticipated inflation

Table 12.1   Comparison of Five-Year Economic Assumptions
in the 1977 OASDI Trustees' Report with Actual Experience,
1977–1981

	Inflation Rate		Real Wage Increases		Unemployment Rate[a]	
Year	Assumed[b]	Actual	Assumed[b]	Actual	Assumed[b]	Actual
1977	6.0%	6.5%	2.4%	1.6%	7.1%	7.0%
1978	5.4	7.6	2.7	0.6	6.3	6.0
1979	5.3	11.5	2.5	−2.7	5.7	5.8
1980	4.7	13.5	2.4	−4.9	5.2	7.1
1981	4.1	10.3	2.3	−1.6	5.0	7.6
1977–1981	28.2	60.0	12.9	−6.9	5.9	6.7

Sources: Assumptions from the *1997 Annual Reports of the Board of Trustees of the Federal Old-Age and Survivors Insurance and Disability Insurance Trust Funds* (Washington, D.C.: U.S. Government Printing Office, 1977); and actual experience, from the 1982 *Economic Report of the President.*
[a] The cumulative unemployment rate shown in this table is the average rate for the period.
[b] Mid-range assumptions.

than before, as long as price and wage inflation occurred in tandem, as they had previously. Some of you may remember the so-called OPEC-II shock of 1979 and the near-runaway inflation that accompanied it. To be fair, this situation was not forecast by anyone. However, over the five-year interval, the 1977 inflation assumptions couldn't have been much further off the mark—actual inflation was more than twice what had been forecast, with the gaps between forecast and actual being particularly wide in the three years from 1979 to 1981.

The performance of real wages was of much more consequence for the finances of the program. Recall that benefits go up automatically with price inflation and revenues go up with increases in wages. What really is of crucial importance to the finances of a pay-go system is the difference between the rate of growth of wages and the rate of growth of prices—which, of course, is equal to the rate of growth of real wages. The system's finances, which had been balanced quite precariously by the 1977 Amendments and the assumptions on which they were based, depended on wages' going up faster than prices by about 2.5 percent per year.

As shown in Table 12.1, the 1977 assumptions about real wages proved disastrously optimistic. On average, wages did not go up as fast as prices, let alone significantly faster, as had been assumed. Whereas the prediction had been that 1981 real wages would be 12.9 percent above their level in 1976; they actually were 6.9 percent lower. When you total up the errors in predicting wages and prices for the period, real wages were more than

21 percent lower at the end of 1981 than had been forecast only five years earlier. As the third set of columns shows, unemployment was higher than anticipated, reducing the number of workers contributing to Social Security's coffers and adding to the financial stress on the system. In fact, the combination of high unemployment and high inflation — "stagflation," as it came to be known — was completely unprecedented and had not even been evaluated in the worst-case scenarios in 1977.

The results of the economy's failure to live up to the 1977 expectations of Congress, President Carter, and the Social Security Administration were disastrous for the finances of Social Security. The system continued its string of deficits, which began in 1975, with the trust fund sinking closer and closer to zero. There were transfers between the OASI (Old-Age and Survivors Insurance) Trust Fund, the Disability Insurance (DI) Trust Fund, and the HI (Hospital Insurance) Trust Fund, but everyone recognized that they were at best a stop-gap measure. None of the funds were in robust shape, so one could not rescue another. For the first time in the history of Social Security, people began talking about the system's literally running out of money and monthly checks' being missed or delayed. It was clear by 1980 that the 1977 Amendments were insufficient to assure even the short-term solvency of the program. In fact, the ability to pay full benefits beyond late 1982 without serious changes in the program was questionable at best.

A Shift in Political Management and Attitudes

In many respects, the same lousy economy that was clouding the future of Social Security doomed Jimmy Carter's re-election chances. Ronald Reagan swept into office in 1981 and hit the ground running with legislation and tax cuts that he believed would stimulate the economy enough to reduce the ballooning deficit. A new term was coined for his alluring blend of economic policies — "Reaganomics." In general, he enjoyed an early legislative honeymoon and was able to enact much of his initial agenda. The string of successes came to a stunning halt when he got to his Social Security proposals. Social Security was a public policy area where Republicans had been off balance politically since Roosevelt. Except when they locked arms with liberal devotees of the program to avoid funding build-ups and to expand benefits, their every move seemed to backfire. Reagan had seen how the 1964 presidential candidate Barry Goldwater had been assailed for his alleged lack of support for Social Security. Seemingly, Reagan learned something from the Goldwater debacle, but not nearly enough.

On May 12, 1981, Secretary of Health and Human Services Richard

Schweiker announced the Reagan administration's plan to "keep the [Social Security] system from going broke, protect the basic benefit structure and reduce the tax burden of American workers."[2] Schweiker unveiled the program and clearly was one of its architects, but David Stockman, the outspoken head of the Office of Management and Budget (OMB), was the person driving the administration's push for early action on this and most of the Reagan economic agenda.[3] Reagan himself was still recovering from the assassination attempt and probably was not involved in the detailed strategy that Schweiker presented.

The proposals were a serious attempt to deal with the looming financial crisis, but the administration showed its political inexperience in not convincing the public and key members of Congress of the need to do anything painful to shore up Social Security. The administration hadn't even sought the counsel of such key members of Congress as the chairman of the Senate Finance Committee, Bob Dole, or pivotal conservative members of the House Ways and Means Committee, such as J. J. Pickle or Barber Conable.[4] Everyone on Capitol Hill was caught by surprise by the distasteful medicine contained in the proposals. Of course, many people were still suspicious that Reagan would try to dismantle the program at his first opportunity, and they read that intention into his plan. Cutting benefits, which Reagan proposed, and raising taxes are not winning political propositions under the best of circumstances, but the Reagan administration didn't even condition people for the need to take such painful steps.

President Reagan Stubs His Toe on Proposals for Social Security Reform

What the Reagan administration proposed in May 1981 was a number of measures, the most controversial of which significantly lowered the benefits for those who chose to retire before the normal retirement age of sixty-five. The benefit at age sixty-two was then and is now 80 percent of the full primary insurance amount that would be payable at age 65. Schweiker and Reagan proposed to make the benefit at age sixty-two only 55 percent of the PIA. Under their proposal, benefits as a percentage of PIA would increase by 1.25 percent per month for every month that retirement was delayed between the ages of sixty-two and sixty-five. That is, while someone would get only 55 percent of PIA by retiring at 62, she would get 70 percent at sixty-three and 85 percent at sixty-four. The actual calculation would be made to the precise month of retirement, as is done now and has always been done since early retirement was introduced. The administration also

proposed phasing out the earnings test under which Social Security benefits payable to persons aged sixty-five through seventy-one were reduced
fifty cents for every dollar earned above some low exempt amount of earnings. The intent of these two elements of the Reagan plan was to encourage
people to work longer, thereby increasing the number of contributors to
the system and reducing the number of retired beneficiaries.

There were several other elements in Reagan's May 1981 Social Security
proposal. He proposed to gradually roll back some of the benefit increases
that had occurred in the 1970s in the initial replacement rate offered by
Social Security by indexing only the so-called bend points in the PIA formula for half the increase in wages for the five years 1982–1987. The effect
was estimated to ultimately reduce the average replacement rate from 42
percent to 38 percent. He proposed delaying the automatic cost-of-living
adjustments for three months so they would take place on October 1 each
year instead of July 1. Finally, he proposed tightening up the administration
and eligibility requirements for disability insurance. Naturally, Secretary
Schweiker tried to emphasize the positive elements of the administration's
proposals. They were that the administration did not plan to cut benefits
for anyone already receiving them; it did not intend to raise the normal retirement age; and, most consistent with Reagan's philosophy, they would
not increase payroll tax rates.[5]

Congress Responds with a Resounding NO!

In everyday parlance, Reagan got his head handed to him on his Social
Security proposals. Not only did the AARP, the National Council on Aging,
and the AFL-CIO attack the plan, but so did virtually all congressional
leaders in both parties. Senator Moynihan (D-NY) thought that cutting
early retirement benefits as much as proposed would make it "financially
impossible to retire at 62."[6] It is hard to argue against Senator Moynihan
and defend the Reagan administration's proposal. It advocated cutting initial benefits for people retiring at sixty-two by more than 30 percent—that
is, they would get only 55 percent of their PIA instead of 80 percent—and
he proposed to do it for new retirees, effective January 1, 1982. Senator
William Armstrong (R-CO) thought that the proposal was a "masterpiece
of bad timing."[7]

House Speaker Tip O'Neill didn't mince words when he called the proposals "despicable . . . a rotten thing to do . . . that robs the system of
its most important feature: the confidence of the American public."[8] The
Democrats were convinced that the proposals were motivated as much by

Reagan's desire to reduce the deficit and hence declare victory for Reaganomics as they were by any wish to save Social Security. Speaker O'Neill coined the phrase that the Republicans were "willing to balance the budget on the backs of the elderly." [9] This charge would be repeated over and over again, to devastating effect. The honeymoon period of the Reagan administration ended on May 12, 1981.

It didn't take long for Congress to move against the Reagan-Schweiker proposals. The Democratic caucus in the House adopted a resolution on May 20 which stated that President Reagan's proposals to reduce early retirement benefits represented "an unconscionable breach of faith with the first generation of workers that has contributed to Social Security for their whole lives." [10] The fact that the Democrats would attack the proposal isn't so surprising. What is surprising is that on the very same day the Senate unanimously (by 96-0) adopted the Senate resolution stating that its sense was that "Congress shall not precipitously and unfairly penalize early retirees."

What must have really stunned the White House was that the author of the resolution was Republican Bob Dole, a leader in the party and chairman of the Senate Finance Committee.[11] Dole surely didn't appreciate having been caught off guard by the Reagan proposal, but his introduction of this resolution was the only way he could defeat a much more strongly worded one from the other party. The latter, accusing the administration of a breach of faith with aging Americans, was written by Senator Moynihan and cosponsored by forty-one additional Democratic senators. The final vote on Moynihan's resolution was 49-48. In the discussion of it, not a single Republican rose to defend the president.[12] Ronald Reagan, Richard Schweiker, and David Stockman couldn't have played their Social Security hand much worse. One top Democratic aide was quoted in *Newsweek* as saying, "That was the stupidest move the Republicans made. . . . Ideology overcame politics . . . and it sealed the fate of a number of Republican candidates." [13] It is possible that this debacle on the part of the Reagan administration is where the saying began that Social Security is the third rail of politics—touch it and you're dead.

The National Commission to the Rescue

Reagan wasn't dead, but on this issue he was in complete retreat. In fact, he retreated to his 1980 campaign position on the subject—he would appoint a high-level bipartisan commission to advise Congress and the White House on how to repair Social Security. This new strategy was announced on September 24, 1981. There is some evidence that the administration had learned a great deal about Washington politics over the summer. First, the fifteen-member National Commission on Social Security Reform was to be truly bipartisan, with one-third of the membership chosen by the speaker of the House, Tip O'Neill, one-third by the Senate majority leader, Howard Baker, and one-third by the president. Reagan announced that two of his five picks would be Democrats.[14] What better time to be bipartisan than when there is unpopular work to be done.

The task of the commission was straightforward: it was to propose realistic long-term reforms to put Social Security back on a sound financial footing and to forge a bipartisan consensus so that the necessary reforms could be passed into law.[15] The composition of the committee was announced on December 16, 1981. It consisted of eight Republicans and seven Democrats; most were household names. Included were Senators Bob Dole, Daniel Patrick Moynihan, John Heinz, and William Armstrong and Representatives (or former Representatives) Barber Conable, Claude Pepper, Martha Keys, and Joe Waggoner. Lane Kirkland, the chairman of the AFL-CIO, represented labor, while business groups had Robert Beck of Prudential and Alexander Trowbridge of the National Association of Manufacturers. Robert Ball was a member and served to represent the interests of Tip O'Neill and the congressional Democrats. The commission was ably chaired by Alan Greenspan, former president Ford's chairman of the Council of Economic Advisors, who though conservative, was widely respected as both knowledgeable and inclusive. Greenspan appointed Robert Myers as executive director of the commission, so the two Bobs, Ball and Myers, were once again in positions of power with respect to Social Security, as they had been for most of the history of the program.[16]

Stalling for Time for Political Gain

The commission was to report its recommendations by December 31, 1982. The fact that the final report wasn't due until after the mid-term elections was important. The Republicans were stung by the complete failure of the administration's first plan to fix Social Security and by the charge that they were trying to eliminate the deficit on the backs of the elderly. Thus, Republican members of Congress were in no mood to stick their necks out again with a plan to either raise taxes, cut benefits, or both. Democrats were finding the charge that Republicans were out to destroy Social Security so effective that they didn't want even to admit that any tough choices needed to be made in the program—at least not before the congressional election.

Figure 12.1   OASI Trust Fund Assets at the End of Each Year, as Forecast in November 1982

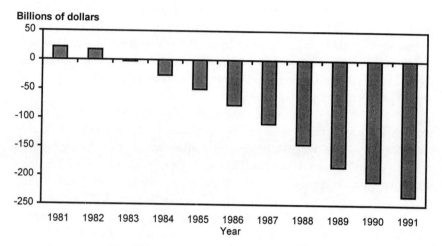

Billions of dollars

Source: National Commission on Social Security Reform, "Actuarial Cost Estimates for OASDI and HI and for Various Possible Changes in OASDI and Historical Data for OASDI and HI," November 1982, Washington, D.C.

The commission held several meetings throughout 1982 but didn't really get down to the hard bargaining until after the elections. The Democrats refused to detail any plan at all, and the Republicans were completely afraid to get out in front once again. When the votes were counted, the Democrats had gained twenty-six seats in the House. Bob Dole said that the Social Security issue alone had caused half the Republican losses. The need to do something could not have been made clearer to the commissioners. Bob Myers prepared a background book for the three-day meeting in November 1982 that laid out the problem quite clearly and contained a large menu of options that had the potential to improve the system's finances.[17]

Figure 12.1 is based on a table presented to the commissioners for that November meeting. To put the numbers in context, OASI was projected to pay out $155 billion in benefits in 1983, rising to $250 billion in 1991. Social Security would be starting 1983 with a trust fund ratio of only 10 percent—that is, the fund at the beginning of the year was only 10 percent of the year's anticipated outlays—and was projected to end the year in the red. By 1991, the negative balance of the trust fund was projected to reach a full year of outlays. Figures like these made it a little hard for anyone to claim that there wasn't a problem. These particular numbers were based on the intermediate set of economic and demographic assumptions. However, the problems were so immediate that even the optimistic set of assumptions presented to the commissioners had the OASI Trust Fund running out of money in early 1984.

The background book prepared by Bob Myers and his staff estimated the impact on the system's finances of well over one hundred possible policy changes. They were grouped into policies concerning (1) coverage, (2) tax rates, (3) alternative sources of revenues, (4) cost-of-living adjustments, (5) level of primary benefits, (6) retirement age, (7) disability benefits, (8) "proposals affecting primarily women," (9) taxation of benefits, and (10) other. Within each category, a large array of options was analyzed. For instance, within "alternative sources of financing," policies such as imposing a new inheritance tax earmarked for the OASI Trust Fund, introducing a 5 percent income tax surcharge, increasing the excise tax on alcohol and tobacco, and imposing an earmarked surtax on gasoline were all evaluated. So too were several possible ways of transferring general revenues into the Social Security trust funds. The printed menu of options was exhaustive, but it was not filled with politically attractive alternatives.[18]

Getting to Work After Mid-Term Elections

Faced with this daunting background book and now that the election was behind them, Democrats were more willing to tackle the Social Security issue. First, on November 11, the commission voted unanimously to accept Bob Myers' analysis of the size of the problem—a $150–$200 billion shortfall between 1983 and 1989 and a long-term (seventy-five-year) deficit of $1.6 trillion.[19] Second, on November 12 Bob Ball and the O'Neill appointees presented a proposal to the rest of the commission. The Republican members didn't have any immediate response except to criticize the Ball plan for relying almost exclusively on tax hikes to save the system.[20] They were looking for guidance from the White House, but Reagan thought it was the commission's job, not his to come up with the proposals. As the December 31 deadline approached, it appeared that this would be yet another ineffective commission. Greenspan asked that they be given a thirty-day extension, but Reagan granted them only an extra fifteen days. The word was also passed to the commission that the White House and the speaker would back any responsible program that received an overwhelming vote in the commission itself.

Two things prevented the commission from quitting unsuccessfully. First, the stakes were very high by now. As time passed, the default date for the trust fund came into sharp focus. The Social Security trustees announced back in the spring of 1982 that the July 1983 checks could not be sent out unless a rescue plan was in place before then. With thirty-six million people depending on the checks, the political consequences of failure were no doubt painfully obvious to every politician in Washington. They were staring down the barrel of a gun on this one. Second, right after the first of the year, Senators Dole and Moynihan began the compromise process. In an op-ed article in the January 3 *New York Times*, Senator Dole wrote that "Social Security overwhelms every other domestic priority." But he also went on to say, "Through a combination of relatively modest steps, including some acceleration of already scheduled taxes and some reduction in the rate of future benefit increases, the system can be saved."[21]

Even though many people had already concluded that the commission had failed in its mission, Moynihan saw a glimmer of hope in Dole's article.[22] Dole had written that some tax increases could be part of the package, and that was a break from the position previously held by the Republicans that they would not support any tax increases. Moynihan and Dole agreed to make one final try to find an agreement and included Ball, Greenspan, and Conable in the last-ditch working group. The White House gave up its strategy of letting the commission come up with the solution on its own and decided instead to work closely with this group of five to see whether a compromise agreement couldn't be reached. The White House negotiators were Stockman, James Baker, Kenneth Duberstein, and Richard Darman.[23] After almost two weeks of nonstop negotiating, led, according to some accounts, by Stockman and Ball,[24] a compromise deal was struck that claimed to be able to improve the system's finances by $169 billion between 1983 and 1989. As was predictable from the start, it was delicately balanced between tax hikes and benefit reductions.

Balanced Compromise in the Face of Default

There were several major elements of the package. First, $40 billion in added revenue would be generated by advancing the scheduled payroll tax increases enacted in 1977. Second, $40 billion would be saved by reducing benefits, by delaying cost-of-living adjustments for six months so that they would occur each January rather than the preceding July. Third, $30 billion would be raised by making 50 percent of Social Security benefit payments taxable for single individuals who had at least $20,000 of other income, and for couples with $25,000, and by earmarking the revenue for Social Security. Fourth, $20 billion would be raised by including newly hired federal employees and employees of nonprofit institutions. Fifth, $18 billion would be raised by increasing the payroll taxes on the self-employed so that they effectively paid both the employer rate and the employee rate. Sixth, $18 billion was to be transferred from general revenues to pay for benefits granted to former military personnel. And seventh, $3 billion would be saved by banning withdrawal from Social Security by state and local governments already in the system.

It is not a coincidence that the two biggest items, numbers 1 and 2, are exactly the same size, the first being a tax hike and the second a benefit cut. Such are the politics of compromise. Similarly, the third item, making benefits partially taxable for middle- and high-income individuals, could be characterized as either a tax increase or a benefit reduction. The fourth item was made possible by the fact that we hadn't completely reached universal coverage. With a pay-as-you-go retirement system, you can always improve short-term finances by bringing in new contributors. Overall, the proposal was precisely balanced between the positions of the liberals and the conservatives. The amazing thing is that in the end the commission succeeded in reaching a true bipartisan compromise—and only two weeks late, at that.

The commission operated under the pressure of a system that was losing $20,000 a minute and was going to default in less than six months. Under that kind of pressure, President Reagan and Speaker O'Neill and Senators Dole and Moynihan set their ideology aside and reached a pragmatic compromise. Not everyone was pleased, by any means. Even the commission had three dissenters—three conservative members, Senator Armstrong, Congressman Archer, and former Congressman Joe Waggoner, opposed the plan because they couldn't support the tax increases it contained. Reagan and O'Neill had both yielded more ground than they had hoped and both were attacked from the extremes of their own constituencies. Nonetheless, the complaints seemed balanced; any plan that had both organized labor and the conservative Right against it just might be well balanced politically.

The Greenspan commission proposals offered the promise of securing Social Security's finances for the 1980s, the 1990s, and the first decade of the twenty-first century. Between 1990 and 2010 the huge baby boom generation would be in its peak earning years, and the numbers of new retirees would be below normal, as the relatively few people born during the Great Depression and World War II entered beneficiary status. These two decades promised to be the salad days of the mature pay-go system. So, in patching things together for the 1980s, the plan offered roughly thirty years of smooth sailing. It had already been known for at least a decade that the system's real long-term crisis would begin in roughly 2010, when the baby boom generation started showing up at local Social Security offices to claim its benefits.

The commission's proposals did little to address the long-term funding problems, even though those had been heatedly debated in their deliberations. The long-term choices were strikingly similar to the short-term ones—raise taxes or cut benefits—but the political pressures to come up with a solution were almost nonexistent. The Democrats on the commission favored a tax increase in the twenty-first century, while the Republicans favored benefit cuts in the form of raising the normal retirement age. Somehow the positions of the players on Social Security have always been quite predictable. In the end, the commission punted on a long-run solution, by leaving that element up to Congress.

Swift Congressional Action Stems Debate

Many anticipated that Congress would hold lengthy hearings on the plan advocated by the commission and felt that its ultimate fate was in doubt. They were wrong. This time Congress acted swiftly. The threat that millions of elderly people would fail to get their Social Security checks by midsummer tended to concentrate the minds of members of Congress. Senator Dole tried to impose the rule that any member who wanted to speak out against the compromise plan should have a plan of his or her own about how to save the system. To the extent that this informal rule prevailed, it set a high price on criticizing the plan. The main issue before Congress was what if anything to do about the long-term funding problems of the twenty-first century.

The debate on improving the long-term outlook for the program was heated and divided. The Ways and Means Committee approved a 5 percent cut in benefits for the year 2000, at that time seventeen years in the future, and a tax hike to commence in 2015.[25] J. J. Pickle, who chaired the Ways and Means Subcommittee on Social Security, had an alternative proposal—namely, to raise the "normal retirement age" to sixty-seven by 2027. Raising the age at which people can get full statutory benefits amounts to an across-the-board cut in benefits. In the end, the House passed Pickle's proposal for raising the age to sixty-seven in the then-distant future. The Senate passed a different version, raising it only to sixty-six, but in conference Pickle's plan carried the day.[26] While this advancement of the retirement age didn't completely solve the long-term problems of the system, it was a sizable step in the right direction.

President Reagan signed the 1983 Social Security Amendments on

April 20, 1983, on the South Lawn of the White House, with Tip O'Neill, Claude Pepper, Bob Dole, Daniel Patrick Moynihan, and Howard Baker sharing center stage. His remark that "this bill demonstrates for all time our nation's ironclad commitment to Social Security" shows how far he had distanced himself from the proposals of his own administration less than two years previously. The president showed his sense of the history of Social Security when he went on to reaffirm "Franklin Roosevelt's commitment that Social Security must always provide a secure and stable base so that older Americans may live in dignity." He concluded by saying, "Each of us had to compromise one way or the other . . . but the essence of bipartisanship is to give up a little in order to get a lot. And, my fellow Americans, I think we've gotten a very great deal."[27]

Chapter 13

Backsliding

*T*he 1983 Social Security Amendments, largely crafted by Alan Greenspan's commission, were supposed to shore up the system's finances for the 1980s and make it possible for the system to fund the retirements of the baby boom generation. When the trustees analyzed all the numbers corresponding to the new reforms in 1983, it was predicted that the Social Security trust fund would initially grow to nearly unimaginable proportions (more than $20 trillion) before being exhausted ultimately in 2063. The reforms and the favorable demographics that could be foreseen for the 1990s and the first decade of the twenty-first century meant that the system should run substantial surpluses for at least the first forty years of the forecasting period. The intermediate, or best-guess, forecast for the future path of the OASDI Trust Fund as of the 1983 Trustees' Report is shown in Figure 13.1.

The combination of the surplus of payroll tax revenues over benefit payments and interest on the accumulated special-issue U.S. Treasury bonds would cause the trust fund to continue to grow until 2045. At that point the intermediate projection was that the system would begin to run a deficit but would be able to remain solvent by selling trust fund assets until 2063, when the fund would be exhausted. Obviously, taxes would have to be increased or benefits cut in order for the system to operate beyond 2063. Nonetheless, with the birth years of the baby boomers ranging from 1946 to 1964, it could be claimed that the 1983 Social Security reforms had fixed the system for the lifetime of the baby boomers. After all, the youngest boomer would be 99 in 2063, so presumably not many of them would still be collecting benefits then.

Figure 13.1 1983 Forecast of OASDI Trust Fund Balances

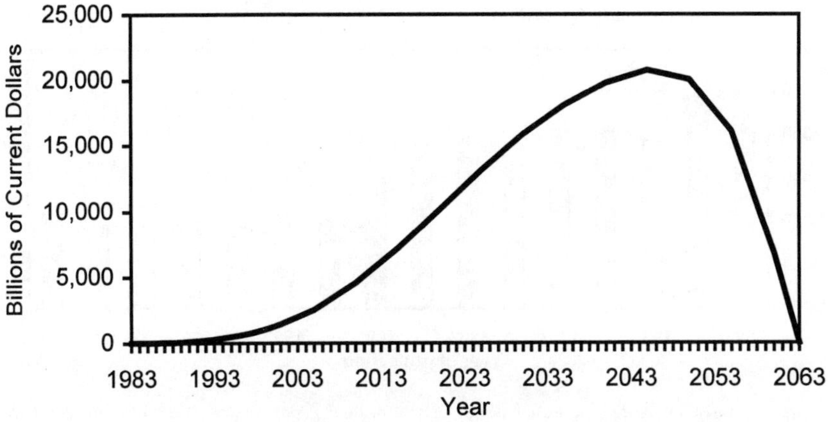

Source: Harry C. Ballantyne, "Long-Range Projections of Social Security Trust Fund Operations in Dollars," Social Security Administration, *Actuarial Notes* (October 1983), p. 2.

New Storm Clouds on the Horizon

The projected date of trust fund exhaustion, 2063 as of 1983, is reforecast annually by the trustees of the system. Unfortunately, in the years after the 1983 reforms, the date kept getting closer, and often by more than one year per year. Figure 13.2 shows the evolution of the date of exhaustion with each forecast year. By 1985 the best-guess forecast date for running out of money had moved up to 2049. By 1994 the date was 2029. The difference between 2063 and 2029 is of course thirty-four years; more important, it is the difference between securing the current level of Social Security benefits for the baby boomers and having to address the imbalances of the system right in the middle of their retirement. In fact, the youngest boomer will be only sixty-five in 2029 and will not even be eligible for full normal retirement benefits for two more years. The projected exhaustion date went up to 2032 as of 1998. Unfortunately, however, the established trend is for the intermediate forecasts to worsen with each future forecast. Members of the baby boom cohorts should certainly not count on the latest projection of solvency until 2032; the problem could easily occur a decade earlier. In fact, the pessimistic forecasts of the 1983–1985 period were far more accurate than the so-called best-guess forecasts. Even the pessimistic forecasts were more optimistic than the actual evolution of events. This is rather remarkable, for in many respects the 1980s and 1990s marked the revital-

Figure 13.2   Exhaustion Date of OASDI Trust Fund, by Forecast Year

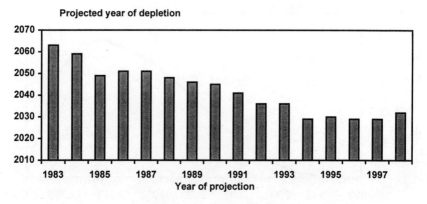

Source: Data taken from sequential issues of the *Annual Report of the Board of Trustees of the Federal Old-Age and Survivors Insurance and Disability Insurance Trust Funds.*

Figure 13.3   Payroll Tax Increase Required for Balance over Seventy-Five Years

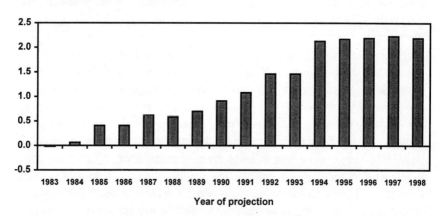

Source: Data taken from sequential issues of the *Annual Report of the Board of Trustees of the Federal Old-Age and Survivors Insurance and Disability Insurance Trust Funds.*

ization of the U.S. economy—it may have done well, but not well enough to live up to the forecasts of Social Security's actuaries.

Another way to look at the deterioration of the system through the 1980s and 1990s is to examine the payroll tax change that the Social Security trustees calculate as being necessary to bring the system into balance for seventy-five years, in their best-guess scenario. Figure 13.3 shows the required tax rate increases by year of forecast, according to numbers published each year by Social Security. The system was thought to be in balance in this sense in 1983 after the adoption of the 1983 Amendments. In fact, it was thought that the payroll tax rate could have been ever so slightly lowered, by 0.02 percent, and still the present value of projected revenues over seventy-five years would equal the present value of projected costs. Again, the system looked decidedly less healthy as time went on. By 1992 a permanent increase in the payroll tax rate of 1.46 percent was thought to have been necessary to bring the system into balance for the succeeding seventy-five years. By 1998 the hypothetical tax hike to balance out the system would have been 2.19 percent. To put the degree of backsliding into perspective, the required tax rate hike to balance the OASDI system in the November 1982 briefing book of the National Commission on Social Security Reform was 1.82 percent. By 1994 the long-term outlook appeared worse than it had before the efforts of Greenspan, Reagan, O'Neill, and the rest of the cast in 1983.

Revisiting the Forecasts of System Operations

Not only did the 1972 and 1977 reforms fail to live up to their forecast effects on strengthening the system's finances, but the same can be said for the 1983 Amendments. Although it is possible that the economy keeps underperforming all reasonable estimates, at some point you have to put the blame on the estimates and not on nature or bad luck. Most of the problem is the incredible rigidity of the design of the system itself. We legislate benefit formulas, the "defined benefits" of the program, for an extremely long-term future and, theoretically at least, legislate future tax rates that will finance the benefits. Only with either remarkable skill or luck will the legislated future taxes exactly fund the legislated future benefits. Although the legislation itself makes the system appear to be without risks, our experience of the 1970s, '80s, and '90s is that the system is actually subject to the considerable risk that the economy won't pan out as forecast by the system's stewards.

The degree to which the future can fail to match earlier forecasts is

Figure 13.4   Three Forecasts of the OASDI Trust Fund Balances

Billions of current dollars

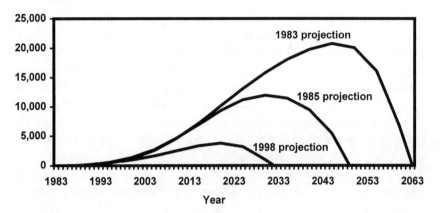

Sources: Harry C. Ballantyne, "Long-Range Projections of Social Security Trust Fund Operations in Dollars," Social Security Administration, *Actuarial Notes* (October 1983), p. 2; *1985 Annual Report of the Board of Trustees of the Federal Old-Age and Survivors Insurance and Disability Insurance Trust Funds;* and *1998 Annual Report of the Board of Trustees of the Federal Old-Age and Survivors Insurance and Disability Insurance Trust Funds.*

shown in Figure 13.4. By 1985 the Social Security trustees were predicting that the trust fund would peak at slightly less than $12 trillion, rather than at the more than $20 trillion figure forecast only two years earlier. While $12 trillion is still a lot of money, the need for a more than 40 percent revision in only two years is not reassuring. By 1998 the peak future trust fund accumulation was being forecast as roughly $3.75 trillion. To be fair, some of the adjustments were due to lower projected rates of inflation, but that cannot explain the huge slide to the left in the date at which the fund is exhausted. Any way you look at it, the forecasts contemporaneous with the 1983 reforms have not stood the test of time. The reforms did allow the system to navigate the 1980s and make it into the clear waters of the 1990s and the first decade of the twenty-first century. What they didn't accomplish, despite the scheduled rise in the normal retirement age, was to make the system viable beyond the third decade of the twenty-first century.

What went wrong with the forecasts in 1983? The first thing to admit is that seventy-five-year forecasts are extraordinarily tough things to do. Imagine someone in 1925 trying to forecast the U.S. economy in the year 2000. They almost certainly would have done terribly. Social Security is trying to evaluate the system's financial condition until almost 2075 as we write. So, though their past performance has been less than stellar, we do

Table 13.1   Contributors to the Change in the
Actuarial Balance of OASDI Between the 1983
and 1995 Trustees' Reports

	Change in Actuarial Balance (percent of taxable payroll)
Balance in the 1983 report	+0.02
Legislative changes	+0.10
Valuation period	−0.55
Economic assumptions	−0.79
Demographic assumptions	+0.83
Methods	−0.93
All other	−0.15
Balance in the 1995 report	−2.17

Source: Appendix 1 of the *Report of the 1994-1996 Advisory Council on Social Security,* vol. 1: *Findings and Recommendations* (Washington, D.C.: Social Security Administration, 1997), pp. 163-164.

recognize that they have a tough assignment. Not only is the forecasting period extremely long, but the program is complex, and some of the key parameters of the economy—such as future birth rates, the rate of real wage growth, and the rate of mortality—are extremely hard to predict.

One can determine the causes of the failure of the 1983 forecast to pan out. The 1994–1996 Advisory Council on Social Security did exactly that in its final report published in January 1997. Table 13.1 lists the separate causes for the deterioration. The story is not that Congress gave away the store. In fact, the most important of the few changes that took place between 1983 and 1995 occurred because of the 1993 legislation to reduce the budget deficit when the percentage of Social Security income that is taxable for middle- and high-income elderly was increased from 50 percent to 85 percent. As shown in the table, the legislative changes actually improved the long-term actuarial balance of the program.

Three big negatives have worsened the outlook. The first is listed in Table 13.1 as "Valuation Period." That simply reflects the fact that the years in the seventy-five-year forecasting window change with each new annual forecast. The year that has just passed is dropped out of the window, and a new one is added from the second half of the twenty-first century. The problem is that even in 1983, the trustees and commissioners knew that they had not balanced the "out years." So, with the mere passage of time, good years drop out of the seventy-five-year planning horizon and they are replaced by distant years when the program is expected to be running a deficit. This effect of passage of time alone accounts for a 0.55 percentage point deterioration in the actuarial balance of OASDI system.

The second cause of the premature unraveling of the 1983 fixes is "Economic Assumptions" in Table 13.1. Assumptions that have not panned out and have had to be modified increased the actuarial deficit by 0.79 percent. The biggest part of this mistake was the same thing that happened in the 1972 and 1977 reforms—namely, overestimating future increases in real wages. The Greenspan commission and the 1983 trustees assumed a long-term rate of growth of real wages of 1.5 percent per year. Although this was below what had been enjoyed in the 1950s and 1960s, it was distinctly above the experience in the 1970s and, unfortunately, the 1980s. By 1995 the trustees had lowered their intermediate estimate for future improvement in real wages to 1 percent per year. Another economic factor which caused the 1983 forecast to go awry was that nontaxable fringe benefits, primarily health and pension benefits, grew more rapidly than expected, reducing the proceeds of the payroll tax.

The third big contributor to the failure of the 1983 intermediate projections to materialize is listed in Table 13.1 as "Methods." In everyday parlance, this probably should be labeled "Mistakes"—and they were whoppers. The biggest methodological mistake was in the assumed age of immigrants. In the mathematical calculations, the Social Security administration treated immigrants as if they were newborns. They assumed that immigrants would have full-length work careers, that they would make corresponding payroll contributions to the system, and that they wouldn't collect benefits for many decades. In fact, the age distribution of immigrants is not so very different from the age distribution of the resident population. This mistake was discovered before the 1985 Trustees' Report and accounts for much of the deterioration in forecasts between 1983 and 1985.

The demographic assumptions built into the 1995 forecast were actually more favorable to the finances of the program than those used in 1983. This explains the fact that changing demographic assumptions brightened the outlook for Social Security. It is our opinion, however, that Social Security may now be too conservative in projecting future improvements in health and longevity. It is likely that going forward, the current demographic assumptions cause the trustees to underestimate the long-term financial problems of OASDI.

We hope all this has convinced you that a pay-as-you-go Social Security system is not without risks. Americans are in this program for their entire lifetime, and the risks are considerable. Think about it—taxes were raised and benefits cut in 1977. Taxes were raised and future benefits cut in 1983.

Now we see that the system has a large long-term deficit. Unless we consider changing its very structure, we will have no choice but to raise taxes and cut benefits once again. There aren't a lot of choices for fixing Social Security other than straightforward tax hikes and benefit cuts—that is, unless we set about designing a system that increases the nation's saving rate and ultimately increases the wealth of our children and grandchildren. But that is getting ahead of our story. Here the point is that the current program is proving to be very risky for young participants, given that the terms offered continue to deteriorate. If a private insurance policy kept raising the premiums and lowering the benefits, one would not hesitate to call it a risky contract. The same should be true for Social Security.

Are the Accumulating Trust Funds Really Added National Savings?

One more thing about the post-1983 period calls for discussion. That concerns the fact that ostensibly the program has been running increasingly large surpluses over the past fifteen years. By the end of 1998 the combined OASI and DI Trust Funds had accumulated approximately $757 billion in special-issue U.S. Government bonds. This amounts to almost two years of benefit payments. The question is whether this "nest egg" represents real wealth created by Social Security to help deal with the future financial problems to be faced by today's young people and those yet unborn. This is particularly important for workers of the 2015–2055 period, who will be asked to support the retirements of the baby boomers. In other words, is this $757 billion real incremental wealth that we can credit to Social Security, and does it represent a down payment on the problems we have been talking about?

The answer to our question depends on what the rest of the federal government has done with the money that Social Security has been turning over to it over the last fifteen years and more in exchange for its collection of IOUs. Was the money saved and invested or did it simply go toward consumption? If it increased the federal government's saving and investment or, more to the point, decreased our federal government's other borrowing and dissaving, then the future population will be wealthier because of the buildup in assets. By contrast, if the extra money that Social Security turned over to the rest of the government simply resulted in more current spending, then future wealth has not increased because of this "accumulation." The savings of one branch of the government would have been exactly canceled out by the dissaving of the rest.

Figure 13.5   Excess of OASDI Contributions over Benefits and "On-Budget" Federal Government Deficits, 1985–1997

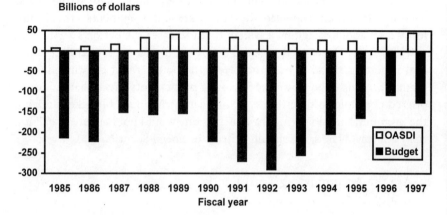

Sources: The Social Security cash-flow surplus was taken from the *1998 Annual Report of the Board of Trustees of the Federal Old-Age and Survivors Insurance and Disability Insurance Trust Funds*, table II.F12. The magnitudes of the on-budget federal government surplus were taken from the *Economic Report of the President*, February 1997, table B-76.

An analogy might help clarify what is going on here. Suppose one adult member of a family is a saver. She saves by turning over her extra money, money earned but not spent, to another member of the family, who promptly gives her an IOU and spends the money on a car. Will the children or grandchildren inherit any wealth from this process? Of course not. On the other, if the second adult had used the money to invest in property, then the answer would be "yes."

The answer to our question whether the Social Security trust fund balance represents wealth that can benefit future generations depends on unobservable or counterfactual behavior. What would federal government spending have been and, for that matter, what would tax collections have been, if the government hadn't had access to Social Security's cash-flow surplus over the last fifteen years or so? The question cannot be answered with certainty, but Figure 13.5 provides some clues. There we see the excess of OASDI revenues, not including interest on the previously accumulated bonds, over costs and the so-called on-budget surplus of the federal government. The figure shows that for the years 1985–1997 the Social Security cash-flow surplus was dwarfed by the deficits in the rest of the federal government budget. To be sure, this doesn't directly answer our question, but it does add to the likelihood that the $757 billion pile of government bonds has not made the future population wealthier.

One of the reasons that Social Security has appeared to be running significant surpluses in recent years is that only one side of the ledger is reported in the annual statement of the federal government's accounts when it comes to this program. When the Social Security actuaries develop their annual projections of the system, they consider its assets and liabilities over the coming seventy-five years. The assets include the current value of the accumulation in the trust fund plus the present value of projected revenue over the whole period. The present value of future revenue is calculated by discounting projected future revenues based on the demographic and economic assumptions underlying their projections. The discounting takes into account the effects of inflation and the time value of money. If the assumed inflation rate is 3 percent and the assumed rate of return on money is 3 percent, next year's revenues would be discounted by the sum of the two, or 6 percent. The estimated assets as of October 1, 1998, were $19.8 trillion. The discounting factor used for calculating the value of future revenues was 6.398 percent. The present value of future liabilities is calculated by discounting projected future benefits by the same discounting factors as in projecting the assets. The estimated liabilities as of October 1, 1998, were $22.9 trillion. The difference in the two is the net actuarial balance of the system. If the difference of assets minus liabilities is positive, it means the system is projected to have a surplus or is estimated to be overfunded. If the difference is negative, it is projected to be underfunded. In this case, it is underfunded by $3.1 trillion.

Figure 13.6 shows the accumulated trust funds and the estimated unfunded obligations of the Social Security system from 1984 through 1998. While this figure looks similar to Figure 13.5, the former showed federal cash budget deficits over the past several years, while Figure 13.6 shows accumulating unfunded obligations in Social Security. Over this period, the trust funds grew from about $32 billion at the end of fiscal 1984 to about $730 billion at the end of fiscal 1998—note that the fiscal year-end balances and the calendar year-end balances differ by about $30 billion. Over this same period, the estimated actuarial balance of the system fell from a net positive balance of $37 billion to a net negative balance of $3.1 trillion. In other words, as we look out into the future and compare the assets of the system to its liabilities, we have run up $3.1 trillion more in obligations over the last fifteen years than we have made in contributions. We have run up a bill of $3.1 trillion for future taxpayers over this period, for which we have not laid aside any assets.

Figure 13.6   OASDI Trust Funds and Estimates of Open-Group
Actuarial Surplus or Deficiency as of October 1, 1984–1998

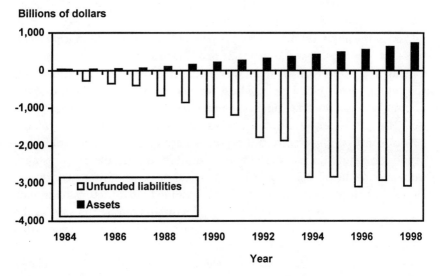

Sources: 1986 Annual Report of the Board of Trustees of the Federal Old-Age and Survivors Insurance and Disability Insurance Trust Funds, p. 58; 1998 Annual Report of the Board of Trustees of the Federal Old-Age and Survivors Insurance and Disability Insurance Trust Funds, p. 103; and unpublished data, Office of the Actuary, Social Security Administration.

To argue that we have been saving anything simply because there is a positive balance in the trust fund is to ignore completely the portion of Social Security that is deep under water. Assume that you start the beginning of a year with no money in your bank account and borrow $10,000 and spend $7,500 of it on consumer goods. No one would consider you richer at the end of the year because you still had a bank balance of $2,500 compared to no balance at the beginning of the year. They would say that you are still $10,000 in debt and, with only $2,500 in your bank account, in need of coming up with an extra $7,500 to get back to where you were at the beginning of the year.

To really answer the question of whether Social Security is contributing to our national saving rate completely, one would have to do a thorough analysis on what the government spent the money on. For instance, does the money go toward investment in roads and bridges? Almost certainly. Is that what the incremental money handed over by Social Security was spent on? We don't know, but somehow we doubt it. But how about money spent on national defense? Is that investment? Arguably. What about agricultural subsidies? Probably not. Education? Probably yes. The space program? Who knows? The point is that much of what the government spends money on can be looked at as investment or part investment and part consumption. However, much of what we spend money on is consumption or expenditure to improve the current lives of our citizens rather than the future wealth of our children and grandchildren. Our tentative conclusion from all this is that today's young will not benefit from the full value of the $757 billion, but only from a fraction of it, maybe half at best. The rest of the money was spent on "us" and not saved and invested for "them."

It may be interesting to review what will happen when the contributions to Social Security begin to fall short of benefit payments in about 2012. At some point slightly later than that, Social Security will need to turn in its bonds to the rest of the federal government and ask for payment. Money will be transferred from the rest of the government to the Social Security system in return for the bonds. Where will the money come from? Presumably from taxes or government borrowing. But these are the same choices that the government would face if the system didn't have the bonds and simply asked for a bailout. The point is that the bonds have helped save the system only if they have resulted in greater investment in the economy and hence in higher productivity and higher wages for those who are going to have to either pay the taxes or buy the bonds. Selling the bonds to the rest of the government doesn't really generate money by itself, because in a very real sense, we are selling them to ourselves. Both the accumulation of these bonds and their liquidation are accounting transactions—they don't guarantee real saving during the accumulation phase and real dissaving during the spend-down phase. All in all, the trust fund balances do not offer much reason to be sanguine about the burden we are passing on to future generations. Let us note at the close of this discussion that this very matter was at the heart of the debate in the 1940s and 1950s over whether the system should be funded. It is still at the heart of the debate today, as we will see in the next part of the story.

Chapter 14

Fundamental Questions

T he research staff at the Social Security Administration periodically develops an analysis to show that Social Security is a vital
program for the income security of the millions of people who receive its benefits. It is the nation's largest single government program. It provides monthly payments to forty-four million elderly, disabled,
or surviving beneficiaries. Social Security contends that among beneficiaries sixty-five and older, nearly 40 percent rely on Social Security for 80 percent or more of their income, and that 30 percent rely on it for 90 percent
or more.[1]

We are convinced that Social Security exaggerates the dependence of
the elderly on Social Security because the SSA uses a survey to analyze its
effects that significantly undercounts the amount of employer-sponsored
pension income that the elderly receive. If the survey undercounts the income from other sources more than it undercounts Social Security income,
it would make Social Security seem more important for the income security of the elderly than it really is. In a comparison that one of the current
authors has developed for 1990, the total pension income reported on the
survey that Social Security uses, the *Current Population Survey* (CPS), was
$154.5 billion. National Income and Product Accounts (NIPA) data devel-
oped by the Department of Commerce for the same year estimated that
employer-provided pensions paid $243.3 billion. The *Statistics of Income*
(SOI) files prepared by the Internal Revenue Service based on federal income tax filings estimated pension income for 1990 at $231.9 billion. But
whether the SSA overstates the importance of Social Security or not, it
is clear that the program plays an extremely important role in providing
income security to the elderly. Given the program's pervasiveness and importance, the public's current perception that the system is not likely to

Figure 14.1   Public Confidence in the Future of Social Security

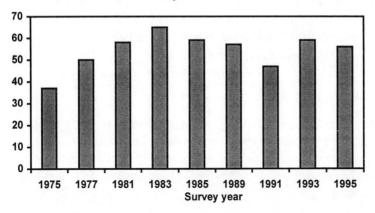

Percent not confident in the system

Sources: American Council of Life Insurance, "Monitoring Attitudes of the Public" surveys by Yankelovich, Skelly, and White (1975–1982) and the Roper Organization/Roper Starch Worldwide (1983–1994), as reported in Jennifer Baggette, Robert Y. Shapiro, and Lawrence Jacobs, "The Polls—Poll Trends, Social Security—An Update," *Public Opinion Quarterly* (Fall 1995), p. 426.

exist in the future is a serious problem. Further, the belief that it is unfair raises a series of fundamental questions that must be explored.

Will It Be There for Us?

In a nationally representative survey conducted during September 1998 by Princeton Survey Research Associates for the educational group Americans Discuss Social Security, 49 percent of the respondents indicated that they believed the Social Security program was headed for major financial trouble. Further, 58 percent indicated that they believed big changes would be needed to correct its problems. Finally, 66 percent indicated that everyone would need to give up something for the program to continue into the future.[2]

The lack of confidence that the current system can continue without significant revision is not new. Figure 14.1 shows the percentage of the public indicating that they were not confident in the program from a number of national surveys done over the last twenty years. The initial survey was done in 1975, before there was a widespread appreciation of the financing problems created by the benefit increases adopted in 1972. The lack of confidence in the system grew steadily from the 1975 survey until 1983, when Social Security's short-term funding crisis was addressed. By 1983, nearly two out of three people indicated a lack of confidence in Social Security. That lack of confidence declined somewhat as the trust funds began to accumulate substantial balances after the 1983 Amendments. Since 1983, as successive Social Security Trustees' Reports have indicated that the trust funds will be depleted toward the beginning of the baby boomers' retirement, the lack of confidence has been rising again.

How Underfunded Is Social Security?

We believe that the underfunding of Social Security is partly to blame for the lack of confidence in the system. Given this possibility, it is important to investigate the order of magnitude of the underfunding in the system and the potential implications for the program and the public's perceptions about it.

The Actuaries' Projections

The nature and magnitude of Social Security's underfunding can be stated most succinctly by showing the income and outgo projections for the OASDI programs from the 1998 Social Security Trustees' Report. Figure 14.2 shows the income and cost rates for the combined programs under the intermediate assumptions for the seventy-five-year projection period. The income rate is the expected revenue for the program, given the existing tax rates in current law. The cost rate is the expected expenditure rate given current law. Both of them are stated as a percentage of covered earnings. Some people look at the estimates in Figure 14.2 and conclude that the system doesn't really have a current financing problem and that policymakers have considerable time to figure out how to deal with it. The reason they are sanguine about dealing with Social Security funding on a delayed basis relates to the surpluses that are being generated by the program currently. The figure shows, however, that the surpluses we are currently generating are much smaller than the deficits that we expect to experience after 2010. The Social Security actuaries estimate that in terms of present value, the system is underfunded over the next seventy-five years to the tune of about $3 trillion.

According to actuaries' 1998 projections, the imbalance in the income rate and the cost rate of the combined OASDI programs over the long-range (seventy-five-year) projection period is 2.19 percent of covered payroll, the equivalent of about $75 billion annually in 1998 dollars. This imbalance is largely being driven by the change in the demographic structure of

Figure 14.2   Estimated OASDI Income and Cost Rates for Selected Years

Percent of covered payroll

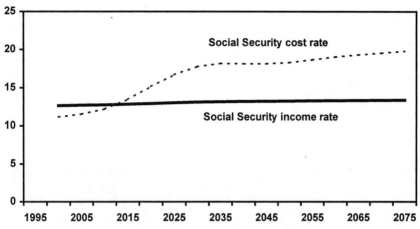

Source: 1998 Annual Report of the Board of Trustees of the Federal Old-Age and Survivors Insurance and Disability Insurance Trust Funds, p. 169.

our population over the next thirty years in combination with the under-lying pay-go financing structure of the system. If we look to the future, the primary reason the system is underfunded relates to the important dependency ratio discussed earlier. In Figure 14.3 we plot the dependency ratios as projected by the Social Security actuaries from today out to 2070. The ratio is currently equal to approximately 0.30, as shown in Figure 14.3, but is expected to rise to about 0.50 by 2030. That means that we will go from roughly 3.3 workers paying taxes today to support each retiree to 2.0 workers supporting each retiree in 2030. If you think of a typical household as having two working parents and a couple of children, by 2030 those two working parents will not only have their children to take care of; they will also have an elderly dependent for whom they finance Social Security and Medicare payments, if current law persists until then. It may be close to the moral equivalent of having grandma move back in with the working family.

In absolute terms, the dependency ratio shift from 0.30 to 0.50 between now and 2030 may seem trivial. But keep in mind that this pesky ratio is a multiplier. Today, the ratio of average benefit to average wage stands at roughly 0.40. When you calculate the cost rate for Social Security—that is, the required pay-go payroll tax rate necessary to finance the benefits being provided—you have to multiply the dependency ratio by the benefits to wages ratio. Doing so today, the cost of the system is around 12 percent

Figure 14.3   Projected Social Security Dependency Ratios, 1995–2070

Ratio of Social Security beneficiaries to covered workers

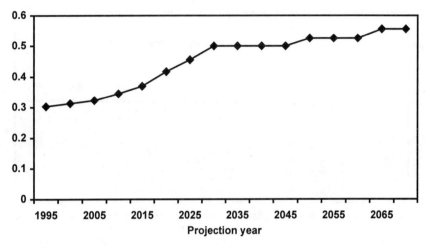

Projection year

Source: Data to develop this chart were acquired from the Office of the Actuary, Social Security Administration.

of covered payroll—that is, 0.30 × 0.40 = 0.12. By 2030, this would jump to 20 percent, assuming that the relationship between average benefits and average wages remains constant—that is, 0.50 × 0.40 = 0.20.

The actuaries estimate that the relationship between average benefits and average wages will decline slightly in future years because of the increase in the system's normal retirement age that is already built into law. But they do not expect it to decline enough to offset the increase in the dependency ratio. That is why the cost line in Figure 14.2 is expected to increase so much between now and 2030. By then the actuaries estimate that the system will cost about 18 percent of payroll, 50 percent more than it does today. If we were facing that higher dependency ratio today, we would have to collect approximately an additional $200 billion in payroll taxes just to support Social Security this year. While President Clinton has been saying that we should save current federal budget surpluses to help solve the Social Security financing problem, the projected revenue shortfalls are larger than anyone believes the budget surplus can credibly become. The added $200 billion we would need this year if we were facing the 2030 financing picture is more than two times the federal budget surplus for the current fiscal year.

The problem that Social Security faces is that if we attempt to continue operating the system under current law, it will certainly come up short of resources by roughly 2030. Some supporters of Social Security note that we will still be able to collect the payroll taxes, and so the situation is not nearly as dire as it might seem. For example, Bob Ball says that Social Security is not "going broke" and that all it faces in 2030 "is a shortfall."[3] He contends that even if policymakers do nothing, the system will still be able to pay 75 percent of benefits provided under current law. To put this conclusion in context, we need only think about the current situation of today's Social Security beneficiaries. The average benefit during 1997 was around $790 per month. If we implemented the 75 percent solution today, the average beneficiary would see that payment immediately reduced to $600 per month. Given the massive dependence that we have created on these unfunded political promises, the mere suggestion that we could reduce benefits across the board by 25 percent is beyond belief.

By the actuaries' estimates, Social Security funding could last until around 2030. But that assumes that the trust funds will be gradually spent down as a supplement to the taxes financing the system. The problem with that assumption is that fulfilling it will throw the larger fiscal picture of the federal government into difficulty. Around 2012, the level of benefits paid by the system will exceed the amount of taxes collected to finance it. Beyond that point, Social Security will become a federal deficit problem, no longer a part of the deficit solution that it has been since the early 1980s. By 2015, Social Security is projected to be in deficit to the tune of $30 billion in 1998 dollars. By 2020, the deficit will have ballooned to $100 billion. This program faces significant challenges, no matter how one looks at it.

The problem we face by delaying action on fixing Social Security is that each year we delay is a year when we could take advantage of the favorable demographics that now exist. The long-range deficit of 2.19 percent of taxable payroll represents a 16.4 percent shortfall in the long-range income rate, which is estimated to be 13.27 percent of covered payroll. But this is an average annual shortfall. This year we will run a surplus, with about 8.7 percent of the income to the trust funds not being spent for benefit payments and administrative expenses. If we do not change the law soon, by 2020, the annual shortfall in income is projected to be 16.2 percent. By 2030 or so, when the trust funds are projected to be depleted, the shortfall will be 32 percent, and it is projected to grow increasingly larger after that. In other words, every year we delay dealing with this problem, it will get worse.

Quibbling over the Numbers

There is currently a debate among Social Security policy analysts over the methods and assumptions that Social Security actuaries use in projecting future costs. That debate, while relatively esoteric, has important implications for our perception of the magnitude of the problem we face and possibly for the way we solve it as well. The actuaries use models that are characterized as being *deterministic* to estimate future costs. Critics of their estimating methods argue that they should be using *stochastic* models to project the system.

In the deterministic approach, the actuaries develop a range of assumptions for estimating the future operation of Social Security. For example, the dependency ratio is sensitive to two particular demographic assumptions. One is the birth rate and the other is the rate of change in life expectancy. It is also sensitive to certain behavioral assumptions about when people start to work, when they retire, and how much they work in between. Social Security actuaries estimate the future operations of the system under three sets of assumptions. Since they develop only a range of three cost estimates, assumptions are paired in specific combinations. For example, focusing just on the demographic assumptions, in one set of cost projections an assumption of high birth rate is paired with one of a relatively low rate of increase in life expectancy. In another set, a low birth rate is paired with a relatively high rate of increase in life expectancy. The first pairing, along with a coordinated set of economic assumptions, results in a lower long-term cost estimate for the system than the second pairing. A third pairing of assumptions is used to develop an intermediate cost estimate. The middle set of assumptions represent the actuaries' best guess about future birth rates and improvements in life expectancy. It is the middle set of assumptions and the resulting projections that are the official estimates that policymakers use in considering changes to the system.

Critics of the deterministic approach argue that the pairings of assumptions that the actuaries use do not necessarily cover the range of contingencies the system faces.[4] For example, they ask why one would only consider the case of high birth rates and low improvement in life expectancy together and not high birth rates and high improvement in life expectancy. The critics also point out that some of the pairings do not make any sense at all. For example, in the low-cost estimates that the actuaries develop, they assume high fertility rates and high labor-force participation rates for women. Typically women who have several children have lower labor-force participation rates than those who have fewer children.

The critics of the actuaries' approach argue that many of the important variables that drive Social Security's costs could play out in a whole range of ways different from those assumed in projecting the system's costs. The critics believe that the modeling of the program should take into account the uncertainty about the important factors affecting system costs. This group of policy analysts argues that we should simulate the future using stochastic models that allow all or most of the important variables to vary over time across a distribution of reasonable ranges. This approach would result in the generation of a wide range of possible outcomes, each of which has an assigned probability of actually occurring.

In some cases, critics of current methods for projecting Social Security's costs are particularly concerned about specific assumptions that the actuaries use. For example, the actuaries assume that the steady improvement in life expectancy that we have experienced in recent decades will slow in the future. One group of academic demographers believes that improvements in life expectancy might actually accelerate in the future.[5] This one variable alone could have a tremendous impact on the dependency variable if people begin living much longer periods in retirement than they do today.

A question that naturally arises from the debate on alternative approaches to modeling Social Security costs is whether the evolution of the program has historically tracked along the lines the actuaries have estimated. Generally, the stochastic models would have resulted in best-guess forecasts similar to the intermediate cost forecasts of the actuaries but would have warned us that the worst-case outcomes were far worse than the trustees' high-cost estimates.

One of the problems in developing public policy estimates that are bounded by degrees of uncertainty is that policymakers do not like uncertainty. When a problem arises, they want to be able to solve it, or at least to adopt policy changes that they can describe to their constituents as solving it. When Social Security was in financial crisis in the early 1980s, the deterministic model allowed policymakers to claim that they had solved the problem by adopting the 1983 Amendments, because the actuaries' projections showed that they had. It is not clear how the same policies would have been greeted under a headline "Congress Adopts Changes That Have a 60 Percent Probability of Solving the Social Security Financing Problem." In retrospect, the public probably would have been better off if something like that had been the message, but putting probability distributions on policy prescriptions may further complicate the process of policymaking itself.

We believe that the most important issue that people should be focusing on today is that we are now at a point in the evolution of Social Security that by widespread consensus, the system is seriously underfinanced. Both deterministic and stochastic models yield this result. Certain aspects of the program have to be changed if it is going to survive as a meaningful and effective vehicle for retirement security.

Is Social Security Fair?

Determining whether workers get their money's worth from Social Security benefits is complicated for several reasons. In the case of retirement benefits, the lifetime accrual process of earning these benefits casts them more in the light of deferred consumption or a means of wealth accumulation than of insurance against a contingency over which the beneficiary has little or no control. In 1997, there were approximately 37.5 million people receiving retirement benefits or dependent or survivor benefits under the retirement portion of the program.[6] Evaluation of the money's worth of these benefits depends on whether the program is an efficient vehicle by comparison with the alternatives for financing benefits across groups of workers and across time.

In a major sense, the efficiency of our Social Security system in giving workers their money's worth in retirement benefits goes back to the discussion in earlier chapters over whether Social Security should serve as an accumulation or banking device or simply an intergenerational transfer device. As we explored earlier, Edwin Witte felt strongly that the banking feature was important if people were to be treated fairly in the long term. Senator Arthur Vandenberg fought, with the help of people like J. Douglas Brown, to make the system an intergenerational transfer device. Vandenberg and Brown, from the opposite ends of the ideological spectrum, won.

The size of the lifetime contribution for retirement benefits, plus the widespread availability of alternative means for accumulating retirement wealth and their broad popularity invites comparisons with Social Security money's worth for retirement benefits to a greater extent than do disability or early-survivor benefits. Finally, the redistributive character of Social Security's benefit structure suggests that direct comparisons with alternative financial investment opportunities might fail to consider an explicit policy goal not captured in such comparisons—that Social Security intends for earners with high wages to subsidize those with lower wages.

Assessing Fairness

Over the years, the rates of return for participating in Social Security have been computed in different ways. While there has been considerable fussing about showing the results in one fashion or another, the story is remarkably consistent once all of the methodological chaff is blown away. Robert Myers and Bruce Schobel, a young actuary who worked with Myers on the National Commission on Social Security Reform in the early 1980s, have demonstrated that early beneficiaries received an extremely good deal in the early years. They showed that a single male with lifetime average earnings who retired at age sixty-five in 1960 would have gotten a benefit from Social Security that was seven times more valuable than what he would have received from investing payroll tax contributions on his wages in government bonds. For the single-earner couple it was thirteen times. For the single male with average earnings who retired in 1980, Social Security benefits would have been nearly three times what would have accrued in a government bond fund. For the single-earner couple at that time it would have been more than five times.[7]

Quantitatively, Myers and Schobel's calculations were done differently from those developed by Dean Leimer and reported in Chapter 7. Their calculations more closely approximated the approach that we used in estimating the windfalls for prototypical workers in Chapter 7, but they were not exactly the same. All of these calculations, however, tell the same story. The argument over the exact methodology for doing the calculations or exactly what is in the calculations is just smoke obscuring the light behind them. Early participants in Social Security got an unbelievable deal compared to other ways they might have saved for retirement. The part of the story in Chapter 7 about high-level earners getting a bigger absolute windfall than those further down has not been widely publicized by Social Security. It is the dirty secret behind the rhetoric of redistribution surrounding the program.

As we look into the future, the story about fairness takes a markedly different turn. Here again, there are different ways of looking at the situation, but once again, the results lead to a consistent set of conclusions. One of the issues is what should be included in the benefit and tax sides of the computations. The simplest analyses of Social Security's "money's worth" typically consider only the contributions for and retirement benefits paid under the OASI program. There are at least two reasons for this. First, considering only the retirement benefits is the simplest way of doing these calculations. Including the benefits paid to young survivors and to disability beneficiaries requires the valuation of three separate benefits and the streams of payroll taxes that support them. Second, the retirement benefit, the early-survivor benefit, and the disability benefit that make up OASDI are each clearly separable, having each been added to the program at a different time, and some analysts believe each should be subjected to a cost-benefit analysis on its own.

Other analysts believe that calculating the Social Security money's worth values on the basis of OASI benefits for retirees alone is inappropriate. They argue that even those workers who survive to retirement age and receive retirement benefits get substantial insurance value from the early-survivor and disability programs. They argue that to ignore the value of the ancillary benefits is to misrepresent the true worth of Social Security, adversely biasing the money's worth ratios. The Office of the Actuary at the Social Security Administration has developed an analysis that includes "direct consideration of disability and survivor benefits" that Myers and Schobel did not include in the development of their analysis.[8] Money's worth ratios calculated under this more comprehensive method were moderately higher than Myers and Schobel's calculations for single males born in 1940 or 1960 with lifetime earnings at the average and maximum levels. For single women born in the same years, the expanded calculations were also higher but the differences were trivial. They do not alter any of the basic conclusions one might draw about the relative fairness of the program across generations.

While using a different basis for calculating money's worth ratios may result in different measures of the value of Social Security's benefits relative to contributions, it has virtually no effect on the trend in the money's worth ratios. Table 14.1 shows the ratios for a number of hypothetical workers on the basis of their lifetime earning levels and their date of birth under current law as developed by the Social Security actuaries. For average- and high-wage single workers born after 1940, the value of benefits, including disability and survivors' benefits, is consistently less than the value of the anticipated lifetime payroll taxes. The projected ratios for workers at each wage level tend to improve for those born after 1960. But these ratios are calculated in accordance with current law and, we know, are not sustainable. This result simply means that many of today's workers will not get even the equivalent of a government bond rate of return on their Social Security contributions.

Policy options that would close the funding gap by increasing payroll taxes would cause further deterioration of the projected money's worth ratios, especially for workers born after 1980 who would likely face a rela-

Table 14.1   Ratio of the OASDI Taxes
Accumulated at Government Bond Rates
to the Present Value of Benefits

Year of birth	Present Value of Benefits/ Accumulated Value of Taxes		
	Single man	Single woman	Married couple
Low-wage earner			
1920	2.24	2.72	5.15
1940	1.12	1.29	2.26
1960	1.02	1.18	2.03
1980	1.16	1.33	2.24
2000	1.21	1.37	2.30
Average-wage earner			
1920	1.51	1.82	3.51
1940	0.84	0.96	1.70
1960	0.76	0.88	1.52
1980	0.86	0.99	1.68
2000	0.90	1.02	1.72
Maximum-wage earner			
1920	1.29	1.54	2.99
1940	0.64	0.74	1.29
1960	0.51	0.59	1.01
1980	0.57	0.65	1.11
2000	0.59	0.68	1.13

Source: Derived from Stephen C. Goss and Orlo R. Nichols,
"OASDI Money's Worth Analysis for Hypothetical Cohorts
—INFORMATION," Office of the Actuary, Social Security
Administration internal memorandum, March 1, 1993, p. 5.

tively full career at the higher tax rates. Policy options that would reduce benefits would likewise cause further deterioration in the projected
money's worth ratios, especially the ratios for workers born after the beginning of the baby boom generation. Because benefit reductions are likely
to be phased in over time, the youngest workers represented in Table 14.1,
those born in 2000, could see the biggest reductions in the value of Social
Security as a result of the policy changes we face. If we wait another ten
years to address the Social Security funding shortfall, it is likely to require
ultimate benefit reductions of more than 25 percent relative to current law

Table 14.2   Projected Ratio of the OASDI Taxes
Accumulated at Government Bond Interest Rates to
the Present Value of Retirement Benefits

Year of birth	Present Value of Benefits/ Accumulated Value of Taxes		
	Low-wage earner	Average-wage earner	Maximum-wage earner
Current law			
1949	0.99	0.78	0.71
1973	1.21	0.95	0.78
1997	1.29	1.01	0.82
Maintain current tax rate reform			
1949	0.94	0.73	0.62
1973	1.16	0.85	0.65
1997	1.19	0.86	0.65

Source: *Report of the 1994-1996 Advisory Council on Social Security*, vol. 1:
Findings and Recommendations (Washington, D.C.: Social Security Administration, 1997), p. 200.

to bring the program into balance. If such reductions occur, the money's worth ratios in Table 14.1 for males born after 1980 would fall to the 0.50 to 0.70 range for single men who earned average wages throughout their working lives and to the 0.55 to 0.75 range for single women with average wage levels.

In the work that the Social Security actuaries did for the 1994–1996 Social Security Advisory Council, they calculated money's worth ratios for three birth cohorts under a variety of policy options that the council considered. They also weighted workers in rough correspondence with the expected occurrence of benefits by recipient type—that is, single males, single females, single-earner couples, two-earner couples, and so on. The results of their projections for present law and a policy alternative that would reduce benefits to live within currently legislated payroll tax rates are shown in Table 14.2.

Any value in Table 14.2 that is less than 1.00 suggests that the worker represented would be better off investing in government bonds than participating in Social Security. The results in Table 14.2, calculated by the Social Security actuaries, suggest that significant numbers of current workers may get less from Social Security than from investing in government bonds. Partly the results in this table reflect the maturing of the system. Partly the results reflect underlying government bond interest rates that are used to calculate the value of the alternative "investment portfolio" to which accumulated Social Security benefits are compared. Because the government bond rates vary significantly over time, it is difficult to appreciate fully how much of the variation in the money's worth ratios is being driven by systemic characteristics of Social Security and how much is driven by the bond rates. Because of this, most economists prefer to look at internal rates of return rather than the money's worth ratios.

This takes us back to the analysis developed by Dean Leimer at the Social Security Administration to show the internal rates of return under the Social Security program across a wide range of birth cohorts. We looked at his results for the early birth cohorts in Chapter 7 on the basis of historical data. Results for later birth cohorts are developed through a simulation model of the system benchmarked to correspond with the actuaries' projections of future Social Security operations. The results of his historical calculations, as shown earlier, and his projections based on current law are shown in Figure 14.4.

The two flat lines in Figure 14.4 juxtapose the real compound returns on large-capital stocks and intermediate government bonds from the period 1951 through 1995 with the cohort rates of return for Social Security. We selected this period because it roughly corresponds with the working career of people who have turned sixty-five recently. The figure is ambiguous in whether such people, on average, would have been better off investing their Social Security contributions on their own or participating in Social Security. We know that most people do not invest all of their retirement savings in stocks, so most would not have realized the full stock returns shown in the figure. We also know that some do tend to invest conservatively, so the intermediate government bond rate might be a reasonable alternative expected return for them. Those investing in a diversified portfolio over their careers would have realized returns somewhere between the two lines, tilting toward one or the other depending on the share of assets held in stocks or bonds over the period. For the cohorts born beyond the mid-1940s, the picture is less ambiguous. The Social Security rate of return under current law does not even equal the intermediate government bond rate of return, essentially the most conservative alternative investment vehicle available to workers. And current law is not sustainable.

Leimer also estimated Social Security rates of return for cohorts of future retirees on the assumption that the payroll tax had been adjusted to de-

Figure 14.4   Real OASI Rates of Return for Specified Birth Cohorts, and Real Compound Returns on Large-Capital Stocks and Intermediate Government Bonds, 1951–1995

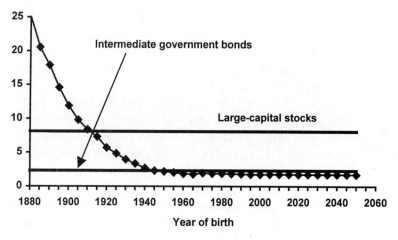

Sources: Dean R. Leimer, "Cohort-Specific Measures of Lifetime Net Social Security Transfers," ORS Working Paper Series, No. 59 (Washington, D.C.: Social Security Administration, February 1994), p. 16, and Ibbotson Associates, *Stocks, Bonds, Bills, and Inflation, 1996 Yearbook.*

liver on benefits promised under current law. His results are presented in Figure 14.5 for cohorts born in 1970 and after. Under this policy scenario, all the cohorts under age thirty today would do somewhat worse than under current law. For the older cohorts, the changes would be relatively small. For the younger ones, they would be quite significant. Under this policy scenario, youngsters in their midteens today could as a group expect to receive rates of return from OASI that are 40 percent less than their parents have realized on intermediate government bonds over their whole life to date. They are expected to be about two-fifths the rate of return Social Security paid to their grandparents and one-sixth that paid to their great-grandparents. These calculations are for whole birth cohorts. The structure of the program assures that large segments of each of the younger cohorts will do much worse than the cohorts as a whole. The implication of the re-distributive structure of the Social Security benefit formula is that average and higher earners will get lower rates of return within the cohorts than those with low earnings. A number of recent research efforts, however, have begun to raise questions whether this is the case.

Is Social Security as Redistributional as Its Supporters Pretend?

A substantial body of evidence shows that adults with lower incomes have shorter life expectancies than people with higher incomes. One study by a group of researchers at the National Institutes of Health was done in the early 1980s. It found that white males aged twenty-five living in families with annual incomes of $5,000 to $9,999 in 1980 dollars had life expectancies of 7.5 years less than their counterparts living in families with incomes above $50,000. At age forty-five the difference in life expectancies at these family income levels was 6.5 years, and at age sixty-five it was nearly 3 years. For white women, the differentials were less but followed a similar pattern.[9]

Life expectancies are important in estimating rates of return under programs like Social Security because they determine the period of time an individual can expect to pay taxes and to receive benefits. Groups that experience disproportionate death rates between the time they begin to work and normal retirement age, or individuals that live for only a short time after retirement get back little in the way of retirement benefits from Social Security by comparison with the payroll taxes levied on their earn-

Figure 14.5 Projected Real OASI Rates of Return Under Current Law and Under Higher Tax Rates Balancing Financing

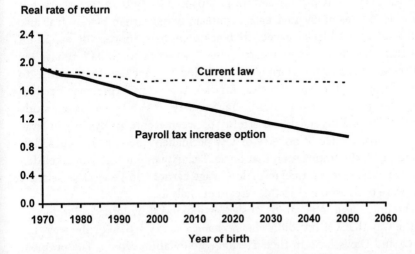

Source: Dean R. Leimer, "Cohort-Specific Measures of Lifetime Net Social Security Transfers," ORS Working Paper Series, No. 59 (Washington, D.C.: Social Security Administration, February 1994), p. 16.

Table 14.3   Cohort-Internal Real Rates
of Return for Single-Earner Couples, for
Workers Born in 1925

Income percentile	Common mortality	Differential mortality
20th	3.52%	2.90%
40th	2.96	3.10
50th	2.78	2.92
60th	2.64	2.78
75th	2.46	2.61

Source: Daniel M. Garrett, "The Effects of Differential
Mortality Rates on the Progressivity of Social Security,"
Economic Inquiry (July 1995), p. 466.

ings. Table 14.3 shows the results of one effort to estimate the implications
of differential mortality rates at varying income levels on rates of return
from Social Security. The results suggest that by controlling for mortality,
workers at the low end of the earnings distribution receive lower rates of
return than those with higher earnings.

The issue of whether Social Security's redistributional characteristics
are offset by shorter life expectancies among workers with low earnings
is further complicated by the fact that the probability of having low lifetime earnings is higher for certain groups in society than for others. For
example, whites on average earn significantly more than blacks. It is also
well known that blacks, especially black men, have shorter life expectancies than their white counterparts. These factors in combination have led
two researchers at the Heritage Foundation to conclude that owing "to
generally lower life expectancies, African Americans experience particularly poor rates of return from Social Security." [10] While one recent study
suggests "that differences in mortality between ethnic groups are, in large
part, a consequence of poverty or low permanent income, as opposed to
genotype," [11] the implication that Social Security might disadvantage African Americans, in particular, or low-wage earners, in general, is serious.
There are two responses to this stream of analysis.

The first is that one can be misled by looking at hypothetical individuals the way that Garrett did in his *Economic Inquiry* article or the way that
Beach and Davis have in their Heritage Foundation report. The problem
is that real-life circumstances are far more complicated than a small set
of hypothetical situations can capture. Looking at the accumulated payroll

taxes that a typical African-American male pays and his lifetime benefits is very different than the distribution of taxes that such men pay. African-American males' lower life expectancy than their white counterparts' means simply that they die at an earlier age, on average. But much of the lower life expectancy occurs in this case because of death at a relatively young age, before the person has paid much in taxes. Many who get to retirement age live a relatively full retirement life. To look only at an average African-American male with respect to Social Security's money's worth is to tend to overestimate the taxes that he would pay and underestimate the benefits he would receive. Both bias the money's worth estimate.

Two researchers at the U.S. Treasury Department and one at the U.S. Labor Department have used Social Security administrative record data on a number of cohorts of beneficiaries to analyze whether the program's redistributive structure is being offset by variations in mortality rate across the earnings spectrum. Their analysis focused on 8,344 workers born between 1917 and 1922. The analysis included OASI benefits and payroll taxes but did not include either DI benefits or the taxes that separately finance those benefits. Their results are shown in Table 14.4. The conclusion from their study is that controlling for differential mortality does diminish the

Table 14.4   Social Security Real Rates of
Return Using Mortality Distributions Either
Adjusted or Unadjusted by Income

	Income class	Real Rate of Return	
		Income-unadjusted mortality	Income-adjusted mortality
Men	Zero	6.61%	6.52%
	Low	6.23	6.17
	Medium	5.59	5.58
	High	4.99	5.04
Women	Zero	8.52	8.38
	Low	9.24	9.19
	Medium	7.66	7.70
	High	6.02	6.12

Source: James E. Duggan, Robert Gillingham, and John S. Greenlees, "Progressive Returns to Social Security? An Answer from Social Security Records," Research Paper No. 9501, U.S. Treasury Department, November 1995, p. 14.

Figure 14.6   Social Security Real Rates of Return for the 1918 Birth Cohort, with Mortality Distributions Adjusted by Income and Race

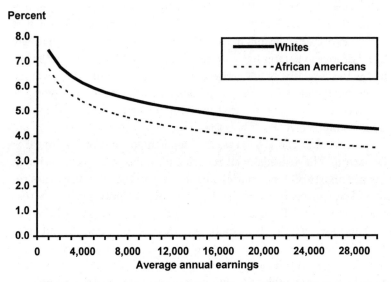

Source: Computed by the authors from data provided by Robert Gillingham and used in the development of a paper by James E. Duggan, Robert Gillingham, and John S. Greenlees, "Progressive Returns to Social Security? An Answer from Social Security Records," Research Paper No. 9501, U.S. Treasury Department, November 1995.

progressivity of Social Security, but not by much, and certainly not enough to offset it.

In their analysis, Duggan, Gillingham, and Greenlees include variables measuring the effects of race on life expectancy. They do not report its effects, however, on their calculations of rates of return on Social Security participation for the cohorts analyzed. We have gotten their equations for estimating rates of return and estimated rates of return at various levels of lifetime earnings for African Americans and the non-African-American workers in the 1917 to 1921 birth cohorts. Those results are plotted in Figure 14.6. The differences are quite sizable. For example, an African-American worker whose average earnings were $10,000 per year would realize a rate of return comparable to that achieved by other workers earning $22,000 per year.

The second criticism of analyses that find that Social Security's progressivity is offset by the lower life expectancy of workers with low lifetime earnings is that these studies do not take into account the full complement of Social Security benefits. In the case of the Beach and Davis study published by the Heritage Foundation, for example, neither disability nor survivors' benefits were considered. Duggan, Gillingham and Greenlees, and Garrett did not include disability benefits in their analyses either. The argument here is that while some segments of the population might expect to die at a younger age than others, those segments would be likely to benefit disproportionately from disability benefits themselves or from benefits provided to their survivors when they die. Although this argument is widely proffered by supporters of the program, it has not been empirically validated. As a member of the 1994–1996 Advisory Council on Social Security, one of the current authors (Schieber) specifically asked, along with other members of the council, that Social Security staff undertake an analysis of this very point. The SSA simply would not develop such an analysis. This issue can be resolved only with data of the sort that Leimer or Duggan, Gillingham, and Greenlees used in their analyses. Only government employees are given access to that data.

Do Rates of Return in Social Security Really Matter?

In the early days of Social Security, there was considerable sensitivity to making sure that the program provided workers with retirement benefits on a basis that at least matched what they could purchase in the private insurance markets. This sensitivity was instrumental in the initial design of the program. The Roosevelt administration's recommendation and the Social Security Act adopted in 1935 called for an initial combined payroll tax rate of 2 percent of covered earnings with 1 percent increments every three years until the combined rate reached 6 percent in 1949. The intent of the more rapid implementation of the payroll tax and its ultimately higher level in Roosevelt's plan was to partially fund a portion of accruing benefits in the early days and provide some funding support in later years through interest earnings on those funds.

The original architects and builders of our Social Security system, such as Arthur Altmeyer, anticipated exactly the situation we face with pay-as-you-go financing. They thought that it would prove to be unfair to future workers, and they did not want to see that eventuality materialize. The rates of return provided by Social Security for future cohorts of retirees are problematic from a public policy perspective. They are likely to generate an increasing set of analyses of the sort that William Beach and Gareth Davis have recently included in a Heritage Foundation report. The Heritage report showed that Social Security is a bad buy for many workers today, and may be an especially bad buy for lower-wage workers in general and minority workers in particular.[12] Bob Myers has written a stern criticism of the way Beach and Davis developed their assessment of the program,[13] but these analyses are likely to further undermine the faith of the American public in the system. The reason we come to that conclusion has nothing to do with the libertarian goals of many longtime critics of Social Security. It has to do with the commonsense assessment of Arthur Altmeyer back in 1945 that it is inequitable to compel workers to participate in a system that costs them more than it would cost to purchase similar benefits through private means. Arthur Altmeyer was not motivated to make this observation by any libertarian philosophical inclinations.

Martha Derthick tells us that Arthur Altmeyer was "Mr. Social Security" to a whole generation of the agency's employees.[14] He was one of the principal builders of the program during its early years and served as its highest official during seventeen of its first twenty years of operation. His observations about the equity of the program merit serious consideration. His observations about the embarrassing situation Congress would face if the current predicament should come to pass warrant hearings of the sort the Senate Budget Committee held in January 1998 on the subject. Congress is no longer in a situation to give out massive windfalls to one generation after another. The prospects for the future do not look a lot brighter than they did for the late generations of investors in the Ponzi scheme described in Chapter 7.

Chapter 15

The Iron Rules of Arithmetic Assert Themselves

*T*he Congress of the United States can write laws affecting many facets of the lives of its constituents. It can implement programs that seemingly allow society to overcome certain fundamental principles of accounting or arithmetic, at least for some period of time. The seeming benefits of such programs may persist for some period of time and may continue indefinitely in certain environments. For many years, Social Security looked like one of those instances where federal policymakers could make each successive generation of workers better off than the one before. Ultimately, however, the laws of arithmetic generally reassert themselves, as they have in the case of Social Security.

In Chapter 7, we discussed Paul Samuelson's consumption loan model that held out the promise that the pay-go financing could provide good returns for successive cohorts of participants in a national retirement plan. For his model to work, however, the economy in which the system operated had to experience substantial growth in the labor force and wages over time. The discussion of Samuelson's consumption loan model and the labor force dynamics that would make it work centered on Figure 7.8. There we saw a hypothetical workforce where each successive cohort of workers was larger than the preceding one, and where individual worker productivity for each cohort was larger than for the one before it.

The structure of the hypothetical workforce that we contrived in explaining Samuelson's concept looked very much like a pyramid. His 1974 *Newsweek* article, quoted at length in Chapter 7, was written at a time when he was looking at a population structure that suggested there would be an ever-increasing pool of workers. The population's age distribution shown in Figure 7.9 looked very much like the pyramid needed to make the model a success. In addition, when Samuelson wrote his article, he was looking back at a history of growth rates of 3 percent per year in Social Security covered wages.

New Demographic Realities

There are essentially three ways to maintain the pyramidal shape in the workforce that Samuelson's model requires, and one of them is limited in its ability to do so indefinitely. The first is for birth rates to be in excess of zero population growth, so there is always a larger number of new workers entering the workforce. The second is to have ever-increasing percentages of the people from one birth cohort to the next engaged in the workforce over their prime working ages. The third is to have immigration that brings young people into the society early in their working careers in sufficient numbers to make up for the shortfall that arises if birth rates fall to or below population replacement rates.

Figure 15.1 shows the shape of the population's age distribution for 1965 and as currently projected by the U.S. Census Bureau for 2000 and 2030. The age distributions in the three panels of the figure reflect the combined effects of birth rates and immigration on the composition of the population. In 1965, the age distribution, shown in the top panel of the figure, was pyramidal to a considerable extent. Today, the population still has a pyramidal shape from age sixty up, but definitely not so for age fifty-five and younger. The 2030 projections by the Census Bureau suggest that below age seventy-five, the population will have little of the pyramidal composition that existed three or four decades ago. The population distribution in the United States is gradually being converted into a shape that is much more rectangular. That squaring up of the population distribution portends that the condition of continuous growth in the labor force that Paul Samuelson laid down in his model can no longer be counted on because we do not have successively larger pools of people available to work at younger and younger ages.

It turns out that the second way of growing the workforce in spite of the squaring of the population age distribution was exercised during the second half of the twentieth century. In 1950, 34 percent of the women in the United States between the ages of twenty-five and thirty-four were in the workforce, compared with 96 percent of the men in that age group. The differences in male and female labor-force participation rates in that period are shown by the distances between the top and bottom lines in Figure 15.2. The differences were consistently about 60 percentage points over the prime working ages. In 1997, 76 percent of the women between

Figure 15.1   Population Structure of the United States by Age, in 1965
and as Projected for 2000 and 2030

U.S. Population Structure in 1965

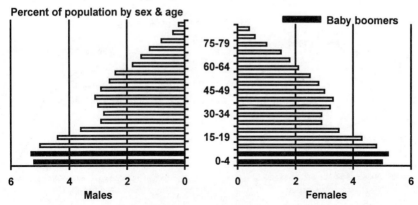

U.S. Population Structure in 2000

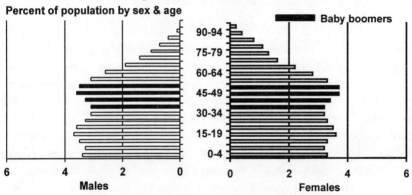

U.S. Population Structure in 2030

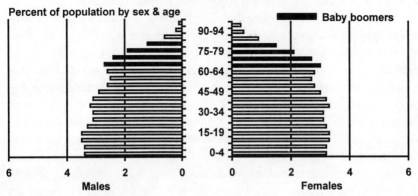

Source: The data underlying this graph can be found on the U.S. Bureau of the Census home page at *http://www.census.gov/ipc/www/idbsprd.html.*

Figure 15.2   Labor-Force Participation Rates by Age and Sex in 1950 and 1997

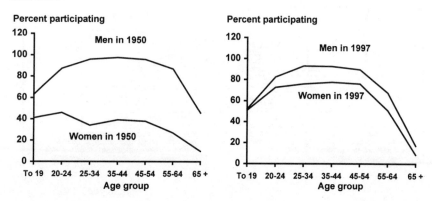

Sources: U.S. Department of Labor, Bureau of Labor Statistics, *Handbook of Labor Statistics* (Washington, D.C.: Department of Labor, August 1989), Bulletin 2340, pp. 13, 14, 19, 20; and *Employment and Earnings* (January 1998), vol. 45, no. 1, p. 164.

the ages of twenty-five and thirty-four were in the labor force. Among their male counterparts, the labor-force participation rate was 93 percent. The differences in the participation rates of men and women that had been 60 percentage points across the prime working ages at midcentury had shrunk to 15 percentage points by the end of the century.

The picture in Figures 15.1 and 15.2 taken together portends a problem regarding workforce growth in the future. As mentioned, the successive birth cohorts coming into the workforce since the baby boom has entered have not had the pyramidal shape that is one of Samuelson's conditions for Social Security to provide decent rates of return for current and future workers. The steadily increasing labor-force participation rates of women, however, have helped to offset the effects of the slowdown in the growth of younger birth cohorts in the top panel of Figure 15.1. Our problem as we look toward 2030 is that the birth patterns after the baby boom are expected to continue at something marginally below population replacement, but we now have little capacity for further expansion in bringing more women into the workforce. Their participation rates today approach those of their male counterparts at various ages. We assume that there will always be some number of people, such as homemakers, who are never formally employed.

The one area where we might be able to manage workforce growth through changes in participation behavior is by keeping older workers from retiring as early as they do now. Men especially are retiring much earlier today than they did at midcentury, as is apparent in Figure 15.2. Purely from the calculus of financing Social Security, encouraging people to work later in life is extremely appealing. But it may be difficult to get people to extend their working lives, given the clear disposition of workers to retire in their late fifties or early sixties and employers' interest in getting them to retire at those ages. We believe that workers who are financially better off will continue to prefer retirement leisure to extended working careers. The labor unions are not likely to surrender easily to pressures to extend their members' working lives.

If birth rates fail us and if labor-force participation from the existing population does not expand, the only remaining alternative to offset the evolving demographic pressure on Social Security is to develop more co-ordinated and aggressive immigration policies than we now have. America has traditionally been considered a melting pot of peoples from all over the world. That perception simply reflects the multiethnic origins of our forebears. Given this tradition, why not invite in even more workers from around the world to help offset the effects of lower birth rates? Part of the answer is that immigration has its own set of associated problems. Immigration into the United States has been relatively high in recent years, but not nearly at the levels experienced at the beginning of the century. Table 15.1 shows the decade by decade immigration rates for the United States from the beginning of the twentieth century through 1990. The immigration rate that is shown in the right-hand column of the table is the number of immigrants into the United States over the decade for every thousand of existing population at the beginning of the decade. Immigration continues to be an extremely important component in our overall population growth and composition.

But the influx is not sufficiently large to solve the concerns about our demographic structure in the twenty-first century. For example, a recent National Research Council study of the effects of immigration on the age structure of our society finds that in 2050, under their high immigration scenario, there will be twenty-seven people over the age of sixty-five for every one hundred between the ages of twenty and sixty-four. In their low immigration scenario, the ratio would be thirty to one hundred. If we translated this full effect into the dependency ratio that we expect to be facing in Social Security by 2030 under current law, the largest conceivable increase in immigration from current levels might reduce the payroll tax needed to sustain the system by as much as 1 percentage point.[1] So the

Table 15.1   U.S. Immigration by Decade,
1900–1990

Period	(000's)	Rate[a]
1900 to 1910	8,795	10.4
1911 to 1920	5,736	5.7
1921 to 1930	4,107	3.5
1931 to 1940	528	0.4
1941 to 1950	1,035	0.7
1951 to 1960	2,515	1.5
1961 to 1970	3,322	1.7
1971 to 1980	4,493	2.1
1981 to 1990	7,338	3.1

Source: U.S. Department of Commerce, *Statistical Abstract of the United States* (Washington, D.C.: U.S. Government Printing Office, 1992), p. 10.
[a]Annual number of immigrants per 1,000 population.

cost of the system might only be 17 percent of covered payroll rather than 18 percent. Such relief comes with a set of associated costs.

Increasing our immigration rate has the potential to help deal with our Social Security financing problem, but it also creates certain challenges. One of these is that immigration is often more appreciated from a distance than it is "up close and personal." Cultural diversity sometimes means social tensions within communities. Multilingual education and communication programs present real costs for government and business. In addition, we may be entering an era where there will be greater competition for the émigrés of the world. We are not the only developed country facing potential shortages of workers in the next century. Countries like Japan, Germany, Italy, and Spain have birth rates that fall far below ours and that portend significant reductions in their workforces unless they turn to immigration to stabilize their populations. Although some of these countries have been less receptive to significant immigration than the United States, economic necessity might drive them to be more open in the next century and to compete with us for the available world labor supply.

Translating Demographics into Reality

Figure 15.3 shows the percentage of the population in the United States that worked in the labor market from 1935 to 1995. The dip in the percentage employed between 1950 and the mid-1960s reflects the impact of the baby boom generation on the population. The baby boomers were born between 1946 and 1964, so they made up a significant portion of the population that was not employed between 1950 and 1965 or so. By this latter date, the baby boomers were beginning to filter into the workforce, and they entered in record numbers, not only because of the size of the group itself, but because the women in the group entered the workforce at unprecedented rates and stayed in it in record numbers. The dip in the labor-force participation rates of women in their mid-twenties in 1950, as shown in Figure 15.2, never occurred for the baby boom cohorts.

Figure 15.4 shows the percentage of the population projected to be working in employment covered by Social Security between 1995 and 2045. It also shows the projected percentage of the population that will be employed on a full-time-equivalent (FTE) basis in covered employment. The FTE measurement is simply a way of accounting for part-time workers in a way that compares their work effort with that of people who work full-time. Under the FTE measure, two people working half-time count as one full-time worker. For all practical purposes, the number of workers as a percentage of the population is expected to hold relatively steady between now

Figure 15.3   Civilian Workers as a Percentage of the U.S. Population for Selected Years

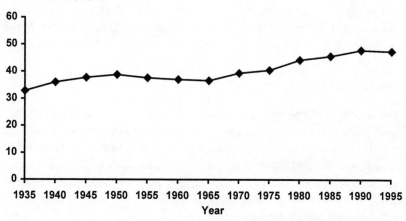

Percent of the population

Sources: U.S. Department of Commerce, Bureau of the Census, *Historical Statistics of the United States, Colonial Times to 1970* (Washington, D.C.: U.S. Government Printing Office, 1975), pp. 10, 126–127; *Statistical Abstract of the United States, 1993* (Washington, D.C.: U.S. Government Printing Office, 1993), pp. 8, 395; and *Statistical Abstract of the United States, 1993* (Washington, D.C.: U.S. Government Printing Office, 1997), pp. 8, 397.

Figure 15.4   Projected Number of Workers and Full-Time-Equivalent
Workers as a Percentage of the Population

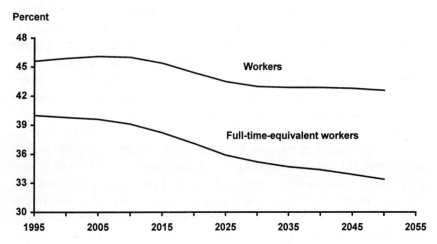

Source: Unpublished data from the Office of the Actuary, Social Security Administration.

and 2010 and then to begin to decline. In other words, as the baby boomers
reach their sixties and become elder boomers, they will drive up the portion
of the population that is retired. As they do so, they will probably shrink
the U.S. labor force for the first time in the country's history. Factoring in
trends in the part-time working patterns of many modern-day workers, the
projections of full-time-equivalency indicate an even greater decline in the
labor force relative to the population than the raw projections suggest.

Disappointing Wage Growth

The second variable that was crucial to the successful implementation
of Paul Samuelson's consumption loan model was the rate of growth in
wages. Table 15.2 shows the compound growth rates in average wage levels
adjusted for inflation in the United States for past decades, from the 1950s
up through the 1980s. The 1990s growth rate includes projections from the
midpart of the decade to the end. Through the mid-1990s, the compound
growth rate for the decade was only about 0.2 percent, so the robust results of the latter part of the 1990s reflect a substantial expected surge in
wage levels. The projections for the 2000s reflect the long-term assumed
rate of growth in average wages that the actuaries use in projecting long-
term costs and revenues for the system. The rate of covered wage growth

that Samuelson had surveyed, from the end of World War II up until he wrote his article in *Newsweek* magazine in 1974, had been 3 percent per year after adjustment for inflation.[2] Part of the reason that he was looking at a higher wage growth rate than that suggested by Table 15.2 is that the table reflects the growth in average wage rates in the whole economy. Samuelson was looking only at the growth in average covered wages. The latter were increasing more rapidly than average wages generally, because of increases in the level of wages subjected to the payroll tax.

Those Really Were the Good Old Days

The prospect of slow growth in the number of workers in correspondence with slow growth in wage rates does not bode well for Samuelson's consumption loan model or our Social Security system. The results show up in the numbers underlying the financing of the system. In Chapter 7 we used Dean Leimer's estimates of the aggregate windfalls paid to the participants in Social Security to show what a good deal the program was for its early participants. We looked only at birth cohorts of the population up to those born in 1910. Understanding why the rates of return in Social Security have been declining requires that we extend that analysis.

In Figure 15.5 we show what Leimer calls net intercohort transfers under Social Security. When he did his analysis, he estimated the transfers in 1989 dollars. Using the trust fund rates of return, we have updated the series to 1998 dollars. Where the value of the net transfer is positive, it means

Table 15.2   Compound Annual Wage
Growth Rates Adjusted for Inflation
(Selected Decades)

Decade	Percent growth per year
1950s	2.58
1960s	1.65
1970s	−0.49
1980s	0.58
1990s	0.85
2000s	0.88

Source: Computed by the authors from the average annual wage indexing series and from projections reported in the *1998 Annual Report of the Board of Trustees of the Federal Old-Age and Survivors Insurance and Disability Insurance Trust Funds*, p. 175.

Figure 15.5   Social Security Transfers to Various
Participant Birth Cohorts

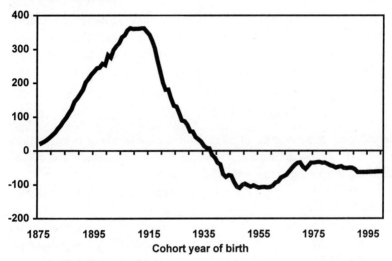

Billions of 1998 dollars

Source: Dean R. Leimer, "Cohort-Specific Measures of Lifetime Net Social Security Transfers," ORS Working Paper Series, No. 59 (Washington, D.C.: Social Security Administration, February 1994), pp. 76–77; and calculations by the authors. Leimer used the interest rate on trust fund assets to convert current dollars into 1989 dollars. We convert the series into 1998 dollars by using corresponding interest rates between 1989 and 1997. All figures are present values as of 1998.

that the birth cohort got back more from Social Security as a group than it would have if it had invested all of its payroll tax contributions in government bonds instead. The cumulative value of the transfers for birth cohorts born up until 1937, the first year Social Security taxes were collected, is $11.4 trillion in 1998 dollars. Where the value of the net transfer is negative, it means that the birth cohort will get back less from Social Security as a group than it would by investing in government bonds instead. Virtually all birth cohorts born after the end of the 1930s can expect to get financial returns that are lower than they would get from investing their Social Security contributions in government bonds. For the birth cohorts born from 1938 through 1998, the cumulative total of the loss is $4.0 trillion. For every man, woman, and child from these cohorts alive today, the $4.0 trillion converts into the average equivalent of between $17,000 and $18,000.

John Geanakoplos, Olivia S. Mitchell, and Stephen Zeldes have developed the analytical linkage between Figure 15.5 and the falling rates of return on Social Security contributions.[3] The pay-go financing allowed tremendous windfalls for early participants that resulted in their astronomical rates of return. For example, the 1915 birth cohort received windfalls by Leimer's estimate that would be worth $340 billion. If workers had made that $340 billion in contributions to their own retirement fund rather than giving it to the 1915 birth cohort as a windfall, the contributions would have generated a positive rate of return. Instead the workers gave their contributions away, in practical terms, and their benefits are based simply on unfunded promises dependent on the willingness of future generations to pay them out of future wages. With the diminishing windfalls as the system matured, rates of return declined. The problem of the decline in windfalls has been exacerbated by the slowdown in wage growth since the end of the 1960s. As we look into the future it will be further exacerbated by the slowdown in the growth of the labor force. Dean Leimer's net cohort transfers are expected to be negative for virtually all the cohorts of retirees reaching retirement age after the turn of the century. Translating this into colloquial English, every birth cohort reaching retirement age from 2000 onward would have gotten better financial returns from investing in government bonds than participating in Social Security's retirement program. Expected rates of return are no longer even the equivalent of what cohorts of workers should be able to get from an extremely conservative investment alternative.

Refining the Insurance Issues Behind
Social Security Retirement Benefits

Part of the concern about the rates of return from Social Security's retirement program relates to the hazards and vicissitudes being "insured" in this case and the way they are covered. We believe that essentially two separate components of the program have been widely discussed and analyzed over the years of its operations. One is a "hazard"; the other is a relative certainty. The confusion between the two has led to significant criticism of the program from a money's worth perspective.

The hazard that Social Security's retirement program covers is the risk that we all face of having an unsuccessful experience in the labor market. The problem a worker has at the outset of a career is that it is impossible to know whether it will be successful or not. The probability of an unsuccessful career experience is not totally random, but it undoubtedly has a certain element of randomness about it. Some people are unsuccessful throughout their whole careers because they lack the human capital that warrants a wage that can support sufficient levels of savings to finance adequate retirement security. Alternatively, many workers are successful for a portion of their career but at some point during it face circumstances that significantly derail their ability to accumulate retirement security on their own. These dislocations can occur because of unexpected illness or other personal problems, because of structural reorganizations of the economy, because of business decisions by the career employer, and because of a host of other forces beyond the control of the worker. To the extent that these problems diminish workers' ability to save adequately on their own to meet their retirement needs and that they are often beyond the control of individual workers, a redistributive social insurance program can help to ameliorate the situation. Since private insurance institutions are not organized to provide insurance of this sort, it makes sense to run the program through an entity much like our Social Security system.

The second element of the program insures workers against myopia in saving to meet their retirement needs during their working careers. The myopia comes in because young workers often do not appreciate the need to save for their retirement and will not do so unless mandated to save. Many people believe that young workers cannot afford to save, but when you think about Social Security as a vehicle for accumulation of wealth, it is clear that from an individual perspective workers are already "saving" a considerable amount. The problem with the saving being done through Social Security is that the payroll tax funds go back out the door as benefits almost as fast as they come in, and the contributions never have a chance to gain any economic horsepower from accumulating interest.

Insuring against workers' myopic views of their own need to save some of their career earnings to support life in retirement is completely different from insuring them against the prospect of a bad labor market outcome. In this case, the requirement that workers make some provision for their own retirement needs can be met in several ways. The government can mandate such insuring through Social Security, as it does now. Alternatively, it could require workers to insure against their myopic tendencies by requiring that they save for retirement through some alternative vehicle.

The provision of insurance to cover these two risks raises widely different implications about the importance of rates of return as they are presented in most money's worth analyses. Rates of return to the "bad labor market experience" element of our social insurance system makes less sense than for money's worth calculations for Social Security suggest, because there is no private market counterpart against which the program's operations can be measured. Even if a worker ends up having a successful career, it doesn't mean that he or she has not derived some value from insurance against the probability of a bad career experience. Just because a homeowner's house doesn't burn down and allow that person to make a claim on the insurance doesn't mean that the homeowner hasn't received value from the insurance.

The difference between home fire insurance and insurance against a bad labor market experience is that the former has a determinable value, based on the probability of a home fire and the value of properties being insured. In the case of insurance against a bad labor market experience, the actuarial determination of value that can be made for homeowner's fire insurance has to be replaced by the social values determined in the court of public opinion and political deliberation. To determine whether the element of the program that corresponds to a bad labor market experience is providing money's worth, policymakers have to weigh the program costs against the relative perceived benefits to society. That is likely to be an inexact process that is driven by political considerations about the relative merits of the needs of retirees and the host of other things that compete for governmental resources. The costs of such a program could be minimized and the target efficiency of benefit delivery maximized in such a program by implementing a means test for benefit qualification. The general reluctance to implement such means tests for these types of programs in Western societies with developed economies suggests that such means testing would be difficult to achieve politically. Given the unwillingness to impose a means test on benefits, an alternative means of minimizing program costs would be to provide a flat floor of benefits to workers at all levels of earnings at an average rate somewhat below current average benefit levels.

Relative rates of return to the mandated retirement savings portion of our Social Security system are extremely important. Once again, the reason relates to the point that Arthur Altmeyer made in his 1945 congressional testimony, cited in Chapter 6, that it is inequitable to compel workers to pay more under this system than they would have to pay under a private alternative. The current system is not an effective capital-accumulation device and because of that is unfair to many if not most current workers and is becoming increasingly so. The problem is that the system is being financed on a pay-go basis. If we wish to make it more efficient in the future than it is now for retirement savings, we have to do more funding than we have been. Alternatively, we could contribute federal revenues from outside the current system that would give the illusion that workers were getting higher returns on their contributions than they can expect under current law. We will investigate the potential for both these options in subsequent chapters. We will first take up the possibility of federal contributions, in the next chapter.

Chapter 16

Social Security
in the Bigger Picture

A s a federal government program, Social Security is just one element, albeit a very large one, of a larger set of federal revenue and expenditure operations. In that context, some policy analysts and policymakers believe it is impossible to talk about Social Security financing without considering it in the larger context. For example, early in his presidency, President Clinton agreed to form the Bipartisan Commission on Entitlement and Tax Reform as a condition for securing Senator J. Robert Kerrey's vote on a deficit-reduction bill. Kerrey is a Democrat from Nebraska who has become concerned about the growing claims made by "entitlement" programs as part of the federal government's total budget.

The Entitlement Commission sounded the alarm about the long-term prospects of government finance in light of the aging of our society and raised the prospect that the entitlement programs run by the government could cause a federal fiscal catastrophe after the turn of the century unless they were brought under control. The commission focused on Social Security, Medicare, and similar programs in the context of overall federal budgeting considerations. From this perspective, federal budgeting has certain similarities with personal budgeting. For example, in our personal budgets if we allocate 20 percent of our available resources for housing and 80 percent for everything else, an increase in housing costs will affect how much we have available for everything else. If housing costs rise enough that we are spending 30 percent of our resources on it, then we have to figure out how to reallocate our other spending so that it only claims 70 percent. Similarly, if Social Security takes up an increasing share of the federal budget in the future, there may be less money available to do the other things that we expect government to do.

Despite the concerns of people like Senator Kerrey, some policy advocates contend that Social Security is different from other government programs because it has its own earmarked payroll tax and has paid its own way over the years. For example, Robert M. Ball, one of the principal architects of our current system, has said, "In connection with short-term budget decisions, there is no good reason at all to consider Social Security. . . . Social Security is a long-term program. People today are paying for benefits that they may not collect for up to a half century."[1] Ball argues that using Social Security as a short-term budgeting device would merely erode confidence in the system, because of the program's long-term nature. But he holds that it is not an effective long-term budgeting device either. On this side he contends: "Another point to be kept in mind is that major permanent cuts in Social Security benefits are not likely to help the deficit over time because such cuts would trigger corresponding cuts in Social Security income. It is unlikely that people could be persuaded to pay higher Social Security contributions than would be necessary to pay for the reduced protection."[2] Bob Ball's position is hardly surprising. He has been involved in every major piece of Social Security legislation expanding the program over the past half-century.

In this case, as in many, differences of opinion can often be explained by scrutinizing the differences in the words used to describe a situation. Senator Bob Kerrey is looking into the future when he raises his concerns about federal entitlement programs. Bob Ball is looking to the past when he says that Social Security has not been part of the problem. From one perspective, Ball's contention is correct: the federal budget has never had a sustained period when Social Security's cash flows have had a negative effect on the federal budget, although there were substantial cash deficits between the passage of the 1972 and 1983 Amendments. From the perspective of accruing liabilities, however, Ball could not be more wrong. It is the liabilities that Kerrey is worried about—and how we are going to pay them. In the case of Social Security and Medicare, those liabilities derive almost totally from legislative actions taken between 1939 and 1972, the period of Ball's tenure at the agency.

The Federal Entitlement Phenomenon

Federal entitlement programs have attracted a great deal of scrutiny in recent years. Entitlements, in the context of federal programs, are benefits for which Congress sets the eligibility conditions in law. Administrators of these benefit programs are given virtually no discretion in interpreting the eligibility conditions. They can only confirm that an applicant for a particular benefit meets the conditions of eligibility. If an applicant is denied eligibility for one of these programs, he or she can seek redress through administrative appeals and the court system, all the way up to and including the Supreme Court.

Entitlement programs are mandated by law and carry on from year to year without congressional votes to continue them. For example, Congress does not have to vote on the Social Security Act this year in order for the program to collect taxes and pay benefits next year. On the other hand, Congress does have to vote on the defense budget and make explicit resource appropriations so that the projects that come under that budget will be financed. The programs that have to be considered each year are categorized as being "discretionary," whereas entitlements are considered to be "mandatory." Just because the latter are mandatory does not mean that Congress cannot change them. For example, the Social Security Act includes a section that reserves to Congress the right to amend the program as it sees fit, a provision that has been upheld by the Supreme Court. Besides entitlement programs, payment of interest on the national debt is considered to be a mandatory obligation.

In fiscal 1997, Social Security and Medicare combined made up just over two-thirds of total entitlement spending. Medicaid benefits, about half of which go to elderly recipients, made up another 11.8 percent of the entitlement budget that year. The Supplemental Security Income program (SSI)—the federal welfare program for needy aged, blind, and disabled people—claimed 3.3 percent of entitlement spending. Federal employee retirement programs claimed another 8.8 percent. In combination, these five programs comprised 91.8 percent of total mandated expenditures for federal programs other than interest payments on the debt. By comparison, the combination of programs that we often think of as welfare—for example, food stamps and child nutrition programs, housing assistance for the needy, and welfare payments to needy families—made up only 6.1 percent of total entitlement spending.[3]

The concern that Senator Bob Kerrey and the Entitlement Commission have highlighted is that mandatory expenditures are taking an ever-increasing share of our federal budget. Figure 16.1 shows the phenomenon over the thirty-five years between 1962 and 1997. In the early 1960s, mandatory spending programs, including interest payments on the federal debt, claimed about one-third of the total federal budget, and Congress had discretionary control over the remaining two-thirds. By the end of the 1990s,

Figure 16.1   The Changing Composition of the Federal Budget, 1962–1997

Percent of expenditures going to various classes of programs

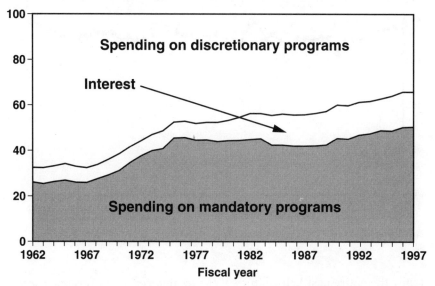

Source: *Historical Tables, Budget of the United States Government, Fiscal Year 1999*, pp. 21–22, 121–130.

mandatory spending accounted for almost two-thirds of total government outlays.

Entitlement Claims Outstripping Increasing Economic Capacity

Another aspect of the analysis developed by the Entitlement Commission related to resources available for policymakers to finance the federal government's operations. Figure 16.2 shows the total tax revenues and fees collected by the federal government, stated as a percentage of gross domestic product (GDP) in each fiscal year from 1952 through 1997. Over the whole period, the amount collected averaged 18.1 percent of GDP. In only eight of the forty-six years did the amount collected vary by more than 1 percentage point from the average, and only twice did the percentage-point variance occur in two consecutive years. While there is no natural limit to government's claim on the economy, clearly political forces have strictly limited the amount that U.S. taxpayers have rendered to it over vir-

Figure 16.2   Total Federal Receipts as a Percentage of Gross
Domestic Product

Percent of GDP

Source: Historical Tables, Budget of the United States Government, Fiscal Year 1999, pp. 20–21.

tually the entire past half-century. If the total government revenue claims
on the economy are limited and Social Security is scheduled to make a bigger claim than currently, then some other government expenditures must
shrink. And as other programs are crowded out, the projected expansions
in Social Security's economic claims will seem less feasible.

The relatively restricted range of resources available to federal policymakers in combination with the historical growth of mandatory programs
led the Entitlement Commission to focus on the future operations of government. The members' conclusions are summarized in Figure 16.3. In regard to the story pictured there, the commission concluded:

In 2012, unless appropriate policy changes are made in the interim,
projected outlays for entitlements and interest on the national debt
will consume all tax revenues collected by the Federal Government.

In 2030, unless appropriate policy changes are made in the interim,
projected spending for Medicare, Medicaid, Social Security, and Federal employee retirement programs alone will consume all tax revenues collected by the Federal Government. If all other Federal programs (except interest on the national debt) grow no faster than the
economy, total Federal outlays would exceed 37% of the economy.[4]

In a more recent analysis, the Congressional Budget Office (CBO) looks at the same set of issues that the Entitlement Commission considered. The CBO concludes that current fiscal environment will continue to "improve over the next decade and then progressively deteriorate because of demographics, health costs and increasing interest payments. . . . The primary forces acting on the budget in the long run come from Social Security, Medicare, Medicaid, and, ultimately, interest payments."[5]

Although the projected federal revenue constraints are somewhat different in the Entitlement Commission's and the CBO's projections, the results of their separate analyses are essentially the same. By 2030, federal entitlement programs are projected to make a claim on the economy that is the equivalent to or larger than the level of revenue claims the government has made on taxpayers over each of the last forty-five years. We are beyond the era when reductions in federal defense programs, our space program, or any other federal initiatives can finance the projected growth of entitlement programs. Indeed, the bottom line is that unless taxpayers are willing to cede more of their resources to the federal government than they have been in the past, entitlement expenditures must be severely reined in if we

Figure 16.3   Projected Federal Outlays as a Percentage of Gross Domestic Product

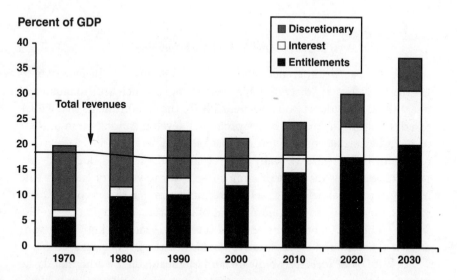

Source: Bipartisan Commission on Entitlement and Tax Reform, *Interim Report to the President* (Washington, D.C.: Bipartisan Commission, August 1994), p. 7.

Figure 16.4   National Defense Expenditures as a Percentage of Gross
Domestic Product

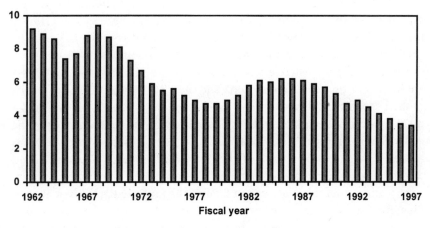

Source: Historical Tables, Budget of the United States Government, Fiscal Year 1999, pp. 21, 44–49.

are to have any hope of eliminating the projected federal deficits over the
long term.

A Political Perspective on Entitlement Spending

In looking at the differences between the programs that the federal budget distinguishes as "discretionary" versus those which are "mandatory,"
one thing to consider is who is responsible for the commitments that we are
taxed to fulfill. The discretionary programs develop a momentum of their
own, to be certain, but Congress must take deliberate action to increase
or diminish their size virtually every year. And Congress does add and
subtract resources for these programs from year to year. For example, the
history of national defense expenditures in Figure 16.4 shows considerable
variation over time in the commitment of resources. If you do not like the
size or composition of defense expenditures this year, you know that your
elected senators and representative voted on the current package. When
we look at Social Security, Medicare, and Medicaid, on the other hand, the
essence of the current programs was voted into law many years ago. Medicare and Medicaid have changed somewhat over the years, but the benefits
being delivered this year are the direct result of legislation voted into law

over thirty years ago. Expenditures under this program today are directly influenced by accommodations made between Lyndon Johnson as president, Wilbur Mills as chairman of the House Ways and Means Committee, Russell Long as chairman of the Senate Finance Committee, and Bob Ball as commissioner of Social Security. The benefit side of Social Security was largely put on automatic pilot in 1972, when Richard Nixon was president and many of the other players who orchestrated the passage of Medicare were still around. Our current political leaders do not have direct control of the largest part of government operations.

The problem that policymakers face with entitlement programs is that they are significantly outstripping the growth in our economic capacity and in the capacity of the government to tax its citizens. The narrow range of variation in revenues collected by the federal government as reflected in Figure 16.2 does not mean that the government could not possibly tax its citizens at higher rates than it has for nearly a half century now. Certainly other governments around the world impose a higher tax burden on their citizens than ours does on us. It does reflect, however, that there are considerable political forces at work that have restricted taxes in the United States, and after nearly a half-century, it is unlikely that attitudes about how much we should give the federal government are going to change very quickly or significantly.

Having Fewer Children Helps, but Not Enough

Bob Ball suggests that Social Security's financing problem is overblown because of the dynamics of the dependency ratio. Ball contends that the Social Security dependency ratio is not an appropriate measure for us to focus on when we consider the burden of the program. He says that we should be looking at the total dependency ratio in society. The total dependency ratio takes into account not only an elderly population that does not work but younger dependents who do not work either. Ball says that "the combined ratio of *all* dependents to workers is not expected to be as high again at any time in the entire 75 years of Social Security forecasting as it was, for example, in the decade from 1960 to 1970."[6] His analysis is misleading on two fronts.

The first mistake that Ball makes is in his computation of the dependency ratio. He calculates the dependency ratio using the number of people between the ages of twenty and sixty-four as the denominator and the residual of the total population as the numerator. The total dependency ratio in a society is the number of people in the population who do not work

Figure 16.5   Total Dependency Ratio in the United States, 1947–1997

Ratio of nonworkers to workers in the United States

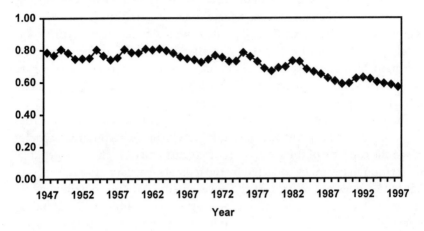

Year

Source: Eva E. Jacobs, ed., *Handbook of U.S.Labor Statistics,* 2d ed. (Lanham, Md.: Bernan Press, 1998), p. 10.

divided by the number who do. In his calculation, he has included in the numerator people under age twenty who work, when they should be in the denominator. He also includes in the denominator people between the ages of twenty and sixty-four who do not work, who should be in the numerator. We have correctly computed the total dependency ratio and report the results in Figure 16.5. In fact the ratio has fallen from the decade of the '60s until the present time. But the decline in the total dependency ratio shown in the figure is not as important in considering the future of Social Security financing as the reason that it has fallen. The decline may be as much the result of the growing Social Security burden imposed on workers over the last three decades as of demographic or other changes in society.

We saw in the last chapter that wage growth stabilized after the 1960s. And not only were wages stabilizing, the ever-growing Social Security payroll tax burden meant that many workers were seeing their inflation-adjusted levels of take-home pay decline. We also saw in the last chapter that women have come into the workforce in unprecedented numbers and stayed at those levels since the 1950s. One possible explanation for women's increased presence in the workforce is that the stabilization of wages meant that the only way families could improve their standard of living over time was to have more earners than earlier generations. As women shifted from being homemakers to being breadwinners, they moved from the numerator of the total dependency ratio to the denominator. But the higher labor-force participation of women since the 1960s has been the major reason that the total dependency ratio has fallen. If the total portion of the population that works declines in the future, as the Social Security actuaries expect and as we showed in the last chapter, the total dependency ratio will start rising again after the turn of the century.

The second mistake in Ball's analysis is more egregious than the first. His assertion that we should be focused on the total dependency ratio rather than on the Social Security dependency ratio suggests that a child dependent and a Social Security beneficiary are equally expensive to support. This is not the case. The CBO has specifically looked into the matter. The staff observes:

> The federal government spent seven times as much on the elderly as it did on young people, in per capita terms. The possible relative decline in the population of children would not make up for the costs associated with the projected surge in the elderly population. In contrast, state and local governments might well benefit from a relative decline in the number of children. But any reduction in the budgetary pressure on state and local governments is likely to be small compared with the increased pressure the federal government will face.
>
> The potential savings for state and local governments from a relatively smaller number of children are not automatic. . . . In addition, expenditures for state and local governments would also increase with the size of the elderly population. State and local spending on medical care and related services for the elderly (largely funded by Medicaid) could skyrocket with growth in demand for long-term care services. Such increased costs could offset any possible reduction a decreasing proportion of children might bring.[7]

The CBO's analysis estimates that federal spending averaged $14,000 per elderly person in 1995, compared with $2,000 per child. Anyone who suggests that substituting a child dependent for an elderly dependent would help offset fiscal demands is either badly mistaken or simply disingenuous.

Entitlement Claims Are Crowding Out Political Prerogatives

The federal policymaking process in Washington, D.C., seems to have gotten more vitriolic and confrontational in recent years than during earlier decades. At the end of 1996, federal budget battles between Democrats and Republicans led to a shutdown of significant parts of government. The environment of those budget talks was very different from the atmosphere during the 1960s as policymakers toiled over Lyndon Johnson's War on Poverty and Medicare initiatives. Those were extremely controversial matters at the time and were hotly debated in the halls of government; but they were debated in the spirit of accommodation and the attempt to find political common ground for moving forward. The environment of the 1996 budget fight was also very different from the periods of crisis that seemed to descend on us during the 1970s, with our oil shortages, runaway inflation, international political embarrassment over American hostages being taken on foreign soil, and concerns about a national malaise. Again, there was always vigorous debate about appropriate policies to deal with these problems, but in the end the political parties came to an accord and resolved the issues together. The political fights over budget priorities at the end of the 1990s seem far less susceptible to compromise than they did during the 1980s, when President Ronald Reagan convinced policymakers from both parties that we should have low taxes and higher defense expenditures. Reagan was willing to sacrifice entitlement programs to make the budget arithmetic balance, in accordance with traditional conservative principles of fiscal responsibility. When members of both political parties in the Congress refused to go along, accommodations were found, albeit ones that led to unprecedented budget deficits. One possible explanation for the heightened conflict over public policy matters in recent years is that political prerogatives concerning public policy have become increasingly limited as entitlements have grown. At the same time, the battle to control the direction of government has become both less and more important.

It has become less important because our political leaders have a smaller and smaller share of the effect of government under their control. We saw earlier that in the 1960s, two-thirds of government expenditures were "discretionary" but that by the end of the 1990s only one-third still fell into this category. Our political leaders could refuse to accommodate each other in the 1996 budget debate, because even in shutting down the government by failing to reach political agreement, they knew that two-thirds of government would continue to function automatically. Other things deemed vital to the safety of the country, like national defense, had to be worked out in any event. So policymakers could make major political statements in "shutting down government" but meanwhile close only a relatively trivial portion of its total operations. If more had been at stake, there would have been more reason and greater reward for finding common ground.

The battle over control of the direction of government has become more important because of the shrinking pool of resources available to policy operatives to implement their agendas. The vast majority of people who run for national office are full of ideas on how to make the country a better place for its citizenry. But putting those ideas into effect takes federal resources, and it doesn't make any difference whether the idea is to cut taxes or to expand an expenditure program of one stripe or another. When the pool of money to fund the ideas that will make the country a better place is shrinking, the fights over the diminishing funds will naturally become fiercer. As they do so, the room for accommodation shrinks further. Arguments with no room for compromise cause polarization. And polarization can lead to people naturally bent on finding common ground to withdraw from the process. The retirements in 1996 of Senators Alan Simpson, a Republican from Wyoming, and Bill Bradley, a Democrat from New Jersey, were both partly in frustration over the loss of civility and of willingness to compromise in the policy debates in which they increasingly found themselves participating.

The inherent forces at play in our society seem inevitably to set us on a collision course between entitlement commitments and taxpayers' willingness to surrender resources to the federal government. Virtually all serious students of the issues conclude that the nation's demographic structure and the resulting commitments in current law to federal entitlements will continue to outstrip the economy. Most students of government fiscal operations acknowledge that expanding government's claim on the nation's resources is going to be aggressively challenged in a society that is not nearly as disposed to pay taxes as are many others. After any serious look at our political options, we would have to concede that policymakers are going to find themselves increasingly squeezed between exploding entitlement expenditures and limited federal resources. This closing vise will leave fewer and fewer options, and we will be less inclined to look toward entitlement programs as part of the long-term solution to our fiscal conundrum. The two of us believe that Social Security has to be one of the programs subjected to scrutiny, not only because of its own actuarial imbalance, but because of the larger set of policy considerations that are on the table.

Balancing Social Security Within the Context of Total Government Operations

In 1998, total expenditures under the OASDI programs will be an estimated 4.57 percent of our gross domestic product. By 2030, the OASDI claim on the economy is expected to rise to 6.79 percent of GDP.[8] In other words, over the next thirty years, Social Security's claim on the economy is expected to grow by about 2.25 percentage points. Some analysts suggest that such a shift in the national resources allotted to this vital retirement program can be achieved without significant difficulty. One of the problems to be faced in rebalancing Social Security is that it is only one of several government programs that will be affected by the aging of our society. The combination of these programs, including Social Security, Medicare, Medicaid, and other federal retirement programs, will place a tremendous strain on the government's fiscal operations.

Figure 16.6 shows the projected increases in the claims on the economy by various federal entitlement programs between 1996 and 2030. The projected growth in Medicare claims is expected to far outstrip that of OASDI. While OASDI is expected to increase its claim against GDP by roughly 45 percent between 1998 and 2030, Medicare is expected to more than double its claim. Some analysts conclude from this picture that we should focus our energies for managing entitlement growth on federal medical programs in general and Medicare in particular. They claim that if we can restrain the rapid growth in the health care programs, we can sustain projected growth in the cash retirement programs.[9]

While it may be necessary to contain federal health programs for the

Figure 16.6   Current and Projected Levels of Entitlement Program Operations as a Percentage of GDP

Percent of GDP

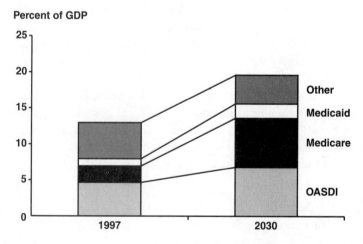

Sources: *1998 Annual Report of the Board of Trustees of the Federal Old-Age and Survivors Insurance and Disability Insurance Trust Funds*, p. 187; and Congressional Budget Office, *Long-Term Budgetary Pressures and Policy Options* (Washington, D.C.: U.S. Government Printing Office, May 1998), Executive Summary, table 2.

Figure 16.7   Average Per Capita Health Expenditures by Age
and Portion of the Population over Sixty-Five

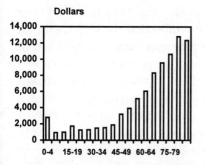

1995 Per Capita Expenditures

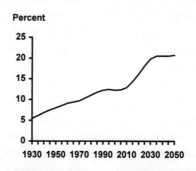

Percentage of Population over Age Sixty-Five

Sources: Roland D. McDevitt and Sylvester J. Schieber, *From Baby Boom to Elder Boom Providing Health Care for an Aging Population* (Washington, D.C.: Watson Wyatt Worldwide, 1996); U.S. Bureau of the Census, *Historical Statistics of the United States, Colonial Times to 1970, Bicentennial Edition*, pt. 1 (Washington, D.C.: 1975), pp. 8–10; and *1995 Annual Report of the Board of Trustees of the Federal Old-Age and Survivors Insurance and Disability Insurance Trust Funds*, p. 145.

elderly, it will be more difficult to accomplish than restricting the cash programs for retirees, for four reasons. First, old people simply use more health care services than younger ones as shown in the left-hand panel of Figure 16.7. People in their eighties use one and one-half to two times as much health care services as people in their mid-sixties. The most rapidly growing segment of the population today is the old-old, people over the age of eighty-five. Second, we will see an explosion in the absolute numbers of older people after the turn of the century. The percentage of our popula-tion over age sixty-five is expected to grow by as much between 2010 and 2030 as it did in the eighty years preceding, as shown in the right-hand panel of Figure 16.7. Together, these phenomena suggest a tremendous in-crease in the demand for health care in the future, with much of it being funded through publicly financed insurance programs for the elderly.

Third, Medicare expenditures will be difficult to reduce because of the excessive price inflation that persists in the health sector of our economy. Medical price increases in the consumer price index in comparison to over-all growth in the CPI have moderated recently. But the ratio of the com-pound growth in the medical CPI to the total CPI has been larger from the beginning of the 1990s through the end of 1997 than it was over each of the previous three decades. The record from the last forty years does not support the conclusion that the recent slowdown in medical price inflation will persist.[10]

Fourth, the continued technological development in the health sector and increasingly intensive treatment of patients will both drive up future health costs. Not only are these technologies expensive in and of themselves; they generally do not cure the maladies that they treat, and they often create new maladies that require additional treatments. As technological medicine extends recipients' lives, they go on to need even more health care services than they would if their lives had not been extended. The numbers of baby boomers who will live to advanced ages are likely to have a tremendous impact on health care consumption rates by 2030.[11]

These four factors compounded drive up the cost of Medicare claims even in the face of program reforms. Current projections suggest that under present law, Medicare's claim on the economy will grow from around 2.3 percent of GDP today to 6.8 percent by 2030.[12] The underlying assumptions in that projection, however, are that we will see some slowing in health price inflation just as the baby boomers' demand for services under the program undergoes a tremendous increase. The actuaries estimating the cost of Medicare, and its trustees, appear to anticipate some kind of systematic reform around 2010, although we are left clueless about what such a change might be. The CBO says of this assumption that it "is optimistic, though, since policies designed to achieve [the] result are not yet in place."[13]

This assumption about the growth in health costs under Medicare is one that should not be taken lightly. To paraphrase Yogi Berra, it may be *déjà vu* all over again. In the very first Trustees' Report published on the program back in 1966, the trustees acknowledged: "Hospitalization costs have increased in the past significantly more rapidly than general earnings levels, and it is likely that this trend will continue for some years. Even in the long run, it is likely that hospitalization costs will continue to rise since the general earnings level has a similar trend—although the current differential between the rates of increase of these two factors will very probably be eliminated or may even be reversed."[14] Later in the report in discussing the cost estimates for the program the trustees said: "The cost estimates assume that hospitalization costs will increase more rapidly than total earnings rates by a net differential of 2.7 percent per year (the actual difference in the period 1954–63) for the first 5 years after 1965. This differential is then assumed to decrease to zero over the next 5 years. Thereafter, hospitalization costs and wages are assumed to increase at the same rate."[15]

The importance of this assumption ties in with our earlier discussions about pay-as-you-go financing of programs like Social Security. In that dis-

Figure 16.8   Ratio of Covered Workers' Average Taxable Earnings to
Average Benefits Paid Under the Medicare HI Program, 1966–1996

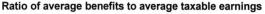

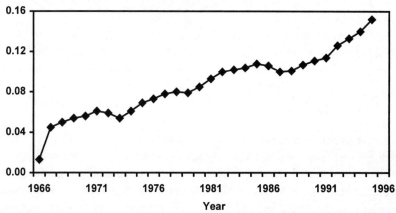

Sources: The total HI benefit payments are taken from the *Social Security Bulletin, Annual Statistical Supplement,* table A1, in the "Health Care" sections of the report. The number of enrollees
is taken from the same report, tables B1 and B2. The average covered earnings were taken from
table 4.B1, p. 167, of the 1997 report.

cussion, we said that the cost of these kinds of programs is driven by two
ratios, the dependency ratio and the ratio of average benefits to the average
covered wages on which the taxes are levied. In the case of the Hospital Insurance program under Medicare, which is also pay-go financed using the
payroll tax, the ratio of average hospitalization costs to average covered
wages is the second of these two important ratios.

The dependency ratio for Medicare tracks the Social Security dependency ratio fairly closely. As we saw earlier, the dependency ratio in Social
Security has been relatively flat since the mid-1970s. The Medicare dependency ratio has been similarly flat. The ratio of average benefits to average
wages for the HI program is shown in Figure 16.8. The pattern over most
of the first thirty years of Medicare's operations was one of average benefits rising more rapidly than average taxable wages. The ratio declined only
four times from one year to the next over Medicare's first thirty years. In
each of those cases, increases in the tax base were being phased in, and
it was the resulting increases in covered wages that drove down the ratio
rather than general increases in workers' wages in excess of the increase
in Medicare benefits. The assumptions underlying Medicare projections
today are not only optimistic; they are totally contrary to the whole his-

tory of the program. The change in this historical trend is being assumed to occur just at the point where a tremendous surge will take place in demand for benefits under the program. Typically, in such circumstances, you would see just the opposite effect from that which is being assumed in Medicare's cost estimates.

The CBO suggests that there are three ways that Medicare costs can be brought under control. The first would be to raise the eligibility age. The second would be to raise the premiums charged to the participants in the program. The third would be to restructure the system.[16] Each one of these suggestions has certain appeal, but each also will garner considerable political opposition.

A major problem that policymakers will have in dealing with the Medicare dilemma is that raising eligibility age does not provide the same leveraging opportunity as it does with Social Security. Specifically, if normal life expectancy at age sixty-five is another eighteen years, increasing the normal retirement age by one year will reduce Social Security claims by roughly one-eighteenth. For Medicare, however, raising the age of eligibility would largely exclude the part of the eligible population that uses the least medical care, because even among the elderly, the older ones use more health care. Even though some people would be excluded on the basis of an increase in eligibility age, the unhealthiest people would still qualify for Medicare benefits because their health status would qualify them as disabled beneficiaries. For those in the lowest income categories, limiting Medicare eligibility would merely transfer them more completely to Medicaid coverage.

Figure 16.9 shows the aggregate effects on caseloads and potential cost reductions from raising the eligibility age under Medicare. The figure does not include the extra potential costs to the government that would result from transferring people from Medicare coverage to other federal health insurance programs. Basically, in the set of bars on the far right in the graph, the story is that if we raised the eligibility age for Medicare today from age sixty-five to age seventy, we would cut out about 28 percent of the currently eligible population. But when you take into account the higher health care use by the remaining older population and those who would qualify for disability benefits, the cost of the system would be reduced by only about 11.5 percent. Getting policy leverage on Medicare is going to be extremely difficult. Our estimate of the effect of raising Medicare's eligibility age to age seventy on program costs is very close to the CBO's estimate of the same provision.

If given an alternative, many people might be willing to pay higher pre-

Figure 16.9   Medicare's Caseload and Cost Reductions for the Aged, with Alternative Eligibility Ages

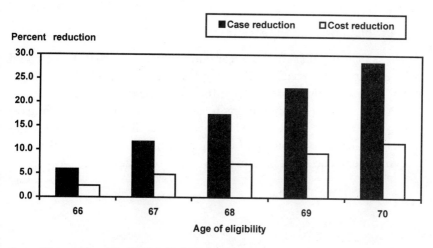

Source: Watson Wyatt Worldwide's Health Policy Simulation Model as described in Roland D. McDevitt and Sylvester J. Schieber, *From Baby Boom to Elder Boom: Providing Health Care for an Aging Population* (Washington, D.C.: Watson Wyatt Worldwide, 1996).

miums for their Medicare coverage. But the history of the program has not tended in that direction. Originally the intent of the program was that the HI benefits would be fully covered through payroll tax financing on a pay-go basis. The second part of the program, however, the Supplementary Medical Insurance (SMI) program, was to be jointly financed, with half the money coming from retirees' premiums and the other half from general government revenues. Over the years, the share that the participants contribute has been considerably below the original target of fifty-fifty sharing. This experience and the potent opposition of the elderly to charges for catastrophic health insurance coverage several years ago suggest that raising premiums will be difficult.

Indeed, we may see substantial restructuring of the health delivery system along the broad guidelines the CBO has suggested. But it seems that the only way the costs of this system can be curtailed will be through reduction in the provision of some services now being offered. It makes little difference whether this is carried out under the auspices of what we call managed care or through the unpopular method of "rationing." Among the elderly, the heaviest users of medical care in society, any curtailments in Medicare will almost certainly be met with strong opposition. Medicare is going to be a much tougher problem to solve than Social Security, no matter how you look at it.

A Problem of Dual Constraints

The conclusion that we draw from this discussion is that the potential rededication of 2 percent of GDP to rebalance OASDI might be tenable if that were the only imbalance that the government were facing. But it is not. As we look for policy options to deal with Social Security, we have to consider rebalancing it in the larger context of the total federal government claim on the economy and within the context of other entitlements that must be financed out of total government revenues.

Part III
The New Realities

Chapter 17

Heathens in the Temple

O ver the years of Social Security's evolution, one of the most effective vehicles for moving the system supporters' agenda forward had been the advisory councils. Martha Derthick identified a number of criteria that were important in making the advisory councils so indispensable. The first was that the membership be limited to persons who were generally supportive of the program. The second was that the staff that did the background work for the councils be drawn directly or indirectly from the Social Security Administration. The third was that the charter of a council be limited to matters that Social Security managers judged to be timely. Derthick observed that if these criteria were met, there was not much chance that such a group of "outsiders would get out of control and produce unwanted recommendations."[1] She went on to say that "it was unlikely that a part-time group of citizens, however distinguished or independent, would question what was firmly established and widely accepted. Social Security executives, watching one after another of these groups assemble, were never entirely sure that they would not do something quixotic. 'I must say I never worked with any council without feeling that it might go off the deep end with inconsistent and peculiar recommendations,' Bob Ball recalled. But they never did."[2] Derthick was right, at least until 1994. And then things went badly awry.

The 1994–1996 Advisory Council on Social Security would end up hopelessly divided in its recommendations, much more so than any earlier council. The majority of its thirteen members would ultimately suggest that Social Security be significantly restructured to include some element of individual accounts. An important motivation for doing so was the general feeling among council members that the Social Security system should be funded to a much greater extent than it had been traditionally. Fundamental questions were raised within this advisory council over whether such funding could be accomplished within the context of a large defined-benefit system run by our federal government. Funding was once again at the heart of controversy over the evolution of Social Security in the United States.

Setting Up the 1994–1996 Advisory Council

The 1994–1996 Advisory Council on Social Security was charged with reviewing Social Security's financing, including its long-term financial status. It was also to look at issues of *adequacy* and *equity* provided by the program to people at different income levels, in various family situations, and among various age groups. It was to consider the increased labor-force participation of women, the changing marital behavior in the population, and the economic status of elderly women. The charter for this council was somewhat broader than most of the previous ones in that the council was given the option of analyzing the relative roles of the public and private sector in providing retirement income security.[3]

The membership of the 1994–1996 Advisory Council on Social Security was not remarkably different from that of earlier councils. Its thirteen members were drawn from the public. The chairman was Edward Gramlich, the dean of the School of Public Policy at the University of Michigan. He had served in various government positions in the past, including the number-two post at the Congressional Budget Office. In keeping with tradition dating back to the original council, three members were drawn from organized labor and three represented the employer community. The other members drawn from the general public included a number of people knowledgeable about Social Security policy or aging and general retirement issues. Among these six was Robert M. Ball, the former commissioner of Social Security.

By the time the council's deliberations had ended, six of the members were old enough to be receiving Social Security, and several of them were. There were five women and eight men. Although the majority of the members of the council were Democrats, there were also Republicans and Independents on it. Fidel Vargas, representing the X Generation, was only twenty-five years old when deliberations got under way. He was the mayor of Baldwin Park, California, and a policy analyst for the mayor of Los Angeles. Most of the council members clearly took their responsibilities very seriously. Among them, the deliberations were not always cordial.

The executive director of the council was David Lindeman. He was nearing the end of a civil service career that included stints at the Office of

Economic Opportunity, the Department of Health, Education, and Welfare (later the Department of Health and Human Services), and the Pension Benefit Guaranty Corporation. Lindeman is a knowledgeable analyst with a deep background in Social Security in the United States and elsewhere throughout the world. More suited to be a teacher or philosopher than a staff director and manager of a diverse study group, Lindeman ultimately lost control of the agenda and the analytical work surrounding proposals being considered by the council. He left the council staff a full year before the final report was completed. Social Security failed to move to reassert control by providing able staff to manage the analytical work done by the council.

The Office of the Actuary at Social Security did massive amounts of work for the advisory council during its deliberations. Most of this work was done under the direction of Stephen Goss, one of the senior actuaries in that office. If there was ever a person that one would want to hold out as an example of what a civil servant should be, Steve Goss would be that person. He worked tirelessly on a great multiplicity of proposals, options, and challenges that the council put to him.

Beyond the Office of the Actuary and its staff, the Social Security Administration's substantive support of the advisory council was minimal. Most of the analytical work, other than by the actuaries, was done through outside contractors or by the advisory council members themselves. The SSA had actually ceded without a fight the second of Derthick's criteria for a successful council, that the SSA staff would do the background work. Indeed, it looked as though the SSA staff, other than in the Office of the Actuary, didn't want to be bothered by the council's deliberations.

The Early Council Deliberations

The 1994–1996 advisory council got off to a regular start. The first meeting was held toward the end of June 1994, with the clear understanding that the council's final report was to be completed by the end of 1995. This council, like the ones that preceded it, comprised people with different levels of knowledge and understanding about Social Security, how it worked, its role in the retirement income security system, and so forth. The initial meetings of the council consisted of a series of presentations intended to give the members a substantive background that could then serve as the basis for considering the financing issues facing the program. There were presentations by research analysts from both inside and outside government. The council set up two technical panels to provide input on various issues. One was to focus on trends and issues in retirement savings. The other was to focus on the assumptions and methodology used in estimating Social Security's future operations.

The panel on Trends and Issues in Retirement Savings (TIRS) noted the financial imbalances in the system indicating the need for benefit reductions or tax increases to bring it back into balance. The panel also developed a set of criteria that the council could use in evaluating proposals to deal with Social Security's financing problems. But the panel members pointed out that their criteria did not provide a clear indication of whether cutting benefits or raising taxes was the preferred approach to modifying the system. On the benefits side, the panel supported raising the early eligibility age for Social Security benefits now set at sixty-two and further increasing normal retirement age, already scheduled to increase starting in 2000. On the revenue side, the TIRS Panel favored increases in the payroll tax over increases in the wage base subjected to the tax.[4]

In addition to its more conventional set of recommendations, the TIRS Panel also raised the prospect of converting a portion of the existing Social Security program to a funded defined-contribution system:

> Many Panel members find promising the proposal to convert part of the Social Security Trust Fund to individual accounts, if the remainder of the Social Security system can still be made solvent. The Panel recognizes the need to coordinate the pattern of any benefit cuts with the pattern of benefits that would be received from these individual accounts.
>
> Most Panel members would prohibit access to the funds for any reason other than retirement, and would mandate that the benefits be wholly or in part distributed in the form of an annuity, rather than permitting a 100 percent lump sum cashout. The Panel was divided on whether the annuity could be best managed by the government or the private sector.[5]

Getting to the Heart of Matters

In late January 1995, Barry Bosworth, an economist at the Brookings Institution in Washington, D.C., presented a paper on Social Security funding at a conference sponsored by the National Academy of Social Insurance (NASI). Bosworth projected that an increase in the payroll tax of 2 percentage points in 1995 and a change in the investment of assets would rebalance the system. He proposed that some of the assets in the system be invested in equities rather than in the federal government bonds that had been the form of investment used by the program from its outset. He estimated that the trust funds could achieve a rate of return that would be 1 percentage point higher than under existing policies. He estimated that pursuing such a policy would have a significant net positive effect on national saving that would drive up the capital stock and ultimately have a secondary positive effect on wages. All of these would be beneficial to the economy and Social Security over the long term.[6]

The council would spend a great deal of time on two points in Bosworth's paper for the remainder of its deliberations. The first was that we needed to increase national saving in conjunction with solving the Social Security financing problem. The second was that the investment of Social Security funds in the stock market would yield higher returns than the historical policy of investing in government bonds would yield.

The advisory council met about two weeks after the NASI conference and Tom Jones, the president of Teachers Insurance Annuity Association and College Retirement Equity Fund (TIAA-CREF) and a member of the council, made a formal presentation on the investment of Social Security assets in the stock market. Jones laid out four alternative investment strategies, each calling for investment of some of the trust funds in the private equity markets. Jones's presentation held out the prospect that changing the investment policy alone would potentially have a tremendous positive effect on Social Security financing. Under his most optimistic scenario, the system would raise an additional $4.4 trillion.[7] At the time, the seventy-five-year projection was that only an added $3 trillion was needed to rebalance the system.

Immediately following Jones's presentation, Barry Bosworth addressed the council and laid out the proposal that he had developed in his NASI presentation. Bosworth's speech, although seemingly supportive of the approach that Jones proposed, put a damper on the recommendation. Jones had simply advocated investing existing funds into the stock market to garner larger returns. He had not, however, focused on the additional recommendation about savings that Bosworth had made. Bosworth was concerned that simply restructuring the investment of the existing trust fund balances would not have any positive effect on the operations of the total economy. Finding policies to grow the economy were crucial, from his perspective. He spoke of "the tendency to look at this as though there's a pie out there and it's fixed and it's going to be divided between workers and retirees." The pie in this case was the gross economic output for the whole economy. His point was that if we couldn't find ways to actually increase the available production of the economy as part of Social Security reform, the issue for the advisory council to resolve was simply "whose tax you're going to increase or whose benefit you're going to reduce."[8] Bosworth denied that that scenario was the only one to be considered.

He maintained that the pie does not have to be fixed, but to make it bigger you have to figure out how to increase saving. He said we could "finance the increased costs of Social Security, which I think are enormous in terms of rates of increase, by saving more, by saving and investing more and earning an increase in national income."[9] In the increase in national income Bosworth saw a ready solution to the Social Security financing problem. If the pie were bigger, if national output were larger, the size of retirees' claims would be easier to deal with in the future. Higher investment returns were part of his solution, but the key was additional savings. He concluded that his proposal would work only "if you do one thing, and that's you truly save the money, if it really flows through capital markets into increased investment. Otherwise, you're playing games."[10]

Bosworth's presentation was followed by one by Joyce Manchester, an economist at the Congressional Budget Office. She reported on an analysis that the CBO had done on Social Security's investment policy, which had concluded "that it doesn't really do any good to change investment policies. The reason is that we were looking only at an unfunded system, in other words, a pay-as-you-go system. We stated very strongly that if you care about the well-being and financial welfare of future retirees, the most important thing you can do is worry about national saving."[11]

Some of the council members argued that Social Security was already contributing to national savings because of the substantial build-up in the trust funds that had occurred after the 1983 Amendments to the Social Security Act. But both Bosworth and Manchester countered that the accumulation in the Social Security trust funds between 1983 and 1995 had not added to national savings, because of the large net deficits that had been run by the federal government over that period. Council members Bob Ball and Edith Fierst disputed that conclusion. Fierst was an attorney in independent practice who would be a vocal defendant of the current Social Security system throughout the council's deliberations. Chairman Gramlich brought the discussion back to point.

> There are two issues, as I understand this. One is the saving issue. That has been well stated by the previous speakers.
>
> The second issue, and I think Joyce would agree with this, is that national saving is what it is, and if all that were done would be to

do what Tom [Jones] wants to do, to change the investment policy of Social Security, then all you're doing—there's no change in national saving. All you're doing is shuffling around who holds various assets and there is no effect on U.S. GDP. . . . The point is that it's possible to make Social Security better off without any change in overall GDP. That is possible under a Jones-type policy. But a Bosworth-type policy would make GDP higher and the system better off by a lot more.[12]

In the discussion that followed, Bob Ball said that he could simply not see Congress "actually put 2 percentage points of payroll right away into building up the Social Security fund when there isn't any emergency. . . . On the other hand, what would be the situation if, instead of immediately doing that, one were to have a tax increase"[13] in 2019 when the trust fund under current law was projected to begin declining? Bosworth responded to Ball's line of reasoning. "You shouldn't be allowed to get away with proposing changes that affect somebody else down the road. You ought to be up front with your proposals. Do it now if you're going to do it."[14] Edith Fierst chimed in, "I think we have to make some benefit cuts, but I'm very resistant to the idea of raising taxes now. . . . It's totally unrealistic to expect Congress to do it."[15]

As the discussion wound down, the two sides were summarized in stark contrast. Ball concluded, "Politically I don't see increasing [the payroll tax] 2 percentage points in the short-term." Bosworth responded, "If the country can't be brought to understand the benefits of expanding the pie, then we don't have to make these divisive choices, if we would just go back to saving something. Somebody says, 'Well, why should Social Security do it?' Because it's a retirement program. That's what the essence of a retirement program is."[16] Ball came back with, "There's really more to it than we've said, too, Barry. . . . That is the ability over time to maintain a large fund as against later on dissipating [it] for other purposes. I don't think the experience in Canada, Sweden, Japan is all very encouraging from that standpoint."[17]

Stephen Zeldes, an economics professor at Columbia University and a member of the TIRS panel, also made a presentation to the council at this same meeting. He suggested that if we were going to accumulate additional funds through Social Security, either by raising taxes or cutting benefits, one way to handle the added funding would be to take the "money and hand it over to people and let them invest" it. He said that one reason for letting workers invest the added funding themselves was that "if you give people some control over their money, they're willing to trade off a bigger cut in benefits than they otherwise would." He suggested that giving people a dollar in a retirement account with their name on it might allow policymakers to reduce future Social Security benefits by more than the equivalent value.[18]

The council reconvened in March 1995 and began a general discussion about the funding matter. Bob Ball indicated that he would be for some advance funding, but only if it were accomplished without individual accounts. Carolyn Weaver attempted to steer the council away from the direction that Ball was clearly headed in. Weaver was an economist who directed Social Security policy research at the American Enterprise Institute in Washington, D.C. She had served for years as Social Security adviser to Senator Robert Dole. She suggested that before getting to specific policy proposals, the council should hold a general discussion about the desirability of prefunding some or all of Social Security's obligations. After that discussion, she suggested, council members would come to a "fork in the road" on funding methods—*if* they thought additional funding was desirable.[19] As the dialogue progressed toward specific proposals, Weaver became more explicit. "You're getting specific enough that I'm getting nervous. I don't know that I would support the government's centrally directing investments in the private sector, where we hope Congress will use index funds. That's what has led me in my writing to talk about long-term reforms that involve a defined-contribution component to Social Security, because I do not think we need direct private investment. But I'm concerned about how you control and decentralize those investment decisions through means other than millions of people making individual decisions."[20]

In this discussion, Weaver began to press for consideration of Social Security reform options that might include individual accounts. Bob Ball went on record clearly as opposing this approach. Edith Fierst weighed in to raise questions about annuitization of benefits at retirement. Weaver insisted that it was premature to focus on specific problems without considering the potential benefits of alternative approaches: "It's important to recognize the benefits of looking at Social Security in different ways and thinking about alternative ways to structure the system."[21]

Taking a Look at First Principles

By the time the council convened for its April 1995 meeting, some of the members were getting frustrated with the continual deluge of information and wanted to get on with drawing up a specific set of recommendations to deal with the undisputed financing problem. This was driving the council back repeatedly to the issues of raising taxes or cutting benefits. But Bob Ball, the elder philosopher of the group that most adamantly supported the current system, had been quite unequivocal in stating that he did not see how an unvarnished, straightforward tax increase could attract the necessary political support. Others less committed to the system were openly hostile to tax increases.

Potential adjustments on the benefit side were forcing into the spotlight the conflict between the traditional goals of adequacy and equity that had successfully been avoided during the phase-in of Social Security. The conflict between these two goals had historically been masked by the trillions of dollars in windfall benefits provided to people retiring up through the 1990s. Now the conflict was driving some members of the council toward revisiting first principles. Fidel Vargas, the youngest council member, went at the issue directly: "The fundamental question, at least to me, is . . . are we talking about keeping the Social Security system the way it is and finding individual things that . . . will get us into balance over seventy-five years, or are we talking about doing something fundamentally different. . . . If we talk about whether individual accounts are a good idea or not, I don't think it's going to deal with the basic question . . . about this as a financing problem or as something more fundamental that's going to change."[22]

Although some council members were willing to revisit Social Security's fundamental goals, not everyone on the council wanted to go there. Tom Jones responded to Vargas that he didn't believe that the council had been asked to examine the government's reasonable role in providing Social Security to its citizens.[23] Carolyn Weaver observed that she could not understand how the council "would evaluate [the] equity or adequacy of any single proposal without a view of what the government is trying to accomplish with this program."[24] Bob Ball weighed in with the opinion that the council needed to reach agreement around specific programmatic changes.[25]

Bob Ball was trying to achieve the same approach and result in the deliberations of the 1994–1996 Advisory Council on Social Security as he had been able to with the 1982 National Commission on Social Security Reform, the Greenspan commission. There he had generally been able to keep the discussion away from the fundamental philosophy of the program and get the members to focus on a "Chinese menu" of marginal adjustments to the system. Each of the marginal adjustments had a price tag. The goal was to get the system back into balance by picking and choosing from the marginal adjustments until the price tags added up to 2.19 percent of covered payroll.

Another of Ball's goals was to attempt to find items that he could include in his menu of choices that he could argue were neither tax increases nor benefit cuts. Raising the necessary revenue to rebalance the system without having to raise taxes or cut benefits made change seem painless within the context of the program's operations. At the February 1995 meeting he stated his position clearly in an exchange with Ned Gramlich, the chairman of the council. It followed a discussion about possible approaches to reducing benefits and the *equity* issues that would be created as a result. Ball observed that he would not want to make the system any more redistributional than it already was. According to Gramlich, the conclusion "just so we've laid all the cards down, is that most of the financing then would have to be in the tax side." Ball responded, "Well, not necessarily. I keep arguing that there are equity changes in this program that are not correctly classified as either tax or benefit cuts."[26]

In order to set forth his perspective on the approach that should be taken by the council, Bob Ball put a proposal on the table at the April 1995 meeting. He offered three provisions that he characterized as being neither benefit nor tax items. He was proposing that the Department of Labor correct the measurement of the consumer price index, to net an added 0.21 percent of covered payroll by his estimate. He wanted to expand coverage to include state and local government employees still outside the system, thereby additionally netting 0.25 percent of covered payroll. He suggested investing a portion of the trust fund in the private equity markets, which would net 0.70 percent of payroll. In the area of "shared sacrifice" Ball proposed to expand the taxation of benefits, thus netting 0.48 percent of covered payroll. Expanding the number of years of earnings used in calculating benefits would reduce the system's costs by 0.28 percent of payroll. Increasing the maximum taxable earnings by $10,000 would net 0.17 percent of covered payroll. Increasing the payroll tax by 0.20 percentage points each on workers and employers would net 0.38 percent. Finally, accelerating the increase in the normal retirement age from sixty-six to sixty-seven, starting in 2006, would net 0.12 percent. If you took into account the interplay between the various measures, Ball suggested, his package would eliminate the system's deficit and allow for an increase in benefits to widows.[27] Ball's selections from his Chinese menu of choices gave the illusion that no one had to suffer a direct benefit reduction to bring the system back into balance. It would require only a tax increase of 0.20 percentage points on workers.

Considerable debate and discussion took place within the council about a number of the items on Bob Ball's list and how they should be scored.

When the option for investing the trust funds in the stock market had first come up, Chairman Gramlich had characterized it as magic rabbit that would offer an alternative to benefit cuts or tax increases.[28] This characterization of the proposed investment policy was transformed into the "magic bunny" as the council's deliberations continued. Though most council members supported expanded coverage of state and local workers, several would have counted that recommendation as a tax increase. Indeed, with the exception of the magic bunny, all the items could be scored as benefit reductions or tax increases. Bob Ball had offered them up without the fundamental discussion that some council members clearly yearned to have.

An Appetite for More than Tinkering

To facilitate a discussion of philosophical issues, Sylvester Schieber, one of the authors of this book, tabled an alternative proposal that attempted to highlight the conflicts between the considerations of adequacy and individual equity under the program. His proposal was based on an analysis of the implications of alternative adjustments to taxes and benefits for workers at different levels of earnings. On the benefit side, the analysis focused on reductions that would be proportional across the earnings spectrum as opposed to reductions targeted at workers at higher earning levels. His conclusion was that Social Security benefit reductions at the bottom of the earnings distribution scale would be far more disruptive, from the perspective of retirement security, than those at the top. To the extent that benefit reductions were to be considered, larger reductions in benefits for workers at higher earning levels might be fairer than proportionate reductions across the board.[29]

Given the lack of support expressed by several council members, including Bob Ball, for straightforward tax increases to rebalance the system, this alternative proposal focused on reducing benefits. Schieber proposed raising the normal retirement age by two months per year, beginning in 2000 and continuing until the retirement age reached sixty-eight in 2017. He called for raising the early retirement age in lockstep with the normal retirement age. Because the increase in the retirement age alone was not sufficient to rebalance the system, he recommended the imposition of a flat benefit across all earning levels. Benefits would be set at a level that rebalanced the system. He proposed a twenty-year phase-in and a voluntary account system that would allow workers to buy back the early retirement benefits lost because of the increase in the early retirement age.

Bob Ball began his critique of the proposal by noting that it would convert Social Security into the bottom deck of a retirement system in which the upper deck was voluntary. He worried that the lack of universal employer-sponsored pensions would leave many middle- and upper-level earners with inadequate resources in retirement. Ball favored redistribution, but not too much of it. Edith Fierst worried that "if we abandon the idea of proportionate return, then we'd have to abandon the idea of the payroll tax."[30] It made little difference to her that Social Security was already projected to be a bad deal for most middle- and high-level earners in the baby boom generation and younger. Gramlich commented that if the system were throwing off submarket rates of return, keeping it smaller as opposed to larger might be in the interest of workers with higher wages. One way to do that was to flatten the benefits provided by the system.[31] Ball then argued that entirely too much attention was paid to rates of return and that some benefits provided by the system were not represented in these economic measures. But when that argument was rejected as supporting further flattening in benefits, Ball countered that "to say that the sole criteria, or even the most important criteria, are not rate of return, isn't to say that there aren't values in the system being related to wages."[32]

Schieber responded that the system was out of balance and either taxes had to be raised or benefits had to be cut. Either one of those was going to change the current gradations in benefits relative to taxes, which affected both equity and adequacy. He admitted that his proposal was extreme, but it was purposely crafted that way to provoke council members to think about their priorities with respect to the policy goals embedded in current law and how those might be changed to serve future participants in the system. Ball pointed to his own proposal as a mechanism for adjusting the system that would require "relatively minor shifts in contribution rates and in benefit cuts."[33] But not all the council members were willing to buy his whole package or even many of its components.

As the discussion evolved, significant differences of perception within the council became more defined. Fidel Vargas saw the system as broken and in need of fundamental change. Tom Jones and Bob Ball saw it as sound, in need of small incremental adjustments. Carolyn Weaver and Fidel Vargas argued that the veil of complicated redistribution should be made more transparent so that the public fully understood how the system worked. Gerald Shea, the director of the Department of Employee Benefits for health, pensions, Social Security, and child care at the AFL-CIO, worried that the move to a flat benefit would erode public support for the system. Edith Fierst's view was that if higher-level earners don't get higher benefits, "the whole system will collapse. . . . If the connection between what they pay and what they get back is totally eradicated, . . . it will kill the support for Social Security."[34]

Gerry Shea captured the essence of one side of the argument. He strongly opposed "cutting benefits unless absolutely necessary." He was even more strongly opposed to "raising the retirement age, because of the differential impact that has on people by virtue of their earnings history." He was in favor of raising taxes if the increase was reasonable. He thought Bob Ball's recommendation of a 0.20 percentage-point increase on workers and employers was "quite modest."[35] The problem the council faced was that the deficit they were trying to eradicate was 2.17 percent of covered payroll. Ball's proposed payroll tax increase wouldn't cover 20 percent of that. The top line in his proposal stated that added investment returns would cover nearly a third of the total shortfall, but Barry Bosworth had made a compelling case that added investment return would help only if some new real savings were added to the system. Several council members didn't accept other adjustments in Ball's package. And Carolyn Weaver repeatedly argued that if the system did get added funding from the kinds of things Ball proposed, some of it should go into individual accounts.

At the May 1995 council meeting Ned Gramlich put a proposal on the table that adopted several of the features from the flat benefit proposal that had been discussed and rejected at the April meeting. Gramlich started from the assumption that no one on the council was willing to put forward an unvarnished proposal to raise taxes to support current benefit levels. Thus, his proposal focused on benefit reductions. Gramlich's plan, though, called for the benefit to be progressive, with wage earners at the top of the pay scale still getting higher benefits than workers at lower earning levels. It would be less progressive than the current system, however, as benefit reductions would be concentrated at the higher end of the earnings distribution scale. The motivation for this approach could be traced back to the earlier discussion about wanting to contain the size of the system, given that it was going to provide extremely low or negative rates of return to future cohorts of retirees. Gramlich proposed substituting a double-decker system not markedly different from the one that the Social Security staff had developed back in the 1940s when Senator Arthur Vandenberg and Representative Carl Curtis had favored such an approach. Under Gramlich's approach, the bottom deck of the retirement plan would pay all retirees a flat benefit—one that would be the same for those with low or high earnings. The second deck would pay a benefit that was proportional—depending on the amount of total covered earnings.

Tom Jones challenged the desirability of reducing benefits so significantly. When reminded that the "only other option is to raise taxes," Jones responded, "That's a debate that should be raised." He then framed the debate within the context of Gramlich's proposed reduction of benefits to eliminate the actuarial deficit and Bob Ball's proposal calling for a 0.20 percentage-point increase in the payroll tax rate on employers and workers.[36] Bob Ball made it clear that he did not like the Gramlich proposal because of the skewed nature of the cuts that it entailed. If there had to be cuts in benefits, he favored across-the-board cuts.[37] Edith Fierst was opposed to cutting benefits. To complicate matters, she was also opposed to raising taxes. Given her dilemma, she proposed raising the retirement age,[38] as though that were not a benefit cut. She also suggested that "maybe the thing to do would be to tax defined-contribution plans, both the employers' and employees.'"[39]

As the discussion unfolded around the Gramlich proposal, the approaches that various council members wanted to pursue were clarified. Ball and several other council members wanted to maintain the current structure of the system and benefit levels to the greatest extent possible. They wanted to find new revenues in a way that such additional money would not have to be characterized as a tax increase. Gramlich and another set of council members were willing to stay within the traditional Social Security framework but were driven to straightforward benefit reductions, for two reasons. First, no one was willing to stand up and advocate a straightforward tax increase. Second, the rates of return on this kind of retirement financing were so poor that they didn't want to expand it. Carolyn Weaver wanted to explore alternative approaches. Several council members, including some working with Gramlich, were sympathetic to Weaver's interests.

Weaver was persistent in pushing for consideration of the issues that would arise if we were to adopt some form of individual accounts as part of Social Security reform. At the May 1995 meeting she once again raised the issue of additional funding versus pay-as-you-go financing and the implications of the latter for the transfer of wealth across generations. She contended that deferring tax increases merely passed on to our children and grandchildren the burden of providing for our retirement. Pursuing her earlier line of thinking, Weaver asked that the proposal introduced by Senators Robert Kerrey and Alan Simpson to include substantial prefunding through individual accounts be put "on the table for serious and detailed discussion" by the council.[40] Her request was not acknowledged by either the chairman or the executive director of the council.

As the meeting wore on, Carolyn Weaver came back two more times to the need for discussion about some form of individual accounts. Toward the end of the day, Chairman Gramlich finally opened the floor for discussion of individualized accounts. The discussion was very general, and little substantive consideration was given to this matter. The staff had done no work on any proposal for individualized accounts, and no one else had materials ready to provide a framework for deliberation. Finally, Bob Ball spoke up. "I don't know how much discussion you want now, but I do think it would be really important for us as a council, before we disband, to have before us a detailed, really worked-out plan."[41]

The June 1995 meeting of the council was relatively uneventful. The actuaries had continued to develop estimates on the two plans that were unfolding in the council's deliberations. There was considerable discussion about benefit levels and the fairness of benefits across generations under the two plans. At this council meeting Edith Fierst advocated taxing employer-sponsored fringe benefits other than health care benefits. She declared that such a tax was another "magic bunny." The chairman of the council had already identified Bob Ball's proposals to expand the taxation of benefits and the investment of the trust funds in private equities to be magic bunnies. Although magic bunnies were generally pulled from the hat with more delight than the painful proposals associated with direct tax increases or cuts in benefits, Tom Jones and Ann Combs challenged Fierst on her recommendations. Combs had served as the deputy assistant secretary of pension and welfare benefit plans at the Department of Labor during President George Bush's administration. The TIRS Panel had recommended against the proposal to tax employee benefits. Jones and Combs raised concerns about the viability of such benefits if Fierst's repeated recommendation were adopted.

Carolyn Weaver observed early in the meeting, "We haven't talked too much about private accounts. This has been something that has been on the table for as long as I can remember. We may have chosen as a group not to talk too much about it, and some people may have chosen not to think too deeply about it. It may not have been presented with very careful statistical analysis of it, but it has been sitting on the table the entire time. And it's something, as everybody knows, I feel quite strongly about, and will be looking toward any proposal that we take seriously toward finding a way to get privatized accounts into that proposal for some portion of Social Security."[42] The council's executive director pointed out that the staff had reviewed the proposal developed by Senators Kerrey and Simpson. The problem was that he had provided no analysis to the council on the Kerrey-Simpson plan.

At its July 1995 meeting the council once again took up the importance of increased savings for growing the national economy and average wage levels. More savings should lead to higher wages in the future, which should reduce the burden imposed by the program. This was essentially the same result that Barry Bosworth had challenged the council to consider some five months earlier. Within the context of the specific proposals that were on the table, the rate of return attributed to the added savings was extremely important. We have discussed in previous chapters the value of funding in financing retirement plans. The higher the return on accumulating funds, the greater the value of funding. Bob Ball and Tom Jones were making a case that their proposed investment of trust fund assets in the private stock market should bring a rate of return higher than several other council members were comfortable assuming in developing long-term projections.

At the end of a presentation on the mechanics of pay-go financing, Lindeman remarked that if "we don't build up a capital reserve in advance, you can assume whatever you want in terms of the discount with the real interest rate. Because you have a higher real interest rate, you discount [future liabilities] at a higher rate. You can make the system's problems look smaller, but it's all a fraud. It's all an illusion, unless you're partly capitalized." [43]

This comment brought Bob Ball back into the discussion once again, defending Social Security's trust fund accumulations as a contribution to the national savings. [44] National savings is the sum of personal savings, business savings, and government surpluses (less government deficits). The repeated characterizations of various elements of Ball's package as "magic bunnies" around the advisory council table suggested considerable skepticism on the part of council members. When Ball observed that he thought "the present Social Security surpluses are contributing to savings," Lindeman observed that he didn't believe that most of the members of the TIRS Panel would agree. [45]

The point of discussion between Ball and Lindeman can never be definitively resolved. This particular argument was exactly the same one that Arthur Altmeyer and Arthur Vandenberg had held repeatedly a half-century earlier. By this stage in the council's deliberations, Ned Gramlich was making the point that we needed to be thinking about increasing Social Security's surpluses in a way that the contribution to national savings was less ambiguous. This discussion ultimately led into a brief discourse by Lindeman on the bill that Senators Kerrey and Simpson had introduced during the 1995 congressional session.

The Kerrey-Simpson bill called for significant reductions in the cost-of-living adjustments (COLAs) provided to Social Security beneficiaries and an increase in the retirement age. The senators proposed using the savings from reductions in benefits outlined in their bill to finance personal investment plan (PIP) accounts. These accounts would be credited each year at a rate of 2 percent of workers' covered earnings. The contributions plus the interest earned on them would eventually replace the reductions in benefits used to finance the accounts in the first place. Barry Bosworth suggested that if the rates of contribution to Social Security couldn't be raised, as he recommended, maybe they could be raised in a reform plan that included individual accounts. To contrast the two approaches, the Kerrey-Simpson proposal amounted to the financing of individual accounts by carving the equivalent of 2 percent of covered payroll out of the existing system, and Bosworth's proposal could be interpreted as a 2 percent add-on to the existing system. This discussion led back to the consideration of whether trust fund assets should be invested in the stock market and whether the plans before the council would add to national savings.

As centered on the Kerrey-Simpson proposal, the discussion was finally headed in the direction that Carolyn Weaver had been advocating for some months. But there were at least three problems with this particular interchange. The first was that the discussion was extremely brief by comparison with the earlier discussion about reform options. The second was that it concentrated purely on issues of savings and financing, without any exploration of the implications of such a plan for the distribution of benefits within or across generations of workers. The third was that the discussion was held at a time when Carolyn Weaver was not present. Afterward, the council broke for lunch. When the council reconvened on the afternoon of July 27, 1995, Edith Fierst took the floor yet again to inquire why the Social Security payroll tax should be applied to employees' fringe benefits. Even though she had raised the issue repeatedly before and seen it rejected by the council, the discussion lasted far longer than the pre-lunch discussion on the Kerrey-Simpson proposal.

Be Careful What You Ask For

As the council concluded its discussions on the afternoon of July 27 and reconvened on the morning of July 28, 1995, it became increasingly clear that Bob Ball was not going to convince certain council members that his package of recommendations was the one they should support. The package of benefit reductions in the plan that was being crafted by the chairman and several other council members was likely to receive substantial support.

No one has ever accused Bob Ball of being a poor tactician. He moved to garner support for his position. Toward the end of the second day of meetings in July, he said, "I would like to see whether our assumptions that people are so averse to any increase in the contribution rate that they'd prefer cuts in benefits [could] be tested in a poll."[46] Considerable discussion ensued over the crafting of questions for such a poll on benefit cuts and tax increases that would not elicit biased responses. There was also talk of the dwindling time in the schedule for the council to prepare its report. The final report was to be written before the end of the year. The council needed to start making decisions if that schedule was to be met. Finally, Carolyn Weaver spoke up: "I'd like to have an honest assessment from the panel about whether or not we intend to meet a deadline. I don't know about the rest of you, but I have a job and a life I'm trying to conduct around this panel."[47]

Bob Ball responded that the council ought not be driven by production schedules but by the substance of the matters it was trying to resolve. He said that, after all, nothing bad would result "except the waste of our own time." Weaver responded, "Right. Which is a fairly enormous cost."[48] It is not surprising that a gentleman in his eighties tending to his life's work and a working mother of two young boys would look at the value of their time differently. Finally, Weaver was pushed to the limit. If they faced no schedule constraints, she said,

> then I'd like to express my great disappointment in the fact that we have never had a careful discussion and presentation on two-tiered systems of personal investment accounts. That we haven't had the World Bank in here to discuss in some detail what the issues are in moving toward a two- or a three-tiered system with a substantial private component or a substantial defined-contribution component.
>
> I've been distressed about that the entire year. And I would very much like to spend our remaining time on that issue only, rather than whether it's thirty-two, thirty-six, or thirty-eight years of earnings that will be used in the calculation of benefits.[49]

David Lindeman tried to make a case that he had covered the issues that Weaver was concerned about in his presentation on the previous day when she was absent. She wasn't convinced. Finally, Bob Ball added, "If we have time for it, I would very much like to have the council thoroughly consider

Kerrey-Simpson."[50] As council members pressed to have some discussion of the issues being raised, Lindeman pushed back. "I must say. . . . there are very large opportunity costs to have a speaker at the next meeting on this issue and do it in the depth that it would have to be done to really lay out all the issues over different kinds of versions of this."[51] Ball responded: "I would love to see this report say we had considered this and decided for this and this reason that it wasn't a good idea."[52] It was easy to see where Ball was headed. But once again, not everyone was willing to go there. Syl Schieber commented on Ball's recommendation:

> I think we have to be very careful about saying we looked at Kerrey-Simpson and we were uninterested in two-pillar approaches or approaches with some kind of real savings accounts, and so forth. Kerrey-Simpson is a variant that's financed in a way that I think a lot of people . . . would not support. There may be other ways, though, that you could finance such an approach and we have spent very little time thinking about them or talking about them.
>
> I know this was put up yesterday, but there was hardly a discussion by the council of this approach to dealing with Social Security financing. There are distributional issues. There are financing issues. There are transitional issues. There are . . .[53]

Lindeman cut in: "Governance issues. There are management issues. There are a whole bunch of issues you'd have to look at if you did this."[54] He continued to make the case that the hour was late and the opportunity costs were such that to pursue this line was not reasonable. When Gerry Shea came out in favor of looking at individual accounts to avoid "serious short-changing of an important issue,"[55] the case was carried. Although Lindeman continued to protest about his inability to line up speakers, and to complain about the time that would be claimed, a full spectrum of council members clearly supported taking a closer look at the matter.

At this juncture Lindeman and his staff could no longer forestall a serious consideration of individual accounts as an element of Social Security reform. Even the strongest proponents of the status quo were saying that the council ought to consider the approach. Others, who had been working on the Gramlich plan, were calling for the same thing. It appeared that Weaver was finally making headway. At the next meeting, on August 31–September 1, 1995, two people from the World Bank made presentations to the council. Dimitri Vitas and Louise Fox were members of the World Bank staff that had worked on a major study of aging around the world and the ways different countries were dealing with it. They had considerable firsthand experience in working with national governments in revising their social insurance systems. Although their presentations were instructive in general terms, they brought little specificity to the issues the United States would encounter in implementing a program of individual accounts.

Michael Tanner of the Cato Institute also did a presentation for the council. Before the meeting, he had distributed materials that explored several issues related to replacing the Social Security system in the United States with a system of individual accounts. A considerable part of Tanner's discussion was about the ability to back out of the current system without having to pay all current workers the full benefit that they have earned under it. Being able to do this would significantly reduce the costs of transition to a new fully funded system. Finally, Louise Fox from the World Bank pointed out that "if you go to [a] funded system, somebody pays twice."[56] After lengthy discussion around the council table, Tanner came back to this point.

> Can I challenge the assumption, though, that a generation has to pay twice? That only applies . . . under some transition financing mechanisms. I mean to the degree you continue on a portion of the payroll tax basis, they pay twice. To the degree that you default and run up a deficit, they pay twice.
>
> If you find that it's funded out of current expenditures of general revenue without increasing tax rates, for example—just a theory—you do not pay twice. I mean, let's just take a wild hypothetical. Let us say you eliminate the hundred billion dollars a year we spend on NATO, and you take that money and transfer it over to Social Security. . . . I think it's a stretch to say at that point that the next generation is paying twice. . . . I would argue that much of the government spending is actually a net social harm or a net negative value, and therefore that we'd be better off [without it].[57]

Sylvester Schieber observed that "Michael [Tanner] does benefit from a wider charter than we have. Ours is fairly wide, but NATO was not included."[58]

At the end of these presentations, the council broke for lunch. At lunch with several other council members, Schieber announced that if no one else would put a specific proposal for individual accounts on the table, he would. When they returned for the afternoon session of the meeting, the discussion started off in very general terms about the implications of moving to an individual-account approach to Social Security reform. Finally Schieber spoke up.

We can talk philosophically about whether or not we should explore this, but it seems to me, given what's going on in the world, for us not to at least explore it is going to suggest when our report comes out that we had a tremendous blind spot.

I think we ought to at least explore it. . . . If we're talking about something that's totally minimalist, then it would probably not be considered . . . a good faith test. . . . I would suggest there's possibly even a model that we already have on the table that could be modified somewhat that would be at least the beginning example for us to walk through and begin to understand the issues. It's . . . the two-tiered system that we're talking about. . . . The two-tiered system that's on the table right now is roughly a fifty-fifty split between the flat benefit on the bottom and the proportional benefit on the top.

One of the things that we might do is . . . run that flat benefit through Social Security and assume that it's over time going to take about half . . . of the payroll tax at its current rate, given the way we've configured it. . . . We can worry about whether we cut it off at 55 or 45 [percent] . . . after we start to get some of the general framework. . . . We want to get to a position where the other half of the payroll tax goes to give people individual accounts. . . .

When we get the general framework laid out, we can . . . work on some of the nits and gnats about . . . how you go about annuitizing things at the end of the day, and so forth.[59]

Sylvester Schieber, Carolyn Weaver, and a number of other council members worked out the specific details of this proposal as the council's deliberations continued.

Some puzzlement has been expressed over why Carolyn Weaver did not put her own proposal for individual accounts on the table. She had written extensively over the years on Social Security and was clearly in favor of discussing the option. Her repeated requests that the advisory council consider individual accounts could leave no doubt about where she stood. Part of the reason she did not offer an independent proposal probably goes back to history, both her own and the Republican Party's. Weaver had worked for Senator Robert Dole on Social Security matters for years. She was his staff assistant on Social Security when Dole was serving on the Greenspan commission in the early 1980s. She had served on the staff of the Senate Finance Committee while Dole was the Committee Chairman. In 1995, she was advising the senator on Social Security matters as he was positioning himself for his run for the presidency. This was an area where Dole, and so Weaver, too, had to be careful.

The individual-account proposal was eventually put on the table at the advisory council as a means to help the council members understand what many people were already talking about. Chile had "privatized" its social security system in the early 1980s. Not only did the country not come apart, but it seemed to have prospered after the move. Australia had adopted a system of mandatory savings accounts in the early 1990s. The system had been introduced by a Labor government and was heavily supported by the organized labor movement in the country. Other countries around the world were considering or adopting similar proposals. Here in the United States, groups like the Cato Institute and the Heritage Foundation had been advocating this approach for years. But serious consideration by people like Martin Feldstein at the National Bureau of Economic Research gave the concept new currency. Having someone like Democratic Senator Bob Kerrey pushing an individual-account proposal gave the idea further cachet. There was no way the advisory council could legitimately ignore it.

The council held what was scheduled to be its final meeting on Thursday, December 14, 1995. Between the October and December meetings there had been a continuing refinement of the proposals that were before the council. Christopher Bender at HR&A had developed a model under contract to the advisory council to help in evaluating the various proposals. His model allowed for the calculation of replacement rates at a given age of retirement across cohorts of workers and at different levels of lifetime earnings. His model also calculated money's worth ratios for these same sorts of workers. This model had been used extensively in developing a comparative analysis of three alternative plans. The first of these was the plan that had been developed under Bob Ball's direction, the "Maintain Benefits," or MB plan. The Gramlich plan was called the double-deck plan. At this juncture, Gramlich's plan did not call for any individual-account reform to Social Security. The plan that Schieber and Weaver had worked out with the other members of the council was called the personal security account, or PSA, plan. According to the analysis, the PSA plan held out the promise of paying benefits that were generally as good as or better than those offered by the MB plan. The PSA also held out the promise of paying benefits far superior to the double-deck plan supported by the chairman of the council. With regard to the money's worth analysis, the PSA plan also performed relatively well and appeared to be the superior plan in the long term.

Bob Ball raised a number of concerns about the implications of the comparative analysis of the plans. But one thing in particular troubled him about the PSA proposal: "It seems to me that with everybody getting their own accounts, there really isn't a very good stopping place if the returns are really bigger."[60] The value of the rates of return on contributions that would be saved under the PSA plan were troubling to several members of the council. Ball worried that "what might happen is that people would find it cheaper to do an SSI type of program underlying an individual-account program and let the system go at that."[61] Schieber responded, "The fundamental question is whether or not the American people will support these two concepts that we have underlying our current system, the adequacy and equity components. We've blurred them up over the years. . . . If the [people are] not going to support them in this kind of mechanism [a PSA], it's not clear to me they're going to support them any more in a mechanism where we . . . gum them up."[62]

Back to the Drawing Board

After the lunch break Bob Ball put a totally new plan on the table for the council to consider. As the afternoon went on, it was clear that Gramlich was going to alter his recommendation as well. Tom Jones, who had been in the Ball camp all along, expressed unhappiness at this development.

I don't understand our process. We have been at work for a year and a half. We've had two expert panels who were charged with vetting ideas and giving objective analyses on various alternatives. We organized a meeting to discuss a final report, and the Saturday before we [get] a fifty-page paper that has not been subjected to any of that expert panel review process. . . . Now we're going to have another plan. . . .
   I think that [if] Syl [Schieber] has a personal plan that he wants to write about and put forth, that's great. And if you [Ned Gramlich] have one, that's great. I just don't understand how these things surface at the eleventh hour and without going through the same process and now get equal standing in a report which is supposed to be a report of this full council, coming out of an eighteen-month deliberative series of meetings.[63]

Schieber immediately responded:

First of all, there have been a number of requests over the eighteen months to include an option that would have as part of it some significant personal account. It had been requested of the staff several times. There was nothing ever forthcoming. In terms of the development of this paper and its late delivery, we have been waiting for analytical numbers to understand these issues and the implications of the various options for quite a number of months. . . . They only came together late last week. . . . There were literally hundreds of pages of numbers.

These were not numbers I generated on my own. I have tried to capture numbers from either contractors that were hired by the council or by the people with the Office of the Actuary in Baltimore. And there has been checking of those numbers.

It's regrettable that it took so long to get this option on the table, but we would be totally remiss in terms of what's going on elsewhere around the world and what's being discussed in our own society and our own policy community to have not investigated this option.[64]

Ned Gramlich added a correction to Jones's statement: "Our technical panel did review at some length individual accounts. They have a lengthy, maybe forty-page discussion of that, and we've always known that that was around the table. . . . I would almost bet that there is more discussion of individual equity, individual accounts in our technical panel reports than there is on equity investment. . . . In fact there has been more analysis of individual accounts than there has been of having the central system invest in equities."[65]

After more discussion of procedures and plan specifications, a straw vote on the three plans was called. Including proxies for missing members, six members of the panel supported the Maintain Benefits plan. The six were Bob Ball, Tom Jones, the three members of organized labor, and Edith Fierst. Ned Gramlich and Marc Twinney supported the plan that Gramlich was now amending on the fly. The remaining five members supported the PSA plan. This group was the most diverse of the three groups in the council. Three of the total of five women on the council joined this group. It included the youngest member of the council and one of the older members. It included two of the three economists on the council. It included two Democrats, two Republicans, and an Independent. Immediately after the vote, Edith Fierst allowed that, "I voted for maintaining benefits, but I don't necessarily buy into the particulars of the plan presented." Marc Twinney added, "I have the same problem with my vote."[66] None of those supporting the PSA plan ever wavered in their commitment, despite intense lobbying by the other two factions to get them to do so.

As the council finished its December 1995 meeting, members hoped to have the final report completed by January 15, 1996. Indeed the council would meet again on April 13, 1996. By now David Lindeman was working for the World Bank, and most of the other staff members who had been involved in the council's work were gone. The contract with HR&A had expired, and the actuaries at Social Security were charged with developing all projections for the three plans that would be included in the final report. The writing of the final report was thrust back on the members of the council.

Ned Gramlich was responsible for the drafting of the general report and the statement supporting his plan, which came to be known as the Individual Accounts (IA) plan. It called for a scaling back of Social Security benefits to stay within the 12.4 percent payroll tax in current law. The scaling back was tilted in such a way that higher earners took a bigger hit than did those at the lower end of the earnings distribution scale. Because of the austerity of the benefit rollbacks, the IA plan called for an added mandatory employee contribution of 1.6 percent of covered payroll to be held in the form of an individual account that would be operated by the Social Security Administration.

Bob Ball continued to tinker with his Maintain Benefits plan up to the very end. He was largely responsible for its evolution and description in the final report. In the closing days of 1996 the support evaporated within this group for centralized investment of the trust fund in the stock market. Instead of calling for such investment, the group called for studying it. This result threw their plan out of balance, because they had no provisions to make up for the income that they counted on from that element of the package, which they had been working with in the deliberations. In the final analysis, this group so dedicated to maintaining the current structure of Social Security and essentially maintaining current law benefits could not cobble together a proposal that would rebalance the system. If those who are totally dedicated to the current structure of Social Security cannot come up with a consensus proposal to secure its long-term financing, it may portend significant problems for the program.

The PSA plan changed very little from its initial design. The disability benefits and early-survivor benefits provided by Social Security were left largely intact. Under the plan, contributions for retirement benefits would be divided in half. The part that continues to go to Social Security would purchase a flat benefit that all career workers would receive by virtue of their contributions. This "adequacy" benefit would be the same for everyone within a particular age cohort who had been earning over a full career. Initial benefits would grow over time at the rate of growth in wages and benefits in payment status and would be indexed by the consumer price index. The equity benefit would consist of an individual account funded at a rate of 5 percent of covered pay. Sylvester Schieber and Carolyn Weaver did the staff work on the development of this proposal and were responsible for the drafting of the statements in the final council report describing the plan and the reasons five members were supporting it. A full description of this and the other options can be found in the final report of the 1994–1996 Advisory Council on Social Security.[67]

In Retrospect

Martha Derthick's criteria for the operation of a successful advisory council were significantly violated in the case of the 1994–1996 council. The fact that the majority of council would vote to significantly alter the system in ways that were contrary to the traditionalists' view of how it should operate showed independence that prior councils had never expressed. The failure to assign adequate staff committed to the traditional program virtually required council members to develop independent analyses and capabilities of assessing issues as they arose. The use of outside contractors and analysts working directly for council members rather than through Social Security staff was an unprecedented release of control over the deliberative process. Finally, the introduction of legislation by Senators Robert Kerrey, a Democrat from Nebraska, and Alan Simpson, a Republican from Wyoming, legitimized consideration of policy options that the council staff had adamantly avoided bringing to the table on a timely basis.

If we look back on the developments in this advisory council within the context of Martha Derthick's criteria for successful councils, it is clear that Social Security let matters get out of hand. Although none of the council members had come to the table hostile to the program, several of them considered the financing problem to be much more significant than Bob Ball wanted to concede. In pushing Ball's perspective, Tom Jones alienated several of the council members who viewed things differently. The failure to consider Carolyn Weaver's repeated requests to look at individual accounts simply made other council members sympathetic to her position. This sympathetic support was heightened even more when they were repeatedly called to entertain Edith Fierst's preoccupation with raising taxes through some hidden mechanism.

To a large extent the 1994–1996 Advisory Council on Social Security turned out so different from earlier ones because the underlying arithmetic of the pay-go system finally caught up with it. No prior council had focused on the issue of fairness across generations to the extent that this one did. Edwin Witte and Arthur Altmeyer had worried that this day would eventually come when they fought so hard for a funded system back in the late 1930s. Though policymakers were able to ride the tremendous surge of windfalls for a long time under the pay-go approach Witte and Altmeyer had feared, the bill was finally coming due. As we showed in Chapter 15, Dean Leimer at Social Security estimated that the last birth cohort of workers to get a windfall from the OASDI system was the one born in 1937. That cohort will reach early retirement eligibility in 1999. Policymakers had been able to give away $11.4 trillion in unearned benefits to the windfall generations. Now they were going to have to start taking some of it back from those born after 1937.

Bob Ball could talk all he wanted about the value of not having your mother-in-law living with you as a reason for supporting Social Security. Around the advisory council table, the prospect that whole generations would not get back what they contributed to the system simply did not pass the test for being fair. Finding sneaky ways to get more money for the system didn't either. In the final analysis, it was not an ideological upheaval that led to such fractiousness on the council. It was a general sense that something was simply not right that moved the majority to support very significant change in Social Security.

Chapter 18

Social Security Today and Marginal Proposals for Reform

*B*efore we talk about different ways to change Social Security to bring its finances into balance in the long run, it seems to make sense to describe in some detail the current deal—that is, the currently legislated taxes and benefits. However, it is important to remember one thing—the current deal is not sustainable. Therefore, just standing pat is not an option. Nonetheless, it should prove useful to know the law as of 1999.

The Current Deal

As we have done throughout so far, we are going to focus almost exclusively on the retirement program within Social Security, meanwhile noting, however, that the other benefits, such as Medicare, survivors, and disability benefits, are extremely important. The reform proposals that we are going to present leave these other programs intact. However, at least one of them (Medicare) faces severe financial problems of its own. Also, we are going to cover only the main points of the law. This presentation is not meant to be sufficiently detailed to enable readers to precisely and accurately calculate their retirement benefits—although most people should come very close. For readers who want more information and are comfortable surfing the Net, the Social Security web site, *www.ssa.gov*, is an excellent source.

The tax side of the program is particularly simple. As of 1999, the OASDI system is financed with a 6.20 percent tax on wages up to $72,600 per year. Both the employee and the employer pay the 6.20 percent tax, so the total tax is 12.40 percent of the first $72,600 of annual pay. For example, if Sheila makes $30,000 in wages in 1999, her payment of Social Security taxes will be 6.20 percent × $30,000 = $1,860. Her employer will deduct the $1,860 from her check, leaving her with a net-of-OASDI tax income of $28,140. Her employer actually has to forward $3,720 to the government in OASDI taxes because of her employment, the $1,860 that was deducted from her paychecks and the 6.20 percent employer's tax as well. Essentially, most economists believe that workers such as Sheila actually bear the burden of the full 12.40 percent tax. That is, if it weren't for the OASDI program, she would have made $31,860 instead of the $28,140 that she made net of the OASDI taxes.

In addition to the two 6.20 percent levies, one on the employee and one on the employer, the Social Security system imposes a 1.45 percent tax on both employees and employers to fund Medicare's Hospital Insurance program. These 1.45 percent taxes are not subject to the $72,600 cutoff, so high-income workers face a total 2.90 percent tax on all their earnings. The overall picture on the tax side, then, is a 7.65 percent tax on the first $72,600 of annual earnings, with a 1.45 percent tax on earnings above that level. Both the employer and the employee face these rates, so the total rate on the first $72,600 of wage income is 15.3 percent. Self-employed workers are treated as both employers and employees, and therefore they face the full 15.3 percent tax on their first $72,600 of net income, and 2.9 percent on income above that level. All these tax rates have been in effect since 1990 and are not scheduled to change, at least according to current legislation. However, the maximum level of earnings subject to the full OASDHI set of taxes, currently $72,600 for 1999, is raised annually to reflect increases in average wages. As we have mentioned before, the payroll tax has risen enormously over the years as the program has been scaled up. For instance, in 1960 the maximum total tax was 6 percent of $4,800 ($288), instead of the 1999 maximum of 15.3 percent of $72,600, or $11,107.80. More recently, the maximum in 1975 was 11.7 percent of $14,100, or $1,649.70, and in 1985 it was 14.1 percent of $39,600, or $5,583.60.

The retirement benefit structure is somewhat more complicated than the tax structure. It takes several steps to determine a retiree's initial monthly benefit. The first step is to update the individual's record of covered—that is, taxed—earnings. Recall that in 1977 the way the system was indexed for inflation was revised. Since 1977, a potential retiree's record of past earnings has been brought up to date by using a national average wage index. The index used to adjust wage histories is based on average historical wages. The averages for the period of 1951 to 1977 represent the average wage level in covered employment. Beyond 1977, the average wage is based on total wages in both covered and noncovered employment. The average wage series for computing the indexing factors used for people turning age sixty-two in 1999 is shown in Table 18.1.

Table 18.1   Factors Used to Compute Indexed Earnings
for Someone Born in 1937

Year	Maximum Taxable Amount	National Average Wage Index	1999 Index Factors	Earnings Required for a Credit
1951	$ 3,600	$ 2,799.16	9.79794	$ 50
1952	3,600	2,973.32	9.22403	50
1953	3,600	3,139.44	8.73595	50
1954	3,600	3,455.64	7.93659	50
1955	4,200	3,301.44	8.30728	50
1956	4,200	3,532.36	7.76421	50
1957	4,200	3,641.72	7.53106	50
1958	4,200	3,673.80	7.46529	50
1959	4,800	3,855.80	7.11292	50
1960	4,800	4,007.12	6.84432	50
1961	4,800	4,086.76	6.71094	50
1962	4,800	4,291.40	6.39092	50
1963	4,800	4,396.64	6.23795	50
1964	4,800	4,576.32	5.99302	50
1965	4,800	4,658.72	5.88702	50
1966	6,600	4,938.36	5.55367	50
1967	6,600	5,213.44	5.26063	50
1968	7,800	5,571.76	4.92232	50
1969	7,800	5,893.76	4.65340	50
1970	7,800	6,186.24	4.43339	50
1971	7,800	6,497.08	4.22128	50
1972	9,000	7,133.80	3.84451	50
1973	10,800	7,580.16	3.61813	50
1974	13,200	8,030.76	3.41512	50
1975	14,100	8,630.92	3.17765	50
1976	15,300	9,226.48	2.97253	50
1977	16,500	9,779.44	2.80446	50
1978	17,700	10,556.03	2.59814	250
1979	22,900	11,479.46	2.38914	260
1980	25,900	12,513.46	2.19172	290
1981	29,700	13,773.10	1.99127	310
1982	32,400	14,531.34	1.88737	340
1983	35,700	15,239.24	1.79970	370
1984	37,800	16,135.07	1.69978	390
1985	39,600	16,822.51	1.63032	410
1986	42,000	17,321.82	1.58332	440
1987	43,800	18,426.51	1.48840	460
1988	45,000	19,334.04	1.41853	470
1989	48,000	20,099.55	1.36451	500

Table 18.1 (*continued*)

Year	Maximum Taxable Amount	National Average Wage Index	1999 Index Factors	Earnings Required for a Credit
1990	$51,300	$21,027.98	1.30426	$520
1991	53,400	21,811.60	1.25740	540
1992	55,500	22,935.42	1.19579	570
1993	57,600	23,132.67	1.18560	590
1994	60,600	23,753.53	1.15461	620
1995	61,200	24,705.66	1.11011	630
1996	62,700	25,913.90	1.05835	640
1997	65,400	27,426.00	1.00000	670
1998	68,400		1.00000	700
1999	72,400		1.00000	740

Source: Social Security Administration.

The annual indexes are derived by dividing average wages earned at age sixty by the average wage in each previous year. For example, the earnings for a worker who turns sixty-two in 1999 are indexed through 1997, when average wages were $27,426.00. The index factor for 1996 is derived by dividing the average wage in 1997 ($27,426.00) by the average wage in 1976 ($25,913.90). The quotient equals 1.05835 and is shown in Table 18.1. Each annual index factor for 1999 is derived in this fashion, on the basis of 1997 average earnings. All the index factors for someone reaching sixty-two in 1999 for years dating back to 1951 are shown in Table 18.1. These factors are used in calculating average index monthly earnings for everyone turning sixty-two in 1999. They are thus only directly applicable to someone born in 1937. The index factors for someone born in earlier years would be smaller, but always equal to the ratio between average national wages when the person turned sixty and the average national wages in the year the earnings were generated. The index factors for people born after 1937 have not been determined yet, because they will not reach sixty-two until 2000 or beyond. As long as average wages continue to climb, the applicable index factors in future years will be larger than those for 1999. All index factors are always 1.0 or greater.

In calculating the AIME, only taxable earnings up to the maximum taxable amount in each year are considered. The actual amount of covered earnings for each year of a worker's career is multiplied by the index for his or her particular birth cohort. After multiplying each entry in the earnings history by the appropriate index factor, the Social Security Administration generates the individual's indexed earnings history. The next step is to calculate the average indexed monthly earnings, or AIME. First, the individual's thirty-five years of highest indexed earnings must be identified. These are the only years that count. If someone worked for forty-five years, the taxes she paid in the ten years with the lowest indexed earnings will not affect her retirement benefits. After determining the thirty-five years with the highest indexed earnings, the Social Security Administration calculates the individual's AIME by simply adding up the indexed earnings in those thirty-five years and dividing by 420. The divisor is 420 because that is the number of months in thirty-five years. If the potential retiree didn't work for thirty-five years, then some of the thirty-five years of highest indexed earnings will be entered as zeros. It is as simple as that. In order to qualify for any retirement benefit at all, one has to have at least forty quarters (that is, ten years) of covered employment (that is, forty credits). The final column of Table 18.1 shows the minimum amount of earnings for a quarter for it to count (that is, to generate a credit). Through 1977 you needed to earn $50 in covered employment for the quarter to "count." Since 1978, the number of credits you earn in a year (up to four) depends on your annual earnings. In 1999 each $740 in covered earnings generates a credit. It takes $2,960 in earnings in 1999 to earn the maximum number of four credits.

Once the AIME has been calculated, it is used to compute the primary insurance amount. Now, we are getting close to the answer—how much will the retiree get per month in initial benefits. The PIA is the amount that a single person would receive at the normal retirement age (currently sixty-five), but the benefit amounts for people in other circumstances (for example, married or retiring at a different age) can be determined directly from the PIA. The PIA formula for 1999 is (a) 90 percent of the first $505 of AIME, plus (b) 32 percent of AIME between $505 and $3,043, plus (c) 15 percent of the amount by which the AIME exceeds $3,043. The dollar figures in the PIA formula are indexed to the national average wage index and are likely to increase accordingly for years 2000 and beyond. There is no legislation on the books to change the percentages. Figure 18.1 plots the PIA formula.

Figure 18.1 plots only the PIA benefit level for AIMEs ranging up to $4,500, because the maximum possible AIME for someone retiring at age sixty-two in 1999 is $4,439. This is the AIME that someone would have if he earned more than the maximum taxable amount for each of the thirty-five years from 1964 to 1998. His PIA would be $1,476 per month. If the present benefit rules remain intact (which would require significant tax increases), the maximum PIA and maximum benefit will go up both because

Figure 18.1   Primary Insurance Amount for Different Levels of AIME

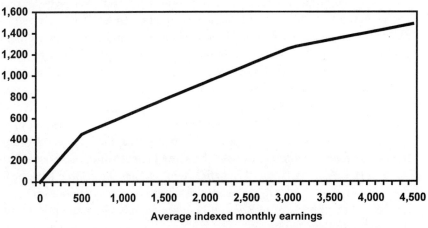

Source: Developed by the authors.

of general wage increases and because of the sharp increases in the maximum taxable amount that occurred in the late 1970s and early 1980s.

The normal retirement age (NRA) begins to advance in the year 2000; that is, the first cohort to face an increased NRA is the one whose members were born in 1938 and who, therefore, turn sixty-two in 2000. For them, the normal retirement age will be sixty-five and two months. It continues to progress at the pace of two months per year until it reaches sixty-six years for those born between 1943 and 1954; it advances again at two months per year for the 1955 to 1960 birth cohorts until the NRA becomes sixty-seven years for those born in 1960 and later. These changes in the NRA were all part of the 1983 Amendments just now beginning to go into effect.

For people who retire before the normal retirement age, the benefit is permanently reduced. The rate of reduction is five-ninths of 1 percent per month for each month that the benefits precede the NRA. For a single person retiring at sixty-two in 1999, the total reduction is 20 percent, meaning that the initial benefit will be 80 percent of the PIA. For people retiring later than sixty-five, their benefit is permanently increased, depending on the exact month of retirement. The rate of increase depends on the person's year of birth. For someone who is sixty-five in 1999, initial benefits increase 0.45833 percent for each month that the commencement of benefits is delayed. The rate of increase in benefits for delayed retirement will be greater for younger cohorts. For people born in 1942 and later, the increase for delayed retirement beyond the normal retirement age will be two-thirds of 1 percent per month, or 8 percent per year. The penalty for early retirement and the bonus for late retirement reflect the fact that early retirees are expected to collect benefits longer than late retirees. The early retirement adjustments are roughly fair actuarially now, and the late retirement adjustments will also be approximately fair for those born in 1942 or later.

Married couples have two choices. If both parties have qualifying covered working careers (that is, they both have forty credits), then they can both get their own benefits. That is, they have the option of being treated like two single people. On the other hand, if one of the spouses does not have a qualifying work record or has one but with a much lower PIA than the other spouse, he or she can get the same benefits due the spouse with the higher PIA. This "spousal benefit" requires that the couple have been married at least one year. How much the spouse receives depends on his or her age when first claiming spousal benefits. If that age is the normal retirement age, then the benefit is 50 percent of the PIA of the spouse (the member of the family with the higher PIA based on his own work record). The bottom line is that married couples have two choices: (1) their separate benefits based on their separate PIAs or (2) the higher PIA and the spousal benefit (50 percent of the higher PIA if the spouse first claims benefits at the normal retirement age; 37.5 percent of the higher PIA if the spouse first claims benefits at age sixty-two). There is a separate maximum family benefit, which applies to one-earner couples; however, the maximum is sufficiently high that it doesn't apply to many couples. There is no maximum for couples who claim their separate benefits.

There are at least two other circumstances worth examining. The first is the benefits for elderly widows and widowers. Elderly widows and widowers can receive 100 percent of the PIA of the deceased spouse if she or he begins receiving benefits at the normal retirement age. Of course, the widow or widower could also choose to receive benefits based on her or his own record, if that generates higher benefits. If the surviving spouse wants to start receiving benefits after age sixty but before the normal retirement age, then an actuarial reduction in the benefits is necessary. If the deceased spouse began receiving benefits before the normal retirement age, then the benefits of the surviving spouse will be reduced if they are based on the earnings record of the departed. If the couple was receiving benefits initially based on 150 percent of the worker's PIA, then the survivor will receive two-thirds as much as the couple was previously receiving. The determination of the benefits of widows and widowers is sufficiently complicated, however, that we cannot describe all the possible circumstances.

People lead complex lives, and this fact leads to many of the complexities of the current system. Nowhere is this complexity more evident than in the area of divorce. Several things must be true for a divorced person to be able to claim retirement benefits based on the contribution record of his or her former spouse. First, the marriage must have lasted at least ten years. The divorced spouse has no claim if the marriage lasted for less than ten years but may be able to claim benefits if the marriage was longer. In the pension business, such circumstances are called "cliff vesting." Second, a person who remarries gives up any claim on the benefits earned via their former spouse. Even here, however, there are exceptions. If the details regarding Social Security's treatment of divorce are of particular interest to you, there may be no substitute for a visit to your local Social Security office.

It is difficult to offer a simple picture of the level of generosity of the current program. For someone born in 1937 who worked full-time from 1964 through 1998 and earned more than the maximum taxable amount for every one of those thirty-five years, the PIA would be $1,476. No one born in 1937 could possibly have a higher PIA. If this sixty-two-year-old began receiving benefits in 1999 and he or she was single, then the initial monthly benefit would be 80 percent of $1,476, or $1,180.80 per month. Once initial benefits have been determined, future benefits are increased once per year by a factor reflecting price inflation. For a hypothetical person who turns sixty-two in 1999 and who just happened to earn the national average wage index amounts shown in Table 18.1 (for thirty-five years or longer), the PIA would be approximately $1,144 per month. Again, such an individual would have to wait until age sixty-five to start benefits to get the full PIA. At that point the replacement rate would be almost exactly 50 percent. For someone who had a long career and who made one-half the national average wage index amounts every year, the PIA would be $658 per month, and the replacement rate would be approximately 57.5 percent. Finally, someone who worked essentially full-time (two thousand hours per year) at the minimum wage for the years 1964 through 1998 would have a PIA of $616.40 per month. If that person were to start receiving benefits at age sixty-two, they would be $493.10 per month.

The current benefits deal is usually characterized as progressive because the replacement of preretirement earnings is higher for lower earners than it is for higher earners. This is due to the shape of the PIA formula shown in Figure 18.1. As we discussed earlier, the program is less progressive than it appears when it is examined on a lifetime basis. The primary reason for the decrease in progressivity is that people with low earnings tend to have shorter lives than those with higher incomes. They have a lower chance of collecting any retirement benefits and tend to receive them for a shorter interval once they have commenced. The reasons for the positive correlation between earnings and life expectancy are multiple, and the causality runs in both directions. People who experience poor health have periods of absence from the workforce and may have limited possibilities for promotion. So in such cases, poor health can lead to lower incomes. But lower incomes also can "cause" poor health. Behavior that harms health (particularly smoking) occurs more frequently in low-income households. And, of course, the poor often do not have access to the best medical care. How much shorter is the life expectancy of low-income individuals is not well known; the trend is a certainty, as is the fact that the differential mortality of rich and poor reduces the progressivity of Social Security.

A Nip Here, a Tuck There

With this general understanding of the current deal, it is possible to examine some of the proposals to bring the system back into balance. Remember, to bring the program into balance in the long run, a combination of tax increases or benefit cuts totaling approximately 30 percent are needed. Nonetheless, our political leaders and some of the program's advocates try to find ways to balance the system that won't hurt. Reducing Social Security benefits has to be one of the most dreaded of political actions. Not surprisingly, there is a great temptation to try to disguise a cut in benefits as something else.

One of the most common proposals for shoring up the finances of the Social Security system is to raise the normal retirement age. It also is easy to justify. In 1940, when Social Security benefits were first paid, the remaining life expectancies for sixty-five-year-olds were 11.9 years for men and 13.4 years for women. Today, the same remaining life expectancies are 15.5 years for men and 19.3 years for women. The improvements (3.6 years for men and 5.9 years for women) are a wonderful feature of the twentieth century in America. However, they naturally place a great deal of financial pressure on a program providing inflation-adjusted life annuities. The 1983 Amendments raised the retirement age, but the increase isn't scheduled to begin until the year 2000. By the time the scheduled adjustments are completed (in 2027), it is quite likely that life expectancies will have increased by another two years. One proposal that is bound to receive a lot of attention in this round of Social Security repairs is to speed up the advance and keep it going. For instance, the Individual Accounts proposal of the 1994–1996 Advisory Council on Social Security proposed to increase the normal

Figure 18.2   The Equivalence for Social Security of Advancing the
Normal Retirement Age and Reducing Benefits

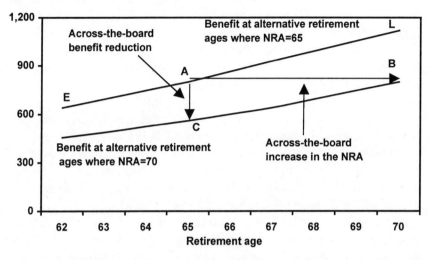

Monthly benefit level in dollars

Source: The actuarial adjustment factors used to calculate these alternative benefits are from the
Office of the Actuary, Social Security Administration.

retirement age to sixty-seven by 2011 and then to index it to increases in
life expectancy. This step alone would eliminate almost one-quarter of the
seventy-five-year actuarial deficit of the system. It also makes sense that
longer work lives accompany longer lifetimes. In fact the extra years of life
that each cohort of Americans has enjoyed have all been taken as extra retirement over the past sixty years. We probably cannot continue to afford
this policy.

Later in the book, we can and will argue the advantages and disadvan-
tages of raising the retirement age. Here we want to make one rather simple
point. Raising the retirement age is equivalent to lowering benefits. It isn't
"similar to" or "a form of," it is *exactly* the same thing. Politicians who favor
increasing the normal retirement age but oppose cutting Social Security
benefits are engaging in complete double-talk. We have already discussed
how monthly benefits are reduced for those who retire early and increased
for those who retire after the normal retirement age. The upper line in
Figure 18.2 shows the schedule of monthly benefit amounts and retirement
ages available to someone with a PIA of $800 per month. If this person
chooses to start receiving benefits at age sixty-five, then he or she will re-

ceive $800 a month; however, this person could also retire at age sixty-two and receive $640 per month (shown as point E) or she could choose any point on the line segment defined by points E and L. For instance, if the start of benefits is delayed until age seventy, the beginning benefit would be $1,120 per month (shown as point L).

Now consider what happens if the normal retirement age is advanced. In order to make the chart clear, consider a major increase in the NRA to age seventy. This means that a person would now have to be seventy in order to get his or her full PIA. The PIA formula would be left unchanged. Before the increase, someone would have gotten 140 percent of PIA by retiring at age seventy—the rule of two-thirds of 1 percent a month applies to those born in 1942 or later. The change from 140 percent of PIA to 100 percent (that is, the movement from point L to point B) is a dramatic decrease in benefits—about a 28.5 percent decrease, to be precise. It is not just the benefits at age seventy that are lower with the new schedule. They are lower for any retirement age. The new choice set is the lower rising line in Figure 18.2.

So far, we have said that we got to this new line or choice-set by moving the normal retirement age up from age sixty-five to age seventy. However, we could have gotten to the new regime by leaving the NRA at sixty-five and simply reducing benefits by about 28.5 percent. That is, we could have lowered the PIA formula so that this person would have received about $570 at age sixty-five (point C) rather than the $800 (point A) before the cut. That sounds pretty painful, right? But that is exactly what raising the retirement age does. It cuts monthly benefits for any retirement age. The bottom line is that distinguishing between cutting benefits and raising the retirement age is all about packaging. There is no real difference.[1]

Another popular reform is to increase the number of years that go into the calculation of the average indexed monthly earnings. Why should only the thirty-five years with the highest indexed earnings count? Why not raise the number of years in the AIME formula to thirty-eight or even forty? After all, many people have forty-year or even forty-five-year careers. Also, from an economic perspective, increasing the number of years that count would improve the connection between contributions and benefits. Despite these rationales, raising the number of years considered in the AIME formula is a benefit cut. We think that tough choices need to be made to fix Social Security, and we are not against making them. We are suggesting only that a cut in benefits be labeled and presented as such. If you include the highest thirty-eight years in the calculation of average indexed monthly earnings, obviously you are going to end up with a lower figure for the AIME amount than if you include only a person's best thirty-five years. The three additional years are by definition worse than the other thirty-five years and will drag the average down.[2] For some people, the extra three years will be zeros. For them, the AIME figure will be reduced by almost 8 percent.

The majority of people in this situation will be women who were out of the workforce for some years to raise children. They will particularly feel the burden of this particular type of benefit reduction. Raising the number of years in the calculation of the AIME has the sound of a "technical correction" to it. It is more than that. Simply raising the number of years to thirty-eight lowers overall retirement benefit payments of Social Security by about 3 percent and solves slightly more than 10 percent of the long-term financing problem. Like raising the retirement age, this measure is often presented as something other than a cut in benefits—we are just suggesting truth in packaging.

Another popular recommendation is to increase the taxation of Social Security benefits. In the 1994–1996 Advisory Council on Social Security this method was recommended by two of the factions submitting a plan. The rationale given for this in most of the council's deliberations was that it would treat Social Security benefits in a way equivalent to the treatment of private employer-sponsored pensions. In order to understand this, we must consider how the federal income tax system treats various kinds of retirement savings.

Table 18.2 shows the tax treatment for a worker's contribution to four different kinds of retirement plans which are widely available. In developing the example we assumed that our worker, George, was in a 40 percent marginal income tax bracket (combining federal and state income taxes) both at the time he made the contribution to the various plans and at the point he retired and received benefits. For the sake of simplicity, we are tracking only a single contribution and we are assuming that George makes it ten years before he retires. In each case, we assume that George is making his contribution on the basis of $1,000 of his gross, before-tax earnings. We are also assuming that the money contributed to the plan accrues interest at a rate of 10 percent per year until it is distributed when George retires. The first column of numbers in the table shows how that $1,000 of earnings is taxed if George makes his contribution to a 401(k) plan. In that case, the money going into the plan is not subject to the income tax when it is earned and contributed to the plan. None of the interest accruing to the plan is subjected to the income tax in the year in which it is earned. When the benefits are distributed, the original contribution and all of the interest are taxed at the 40 percent rate we postulated earlier. In this case, George

Table 18.2   Federal Income Tax Treatment of Employee Contributions
to Alternative Forms of Retirement Accounts

	401(k)	Traditional IRA	Roth IRA	Employer DB Plan
Initial worker earnings from which savings come	$1,000.00	$1,000.00	$1,000.00	$1,000.00
Income tax	—	—	400.00	400.00
Initial investment	1,000.00	1,000.00	600.00	600.00
Balance at end of year				
1	1,100.00	1,100.00	660.00	660.00
2	1,210.00	1,210.00	726.00	726.00
3	1,331.00	1,331.00	798.60	798.60
4	1,464.10	1,464.10	878.46	878.46
5	1,610.51	1,610.51	966.31	966.31
6	1,771.56	1,771.56	1,062.94	1,062.94
7	1,948.72	1,948.72	1,169.23	1,169.23
8	2,143.59	2,143.59	1,286.15	1,286.15
9	2,357.95	2,357.95	1,414.77	1,414.77
10	2,593.74	2,593.74	1,556.25	1,556.25
Taxes at distribution	1,037.50	1,037.50	0.00	222.50
Disposable benefit	$1,556.25	$1,556.25	$1,556.25	$1,333.75

Source: The example here was derived by the authors.

ends up with a net-of-tax amount of $1,556.25. The tax treatment of a traditional IRA is exactly the same as that of the 401(k).

The third column of numbers shows how George's contributions would work if he contributed his money to a Roth IRA. In this case, he has to pay taxes on his earnings before he contributes it to the plan, but he does not have to pay taxes on the distribution at the end. As you can see, it makes no difference under the assumptions we have set out whether George participates in a traditional IRA or a Roth IRA. In both cases he has precisely the same amount to spend at the end of the ten-year accumulation period. Policymakers adopted the Roth IRA because it still gave retirement savers the same benefit as traditional IRAs but allowed the federal government to collect its taxes on earnings in the period earned rather than when benefits are distributed. If you compounded the taxes collected under the Roth IRA by the 10 percent interest assumption we are using here, you would see that the value of the taxes collected by the government is actually the same as with the traditional IRAs or 401(k) plans. Some people prefer to participate in a traditional IRA over a Roth IRA because they believe that they will be in a lower marginal tax bracket when the distributions are made at retirement. If that happens, they can actually reduce their lifetime federal tax liability by participating in the traditional plan compared to the Roth plan.

The fourth column of numbers in Table 18.2 shows how employee contributions are treated when the employee has to contribute to a defined-benefit plan in the private sector. In this case, George would have to pay taxes on his earnings prior to making the contribution. At the end of his career he would also have to pay taxes on the total value of the distribution over and above the initial contribution which had already been taxed. In this regard, the tax treatment of employee contributions to defined-benefit (DB) plans is not nearly as generous as it is for defined-contribution plans. Some people argue that this is one of the reasons that defined-contribution plans have become so much more popular in recent years.

Paradoxically, employer contributions to both defined-benefit and defined-contribution plans are treated the same way employee contributions to 401(k)'s and traditional IRAs are treated. When the employer makes the contribution, it is with pretax money. The benefits accumulate tax-free until distribution, and then they are taxed as they are paid. The difference in the tax treatment of employer and employee contributions to defined-benefit plans creates a classic arbitrage situation. If George wants to make a sufficient contribution to his defined-benefit plan that he gets the same disposable income at retirement as he would get from participating in a 401(k) plan, he will have to contribute the net after-tax proceeds on $1,167 of earnings. If the employer makes the contribution, the net contribution against George's earnings is only $1,000. So the employer can give George the equivalent of $1,167 at a cost of only $1,000. Economists are convinced that these contributions are part of the compensation bill and that the employer is generally indifferent whether he pays George $1,000 in direct pay or puts it in a pension plan if George wants a pension. It just makes sense for the employer to pay the $1,000 into the plan rather than for the employee paying $1,167. Private sector employers have figured this out. In 1995, for example, less than 2 percent of all of the contributions made to private defined-benefit plans were employee contributions.

When the advocates of increased taxation of Social Security benefits on the advisory council were confronted with the fact that almost no contributions going into private sector retirement plans were treated the way they recommended, they changed the rationale to say that their proposal complied with the tax treatment of public plans. They used this rationale to propose that all Social Security benefits over and above the actual payroll taxes paid by workers should be taxed. They do not propose to tax the portion of benefits purchased with the employee's payroll tax, because employee payroll tax contributions are made from earnings that are taxed at the time they are earned.

This rationale for increasing the taxation of Social Security benefits is only partly correct. First of all, public employers have been moving in the same direction as their private counterparts in offering plans that work like 401(k) plans. So an increasing share of retirement contributions for public employees receives exactly the same tax treatment as the overwhelming majority of contributions to private plans. In addition, many public employers are not any more disposed to have their workers pay extra federal income taxes than are private employers. The law allows public employers essentially to work out a deal with their workers that gives them exactly the same tax treatment on Social Security contributions as private workers get on their 401(k)'s and IRAs. Specifically, they can trade employees direct cash wages for picking up both ends of the payroll tax. In that way, the employee gets the same opportunity to make efficient use of the wage budget. It is a benefit to both the employer and the employee. The point is that the proposal to increase the taxation of Social Security benefits is simply another way to reduce benefits. To hide behind the rationale that the proposed tax increase is consistent with the tax treatment of other retirement plans is largely misleading.

Another reduction in benefits that is often proposed is to reduce the indexation of benefits by the full consumer price index. The indexing of benefits according to the CPI was intended to give beneficiaries cost-of-living allowances that would prevent the purchasing power of their benefits from declining over time. The reason that some people advocate cutting the COLA is that there is evidence that the current CPI exaggerates true increases in the cost of living. The CPI is developed by doing periodic surveys of the purchasing habits of consumers. The Department of Labor (DOL) then constructs "market baskets" that represent the consumption patterns of the general population. Each month it sends people to retail outlets all over the country to price the items in the market baskets. Analysts then calculate from month to month how the price of the market basket changes. Social Security benefits are indexed by the annual changes in this index.

Critics of the CPI have pointed to two specific problems with the index. The first is that the CPI has traditionally not accounted for changes in the way people actually behave. If the price of beef goes up significantly, many people substitute chicken or something else for the beef that they ate at lower prices. Another problem with the index has been that it is hard to capture the extent to which prices for many products rise over time, because of improvements in the quality of the product. Finally, the consumption surveys that the DOL does as the base for developing the market baskets are often done a decade or more apart. Over the period of a decade, thousands of new products are introduced in the marketplace. People substitute one product for another. Maybe the cost of going out to the movies has gone up significantly in recent years. But the ability to watch them on a VCR at home may actually mean that people spend less on movies than they used to.

The DOL has been working to improve the CPI and contends that the criticisms now exaggerate its problems. Supporters of full Social Security indexation worry that proposals to reduce the CPI by some arbitrary amount will end up leading to reductions in the purchasing power of benefits. If that happens, people with long life expectancies in retirement will end up having larger benefit reductions than people who live a shorter length of time. Reductions in purchasing power would defeat the goal of providing people with a "real" annuity during their retirement period. There is particular concern that proposals to slash the CPI would reduce the benefits of women especially. With women's significantly longer life expectancy, it would no doubt have a larger effect on their lifetime benefits than it would on those of their male counterparts. Critics of proposals to limit COLAs point to the high rates of poverty among older single women as evidence that proposals of this sort are particularly ill-conceived. Such critics argue that if we need to reduce benefits, we would be better off doing it across the board by reducing initial benefits in one of the ways discussed earlier and then allowing the lower level of benefits to be maintained through full CPI indexation during retirement.

Some proposals have more transparent benefit reductions in them. For instance, the Individual Accounts plan advocated by two of the thirteen members of the 1994–1996 Advisory Council on Social Security called for modifying the percentages in the PIA formula. Instead of the current 90 percent, 32 percent, and 15 percent figures, the IA plan would gradually adopt a formula with 90 percent, 22.4 percent, and 10.5 percent. There can be no mistaking this for anything but a benefit cut, as is illustrated in Figure 18.3. The figure shows the current PIA formula and the new proposed one in the IA plan. It is a crystal-clear benefit cut for everyone except those with the lowest levels of average indexed monthly earnings. The magnitude of the long-term financial problems of the system is apparent if you note that this benefit cut solves only slightly more than half of our seventy-five-year actuarial deficit. The same IA plan called for raising the normal retirement age, increasing the number of years in the AIME formula, and

Figure 18.3   Current Law and Proposed PIAs Under the 1994–1996
Advisory Council on Social Security IA Plan

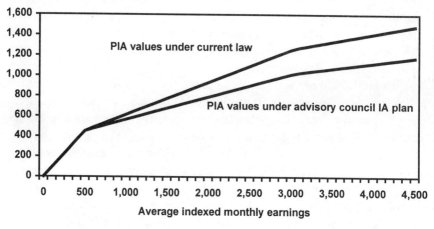

Source: Developed by the authors.

lowering spousal benefits, and it counted on a change in the measurement
of the CPI in ways that would result in calculation of future rates of inflation as lower by 0.21 percent per year. The point of all this is that balancing
Social Security's books requires either substantial benefit cuts or tax increases. The IA plan offsets these many benefit cuts with the proceeds of
a new mandatory individual account funded with a required contribution
from employers and employees totaling 1.6 percent of covered payroll.

No More Pulling Rabbits Out of the Hat

Restoring the solvency of Social Security is important, but it is not going
to be painless. If we stay within the general outlines of the current system,
then benefit cuts or tax increases totaling roughly 30 percent are required. If
we move to a new structure involving mandatory individual accounts, then
payroll deductions will have to be increased to fund these accounts. The
problem cannot be fixed for free. Finding the benefit cuts and the tax increases in some of the proposals can be difficult. Both politicians and advocates of the proposals have an incentive to disguise the painful aspects of
their plans. If you cannot find sizable doses of painful medicine in a particular proposal, you should be suspicious about whether it really has the goods
to solve the problem. Our motto has become "No more rabbits," referring

to one of the favorite tricks of magicians. It will not serve us well if we try to trick ourselves that we have solved Social Security's solvency problems with a few painless remedies. All we will have done is pass the problem along to our children and grandchildren with compounding interest.

Despite our plea for realism about the magnitude of the problem, we do think that some ways of dealing with it are better than others. For a number of reasons we favor relying less in the future on an unfunded defined-benefit Social Security system. First, patching this system up has proved extremely difficult. We tried it in 1977; that attempt failed rather completely. We tried it in 1983; that fix worked longer, but it too has fallen way short of its promises. Our best guess is that another round of nips and tucks (and they won't be small ones) will be about as effective as the previous two rounds. The basic problem is that our current system legislates benefits as if they can be delivered without risk. There are almost no real or financial assets, risky or otherwise, behind those promises. The only real asset of our current system is the taxes that future generations will pay. That is the all-important source of revenue for the system, but it is not without considerable risks, as we have seen over the last thirty years. It depends on such things as future fertility and mortality rates, labor-force participation rates and retirement behavior, and the growth in real wages. The future evolution of these key determinants in a pay-go system is extremely hard to predict. You can't offer "safe" benefits funded by risky revenue sources without running into one financial crisis after another. And that, of course, is exactly what we have experienced ever since Social Security reached maturity in the mid-1970s.

Chapter 19

A Framework for Understanding the Options for Social Security Reform

Social Security can be reformed in a variety of ways. Indeed, a broad range of proposals have already been widely discussed within policy circles, by the media, within academia, and by other interested parties. Some people want to stay with the current system and benefit levels at all costs. Others want to stay with the current approach but curtail the system to stay within current tax rates. Some want to do away with the system altogether and completely replace it with a system of individualized saving accounts. Yet others fall somewhere in between completely standing by the current system or completely replacing it.

Consideration of options for Social Security reform is plagued by a tendency to group approaches into broad categories. In the case of the reform options being discussed today, these categorizations are frequently misleading. In addition, descriptions of various options are being presented in ways intended to be dismissive or to inhibit public dialogue. When the press or political pundits describe a particular proposal as "radical," they often intend to discourage people with "centrist" tendencies from seriously considering the approach. The use of such terms cannot possibly lead to an informed discussion of options. In this chapter we lay out a framework for understanding what various options might achieve. Using this framework, we show how other countries have organized their retirement systems. And we then show how proposals to reform our own Social Security system can be classified within the framework. It makes it possible to classify virtually all of the proposals that are now on the table.

The Policy Field of Social Security Reform Options

Much of the current debate about Social Security reform is being conducted around the concept of "privatization." This term has come to have

Figure 19.1   Field of Social Security Policy Reform Options

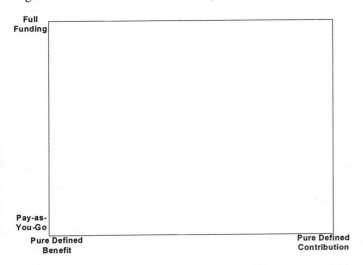

Source: Developed by the authors.

so many meanings that it is confusing the discussion about the various ways we might reform the first tier of our nation's retirement system. Part of the Social Security reform debate is over the desirability of funding the system more than is provided for under current law. That part of the debate flows directly out of the discussion that has permeated our story up to this point. Another part of the debate is whether we should continue to have complete dependence on the defined-benefit approach in current law or should move more toward a defined-contribution system. That part of the debate has received less attention thus far.

To help clarify the discussion about Social Security reform that is under way in this country today, we can think of the debate within the context of Figure 19.1. It defines the field of policy choices we face by bringing together the issues of funding and plan structure. Currently Social Security is a defined-benefit program financed largely on a pay-go basis. Within the field of policy choices, the program is now close to the southwest corner of the figure. Some policy advocates would have us stay there. For example, while Senators Daniel Moynihan and Bob Kerrey's proposal would allow workers to set up individual accounts voluntarily, it would adjust payroll tax rates and benefits within Social Security so that it ran on a strict pay-go basis in the future.

Others would have us maintain the current DB structure but attempt to fund it more than now. They propose partial funding because the interest on the accumulated fund would help lower the payroll taxes needed to pay future benefits. If their proposals were adopted, we would stay on the western boundary of the policy field but move north from the corner. The accumulation of funds, of course, would raise questions about what to do with the money. Higher average rates of return in the stock market relative to government bonds leads proponents of this approach to suggest that some of the proposed funding should be invested in equities. Many policy analysts oppose this approach because they do not believe the government can accumulate wealth to the extent implied, and if it did, they are concerned about governmental intrusion into private capital markets. We will consider the debate over whether to invest in equities inside or outside of Social Security in some detail in Chapter 21.

How Other Countries Have Organized Their Retirement Security Systems

Often the most compelling reason for doing something in one particular way is that "it is the way we have always done it." Another is that "it is the way everybody does it." One of the interesting things about the provision of retirement income security around the world is that many countries have changed their retirement systems significantly in recent years. And many of them no longer provide retirement income protection for their general working population in the fashion that we do in the United States.

The situation that the United States faces with the aging of its population is not particularly different from that faced by most countries around the world. The share of the population over age sixty in the United States today and projected up through 2030 is nearly identical to the share of the population over sixty in Australia, Canada, and New Zealand. Around 24 percent of the population in West European countries like Germany and Italy is over age sixty today, compared with around 17 percent in the United States. This differential is expected to persist through the first quarter of the twenty-first century as our populations age in lockstep. The population in Latin America is much younger than in the United States, with only 6 percent over age sixty in Mexico and Venezuela, about 9 percent in Chile, and 14 percent in Argentina. By 2030, the populations in these countries over age sixty are expected to make up 16 to 21 percent of the totals, compared with 28 percent in the United States. In Asia, the Japanese population is older than ours and aging rapidly. Today the percentage of Japanese over sixty is about 3 percentage points higher than in the United States. By 2010,

Figure 19.2   Location of Selected Nations on the Field of Social Security
Policy Options for Providing Retirement Income Security

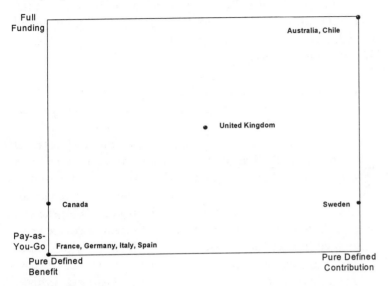

Source: Developed by the authors.

that differential is expected to swell to 10 percentage points. The developing countries in the Asian section of the Pacific Rim, like South Korea and
Malaysia, tend to have younger populations today than the United States
does but can expect to have populations over age sixty in proportions similar to the United States by 2030.[1] While some countries may have older or
younger populations than we do now, most are aging in a fashion similar to
ours. Many other countries with aging populations, however, are moving
more aggressively to control their social insurance programs for the elderly.

Turning back to the policy field that we have just described, we have
plotted where a number of countries are now positioned in that framework in Figure 19.2. There are still substantial numbers of countries in
the pure pay-go defined-benefit area. Many of these countries are facing
far more substantial challenges to their systems than we are. Their fertility rates tend to be lower than ours and their dependency rates higher.
In addition, these countries tend to have extremely generous benefits relative to ours.[2] The combination of high dependency ratios and high benefits
relative to wages means that these countries' national retirement plans are
generally considerably more expensive than ours. The present value of net
public pension liabilities—that is, the extent to which liabilities exceed as-

sets and projected future taxes—is equal to at least 100 percent of current gross domestic product in Japan, Germany, and France. In the United States that value is around 25 percent of GDP. By 2030, one estimate is that the unfunded liabilities in the United States, Germany, France, and Italy will equal their GDP. In Japan, they are projected to equal 300 percent of GDP by then.[3] Because these plans are similar in structure to ours, we will not describe them further here.

The Canadian pension system is shown in the field as being a defined-benefit plan but having some funding. Until 1998, the system was run largely on a pay-go basis. The accumulated fund behind the plan was equivalent to two years of benefit payments, quite similar to the U.S. Social Security system holdings. The Canadian system is a two-tier program with universal eligibility for the bottom tier but with a "claw-back" provision—that is, a means test—for retirees with substantial income. The second tier for the system is known as the Canadian Pension Plan (CPP). At the end of 1997, the contribution rate for the plan was 6.4 percent of covered pay. Legislation adopted in 1998 will increase the payroll tax to 9.9 percent of covered pay by 2003, after which point it is projected to be level. The payroll tax was not collected on the first $3,500 of covered earnings in 1998, nor on earnings above $36,900. The significant increase in the payroll tax under this legislation, coupled with some moderate benefit adjustments, was based on the estimate that the system's costs would reach 14.2 percent of covered pay by 2030. The accelerated increase in the tax and benefit modifications was an attempt to prefund some of the obligations that will accrue between now and 2030. The goal is to take advantage of the returns on accumulating assets to help defray some of the costs of the system as Canada's baby boom generation makes its claim on the system. In the coming years, the trust fund is projected to grow to roughly the equivalent of five years of benefits. The intent is to invest the funds in a diversified portfolio of securities in the hope of getting higher returns than on the government bonds in which the fund had been invested in historically.[4]

Sweden is shown in the figure as having a system with some funding but with retirement benefits provided purely from a defined-contribution environment. This is based on reforms adopted during 1998 and being phased in on a gradual basis. Their old plan was a pay-go-financed defined-benefit plan. People born in 1937 and earlier will receive their pension under the old system. Those born between 1938 and 1953 will receive part of their retirement benefit based on the old system and part on the new, because of a gradual phasing-out of the old benefit and a gradual phasing-in of the new. Those born in 1954 and later will receive benefits purely under the new system. The placement of Sweden on the policy field is a representation of where the retirement system will be once the new provisions are fully phased into operation.

Sweden's revised retirement system requires contributions of 18.5 percent of pay on earnings up to $37,000 per year. Of that, 16 percentage points of the contribution are used to finance current benefit payments to retirees. The extra 2.5 percentage points are contributed to a "premium reserve account" that will earn interest during a worker's career. The worker can choose an investment manager for his or her account. Since roughly 85 percent of the total contributions is still used to finance pay-go benefits, we have plotted Sweden's position only about 15 percent of the way up the pay-as-you-go versus fully funded dimension of the policy field. Workers' contributions under the pay-go element of the new system are credited to individual accounts based on each individual worker's level of earnings and taxes paid. The account is also credited with an interest accrual each year equal to the rate of growth of incomes in the economy. Since the contribution is actually spent to finance current benefits, these accounts are phantom accounts, in that they do not hold accumulating real wealth. Accounts of this sort are often called notional accounts. At retirement, a worker's individual account will be converted to an indexed annuity. The index is the average income growth in the economy. The size of the initial annuity will be based on the life expectancy of the birth cohort to which the worker belongs and his or her age at retirement.[5]

Sweden's old retirement plan was similar to the U.S. Social Security system in that it used the best years of earnings from a worker's career. In that regard, the benefit is calculated according to rules that have no simple or clear connection to a worker's contributions to the system. Sweden wanted a more direct link between contributions and benefits and eliminated most subsidization across the wage spectrum in its new approach. To the extent people have unsuccessful work careers, they have a supplemental pension supported by general tax revenues. People can retire as early as age sixty-one under the new system and will receive a benefit that is 72 percent of the benefit they would receive by waiting to age sixty-five to start taking their pension. If they wait until age seventy, their benefit would be 157 percent of the age sixty-five benefit. The incentives to work extra years are clearly stated and are there for workers to take or leave. In moving to a defined-contribution system of this sort, the effects of increasing life expectancy are automatically recognized by the system. The issue of setting normal retirement ages is also largely eliminated.

The United Kingdom is one of the few major developed economies in the world that does not face a serious long-term financing problem for its national retirement program. Whereas we mentioned earlier that several continental European countries and Japan have pension obligations in excess of current assets and projected revenues that are equivalent to their GDP, the projected difference between the United Kingdom's projected public pension revenues and liabilities between now and 2050 is about 5 percent of GDP.[6] We have depicted the United Kingdom as being somewhat in the middle of the policy field on social security provision and financing.

The United Kingdom has a two-tiered public retirement system with voluntary employer-sponsored pensions as the third tier. The bottom tier of the U.K. system is the Basic State Pension, an old-age benefit floor that everyone qualifies to receive. The benefit at the end of 1997 was around $100 per week, about 15 percent of the average wage for male full-time workers. The benefit is taxable as income. It grows over time with the rate of growth in prices rather than wages, so its replacement of workers' final earnings is declining over time. This feature is a significant reason the system's costs are under greater control than those in other developed countries running pay-go systems. The value of benefits in 2030 would be about 70 percent higher under wage indexing than price indexing of the system.[7]

The second tier of the U.K. system is called the Supplemental Earnings-Related Pension Scheme, or SERPS for short. The government allows workers to opt out of this second tier of their system, and about 83 percent do so. These workers are required to use employer-based pensions or personal pensions if they opt out of the state-provided system. In that regard, the SERPS program establishes the minimum benefits or contributions that must be provided for by workers who opt out of the state program. The upper earnings limit for coverage under the SERPS system is also indexed by increases in prices, and so the value of the SERPS pension will decline relative to wages in the future.[8]

The reason that we put the United Kingdom roughly in the middle of the policy field is that the benefits for workers who contract out of the state plan are funded. While some of these benefits are actually provided through employer-sponsored defined-benefit plans, the indexation provisions for benefits for workers who leave jobs prior to the end of their career make them essentially the equivalent of defined-contribution arrangements. In addition, the trend in the United Kingdom away from defined-benefit and toward defined-contribution plans at the employer level is following that in the United States. It is possible to quibble that we have the United Kingdom placed a little too low or too high on the funding scale, or too much toward the DB or DC ends of that dimension. The point is that it is well out in the middle of the policy field in its provision of retirement security to workers.

The approach to Social Security reform that has received by far the most attention from the press and policymakers around the world in recent years is that of Chile.[9] Chile's 1981 reform of its pay-go retirement plans was revolutionary at the time. The government basically transformed its pay-go-financed defined-benefit system into private individual retirement accounts that are mandatory, fully funded, fully vested, and completely portable. Because of its structure and nature, we place it in the upper-right-hand column of the policy field in Figure 19.2. Workers must contribute 10 percent of earnings to their retirement accounts. Currently, they can choose from a relatively narrow range of funds offered by highly regulated, specialized fund management companies. Workers are also required to purchase term life insurance and disability insurance, offered by the same pension managers. The combined contributions covering retirement, life and disability insurance, and administrative expenses are about 13 percent of payroll, roughly comparable to contributions in the U.S. system for retirement, survivors, and disability benefits. On retirement, Chileans can choose between a phased withdrawal of their account balances or an inflation-indexed annuity sold by insurance companies.

The new system has been extraordinarily successful, primarily because of the very high real rates of return, averaging about 14 percent per year since inception. Total assets in the private accounts have grown extremely rapidly from less than 1 percent of GDP in 1981 to 10 percent in 1985, 25 percent in 1990, and 43 percent in 1994. Private capital markets, relatively undeveloped before 1981, have flourished with the evolution of the pension system. As of 1994, the pension funds held 55 percent of all government bonds, 62 percent of mortgage bonds, 59 percent of corporate bonds, and 11 percent of corporate equities.[10] Current regulations restrict pension funds to holding less than 30 percent of their assets in equities and less than 12 percent in non-Chilean assets. These limits are likely to be eased in the future. It is worth noting that less than 2 percent of the assets are held externally. The Chilean gross rate of saving has gone from 9.4 percent of GDP in 1982 to 12.5 percent in 1984 and 18.9 percent in 1986 and has been at roughly 25 percent since 1988. Because the country was experiencing widespread changes and a massive privatization of basic industries, it is impossible to attribute the large increase in savings to the pension reforms alone. However, most analysts credit the pension system with a major role in increasing the rates of saving.

A number of special features of the Chilean reform deserve mention.

First, the demographics of Chile are sharply different from those of the United States or other developed countries, and this made the transition from a pay-go system to a funded system much easier. There were more than nine people of working age for each retiree in Chile in 1981, compared with about 3.25 currently in the United States. Second, the Chilean government was running a large fiscal surplus when it made the transition, and this allowed it to fund the costs of transition out of general government revenues. Third, the Chilean plan guarantees participants a minimum rate of return and a minimum pension, but the guarantees offer less than meets the eye. Basically, the Chilean taxpayers are putting a floor under the outcomes experienced by the Chilean pension participants. Of course, there is a very large overlap between the taxpaying population and the pension participant population. Presumably the risk inherent in the investments in the pension funds is still present in the economy, despite the "guarantees." Fourth, the very favorable returns on financial assets and the huge cash flows into pension funds may be interrelated. Thirteen years is still a short history for a national pension plan. There is a question about how such a scheme will fare when it is mature or when it faces the kind of aging population, and perhaps net withdrawals, that the United States is likely to face in 2020–2040. Finally, one shortcoming of the Chilean system is that it is relatively expensive to administer. Despite these qualifications, the Chilean pension reforms appear to have been a big success, and similar reforms have already been undertaken or are under consideration across much of Latin America and elsewhere around the world.

At least on the surface, Australia seems to have embarked on an equally significant reform but quite different program of retirement income provision. The basic Australian government pension system or Old-Age Pension as it is called, has been in operation for over eighty years. Today it provides a foundation and an important source of income for those individuals who have not had the opportunity or have failed to build up sufficient retirement savings. It is financed from general revenue taxes. The full pension payment under this "first pillar" of the retirement system represents approximately 25 percent of average weekly earnings.

The benefit provided under the Old-Age Pension is subject to a set of means tests. The first of these is an assets test. The assets test does not consider the value of an owned residence, and it also excludes additional assets from A-$125,750 for a single homeowner to A-$268,500 for a non-homeowning couple. For people with assets above the specified amount, the Old-Age Pension amount is reduced by A-$3 for every A-$1,000 of excess. There is also an income test. A single person with income of less than

A-$100 per fortnight or A-$176 for a couple will receive the maximum benefit. The benefit is reduced gradually, and no benefit is provided at income levels above A-$806.40 for a single person or $1,347.20 for a married couple.

During the 1980s, concerns arose about the cost of Australia's Old-Age Pension system because the high rates of qualification for benefits make it relatively expensive. Fully 81 percent of the elderly qualify for some benefits under the program, and two-thirds of them qualify for full benefits. The prospect that the baby boom generation was coming to retirement age sparked an interest in finding an alternative means of providing retirement security in the future. Today, approximately 15 percent of the population of Australia is over age sixty-five, and that percentage is expected to grow to 23 percent by 2030.[11] While the evolving demographics of the society pose a problem for the Old-Age Pension system, in 1983 the concern was that only 40 percent of the workforce was covered by voluntary employer-sponsored superannuation systems.

The Superannuation Guarantee Charge Act of 1992 was implemented in July of that year in Australia. The act required employers to contribute into complying superannuation funds a specified percentage of income in behalf of employees. In 1997 it was 6 percent of pay. On July 1, 1998, it went to 7 percent; it will be 8 percent as of July 1, 2000; and after July 1, 2002, it will be set at 9 percent of pay. In addition to employer contributions to plans, workers' reliance on the state for security against retirement needs appears to have declined sharply as the system has been implemented. The Research Unit of the Association of Superannuation Funds of Australia estimates that voluntary contributions made on top of mandated contributions equal an average 4 percent for all employees covered by compulsory superannuation. Today, roughly 91 percent of all workers are covered under the mandated superannuation programs. This second pillar of the retirement system will not eliminate the first pillar of the system for workers who fare badly in the labor market throughout much of their career but should eliminate the dependence on it over time for the majority of workers. That is why we have put Australia with Chile up in the top right hand corner of the policy field in Figure 19.2. Both countries have mandated a savings program to basically eliminate the public's dependence on pay-go systems, although both have kept a floor guarantee under their mandated savings programs.

A Range of Options for Reform in the United States

Much of the discussion about Social Security reform in the United States since early 1997 has been over whether we want to "privatize" our system

Figure 19.3   Location of Specific Proposals in the Field of Social
Security Policy Reform Options

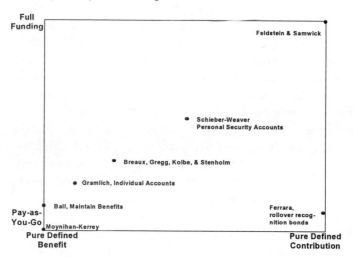

Source: Developed by the authors.

or not. This discussion of options generally confuses the concept of privatization with the proposed shift from a defined-benefit (DB) plan to a defined-contribution (DC) system. In fact, the range of options on the table is little different in their mapping from that of various countries around the world as mapped in Figure 19.2 and discussed above in the context of how specific countries have approached their national retirement systems. Figure 19.3 shows a range of specific policy proposals that have been developed for consideration of how we might reform our retirement system. This set of proposals is not meant to be exhaustive but to represent the range of options that we believe are on the table. By not including others, we do not mean to imply that they are not as deserving of consideration as the ones we have included. The point is to explain the nature and range of options, and we believe this set fully exemplifies both.

The plan shown as "Moynihan-Kerrey" is the proposal put forward by the two senators and discussed in detail in Chapter 20. It would move the system back to pure pay-as-you-go financing. The shift back to pay-go would result in a short-term reduction in the payroll tax followed by later increases. The payroll tax under this plan would get back to current rates by 2030 and rise moderately above current rates thereafter. This proposal depends heavily on a set of benefit reductions to achieve the ongoing balance between revenues and benefit costs.

The "Ball, Maintain Benefits" plan is the plan sponsored by Robert Ball during the 1994–1996 Advisory Council on Social Security,[12] as discussed in Chapter 17. Ball's plan called for the expanded taxation of Social Security benefits such that all benefits in excess of employee contributions would be included in taxable income for determining federal income taxes. In addition, he called for general revenues now going into the Medicare Hospital Insurance (HI) trust fund from the taxation of Social Security benefits to be diverted into the OASDI trust funds. Ball called for the expansion of coverage to include the last groups of state and local government workers not now covered under Social Security. He called for expanding the number of years of earnings that are used to compute benefits from thirty-five to thirty-eight. In 2045, he calls for an increase in the payroll tax rate equal to 1.6 percentage points. Finally, he called for investing 40 percent of the Social Security trust funds in the stock market.[13]

In the final days of deliberations by the 1994–1996 Advisory Council on Social Security, the group of six members that had been supporting Bob Ball in the development of his proposal had serious second thoughts about a number of its provisions. Specifically, the support for the increase in the number of years used in calculating benefits caused concerns because it meant some benefit reductions for people who had fewer than thirty-eight years of relatively full earnings. This was the only direct benefit reduction in the whole package, representing a benefit reduction on average of only about 3 percent for future beneficiaries. In addition, and far more seriously, the support for the investment in this plan of the trust funds in the stock market evaporated at the end of the council's deliberations. In the final report, the group of six members who had been supporting the development of the proposal ended up suggesting that the government should study and examine a plan that would invest some of the money in the markets.[14]

Ball's plan calls for somewhat more funding than under the current system, but for keeping the system purely a defined-benefit program. Because of that, we post Ball's plan somewhat above the bottom left-hand corner of the field of Social Security reform policy options shown in Figure 19.3. Mind you, the plan put forward by the Ball faction of the 1994–1996 Advisory Council on Social Security would not achieve nearly the level of funding shown in the figure. By failing to endorse the investment of trust fund assets in the stock market, they took off the table the single biggest money-maker in their whole proposal, accounting for nearly 40 percent of the total fixes in the package that Ball had molded.

Most of the provisions in the Ball proposal would have very little effect on the rate of national saving. Certainly, moving money from Medicare, which is facing its own financing crisis, to OASDI would not increase the rate of national saving. Moving state and local workers into Social Security would actually decrease the rate of national saving because in most cases we would end up substituting funded benefits under their existing retirement plans for Social Security benefits that would never come close to being funded at the level of these other plans. Increases in the payroll tax to support Social Security that would remain funded at a level significantly below full funding would be likely to lead to reductions in other savings for retirement, as discussed earlier, in Chapter 18. The rebalancing of the trust fund portfolio would not add savings either. Alan Greenspan put it this way when testifying before the Social Security Task Force of the Senate Budget Committee:

> As I have argued elsewhere, unless national saving increases, shifting Social Security trust funds to private securities, while likely increasing income in the Social Security system, will, to a first approximation, reduce non–Social Security retirement income to an offsetting degree. Without an increase in the savings flow, private pension and insurance funds, among other holders of private securities, presumably would be induced to sell higher-yielding stocks and private bonds to the Social Security retirement funds in exchange for lower-yielding U.S. treasuries. This could translate into higher premiums for life insurance and lower returns on other defined contribution retirement plans. This would not be an improvement to our overall retirement system.[15]

Possibly what is most amazing about the development of the Ball plan in the advisory council was the failure of this group of dyed-in-the-wool supporters of the existing Social Security system to find a way on which they could agree to bring it back into balance. If the adamant supporters of the system cannot come to agreement on how to reform the system within its traditional guidelines, the policy analysts and policymakers who see the current arrangement as flawed will have an even harder time embracing traditional reforms.

The "Gramlich, Individual Accounts" plan is the one sponsored by Edward Gramlich during the deliberations of the 1994–1996 advisory council, as discussed in the chapter on the council. He would scale back the current defined-benefit system to remain within the range of the current payroll tax rates and add a small individual-account system financed with mandatory worker contributions. Gramlich would achieve his reduction in benefits partially from across-the-board cuts gained by raising the retirement age and partially from further reductions targeted at higher earners. The latter reductions would be accomplished by adjusting the benefit formula. His plan calls for the normal retirement age to increase from sixty-five to sixty-seven at a rate of two months per year starting in the year 2000. After that it would increase at the rate of increase in life expectancy. The benefit formula would be adjusted such that the 32 percent factor applied against average indexed monthly earnings would be reduced gradually to 22.4 percent, and the 15 percent factor would be reduced to 10 percent. Gramlich called for the same tax treatment of Social Security benefits as Ball did. He also called for expanded coverage of state and local workers and for increasing the computation period to thirty-eight years.[16]

Gramlich was not comfortable with the level of benefits that resulted when he scaled back Social Security to stay within current legislated rates of 12.4 percent of covered payroll supporting the system. That is what motivated him to propose the system of individual accounts on top of his reduced level of Social Security benefits. The proposal calls for workers to contribute 1.6 percent of their covered payroll to individual accounts. The contributions would still go to Social Security, which would set up an administrative system to handle them. The government-run accounts would offer workers limited opportunities to diversify their investments over their working lives. In some regards, this would be like a government-run, mandatory 401(k) program. Benefits in this part of the system would be given the same tax treatment as most employer-sponsored retirement plans are now accorded.[17] Gramlich's plan would end up being somewhat more funded than Ball's and would have about 15 to 20 percent of the benefits provided through a defined-contribution mechanism as the system matured, which accounts for our placement of the plan in Figure 19.3. Gramlich and one other member of the 1994–1996 Advisory Council on Social Security supported this plan.

The next plan, slightly higher and to the right of Gramlich's, the "Breaux, Gregg, Kolbe, & Stenholm" (BGKS) plan, developed by the National Commission on Retirement Policy, a group organized by the Center for Strategic and International Studies (CSIS) in Washington, D.C. The label in Figure 19.3 relates to Senators John Breaux, a Democrat from Louisiana, and Judd Gregg, a Republican from New Hampshire, and Representatives Jim Kolbe, a Republican from Arizona, and Charles Stenholm, a Democrat from Texas, who served as co-chairmen of the CSIS panel. They have also introduced legislation incorporating the elements of the proposals put forward in the CSIS package.

In certain regards, the BGKS proposal is similar to the Gramlich IA plan.

The BGKS plan includes individual accounts that would be centrally managed through the government. Their contribution rate to these accounts would be 2 percent of covered pay rather than the 1.6 percent that Gramlich supports. Both proposals would rebalance Social Security largely depending on benefit reductions targeted more at the workers with higher earnings than at those at lower levels. There are two primary differences between the two proposals. The first is that the BGKS proposal has a minimum-benefit guarantee tied to the poverty level, such that a worker with 20 years of covered earnings would get a benefit at least equal to 60 percent of the poverty line. This minimum-benefit guarantee would increase 2 percent per year up to forty years of covered employment, at which point it would reach 100 percent of the poverty line. Gramlich did not include such a provision in his recommendations. The second major difference between the two is that the BGKS would cut average Social Security benefits more than Gramlich would, primarily through more-accelerated increases in the retirement age. The greater reduction in benefits that would result from this provision would fund the individual account in the BGKS plan.[18]

We include the BGKS plan in this description of reform options because of the important distinction between it and the Gramlich plan in the way the system can be reformed to include some level of individual account. Gramlich's individual account is an add-on to the current system, in that he would require workers to contribute an extra 1.6 percent of covered pay, over and above what they contribute now. The BGKS plan, on the other hand, proposes to fund the individual account on the basis of benefits "carved out" of the existing system. The difference between the two plans may not seem very significant if you don't pay attention to how the individual accounts are financed. The Gramlich plan should, on average, provide bigger benefits down the road than the BGKS because it costs 1.6 percent more of covered payroll. The BGKS plan will make some of that up by having 2 percent, versus 1.6 percent, go into a funded account. But the difference in the amount going into the individual account is not likely to be enough to make up for the differences in the OASDI benefits coming out of the remaining element of the traditional system.

We have put the BGKS plan above and to the right of the Gramlich plan because the individual account would be financed by 2 percent of covered wages out of the total 12.4 percent to finance the system. In other words, 16 percent of total contributions would be going into funded individual accounts. In the Gramlich plan, only 1.6 percent of covered pay out of total contributions of 14 percent of covered pay would be going to the individual accounts. In this case, the individual-account contribution is only 11 percent of the total.

The "Schieber-Weaver, Personal Security Accounts" plan is the PSA plan developed by Sylvester Schieber and Carolyn Weaver during the deliberations of the 1994–1996 Advisory Council on Social Security. This plan calls for a combination of carve-outs and add-ons relative to the current system. The plan would restructure the Social Security system significantly. It would leave disability and early-survivor benefits within the existing framework. It would split the retirement portion of the current system in half. In other words, 5 percent of covered payroll now available to support retirement benefits in Social Security would still go to the system. The other 5 percent of covered earnings would go into individual accounts. Under the PSA plan, the retirement benefit provided through Social Security would be a flat benefit. This benefit was intended to finance the redistributive "adequacy" aspect of the new system. The benefits earned through the individual accounts were intended to finance the "equity" aspect of the new system. The members of the advisory council supporting the PSA felt that the internal Social Security benefit needed to be flat to protect workers at the bottom end of the earnings distribution. Indeed, this type of benefit then becomes a true protection against the probability of a bad labor market outcome. The motivation for making the first-tier benefit in the PSA plan flat is exactly the same as the motivation in Gramlich and BGKS for targeting benefit cuts more at workers with higher wages than at those lower in the distribution scale.[19]

The PSA plan called for increasing retirement ages along the lines included in the Gramlich plan. It also called for increasing coverage to include the remaining state and local workers outside the system. In the case of the PSA, the partial shift from a government-funded plan to the PSA would not have the adverse effects on retirement funding that would exist in Ball's or Gramlich's plan. Having all workers participate in the redistributive first tier of the PSA plan also seems equitable, given that 98 percent of the total workforce has been forced to participate in such a system.

The PSA plan is quite explicit in stating that there are transitional costs associated with a shift from our current pay-go system to a system that is significantly funded. If we wish to do more funding than we have in the past, someone has to put some money into the bank. But that feature of the PSA has nothing to do with the shift from a pure defined-benefit approach to providing Social Security to one that includes a combination of DB and DC elements. The added contributions come because of the added funding. In developing the PSA, Schieber and Weaver insisted that the costs of their proposal should be as clearly stated as possible. They proposed a transition financing mechanism of 1.52 percent of payroll to handle the costs of changeover from the existing system. At the end of seventy years, this would have completely financed the transition, with more than half of the total retirement system being fully funded at that time. The PSA plan would provide roughly half of total benefits through a defined-benefit approach and half through defined-contribution accounts. The combination of the added funding and the rough splitting of the DB and DC components is the reason we put the PSA plan in the middle of the policy field in Figure 19.3.

In the earlier discussion about the way that various countries around the world have organized their provision of retirement security, we mentioned the interesting approach that Sweden has taken. Certainly, in revising our own system we could do something like what Sweden has done, but some critics would still find fault with such a system on at least two grounds. The first is that the system is still being operated on a pay-go basis. The second is that the retirement system is still being operated through the government. Some policy analysts believe the government ought to withdraw completely from the retirement business, except for providing welfare benefits for people at the very bottom of the economic ladder. One of the analysts who feel this way is Peter Ferrara, who has worked on Social Security reform for years for the Cato Institute in Washington, D.C. Ferrara has proposed the use of recognition bonds as a mechanism for the government to get out of the Social Security business almost immediately. Such bonds would be issued to people on the basis of their accrued benefits under the existing system. He argues that it would not have to be a dollar-for-dollar conversion of benefits accrued under the current system to bond value, because workers still in the system could divert their future payroll taxes to invest in financial assets that would generate higher returns than in the current system.[20]

If we took Ferrara's model, which calls for issuing workers a government bond related to their accumulated benefits in Social Security and shutting the Social Security system down, we could create a system something along the lines of Sweden's, but without the government's having to play any managerial role at all. Individual workers would hold their own bonds and cash them when they reached retirement age. If the government simply issued new bonds to refinance the bonds being cashed, we could roll forward the current unfunded liabilities in the system indefinitely. John Geanakoplos, Olivia Mitchell, and Stephen Zeldes have looked into this type of potential reform financing. Their conclusion is that transforming our Social Security system in such a fashion would not garner us any added economic benefits over continuing to run the current system on a pay-go basis.[21] The Ferrara approach, with perpetual refinancing of the recognition bonds as they come due, would result in a system located toward the bottom right-hand corner of the policy field depicted in Figure 19.3.

Finishing out the set of plans that are shown in Figure 19.3 is the plan in the upper-right-hand corner of the policy field labeled Feldstein & Samwick.[22] Martin Feldstein and Andrew Samwick are economics professors and members of the National Bureau of Economic Research. They estimate that the long-term implicit rates of return are so poor that our existing Social Security system could be replaced with a funded system that would cost about 2 percent of payroll—no, it is not a typing error, we meant "two," as in 2 percent. In developing their analysis, they assumed that added saving from funding would be invested and "earn a real rate of return for the nation that is equal to the pretax marginal product of capital. For the past thirty-five years, this has averaged slightly more than 9 percent."[23]

In devising their plan, Feldstein and Samwick assumed that contributions to private accounts would be phased in over a twenty-five-year period. As the benefits begin to flow out of the new funded accounts, benefits from the old pay-go system would be phased out. In their analysis, the authors acknowledge that their baseline calculations did not take into account the variability of rates of return over time or the problem of buying actuarially fair annuities. They suggest that the risks associated with these contingencies would require somewhat higher savings rates than their baseline assumptions implied. Although they did not provide specific estimates of how much would be required, they did observe that preliminary simulations suggested it would still be significantly less than the 12.4 percent required to finance the current system.[24]

One problem that Feldstein and Samwick point out in their analysis is that of getting from here to there, or from today's pay-go system to one that is fully funded and providing benefits comparable to those from the current system. The authors of the plan estimated that during the transition to their proposed system the early cohorts would incur some small loss on their overall contributions to the combined systems. For the first group it would be around 2 percent of covered payroll. These added costs would persist but would decline gradually for about thirty-five years and then be eliminated.[25] The point that Feldstein and Samwick make is that there is no free way to go from pay-go to funding.

The estimated transition costs that would be entailed in implementing the PSA proposal has been the subject of significant criticism of the plan, but they are not unique to it. Every proposal to reform Social Security to bring it back into balance, no matter what the approach, has significant transitional costs associated with it because our starting point is that the current system is underfunded to the tune of $3 trillion. In the Gramlich IA plan, part of the transition price is in the reduction of benefits relative to current law. Such benefit reductions are just as much a cost as tax increases. The other part of the transition cost in the IA plan is the added contribution of 1.6 percent imposed on workers. In the BGKS plan the transition price is all covered through benefit reductions. In the Kerrey-Moynihan plan the transition price is primarily one of benefit reductions. Even to "maintain benefits," Bob Ball is ultimately going to have to come up with a way to raise significant new revenues over those mandated in current law. He first has to raise $3 trillion to cover existing unfunded liabilities. Then he is going to have to raise even more revenue if he wants to create added funding that will add to the levels of national savings. Otherwise, as Alan Greenspan points out, his financing proposal will do nothing to lessen the burden the baby boomers' retirement will place on future generations. To argue that any of these plans do not have transition costs associated with them is simply to be disingenuous.

Thinking About Reforms Within the Framework

The presentation of options within the framework laid out here does not answer questions about many of the details of specific options. For example, the Gramlich IA plan in Figure 19.3 calls for the government to run the individual accounts. The Schieber-Weaver PSA plan would allow workers to invest their accounts the way they do their 401(k)'s or their IRAs. The fact of the matter is that these are technical details peculiar to specific proposals. How they might be resolved would depend on a host of factors that we will take up later. They are not crucial at this point for understanding what the various proposals are attempting to achieve. The framework is completely adequate to help explain how virtually all proposals now on the table would address the issues of funding and the relative roles of defined-benefit and defined-contribution approaches to achieving it.

Relying on this framework offers no optimal solution to the Social Security reform conundrum that we face. But it does begin to allow an analysis of reform options on the basis of specific sets of principles and assumptions. Before considering the desirability of specific proposals, it is important to identify the principles and assumptions that are relevant to devising and evaluating reform options. The broad range of proposals now on the table implies that the principles and assumptions that various reformers advocate are not universally embraced. We suspect, however, that much of the opposition to specific reform options has been the result of people's not looking closely at what they might achieve. Part of the problem is that people are often put off by mischaracterizations of specific proposals rather than by disagreement with the principles and assumptions behind them. In the next two chapters, we look at some of the issues raised by two general approaches to reform. First, in Chapter 20, we look at issues raised by reverting to a pure pay-go approach to Social Security funding.

Chapter 20

The Return to Pay-Go Financing

One possible approach to Social Security reform is to return to the pure pay-go financing that was advocated by many early policymakers and ultimately cast into law in 1972. In this chapter we look at the underlying motivations for returning to pay-go financing now and what the implications of such a policy would be.

Why We Might Want to Use Pay-Go Financing

In Chapter 17 we summarized a debate that persisted throughout the deliberations of the 1994–1996 Advisory Council on Social Security over whether the accumulations in the Social Security trust funds represented real savings or not. In that debate, Robert Ball argued that trust fund accumulations represented real funding and thus a contribution to national savings. Several people making presentations to the advisory council concluded otherwise. This is a very old debate, spanning virtually the whole life of the Social Security Act.

In 1937 Senator Arthur Vandenberg argued that the proceeds of workers' payroll taxes "are currently diverted to foot the general bills of the Government." He went on to trace the nature of his assertion by following the collection of a billion dollars in payroll taxes.

> The Treasury collects the billion in pay-roll taxes. . . . The Treasury gets a billion in cash. It goes into the general fund. . . . Congress then takes it out of the Treasury by appropriating a billion to the reserve. . . . So the Social Security Board hands the billion in cash back to the Secretary of the Treasury and takes from him a special . . . IOU. . . . The Secretary of the Treasury has the billion of money. . . .

He can use the billion either to retire regular Government-debt obligations in the general market or . . . he can apply it on his current operating deficit. As things are now going, we shall have deficits. . . .

What has happened, in plain language, is that the pay-roll taxes for this branch of social security have been used to ease the contemporary burden of the general public debt or to render painless another billion of current Government spending, while the old-age pension fund gets a promise-to-pay which another generation of our grandsons and granddaughters can wrestle with, decades hence.

It is one of the slickest arrangements ever invented. It fits particularly well into the scheme of things when the Federal Government is on a perpetual spending spree. It provides a new source of current revenue, which while involving a bookkeeping debit, providentially eases the immediate burden of meeting current debts and deficits.[1]

Arthur Altmeyer at the Social Security Board saw it differently. In response to a set of questions about funding that Senator Vandenberg had sent him in 1943, Altmeyer responded:

The social security contributor benefits by increased contributions and their investment in two very important ways. First, because the collection and investment of these contributions at this time help to combat inflation. . . .

The second reason why social security contributors benefit from this increase in rates is that future annual government expenditures will be proportionately lower. This is because the government debt in the hands of banks and other private investors will be that much less. Or, putting it another way, the Government will pay to the Trust Fund what it would otherwise have been obliged to pay to those banks and other private investors. In other words, instead of having to make two payments—one to the Trust Fund and another to the banks, the government will only have to make the one payment to the Trust Fund.

Some people have said that the fact that the Government will be required to levy taxes to redeem the Government obligations issued to the Trust Fund means that the social security contributors are being taxed twice for the same purpose. This, as you know, is not true. The truth is that the social security contributors are taxed only once to pay for their benefits when they make their regular contributions. As taxpayers they may also be obliged to pay taxes to redeem Government obligations issued to the Trust Fund but when they do they are paying for the cost of the war and not for the cost of social security benefits. They would have to pay these taxes to cover the cost of the war whether the bonds are sold to the Trust Fund or to individuals or to financial institutions.[2]

Very few people begrudged the government its borrowing to help finance the military effort during World War II. But the question of what the government has been doing with the accumulating Social Security trust funds continues in more modern times. When Barry Bosworth from the Brookings Institution made his presentation to the 1994–1996 Advisory Council on Social Security on increasing saving through Social Security, he claimed that policymakers had been "playing games" with the funds. He used an analogy in which parents set up a savings account to finance college tuition for their children but keep going in and borrowing from the fund and placing an IOU in it to represent the amount borrowed. That, he said, was exactly what the government was doing with the Social Security fund. "It just takes the Social Security surplus and makes it available for other funds and uses it to finance our consumption."[3] He admitted that today's workers would try to reclaim the trust fund accumulation when they reach retirement age. But he argued the contributions were being spent to finance current consumption for current generations of taxpayers, not saved.

Bob Ball did not buy Bosworth's assessment or that of several others presenting to the advisory council. He claimed that "it's a political judgment as to whether Social Security isn't already contributing to savings by reason of the fact that it has reduced the government's dissaving, if you think that the Congress would not have come any closer to balancing the budget anyway."[4] Within the advisory council there was finally agreement that the issue could not be resolved. But that does not mean that both perspectives don't get rolled into contemporary policy debates.

In August 1998, the Senate Finance Committee held hearings on retirement income policy in the United States. At the opening session of the hearing, Ken Apfel, the commissioner of the Social Security Administration, testified. In that session, Apfel argued that the payroll tax revenues in excess of benefits now coming into the program must be saved so the system remains "solvent" until 2032 rather than 2020. Senator Robert Kerrey said in response:

> We are not prefunding. . . . Are we holding the money in reserve someplace? We are not prefunding! The idea in 1983 was that we would prefund the baby boomers. We began to use it immediately for the expenditures of general government. We didn't prefund anything. What we are doing is asking people who get paid by the hour to shoul-

der a disproportionate share of deficit reduction. That's what we're doing! And the beneficiaries on the other hand, they suffer under the illusion inflicted by us very often, that they have a little savings account back here. They are just getting back what they paid in. They don't understand that it's just a transfer from people that are being taxed at 12.4 percent.[5]

Apfel replied that one of the biggest issues facing the Social Security system was whether there should be a significant amount of prefunding or whether the financing should be returned to the pay-as-you-go basis. The exchange between Commissioner Apfel and Senator Kerrey in 1998 was an eerie echo of those between Commissioner Altmeyer and Senator Vandenberg more than a half-century earlier. The inability to certify that funding through this centralized mechanism is true funding has led many policy analysts to search for another way.

Two groups of Social Security policy analysts and policymakers have come to the conclusion that the federal government cannot successfully fund Social Security as it is now configured. One group advocates that we return the system to pure pay-go financing. That approach to Social Security financing has significant implications for program participants. The other group advocates that we change the system so the funding can be carried on outside government beyond its ability to divert Social Security funding into spending programs that finance current consumption. That approach to Social Security policy, which will be analyzed in Chapter 21, also has significant implications for program participants.

Going Back to Pay-as-You-Go Financing

After the 1983 Amendments, it looked as if there would be substantial funding for the baby boomers' retirement claim on Social Security. The initial funding estimate developed just after the passage of the 1983 Amendments has been repeatedly revised downward. Despite the downward adjustment in long-term funding projections, the trust funds have grown fairly rapidly since 1983. At the end of 1998 the Social Security funds held around $760 billion. This may seem like a lot of money; in fact, it is not, by comparison with the system's liabilities. It is roughly the equivalent of two years of benefits.[6]

Over the years, a general consensus has developed that running Social Security on a pay-go basis does require that some contingency fund be accumulated. Most people familiar with the program believe the contingency fund should be roughly the equivalent of one year's worth of benefits, significantly less than that put forward in the Morgenthau rule of 1939. The reason the contingency fund is needed is that variations in the economy's performance make running the system purely on a pay-go basis impossible. For example, during economic downturns, the typical increase in unemployment means that tax collections are reduced. In addition, people on the cusp of retirement tend to retire at higher rates than during boom times and thus drive up the number of beneficiaries. Both of these trends would have an immediate adverse effect on the cost of the program if it were being run on a pure pay-go basis. If the program were run that way, economic downturns would require immediate increases in the payroll tax, which would act as a further damper on the economy. With the contingency fund, such economic variations can be weathered, and the system tends to have a generally expansionary rather than contracting effect on the economy over the business cycle. Given that the trust funds currently hold roughly two years' worth of benefits, while only one year's worth of benefits is required to meet the contingency fund test, the system is funded above pay-go status by the equivalent of around one year's worth of benefits.

Not only does the trust fund hold more than most people regard to be the required contingency fund for adequate funding on a pay-go basis; it also took in about $100 billion more in revenue, counting interest, than it paid out in the form of benefits during 1998.[7] If the contingency requirements have already been met and the program is taking in more than it needs to meet current benefit obligations, it presents policymakers advocating a return to pay-go financing with the opportunity to offer a payroll tax cut immediately. This is shown in Figure 20.1. In the figure we plot the cost rate minus the income rate, both stated as a percentage of covered payroll as based on the Social Security actuaries' projections in 1998. The cost rate is simply the level of benefits and administrative expenses stated as a percentage of covered payroll under current law. The income rate is the level of projected revenues stated as a percentage of covered payroll.

The difference in the cost rate and the income rate in Figure 20.1 is roughly the change in the payroll tax that would be needed to pay out benefits under current law on a pay-go basis in the future. Where numbers represented by the bars are negative, the figure suggests that we could cut the payroll tax relative to current law. Where they are positive, it suggests that the payroll tax would have to be raised. In fact, the potential for cutting the payroll tax in the early years shown in the figure is underestimated, because we have more money in the trust funds today than the contingency reserve would require.

Figure 20.1   Current Social Security Cost Rate Minus Income Rate
Under Current Law

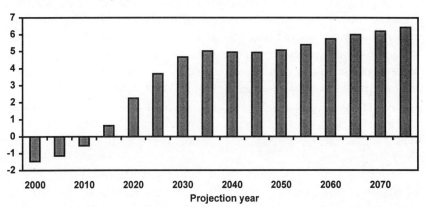

Percent of covered payroll

Source: 1998 Annual Report of the Board of Trustees of the Federal Old-Age and Survivors Insurance and Disability Insurance Trust Funds, p. 169.

There is another way to consider Figure 20.1. The bars also can be in-terpreted as representing how much benefits would have to change if we wanted to run the system on a pay-go basis at current tax rates. From this perspective, a bar with a negative value implies that benefits could be in-creased and bars with a positive value imply that they would have to be reduced. No matter which perspective one takes, the adjustments to the system would have to be very large to accommodate the retirement of the baby boom generation. The cost rate for the program in 2030 is 36 percent greater under projections based on current law than the income rate.

Changing the Tax Schedule to Support Pay-Go

Staying with current law benefits while moving to pay-go financing would require added tax revenues of 20 percent above projections based on current law in 2020, 30 percent by 2025, and 40 percent by 2030. To put this in context, anyone of age thirty or below today would face a payroll tax rate in 2030 that is 40 percent higher than we are currently paying. Anyone who has yet to start kindergarten would face a whole career of payroll tax rates that we are not willing to levy on ourselves today. If the current projections on the payroll tax needed to support the Medicare Hospital Insurance program are added in, the increase in the tax revenues needed to support the two programs would be 57 percent higher in 2030 than it is today.[8] This is a payroll tax rate that is 8.9 percentage points higher than what we now pay.

The prospect of raising the payroll tax rate by the order of magnitude necessary to preserve Social Security in a pay-go financing scenario seems remote. Looking back to the deliberations at the 1994–1996 Advisory Council discussed in Chapter 17, the most ardent supporters of Social Security were not even willing to advocate an increase in the payroll tax of 2 percentage points. But let's assume for a minute that policymakers did decide to raise the payroll tax along the lines implied by Figure 20.1 in order to preserve the standards of living of retirees. We are convinced that in the long run such a policy would nonetheless lead to reduced standards of living for retirees.

Economists generally think about retirement security in the context of workers' attempting to accumulate sufficient retirement resources so they can maintain preretirement standards of living once they quit working. This model is consistent with the aspirations of workers. In surveys about retirement goals, two-thirds or more of the respondents generally say that they wish to maintain their current living standards. To the extent that Social Security is a tax on earnings, it lowers the standard of living that workers can achieve during their working career because it lowers their disposable income. If we raise the payroll tax on workers, we further lower their preretirement standard of living.

For the vast majority of workers, Social Security benefits are not large enough in and of themselves to support a standard of living in retirement that is equivalent to what beneficiaries achieved during their working lives. In order to make up the difference between what Social Security provides and what it takes to maintain preretirement living standards, workers have to save some of their earnings. Some of them do this on their own. Others do it through employer-sponsored pension and savings plans. Others do it through a combination of employer-sponsored plans and personal savings outside such plans. The saving that workers do during their working career also reduces the preretirement standard of living because the portion of wages that is saved is not available to the worker to consume. In this regard, the interaction between personal saving and the level of the payroll tax is important.

To see how this works, consider a hypothetical case where a worker, Jane, earns $30,000 per year. For the sake of simplicity, we will assume that her pay remains constant over time. Assume that Jane pays $3,000 per year in payroll taxes. Once again, for the sake of simplicity, assume that beyond the payroll tax, Jane doesn't have to pay any other taxes on her income, either before or after she quits working. While Jane is working, let us assume that she has $3,000 in work-related expenses that she would not incur if she were not working. These expenses include such things as her commuting costs to get back and forth to work, the work wardrobe that she has to maintain, and the added costs for eating away from home during her workdays.

After Jane pays her payroll taxes and other work-related expenses, she is left with $24,000 to spend on consumer goods or to save. As Jane looks to the future and considers the way that Social Security works, she estimates that when she gets to retirement she will receive a Social Security benefit of $15,000 per year. For the sake of simplicity, we will assume that Jane's Social Security benefits are not taxed when she retires. If she doesn't save anything during her working career to supplement Social Security, when Jane retires, her disposable income will drop from $24,000 per year to $15,000. But let's assume that Jane decides to save $1,000 per year over her working career, invests it, and accumulates sufficient assets that when she retires, she can buy a supplemental annuity that pays her an annual benefit of $8,000 for the remainder of her life. By doing this, Jane can balance her preretirement and her postretirement standard of living. The savings of $1,000 per year reduces her preretirement standard of living to $23,000 per year, and the annuity of $8,000 per year added to her Social Security benefit of $15,000 per year gives her a total retirement income of $23,000.

Now let's assume that as Jane is embarking on her career, her payroll taxes go up from $3,000 to $4,000 per year because policymakers decide that the added taxes are needed to make sure they can actually pay Jane $15,000 per year in Social Security benefits when she retires. Her $4,000 in payroll taxes plus her $3,000 in other work-related expenses reduce her disposable preretirement income from $24,000 before the tax increase to $23,000 after it. If Jane saved $1,000 per year to purchase an annuity of $8,000 per year when she retires, her preretirement disposable income would be $22,000. But her combined annuity and Social Security income would be worth $23,000 in her retirement. So to rebalance things between the period before she retires and the period after, Jane would reduce her savings somewhat, let's say to $870 per year that will allow her to purchase an annuity at retirement of $7,130 per year. Jane's preretirement disposable income in this case is $22,130—her disposable earnings of $23,000 minus the $870 that she saves. Her postretirement disposable income is also $22,130, the sum of her Social Security benefit of $15,000 and her annuity of $7,130. Once again her preretirement and postretirement standards of living are the same. The moral of this story, however, is that by raising Jane's payroll taxes we actually reduce her need to save. Before taxes were raised, she saved $1,000 per year, but afterward only $870. In addition, the move to keep Jane's Social Security benefit intact actually reduced her standard of living both before retirement and after it.

If we assume that policymakers raise the payroll tax sufficiently to run Social Security on a pay-go basis in the future, we estimate that it would have to go up by about 40 percent over current rates by 2030. An increase in the payroll tax to maintain the level of Social Security in current law would actually reduce the need for workers to save on their own or through their pension plans, just as it did for Jane in the hypothetical example above. The reason is that the increase in the payroll tax and the resulting reduction in the preretirement standard of living actually reduces the amount of supplemental income a person would need in retirement. Under our assumptions we have stipulated that current Social Security benefits will continue to be provided—indeed that is the sole motivation for raising the payroll tax. In work that we have done elsewhere, we estimate that raising the payroll tax to support Social Security by 40 percent would reduce target savings rates for prototypical workers by 2 to 2.5 percent of earnings over their working careers. We estimate that it would reduce their retirement incomes by 9 to 10 percent relative to their preretirement earning level. If their target consumption level ranged from 65 to 75 percent of final earnings, which is fairly normal, this represents reductions in retirement consumption levels of up to 15 percent.[9]

Our political leaders may not have a full grasp of the nuances of the economic models that we use to draw the conclusion that protecting Social Security benefits in some cases could reduce retirees' standards of living. But they do understand that the payroll tax is already an extremely burdensome tax and that letting it run free to deliver currently legislated obligations is a problem. That is what motivates policymakers like Senators Bob Kerrey and Daniel Patrick Moynihan to craft their proposal the way that they have. They are advocates of going back to pay-go financing of the system because they do not believe that the accumulation in the trust fund now occurring is resulting in added savings in the economy, or that it is truly funding future obligations. But most of the adjustments they propose are on the benefit side of the program.

Changing the Benefit Schedule to Support Pay-Go

There are an infinite number of ways that Social Security benefits can be reduced to bring the system back into balance. In the earlier work that we did, cited above, we looked at broad generic reductions in benefits in order to understand the distributional implications at different income levels. In our work we looked at reductions across the board versus reductions off the top of the benefit distribution. If you reconsider the example of Jane, benefit reductions will have similar implications for her need to make provision for her own retirement as will proposals to raise her taxes. If we cut Jane's Social Security benefits by 40 percent, she is going to have to save more on her own if she wants to be able to maintain a relatively constant standard of living across her working career and retirement. As in the earlier example, though, the need to increase her personal savings will cut down on the level of consumption she is able to achieve during her working life.

While there are similarities between benefit reductions and tax increases in their effects on people like Jane, there are also some significant differences. We saw in the earlier example that increases in the payroll tax actually translated through the system to a reduction in Jane's need to save outside Social Security. In the case of benefit reductions, the result is just the opposite. If we cut Jane's Social Security benefit, we increase her need to save. If you buy the economic perspective that we ought to pursue policies that encourage more saving, you would probably favor policies that encourage saving rather than discourage it. Added saving leads to added capital formation in the economy, which, in turn, leads to rising wages for workers, which make them better off over time.

Understanding the Generic Rules of the Road

We estimated earlier that prototypical workers facing a 40 percent increase in their payroll tax would end up reducing their rates of savings by 2 to 2.5 percent of earnings pretty much across the earnings spectrum. We also estimated that the combination of the higher payroll tax and the reduced savings would reduce retirement consumption by up to 15 percent. When we look at the effects of reducing benefits by 40 percent, we estimate that it would require increases in personal savings to make up for some of the reduction. We estimate that the increased savings would be in a range of 2 to 4 percent of earnings for a young worker. Our estimates of the reductions in the standard of living in retirement are only one-quarter to one-half what they would be if we merely pursued a pure payroll tax increase of 40 percent.[10]

The reason benefit reductions have less onerous effects than tax increases has to do with the relative inefficiency of pay-go retirement systems. Looking to the future, the money we pour into the pay-go system would net us extremely poor rates of return. As we pour more and more

Table 20.1   Distribution of Wealth Among the Near-Elderly

Position in the wealth-holding distribution	Personal financial wealth	Social Security wealth	Pension wealth	Total wealth
	Retirement Purchasing Power from			
Bottom 10th	3.4%	93.6%	3.0%	100.0%
1/3 from bottom	18.1	63.4	18.5	100.0
2/3 from bottom	29.9	35.7	34.4	100.0
Top 10th	65.2	10.2	24.6	100.0

Source: James F. Moore and Olivia S. Mitchell, "Projected Retirement Wealth and Savings Adequacy in the Health and Retirement Study," presented at the 1998 Pension Research Council Symposium "Forecasting Retirement Needs and Retirement Wealth," April 27, 1998.

into the payroll tax, it siphons money off from other forms of savings that would provide much higher returns. When we cut benefits, we actually encourage people to save in a fashion that will net them a relatively high return on average. In both cases, workers end up having to devote more of their earnings to provision for their retirement. In the case of the higher payroll taxes, the added resources would be used much less efficiently than in the case of added saving outside the pay-go system.

One issue that must be kept in mind as we think about how we might go about reducing benefits is that the playing field is not level for all the people who might be affected. This point is best explained by adapting an analysis developed by Olivia Mitchell and James Moore in a study they did at the Wharton School at the University of Pennsylvania.[11] Their analysis uses the Health and Retirement Survey (HRS) being sponsored by the National Institute on Aging. The HRS is being conducted on a representative sample, drawn from the general population, of people who were between the ages of fifty-one and sixty-one in 1992. Sample members are being interviewed every two years. Mitchell and Moore have used this data set to estimate the participating households' levels of wealth. They include four classes of wealth in their calculations. These are (1) net financial wealth, including saving, investments, business assets, and nonresidential real estate less outstanding debt not related to housing; (2) net housing wealth, or the current market value of the residential housing less outstanding mortgage debt; (3) pension wealth, or the present value of employer-sponsored retirement benefits; and (4) the present value of Social Security benefits.

We have derived Table 20.1 from their analysis. The derivation does not include housing wealth in the calculation of the wealth distributions because most homeowners do not sell their homes at retirement, or if they do, they tend to buy another one. Our definition of wealth in this case would include business assets and nonresidential properties. We are interested in looking at the assets in these people's portfolio that can be expected to generate a stream of income they can use to buy groceries, go to the movies, and so forth, during their retirement. The results are instructive.

The people at the bottom of the wealth distribution scale hold almost all their wealth in the form of Social Security. Those people one-third of the way up in the distribution still hold nearly two-thirds of their wealth in that form. Those who are two-thirds of the way up in the distribution have rough parity in their holdings between Social Security, pensions, and other financial wealth. Those at the top of the wealth distribution scale have almost no dependence on Social Security. The retirement security risks associated with potential reductions in Social Security benefits are clearly not randomly distributed across the wealth distribution.

The wealth distribution reflected in Table 20.1 has profound implications for retirement policy. The results say that any Social Security reform proposals that cut benefits across the board are going to have a disproportionately large effect on the retirement consumption potential of the people who are at the bottom end of our economic ladder. The people at the upper end of the ladder will hardly notice the implementation of such proposals. Proposals that significantly raise the retirement age, reduce COLAs across the board, or reduce the benefit formula on a pro rata basis are policies of this sort.

A Look at the Kerrey-Moynihan Proposal to Return to Pay-Go Financing

In Chapter 19 we laid out a number of issues to watch in any Social Security reform proposal that would either raise taxes or cut benefits. The analysis may seem to be relatively dismal. It is merely an indication that the problems we face are significant. The Social Security system today is underfunded between 15 and 35 percent, depending on when we address the issue. To us that degree of underfunding seems substantial. The program cannot be rebalanced without significant cuts in benefits or increases in taxes. Although there is a set of different proposals on the public stage that try to rebalance the system in one way or another, there is really only one formal proposal before the Congress to rebalance the system through pay-go means. That is the proposal that has been put forward by Senators Kerrey and Moynihan.

On March 16, 1998, these senators introduced the Social Security Solvency Act of 1998 (S.1792). The measure called for the reduction of the payroll tax supporting the OASDI program from 12.4 percent of covered earnings to 10.4 percent. In 2025, it would rise again to 11.4 percent. In 2030, assuming the actuaries' projections were correct, it would rise back to current levels, 12.4 percent. In 2045 it would rise to 12.7 percent, in 2055 to 13.4 percent, and in 2060 and thereafter to 13 percent of covered pay.

There were two other revenue elements in the Kerrey-Moynihan proposal beside the shift to pay-go financing. The first would raise the amount of wages subject to the payroll tax to cover about 87 percent of wages in the total economy by 2003. The underlying premise on this part of the recommendation was, "Historically, about 90 percent of wages have been subject to the tax."[12] Earlier we saw that the "esthetic logic" that led J. Douglas Brown and his associates on the Committee on Economic Security in 1934 to pick $3,000 as the amount of wages to cover under the payroll tax in 1937 lives on today. There is virtually no rationale to support Social Security's taxing 90 percent, 87 percent, or any other percentage of total earnings—except that the supporters of the program need revenues. Finally, the Kerrey-Moynihan bill calls for expanded taxation of the Social Security benefits and claims that it would provide the same tax treatment as is accorded private pensions. Although this is technically true, it is not in accordance with the tax treatment accorded 99 percent of the private employer–sponsored retirement benefits provided in this country today. The last revenue element of this proposal calls for the expansion of Social Security coverage to include the last groups of state and local workers who remain outside the system.

Compared with Moynihan's 1990 legislation proposing a return to pay-go financing, the Kerrey-Moynihan bill of 1998 would not depend nearly as much on increasing the payroll tax rate in the future. The primary reason that smaller future increases in the payroll tax would be required is that their package contains changes on the benefit side of the program. They would index benefit payments in the future by the increase in the consumer price index minus 1 percentage point. They would increase the number of years of earnings that are considered for determining benefits from thirty-five to thirty-eight years. Finally, they would accelerate the increases in normal retirement age that are in current law. Currently the normal retirement age is to increase from age sixty-five to sixty-six between 2000 and 2005. Then it would increase from age sixty-six to sixty-seven between 2022 and 2027. Kerrey and Moynihan would have the normal retirement age increase at a rate of two months per year from 2000 until 2017 and at a rate of one month every other year beyond that. Under this plan, the normal retirement age would reach age sixty-six in 2005, age sixty-seven in 2011, age sixty-eight in 2023, and age seventy in 2073.

The Kerrey-Moynihan proposal would allow workers to contribute their portion of the proposed payroll tax cut to individual retirement accounts. If a worker were to contribute his or her 1 percent reduction in the tax rate to such a plan, the employer would be required to match it with the other half of the payroll tax reduction. Some analysts see this as a significant step in the direction of individual accounts by Senator Moynihan, a longtime supporter of the current Social Security system. Others see the voluntary nature of the individual accounts as only a marginal extension of current voluntary retirement savings opportunities.

The aggregate structure of the Kerrey-Moynihan proposal is captured in Figure 20.2. The left-hand panel of the figure shows the income rates stated as a percentage of covered payroll for the system under current law and under the Kerrey-Moynihan bill. In the early years, the payroll tax would be reduced somewhat from the level in current law. By 2015, total payroll tax collections under the pay-go proposals would be about 13 percent lower than in current law. After 2020, they would start going back up. By 2030, they would be back up to the level specified in current law. Payroll tax collections would continue to rise gradually until they exceeded collections under current law by about 7 percent in 2060, and they would remain around that level thereafter. Over the seventy-five year period on which Social Security projections are based, the net effect of the payroll tax adjustments would be to reduce the payroll tax relative to current law by 0.71 percent of covered payroll over the period.[13]

The right-hand panel in Figure 20.2 shows the benefit rates under current law and under the Kerrey-Moynihan proposal. This is the cost of providing benefits under the alternative financing approaches stated as a percentage of covered payroll. Almost from the outset, benefits under the Kerrey-Moynihan proposal would be worth significantly less than under current law. By 2010 benefit levels would be 10 percent below current law, by 2020 they would be down 20 percent, and they would level off at about 75 percent of benefits under current law by 2030. The overwhelming majority of the adjustment of the system under the Kerrey-Moynihan proposal would come on the benefit side of the program. Indeed, benefit adjustments would be larger than the total underfunding in the current system because of the net payroll tax cut embedded in the proposal.

Table 20.2 shows the specific set of adjustments to the system and the net effect on the system's costs for the seventy-five-year projection period.

Figure 20.2   OASDI Income and Cost Rates Under Current Law
and Senators Kerrey and Moynihan's Pay-Go Proposal

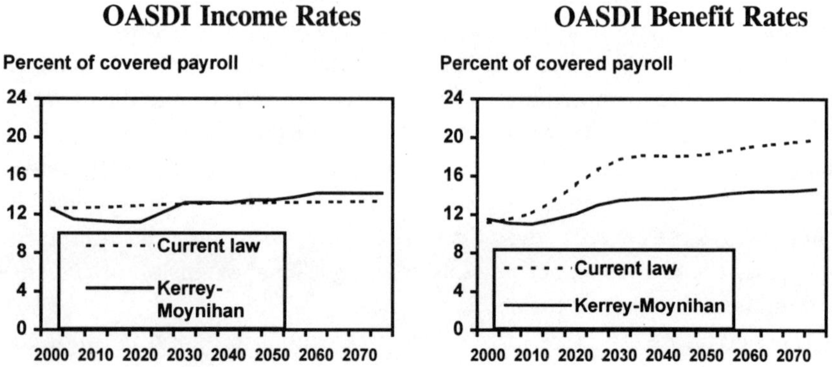

OASDI Income Rates

Percent of covered payroll

OASDI Benefit Rates

Percent of covered payroll

Sources: 1998 Annual Report of the Board of Trustees of the Federal Old-Age and Survivors Insurance and Disability Insurance Trust Funds, p. 108; and unpublished data from the Office of the Actuary, Social Security Administration.

In classifying the various provisions, the proposal to reduce the COLA adjustment and the increase in the normal retirement age would be considered across-the-board cuts. They would affect workers with high levels of earnings and those with low earnings on a proportional basis. As we discussed earlier, though, relative to total retirement security they would have a much harsher effect on those at the low end of the benefit distribution scale than on those higher up in the distribution. Here is where nearly two-thirds of the total positive savings for the system would be realized. Increasing the years of computation would also take a heavier toll on beneficiaries with relatively low levels of benefits. The proposal to raise taxes on benefits would cut fairly far down into the benefit distribution, although it would most certainly spare those at the very bottom. As noted earlier, it does raise a set of equity questions on its own because it moves further from the way in which most retirement plan benefits are treated under federal income tax law.

The proposal to expand coverage to include the last remaining state and local workers hired after 2000 in systems not now covered by Social Security is easy to defend on an equity basis. Social Security is a redistributive program, and there is no reason that a select group of workers who have higher-than-average salaries in the economy should be excluded from the system. The reason for the sizable positive effect on the program is that the new workers covered would pay taxes for quite a number of years, on

Table 20.2   Estimated Long-Range OASDI Financial Effect of the
Kerrey-Moynihan Social Security Reform Proposal

Provision	75-Year Actuarial Balance
1. For 1998 and later, reduce automatic benefit increase by 1 percentage point.	1.41
2. Beginning in 1999, subject OASDI benefits to income tax in a manner similar to that prescribed for benefits received from private and government defined-benefit employee pension plans. (All current threshold levels for taxing OASDI benefits are immediately eliminated.)	0.40
3. Extend OASDI coverage to all state and local government employees hired after the year 2000.	0.25
4. Increase maximum computation period from thirty-five years to thirty-six years for those first eligible in 2001, thirty-seven years for those first eligible in 2002, and thirty-eight years for those first eligible after 2002.	0.27
5. Increase normal retirement age (NRA) eventually to age seventy. The NRA increases by two months a year from sixty-five under current law, beginning with individuals attaining age sixty-two in the year 2000, until it reaches sixty-six for individuals attaining age sixty-two in the year 2005. Current law then leaves the age at sixty-six for several years, but this provision would continue to phase the NRA upward by two months a year until it reaches sixty-eight for individuals reaching age sixty-two in 2017. After 2017, the NRA continues upward by one month every two years until it reaches seventy for individuals reaching age sixty-two in 2065.	0.68
6. Effective January 1, 2003, eliminate the retirement earnings test for beneficiaries age sixty-two and older.	0.00
7. Raise the OASDI contribution and benefit base to $85,000 in 2001, $92,000 in 2002, $97,500 in 2003. After 2003, resume indexing the contribution and benefit base using the average wage index.	0.25
8. Change the OASDI payroll tax beginning in 1999 to 11.4% for 1999-2000, 10.4% for 2001-2024, 11.4% for 2025-2029, 12.4% for 2030-2044, 13.0% for 2055-2059, and 13.4% for 2060 and after.	−0.71
Total for all provisions, adjusted to take into account interactions	2.25

Source: Office of the Actuary, Social Security Administration.

average, before getting any benefits. Including these workers would provide the last benefit of the start-up phenomenon of front-end infusions
of money with delayed benefit obligations. In the longer-term, once the
start-up benefit is realized, the addition of these workers will have little
net positive effect on the system. The politics of covering these workers is
likely to be extremely difficult. The largest remaining groups of uncovered
workers are in California, Colorado, Ohio, Texas, Louisiana, and Massachusetts. The systems that remain outside Social Security coverage feel
strongly about remaining outside the system for the most part. Most of the
people in these systems belong to unions or organizations that have substantial political clout with their federal representatives in Congress. It is a
formidable set of states that is likely to oppose the expanded coverage measures. Even though the politics may be against moving finally to universal
coverage, the redistributive nature of Social Security and the near universality of coverage suggests that all workers ought eventually to be brought
into the system. We can think of no justification for continuing to exempt
a group that has higher-than-average salaries and most of whose members
ultimately gain coverage anyway through alternative employment.

The combined effects of various elements of the package on benefit levels
are shown in Table 20.3. Here we show the estimated average monthly
benefits for workers with various levels of lifetime earnings who are projected to retire in 2025 and 2070. The benefit levels are shown in constant
1998 dollars under current law and under the Kerrey-Moynihan proposal.
The table is showing particularly the combined effects of raising the retirement age and curtailing the COLA adjustment process under the pay-go
proposal by comparison with current law. To understand the effect of the
retirement age increase, compare the benefits at age sixty-five under current law with benefits at age sixty-five under the pay-go plan. To understand the effect of the COLA curtailments, compare the continued deterioration in benefits from age sixty-five to age ninety-five.

It is easy to be critical of the Kerrey-Moynihan proposal because the
long-range reductions in benefits seem so austere, but the proposal is a
good indication of the kind of choices we face if we do not consider moving
toward more funding of the system. More funding may mean more contributions up front, rather than reversion to the pay-go approach advocated
in this proposal. In the long term, however, more funding—a greater accumulation of assets—holds out the promise of a larger economy, a lighter
burden on future workers, and greater retirement security than can be
provided under the pay-go approach. We agree with Senators Kerrey and
Moynihan that more funding will be extremely hard to achieve if we con-

Table 20.3   Estimated Monthly Retirement Benefits to Single Earners
Retiring at Sixty-Five in 2025 or 2070 (Intermediate Assumptions of the
1997 OASDI Trustees' Report)

| | Benefits at Various Ages, Expressed in 1998 Dollars | | | | | |
| | Current law benefit paid at age | | | Pay-go benefit paid at age | | |
	65	80	95	65	80	95
Retiring at age 65 in 2025						
Low earner	$ 614	$ 614	$ 614	$ 544	$ 470	$ 407
Average earner	1,014	1,014	1,014	899	777	672
High earner	1,339	1,339	1,339	1,188	1,027	888
Maximum earner	1,624	1,624	1,624	1,524	1,317	1,139
Retiring at age 65 in 2070						
Low earner	906	906	906	711	614	531
Average earner	1,496	1,496	1,496	1,173	1,014	877
High earner	1,977	1,977	1,977	1,550	1,340	1,159
Maximum earner	2,391	2,391	2,391	2,052	1,774	1,533

Source: Office of the Actuary, Social Security Administration.

tinue to attempt funding through the mechanism for Social Security financing that has been in place since 1935. But we also believe that the potential benefits from funding make it worth the effort to move in that direction. In the next chapter we look at two very distinct ways of increasing the funding of this important pillar of our retirement system. Wanting to fund our retirement system is not enough to solve our current Social Security financing problem. We have to have practical ways of doing it if the added funding is to be effective.

Chapter 21

Wanting to Fund Is Not Enough

W hen Barry Bosworth from the Brookings Institution in Washington, D.C., appeared before the 1994–1996 Advisory Council on Social Security, he strongly advocated adoption of Social Security reforms that would add to national savings. He proposed increasing the payroll tax and building up our retirement reserves. When Robert Ball responded that he couldn't see such a policy being adopted as part of Social Security reform, Bosworth replied: "Well, why should Social Security do it? Because it's a retirement program. That's what the essence of a retirement program is, to save. . . . The right thing to do with a retirement program is to restore savings principles. Why is that so controversial?"[1]

The answer to Bosworth's question lies at the heart of much of the controversy that has surrounded Social Security since August 14, 1935, when Franklin D. Roosevelt signed the original bill setting up the program. Once again, we are debating whether we want to fund Social Security or not. If we conclude that we want to fund it more than we have in the past, then how we go about it is another difficult issue to resolve. Those who want to fund the system to a greater extent than we have in the past come to a fork in the road when they start to address the way to do so. Down one path lies the suggestion that we should once again accumulate assets through the Social Security trust funds and that we should invest some of the funds in the private equity markets. Down the second path lies the suggestion that we should accumulate the added funding through a system of individual accounts.

People determined to take one fork in the road on additional funding are generally adamantly opposed to taking the other route. Those who want to

346

fund through individual accounts raise concerns that the repeated failures to achieve funding in the past are simply the prelude to another failed attempt to fund the accruing obligations under the system. Those who want to fund through the central system believe that the essence of Social Security's goals may be endangered by going that route.

Issues Raised by Funding Social Security Centrally

One conceivable way to fund more of Social Security's obligations than we have in the past is simply to run a balanced government budget for other federal operations over the next couple of decades and to use whatever extra OASDI surpluses we can create to buy back outstanding government debt. The dynamics of that approach dictate that as the Social Security trust funds buy back debt held by the public, those who have previously invested in government bonds take the cash they received for those bonds and invest it in something else. In a macroeconomic context, it makes little difference who holds government bonds and who holds other assets. What is important is the total amount of wealth in the economy.

While the macroeconomics of who holds government bonds and who holds other assets may be neutral, to Social Security who holds what may be important. At issue is the simple observation that over long periods, stocks seem to pay higher average rates of return than bonds.[2] This observation has driven the advocates of increased central funding of Social Security to further advocate that the added funding be invested in the stock market. They have at least two rationales for doing so. The first is that if added national savings are created through Social Security funding, then Social Security ought to reap the reward of the higher returns generated by the added capitalization of the economy. The second is that higher rates of return on the trust funds reduce the size of the revenues that have to be raised through other changes required to rebalance the system. No one disputes the underlying logic for the proposal to build up the trust funds, but the opponents of this approach to Social Security reform oppose it on at least three grounds.

The first reason that many critics oppose the proposal to build up a significant central trust fund is that they do not believe the added funding will materialize. This is simply an extension of the debate that has gone on about funding of the system since the outset. At some point, one has to wonder how long this debate will continue. The second reason many oppose the centralized funding of Social Security is that they do not favor the concentration of economic power within the federal government.

Advocates of private investing say the central funds would be invested passively in large-market indices. Some estimates suggest that the Social Security trust funds could come to hold 5 to 10 percent of the equity base in the economy. Opponents say accumulation of this economic control would raise questions about corporate governance and conflicts of interest. Some advocates of Social Security's becoming a private investor in the market will point to funded state and local pension plans as an example of public entities' successfully funding their plans and investing in private capital markets. A closer look at the track record is not so reassuring.

One of the concerns about the federal government's becoming a major investor in private equities is that it would create a conflict of interest. As a hypothetical case of how such conflicts might arise if Social Security became a major investor in private equities, consider the potential investment in the tobacco industry. On the one hand, the government as a major owner of tobacco company stock would have a fiduciary responsibility to guard the financial well-being of the participants in Social Security and to do nothing to threaten the value of the assets in its retirement portfolio. On the other hand, the government in its role as regulator of industry in the interests of public health might be required to pursue policies that would conceivably reduce the value of tobacco stock significantly. In looking at the Social Security reform proposal outlined in President Clinton's 1999 State of the Union address, where he called for the Social Security Administration to invest in the stock market—the same speech in which he threatened to sue tobacco companies—we see the conflict highlighted. How can these conflicts be resolved, and how can the government be constrained from directly intervening in the management of corporations as it fulfills its duties?

Roberta Romano has developed an extensive review of state and local retirement plan investment patterns, published in the *Columbia Law Review*.[3] She has found that public pension funds have been far more active in corporate governance in recent years than other institutional investors. She concludes that "there are no practical solutions to the problem of political influence on public pension funds short of a substantial restructuring of the funds toward defined contribution plans."[4]

The other issue, also a matter of corporate governance, has to do with social investing. Here the record of public plans is extremely checkered. Romano offers many examples. In the mid-1970s, New York State and New York City pension funds were essentially forced to buy New York City bonds to forestall insolvency. Public plans in Pennsylvania were pressured to help finance a Volkswagen plant as an inducement to get it to locate there. The plant closed a decade later, and a substantial amount of the original loan had to be forgiven to get another tenant into the facility. In the early 1990s, the governor of California pressured the state's public plan to undertake investments intended to stimulate the state economy. The Kansas pension fund invested heavily in local businesses and sustained substantial losses. Many states invest in privately insured mortgage-backed securities to aid local housing markets but garner less-than-competitive returns. Minnesota passed legislation authorizing international investment with up to 10 percent of its public funds. When the investment board moved to implement the authority, organized labor, believing that it threatened local jobs, fought the move. In tallying up the prevalence of these kinds of provisions, Romano found that eighteen states had statutory instructions to foster local economic development and seven states had pension fund board or investment board policies to do so. She found in the early 1990s that eighteen states had legislative restrictions on investing in companies doing business in South Africa and six had pension fund board or investment board policies against investing in them. She found that ten states had legislative restrictions on investing in companies that did business in Northern Ireland and that two had pension fund board or investment board policies against investing in those companies.[5] This behavior is widespread among public plans in this country.

Social investing by public pension plans is also widespread in areas outside the United States. The World Bank noted, in its seminal study on the problems of aging and public pensions around the world, "As government gets privileged access to large pension reserves, it may be induced to spend and borrow more. Borrowing from the pension fund is less transparent than that from the open capital market."[6] At the end of June 1998, Malaysia opened a new top-of-the-line airport in Kuala Lumpur. It was largely financed by a loan of $373 million from the Employees Provident Fund (EPF) at less than market interest rates.[7] If that were all the Malaysian authorities had been up to, workers might not have been too concerned. In the fall of 1997, they announced the use of the EPF assets to reverse the declines they had been experiencing in their stock market. When their support program for the market began in September 1997, the Kuala Lumpur Stock Exchange index was at around 780. By mid-December it was under 560.[8] The World Bank reported that the National Investment Bank of Egypt credits its pension system with negative real interest rates. In Ecuador, mortgage and personal loans to members of the elite accounted for 19 percent of the loan portfolio. Mexico and Venezuela channeled pension funds to housing subsidies that were realizing below-market returns.[9] The list goes on.

Possibly the most telling example of the kind of pressure that might be raised if the Social Security system were to pursue this policy came in an exchange during the deliberations of the 1994–1996 Advisory Council on Social Security. Edith Fierst asked the council members representing organized labor, "How would your people feel about a fund of this kind investing in non-union establishments, anti-union establishments?" Gloria Johnson from the AFL-CIO's executive council replied, "I think it would create some concerns, great concerns." Carolyn Weaver sought clarification of the point by asking if organized labor would have a problem with passive investment policies through an index fund, for example, the "stocks listed in the S&P 500." Gerald Shea, a senior assistant to John Sweeney, the president of the AFL-CIO, responded, "We've certainly taken the position . . . much more favorable to targeted investments than some other people at this table might." [10] Months later, Carolyn Weaver came back to the same issue. "Suppose you do try to invest in a broad equity fund . . . and that equity fund includes companies that have . . . damaging environmental policies, unfavorable labor policies, you name it." She recalled that when the question had been posed earlier, one of the representatives of organized labor had responded, in Weaver's words: "Well, no, I'm not sure we could just sit back and let them be passively invested." Gerald Shea from the AFL-CIO clarified: "I think I responded positively as long as it was buy American and build union." [11]

In Canada, where they have recently adopted legislation that will create a significantly larger fund than currently—roughly the equivalent of an additional three years of benefit payments—the investment in private markets is scheduled for early 1999. As we do in the United States, the Canadians have talked of these funds' being invested in market index funds. Gail Cook-Bennett is the chairwoman of the board that will oversee that investment. In an interview in late 1998, Cook-Bennett described an investment strategy that the reporter described as "index-based, but with a little wiggle room." Cook-Bennett indicated that for the first three years the board was required "to substantially replicate indices." But she added that "it's almost impossible to replicate" indexes all the time. Following the initial period when they are required to track the indexes they choose, she added, "the board can recommend . . . that we go active in the domestic market." [12]

Those who oppose the central accumulation of assets in the Social Security trust funds for investment in private equity markets base their opposition on what they see around them. They point to what has gone on with state and local governmental funds and what has gone on with public funds elsewhere around the world. They point to the position that powerful interest groups are likely to take on how the money should be invested if we accumulate it. Given their concerns about this approach to Social Security funding, they take another direction in their support for Social Security reform. Some advocate that we go back to the pay-go financing discussed at length in the preceding chapter. Others advocate that we fund, but that we do it through individual accounts. That approach also raises a number of questions.

Issues Raised by Funding Social Security Through Individual Accounts

Robert Ball calls the Personal Security Account (PSA) plan supported by five of the thirteen members of the 1994–1996 Advisory Council on Social Security radical. He is concerned that other individual-account proposals, like that advocated by Edward Gramlich, the former chairman of the council, may be perceived as "acceptable compromises." But Ball says, "They really are not."[13] Ball and others raise criticisms of proposals to reform Social Security that include individual accounts.

Individual-Account Options Threaten Redistribution

One of the guiding principles of Social Security in the United States from the outset has been that it should be redistributive. People with lower earnings over their working lifetimes are supposed to get back relatively more in benefits than workers with higher earnings. Those opposed to plans like the PSA and Gramlich's IA plan worry that the redistribution becomes too apparent. They are worried that if redistribution becomes too apparent, people will no longer tolerate it. As a reminder, the PSA plan would basically split the Social Security retirement benefit in two. The benefit provided through Social Security would be a flat universal benefit for full-career workers—that is, equal benefits for workers with low or high earnings. The benefit provided through the PSA would be whatever 5 percent of covered wages would support. It would be a much larger benefit for workers with high earnings than for those with low earnings. In combination, the flat benefit and the PSA benefit would have redistributive characteristics very similar to those of the current benefit structure. Gramlich's IA plan would curtail Social Security benefits more for workers with high earnings than for those with low earnings by adjusting the program's benefit formula. But here again, his individual accounts would roughly rebalance the combined system to resemble the current benefit structure.

Both proposals, however, would more clearly separate the adequacy and equity elements of the program than does current law.

From the outset of the program there has been at least a conceptual tension between Social Security's goal of providing adequate support for retirees who had low earnings throughout their lives and its goal of providing workers with an equitable return on their contributions to the system. This tension between adequacy and equity was masked for years by giving away $11.4 trillion worth of windfalls to people retiring during the first sixty years of the program's operations. We saw in Chapter 7 that the program gave away more money to people with high earnings than it did to those with lower earnings.

In order to explain why the conflict between Social Security's adequacy and equity goals has not been controversial until now, consider the example of a married couple retiring in 1970. Assume that the husband, Bob, was sixty-five years old at the time and that his wife, Lois, had never worked outside the home and so had never paid any payroll taxes. Assume that Bob had worked in covered employment steadily from 1937 on. Assume that both Bob and Lois lived to their normal life expectancy after retiring at age sixty-five. Considering the benefits paid to both Bob and Lois, if Bob had lifetime covered earnings that were about half the national average wage, he and Lois would have received benefits that were worth about fourteen times the value of his and his employer's payroll taxes on his earnings, accumulated with interest. If Bob's pay was always at the maximum level for taxable earnings, he and Lois would have gotten benefits that were worth about eight times the value of lifetime payroll taxes plus interest. It would appear that the Bob with low earnings got much better the deal of the two. In fact, the Bob with maximum earnings received more than $250,000 of free benefits (in 1998 dollars) compared with only about $175,000 for the Bob with low earnings. In relative terms, the Bob with low earnings did get a better deal. But the Bob with maximum earnings would have been awfully hard put to make an argument that he was getting cheated in the deal. People like the rich Bob getting a quarter of a million dollars for free were perfectly happy to let the program give the poor Bobs lower down on the totem pole a larger *relative* benefit. Redistribution in this kind of environment was something that was easily tolerated.

The problem with the Bob and Lois scenario is that Social Security's start-up free money is now almost totally gone. Using Social Security's own analysis developed by Dean Leimer in its Office of Research, Statistics, and Evaluation, the last birth cohort that will get free money from the Social Security retirement program, in the aggregate, is the group of people born in 1937.[14] This group becomes eligible for Social Security retirement benefits in 1999. As the free money party is coming to its end, the tension between the adequacy and equity elements of the program is going to become a great deal more noticeable. Consider the case of Bob and Lois's grandson, Matt, who was born in 1960 and is married to Gretchen. If Matt's annual pay level is about half the national average over his working career and if Gretchen never works outside the home, the Social Security actuaries estimate the value of Matt and Gretchen's benefits will still be about two times the value of Matt's and his employer's payroll taxes.[15] In doing this calculation, the actuaries compared what Matt and Gretchen would get from Social Security to the money they would have if, alternatively, they had invested the payroll taxes in government bonds. If Matt always earns at the maximum taxable level, his and Gretchen's expected lifetime benefits will be almost exactly equal to what they would get from investing their payroll taxes in government bonds. But there are two problems with this scenario.

The first problem is that Social Security is underfunded during Matt and Gretchen's retirement by about 30 to 40 percent. That means the Matt and Gretchen with low pay might expect to get back something between 1.2 and 1.5 times the value of his lifetime contributions to the system, not double the value, as current law offers. It means the Matt and Gretchen with high pay can expect to get back around 60 to 70 percent of the value of their lifetime contributions, not the full equivalent. Now redistribution means more than that the Matt earning $15,000 per year will get a better deal than the Matt who earns $65,000 per year. Redistribution means that the richer Matt won't even do as well as he could do investing in plain old government bonds, which in themselves aren't such a terrific deal. But that's not all.

The other problem with the scenario relates to Gretchen. If she is the same age as Matt, she would be thirty-nine in 1999. How many thirty-nine-year-old women do you know who have never worked outside the home? If both Matt and Gretchen work, the program treats them a lot more like single workers than like a one-earner couple. The Social Security actuaries estimate under current law that the program would give a single Matt with low earnings a benefit worth almost exactly the value that his payroll taxes would have earned by being invested in government bonds instead of in the program. For the Matt with high earnings, it would give him almost exactly half the value of his contributions. And again, this is before the inevitable rebalancing of the system. The iron rules of arithmetic ensure that it will be rebalanced. Under a Kerrey-Moynihan proposal, the single Matt with low earnings is facing a benefit that is around 70 percent of the value of his lifetime contributions if invested in government bonds. The Matt with high earnings is looking at a benefit worth about 35 percent of the value of his contributions. The supporters of the program say, "But there's a lot of value in disability and survivor benefits in the program that is not reflected in the retirement system." The actuaries' calculations reported here include the value of disability and survivor benefits.

The problem we are facing with Social Security's redistribution is that Matt and Gretchen are having to clean up after the good times that Bob and Lois had on Social Security. The people who are trying to hide the cost of the clean-up are afraid that the Matts and Gretchens with high earnings are not going to be nearly as supportive of a redistributional system as the Bobs and Loises with high earnings were. They understand very clearly that this is not a pretty picture. It is exactly the situation that Arthur Altmeyer suggested in the early 1940s would be embarrassing for future congresses to handle. And indeed, as J. Douglas Brown predicted, he and Edwin Witte are now dead, and Congress must sort out the situation.

The PSA plan deals with this adequacy versus equity conflict in two ways. In the creation of the flat benefit it continues the redistributional aspect of Social Security. It essentially converts the adequacy element of the program into a truer social insurance, where workers all contribute proportionately against the prospect of a bad labor market outcome. Though contributions are proportionate, benefits are not. Those who actually have bad labor market outcomes benefit quite disproportionately from this segment of the system. The tax treatment of benefits accentuates this "social insurance" structure further. The PSAs themselves convert the equity element of the program into a true vehicle for retirement savings that will accumulate returns at the rate of return on capital. Inevitably, any system is judged against market returns. Will people support the actual redistribution in the system if they fully understand it? We cannot guarantee that they will. But we can guarantee that they will figure out the redistribution in the current system no matter how much the devotees of the status quo try to hide it. Either way we have to deal with the public's willingness to support redistribution.

People Will Not Know How to Invest

Another criticism of personal account reform options is that many workers will not know how to invest if they are forced to accumulate a share of their retirement wealth through a defined-contribution system.[16] This may be an interesting theory but it flies in the face of what is happening all around us. Ignoring what is going on all across Latin America and what has happened in places as diverse as Australia and Sweden, we have only to look at our own backyard to see another story. Here in the United States, there has been a revolution in the pension industry, as defined-contribution plans in general, and 401(k) plans in particular, have become the pensions of choice over the last twenty years. During the late 1970s, there were approximately twice as many active participants in private defined-benefit plans as in private defined-contribution plans. Today, the situation is almost exactly reversed. This shift from defined-benefit to defined-contribution pension plans has been accompanied by a shift from firms to individuals in the responsibility for financing and managing retirement accruals. In 1975, nearly $2 out of every $3 contributed to private retirement plans went into defined-benefit plans. By 1994, nearly three-fourths of the contributions going into private pension plans went into defined-contribution plans. And by then, contributions to 401(k) plans exceeded contributions to all other private plans combined.[17]

One of the reasons that many low-income workers do not have any idea how to invest today is that they have never had any reason to learn how to invest. If you never had any money to invest or any prospect of having any in the future, why would you bother learning how to do it? Given a reason to learn about these things, however, people can learn. Not only have people in this country moved into retirement plans where they are called upon to invest their savings; they have learned how to invest in them.

Table 21.1 shows the percentage of 401(k) balances held in equities at the end of 1995 in a sampling of such plans. The workers in these plans could choose where to direct their contributions and how to allocate their total balances. The information in the table reflects patterns of investment that most people would find to be reasonable. Younger workers tend to hold more of their retirement savings in the form of equities than older ones. Not only is this true in the aggregate, but it is consistently the case at every level of earnings. Most investment advisers would recommend such a pattern. Workers at higher levels of earnings generally hold more of their retirement assets in equities than those at lower levels. Not only is this true in the aggregate, but it is generally the case within each age category. Once again the pattern is consistent with reasonable expectations. When one compares the two sections in the table, the patterns of investments by men and women are remarkably consistent. In the extended analysis behind this table, the authors concluded that women are as effective in their

Table 21.1   Percentage of Total Balances Allocated to Equities by Participants in 401(k) Plans, by Gender, Age, and Wage Level in 1995

Age group	Wage Levels of 401(k) Account Holders (in Thousands of Dollars)								
	10.0–14.9	15.0–24.9	25.0–34.9	35.0–44.9	45.0–59.9	60.0–74.9	75.0–99.9	100.0+	Total
Women									
20–29	55%	57%	60%	67%	67%	75%	72%	30%	58%
30–39	48	52	56	63	66	67	74	77	55
40–49	49	51	51	60	59	60	68	70	52
50–59	42	46	48	56	58	61	60	69	46
60–65	40	37	43	48	61	49	50	87	39
Total	47	51	53	61	62	63	69	72	52
Men									
20–29	58%	46%	57%	64%	70%	72%	83%	84%	57%
30–39	50	45	51	59	63	68	72	78	59
40–49	47	39	39	53	57	60	63	71	54
50–59	39	31	32	44	49	54	57	64	46
60–65	32	23	28	41	40	56	50	61	40
Total	48	40	46	55	59	62	64	71	54

Source: Robert L. Clark, Gordon P. Goodfellow, Sylvester J. Schieber, and Drew A. Warwick, "Making the Most of 401(k) Plans: Who's Choosing What and Why," a paper presented at the 1998 Pension Research Council Symposium, "Forecasting Retirement Needs and Retirement Wealth," the Wharton School, University of Pennsylvania, Philadelphia, April 27, 1998.

use of 401(k)'s as men. Women were found to participate and contribute at rates as high as those among their male counterparts, and their investment patterns appeared to be more rational than men's in some instances.[18]

Individual-Account Plans Put Workers at Increased Risk

In his recent book entitled *Straight Talk About Social Security,* Robert Ball argues against incorporating individual accounts as part of Social Security reform because such a change "increases risk for the individual."[19] The issue of the risks associated with alternative ways of dealing with our provision for retirement security is such a large one and so misunderstood that we have devoted all of the next chapter to it. That is why we merely mention the potential problem here without addressing it.

Administration Costs for Individual Accounts
Would Consume the Benefits of Funding

Among the issues that repeatedly arise in the discussion of Social Security reform options that include the element of individual accounts is the administrative feasibility and cost of running the accounts. For example, the recently released report of the National Academy of Social Insurance on "privatizing Social Security" raises the issue directly. It notes that one of its panel members does not believe that "an individual account system for over 140 million workers, with less than an 18 to 24 month lag in account recording, is feasible at acceptable administrative costs in the absence of new technological developments, including moving 5.5 million small employers from paper filing to automated filing."[20] In an analysis of the Chilean retirement system, Peter Diamond, who chaired the NASI panel, raises the question of whether an individual-account system "is desirable, because compulsory savings are less attractive when costs are eating up a large fraction" of the savings.[21]

We are not going to spend much time on the administration issue in this forum, although we have written a paper together proposing an organizational structure to handle the administration of the system. This structure would heavily rely on existing structures and institutions to set up and run the system. We believe the added costs would be relatively marginal. We believe that within no more than three or four years, the average annual costs would be less than 0.5 percent of assets under management if we have sizable accounts of the order of magnitude that we lay out in Chapter 23.[22] We offer two observations to bolster our case.

One observation concerns Australia and its retirement system. Australia began the implementation of a national program of individual accounts in 1992. The Australian system of individual accounts is organized completely outside the government. Other than the funds offered to individuals, virtually all the investment of the superannuation accounts now takes place in an environment of pooled funds, largely through employer- or union-sponsored plans. Certainly compared with Chile, often cited as a model for national individual-account retirement reforms, Australia appears to have a cost-effective system of retirement funding based on the twin elements of mandating contributions and offering a large number of superannuation accounts on a group basis, through industry funds.

The Association of Superannuation Funds of Australia estimates that the average administration costs of the system equal A-$4.40—that is, U.S.-$2.85 —per member per week. In U.S. currency terms, administrative costs at

Table 21.2   Administrative Costs as a
Percentage of Assets Under Management in
Australian Individual-Account Superannuation
Funds, 1996–1997

Number of members in the plan	1996	1997
1 to 99	0.689%	0.619%
100 to 499	0.849	0.673
400 to 2,499	0.803	0.797
2,500 to 9,999	0.854	0.837
10,000 or more	0.922	0.846
Total	0.900	0.835

Source: Australian Bureau of Statistics, Belconnen, Australian
Capital Territory, tabulations of a joint quarterly survey done
by the Australian Bureau of Statistics and the Australian Prudential Regulation Authority.

this rate for a system that held average balances of $1,000 would be nearly
15 percent of assets per year. For a system that held average balances of
$5,000, it would drop to 3 percent per year. For one that held average bal-
ances of $10,000, administrative costs would be 1.5 percent per year. By
the time average account balances got to be $30,000, administrative costs
would be under 0.5 percent per year. This pattern is important because it
reflects the pattern of accumulating balances in a retirement system like
Australia's as it is being phased in.

The administrative costs for Australia's national system of individual accounts, stated as a percentage of funds under management for 1996 and
1997, are shown in Table 21.2. The expenses reported here include those
associated with administration of the accounts, investment of the assets,
and other expenses related to running the system. This program is still in
the relatively early stages of implementation, meaning that future costs as
a percentage of assets should be considerably smaller than they were at the
end of 1997. Even though the program was only four years into implementation, the cost of plan administration in 1997 was below 0.85 percent of
assets in individual workers' accounts.

The cost of administering the Australian system of individual retirement
accounts organized at the employer level is below the range of administrative costs used in assessing the viability of the PSA proposal developed by
the 1994–1996 advisory council members. We believe that if the Australians
can figure out how to set up and administer a program of this sort at this

level of costs, the United States should be able to do so as well. No other country in the world has financial markets as efficiently administered as ours here in the United States. One other important consideration in our conclusion is that no other country in the world has the experience that we do in running retirement programs set up and administered to support individual workers saving and investing for their retirement. No other country has anything that comes near matching the 401(k) system in this country.

In the United States, the disclosure of tax-qualified plan operations that the federal government mandates from plan sponsors requires reporting of a range of plan costs, including the administrative costs charged to the plan. We have tabulated the administrative costs reported on the public disclosure form, Form 5500, for 401(k) plans during their 1995 plan year operations. We included only plans that had been in operation for at least three years. We included only plans that had been operating for a while, because we were interested in measuring true operating costs, not start-up costs. Those results are shown in Table 21.3. The table shows the mean and median administrative costs, stated as a percentage of the average of beginning and ending balances in the plans for the year.

From Table 21.3 it is clear that substantial economies of scale are related to various aspects of the administration of 401(k) plans. One should be careful in interpreting the costs for smaller plans because there were

Table 21.3   Administration Fees in 401(k) Plans, by Plan Size in 1995, Stated as a Percentage of Total Assets in the Plan

Active participants	Employer Subsidizes Administration		Plan Pays All Administration	
	Average	Median	Average	Median
1–10	0.701%	0.223%	1.852%	0.445%
11–25	1.100	0.780	1.372	0.982
26–50	2.840	0.471	1.360	0.863
51–100	0.529	0.296	0.907	0.682
101–250	0.436	0.201	0.763	0.557
251–500	0.422	0.202	0.716	0.487
501–750	0.332	0.161	0.613	0.405
751–1,000	0.375	0.180	0.462	0.314
1,001–5,000	0.302	0.145	0.343	0.176
5,001–10,000	0.276	0.106	0.291	0.148
10,001 or more	0.198	0.100	0.226	0.118

Source: Tabulations of the Department of Labor's Form 5500 files.

very few of them in the tabulation. In each of the two classes of smallest plans, there were twenty or fewer plans. And in the size class of twenty-six to fifty participants, there were fewer than forty in both cases. In addition to demonstrating economies of scale in plan administration, the table also suggests that there is considerable employer subsidization of the cost of running these plans. There are approximately three times as many plans where the employer is subsidizing some costs as plans where all costs are paid out of the plan. We believe that employers already running individual-account plans could put in place parallel systems that would have extremely low marginal costs. The infrastructure is already in place. For those without plans, we believe that an extremely low-cost option is possible.

Some costs embedded in Table 21.3 would not be likely to occur in an individual-account program created as an element of Social Security reform. First of all, we would not anticipate that the costs associated with processing loans under 401(k) plans would be relevant in a mandatory savings program. The loan provisions in 401(k)'s arise because of the voluntary nature of the plans. If people did not have a way to get access to their money in time of hardship, many of them would not voluntarily put it into such plans. Given that we are talking about a mandatory account system for Social Security, that issue goes away. In addition, 401(k) plans require discrimination testing to make sure that higher-income workers do not take disproportionate advantage of the tax benefits in these plans. These would not be required in a PSA-type system. The second thing that would drive down administration costs in a PSA system is that the trustees' fees and the record-keeping fees show tremendous economies of scale in other analyses of administration costs associated with 401(k) plans. For example, record administration costs have been shown to drop below 10 basis points—that is, 0.10 percent—per year, and trustees' fees have been shown to drop below 1 basis point for plans with as few as two thousand participants.[23]

If we can devise a relatively efficient way to group workers into large systems, the costs of the remaining administrative functions should be even lower. Finally, we believe that the actual fees associated with money management in a national mandatory savings program could be driven almost to zero. If we assume that they might be as high as 15 basis points—that is, 0.15 percent of assets under management—the total cost of administering the system could be under 25 basis points. While this might seem optimistic to some, we note that it is possible to buy retail funds with annual costs at or below this level. We certainly believe it is possible to devise a mass-scale system that would at least match what individual consumers can buy from a storefront today.

Table 21.4   Sample of Cost-Effective Mutual Fund Products Available Today

	Description	Small-Account Fee	Annual Total Expenses	Minimum Initial Investment	Minimum Initial IRA Investment
Fidelity Spartan Market Index	S&P 500 Index fund	$10 for assets < $10,000	0.19%	$10,000	$500
Fidelity Asset Manager	Asset allocation with stocks & bonds	$12 for assets < $2,500	0.77%	$2,500	$500
Schwab 1000	1,000 largest market cap stocks	NA	0.46%	$1,000	$500
Schwab Total Bond Market Index	Lehman Bros. Aggregate Bond Index	NA	0.35%	$1,000	$500
Vanguard Index Trust Small Cap	Russell 2000 Index fund	$10 for assets < $10,000	0.23%	$3,000	$1,000
Vanguard Index Trust 500	S&P 500 Index fund	$10 for assets < $10,000	0.19%	$3,000	$1,000

Sources: The Internet web sites for each of the companies listed.

One test regarding what fees might be for individual accounts is to look at the terms offered on retail products today. Table 21.4 shows several of the product offerings from three of the largest mutual fund companies in the United States. It is not meant to be a comprehensive survey, but it does contain a selection of widely available, cost-effective ways to participate in financial markets. In all cases, the source of the information in the table is the 1998 prospectus of the fund. Total expenses for the index fund products fall below 50 basis points, and the expenses for two of them below 20 basis points. Four of the funds charge small annual fees for accounts under $10,000. All of them have special low minimum-initial-investment amounts for IRA accounts: four of them set the amount at $500, and the other two set a $1,000 minimum. People who doubt the ability of the financial services sector to offer cost-effective Social Security individual accounts have to answer the question why it should be a problem when offerings such as these are available in the IRA marketplace. All these products appear to offer inexpensive ways for small account holders to participate in diversified portfolios. It is not clear why the costs of Social Security's individual accounts need to be higher.

Individual-Account Plans Will Weaken the Disability Benefits in the System

Both the PSA and the IA plans developed by the 1994–1996 Advisory Council on Social Security would result in reductions in disability benefits of nearly 30 percent when the programs were fully implemented. Both plans have been criticized on this score by opponents of individual accounts.[24] Two issues are important to consider in this case. The first is that Social Security's Disability Insurance (DI) program will itself be nearly 30 percent underfunded by 2030. The advisory council did not consider how to adjust the DI program to bring it back into balance. The issue never made it onto the agenda for discussion by the council. At least some of the council members did not think that it was appropriate to assume that future taxpayers should be required to ante up higher payroll taxes to support this aspect of Social Security without somebody's first taking a careful look at the program. As a result, they took the position that they would commit resources at the level in current law, but no more than that until a formal review was undertaken. They did not explicitly conclude that current benefits should go up or down, just that they should not commit more resources to the program without anybody's giving it serious consideration.

The Social Security Advisory Board recently issued a report on Social Security's disability programs that highlighted a number of serious administrative issues that exist with the current system. The advisory board was established with legislation making the Social Security Administration an independent government agency in 1994. It comprises members appointed to six-year terms by the president and leaders of Congress. In its report on Social Security's disability programs, the board called for Social Security to make the disability determination process more equitable and consistent. It called for strengthening of the public's trust in the system and helping disabled individuals continue at or return to work. Finally, it called for the SSA to initiate research to help policymakers understand changes in the program's dynamics and how to respond to them.[25] Until evaluations and recommendations like these are addressed, it seems totally inappropriate to assume that public policymakers should simply pour more payroll taxes into the DI program.

Beyond the inadequacy of currently legislated payroll tax rates to support the DI program and questions about how the program is being operated, reform of Social Security does not have to automatically reduce disability benefits. If we wish to continue to support the DI at the level of benefits embedded in current law, we merely have to raise the revenues to support it at that level. We would find it odd, however, that proposals to reduce other benefits provided through Social Security would not at least consider whether DI benefits should also be adjusted.

Individual Accounts Will be Subject to Preretirement Distributions

The critics of making mandated individual accounts an element of Social Security reform argue that workers holding the accounts and "facing health emergencies, tuition payments, or other major expenses would want access to their 'own' funds in such situations. Based on experience with IRAs and 401(k) plans, it can be confidently predicted that political leaders would acquiesce."[26] One extremely important distinction between IRAs or 401(k) plans and mandated retirement accounts would be the mandate. If someone voluntarily puts money into an account, to tell that worker after the fact that he or she cannot take it out for an emergency would make it seem as though the account was not truly voluntary in the first place. A mandatory contribution to an account in lieu of a contribution to Social Security would be a different matter.

One thing that the Congress will face if it allows workers to tap mandated accounts before retirement is that those workers will reach the end of their careers with assets insufficient to meet their retirement needs. If that were to happen, the same people would almost certainly appear hat in hand on the steps of Congress, expecting to be bailed out of their plight. Our intuition is that if Congress does begin to find ways to relieve itself of the dire problems posed by the current federal commitments to entitlement programs aimed at the elderly, it is likely to be extremely reluctant to reverse course. If Congress allows holders of mandated accounts preretirement access to them, it would put itself right back in jeopardy of the same entitlement demands that it had set the accounts up to relieve in the first place. We believe Congress can hold the line. Can we guarantee it? No, but then, the advocates of central funding cannot guarantee that Congress would hold the line on that funding, either. In the latter case, there is a long track record of it not being able to do so. We believe that the restraint would be much greater on the part of Congress to spend down the added savings in individual accounts than to spend assets directly at its disposal.

Personal Security Accounts Will Not Provide
Retirement Security

The opponents of the PSA proposal at the 1994–1996 Advisory Council criticized the accounts because they did not require the holders to annuitize the accumulations at retirement. The critics concluded that "inevitably, many retirees will underestimate the amount of money they need to last through their retirement and will use the funds for other purposes."[27] As with many issues of this sort, a set of competing considerations have to be balanced. On the one hand, the public does have an interest in making sure that retirees do not spend down their assets in order to qualify for means-tested benefits. On the other hand, to force people to annuitize wealth beyond levels that would protect the public from individuals' making undue claims on public programs is beyond the scope of public interest. Finally, insisting that workers annuitize their assets at retirement means forcing individuals to purchase annuities regardless of their relative price on the retirement date. Annuities are highly sensitive to interest rates, and the date of retirement could arbitrarily determine whether workers have relatively low or high retirement incomes. In addition, mandatory annuitization discriminates against people with relatively low life expectancies at retirement. Resolving these issues requires care. But they can most certainly be addressed and resolved to satisfy policy goals, once such goals are carefully stipulated.

Transition Costs of Going from Pay-Go to a More Funded System

One of the problems created by a shift from a pay-as-you-go retirement system to one that is partially or fully funded is that previously accrued but unfunded liabilities continue to mature during the transition period, at the same time that future benefits are being prefunded. When the system is financed with a payroll tax, the implication is that a relatively limited number of workers will have to pay off the maturing liabilities on a pay-as-you-go basis while prefunding their own retirement security.

Of the proposals developed by the 1994–1996 Advisory Council, the transition cost is clearest for the PSA proposal, because people who are currently retired or close to retirement at the transition date would continue to receive benefits roughly in accordance with the benefit levels under current law. Those between the ages of twenty-five and fifty-five on the date of transition would also receive a share of their total benefits as determined under current law. In the PSA case, the benefit stream promised by current law would persist for some time. It would gradually taper off as people receiving old-law benefits gradually died off, but the tax rebates for the PSAs would begin immediately; additional funds, therefore, would be required to meet projected benefits during the transition.

The clarity of transition costs associated with the PSA proposal by comparison with such costs for other proposals should not be confused with the relative size of transition costs associated with various proposals. For example, the Maintain Benefits plan to eliminate the currently projected funding deficit in Social Security would have to close the $3 trillion in unfunded liabilities under the current system. The actuaries estimate that the higher return on assets in the MB proposal would eliminate about one-third of the unfunded liability. That means the MB proposal has to somehow include an additional $2 trillion in revenue increases—that is, new taxes—or a similar reduction in benefits, or some combination of the two. In addition, MB also recommends raising the ultimate trust fund balance to the equivalent of 4.7 years of benefits as opposed to the current balance of 2 years. In current terms, that would be the equivalent of having to raise another $1 trillion or so. That means the MB proposal has transition costs of around $3 trillion associated with it. At the end of the day, however, the MB plan would create just a fraction of the funding associated with either of the other proposals developed by the advisory council. It also would not create the same level of funding as proposals like that sponsored by Senators Breaux and Gregg and Representatives Kolbe and Stenholm, as discussed in Chapter 19.

Edward Gramlich, the chairman of the 1994–1996 Advisory Council on Social Security, claims that his IA plan does not pose transition costs for the government and would not cause it to do any additional "explicit" deficit financing. His plan does include a requirement, however, that workers would have to contribute 1.6 percent of covered payroll into individual accounts. The value of the scaling-down of benefits provided through Social Security under his plan is roughly $3 trillion. The present value of the total added contributions that would be required under his plan would be roughly $2.3 trillion in 1998 dollars over the valuation period. If the mechanism that Gramlich would use to finance his individual accounts is not considered a transition cost within the context of Social Security reform, the concept of transition cost is being extremely narrowly and technically defined. The added contributions under his plan are slightly more than the added contributions that would be required under the PSA plan.

The plans that would carve out the financing of individual accounts from existing benefits would also entail transition costs that may not be fully appreciated. For example, the one that has been sponsored by Senators Breaux and Gregg and Representatives Kolbe and Stenholm, discussed in Chapter 19, has two sets of such costs. First, they are closing the unfunded liability in the current system, a cost of $3 trillion. In addition, they are cutting benefits further in order to fund individual accounts to the tune of 2 percent of covered payroll. The cost of that is approximately an additional $2.7 trillion in benefit reductions. All of these plans have significant costs associated with them. The simple fact is that all the plans start in the same hole—a $3 trillion hole. In addition, all the plans seek to do more than just fill in the hole, some more than others. There will be costs associated with every option.

Financing Transition Costs

Transition costs under the various proposals could be financed in several ways. We have already talked about explicit additional contributions in the plans like that offered by Ned Gramlich to the advisory council and explicit additional benefit carve-outs in plans like that of Breaux, Gregg, Kolbe, and Stenholm. A new option that has caught some people's attention is to use budget surpluses to finance transition costs, especially since President Bill Clinton suggested that we use federal budget surpluses to help "save" Social Security. If the federal budget, outside Social Security financing, were to operate in substantial surplus over an extended period of years, such a surplus could be used to cover transition costs.

In the early years, the transition costs under the PSA proposal, to take an example, would run nearly $9 billion per year. In terms of present value, they would still be running $60 billion per year after twenty years. Certainly, federal surplus revenues could help to defray the costs associated with moving to such a plan. If the surpluses in other parts of the federal budget were insufficient to cover the full transition cost, added financing would be required. But no one should be misled about the use of budget surpluses to finance a transition in the financing of our Social Security system. A dollar that goes into financing such a transition is a cost no matter where we get it. It is a cost even if we free it from other activities that the government might engage in, because each dollar taken from other federal coffers could always be spent on something else, whether roads, defense, or tax cuts.

Some policy analysts advocate that we reduce or eliminate other sorts of government spending in order to finance the transition. For example,

Peter Ferrara and Michael Tanner advocate selling a specific set of federal assets, which could net us $375 billion, by their estimate. In addition, they give us more than six pages of government programs that could be cut back to generate savings of $143 billion per year.[28] Though all of us might have a favorite example of government expenditures on programs that we would be willing to live without, the current structure of the federal budget has been developed over many years through a pluralistic process of reconciling widely varied public priorities. It is unlikely that we can radically alter all these earlier priorities to garner the marginal resources needed to meet the costs implied by this proposal. If we can, the policy shift proposed here could be easily accomplished. But once again, taking money from other activities should not be misconstrued as eliminating the cost associated with the transition from a pay-go system to one that is partially funded. We may be able to hide some of the costs of the transition, at least at the margin, but hiding them does not mean eliminating them. It makes no difference whether we are dealing with cleverly designed MB plans or plans intended to move us fully to a private world of defined-contribution plans such as the one Ferrara and Tanner advocate.

Another option for financing the transition is to merely issue government bonds as the liabilities come due, thus converting unfunded statutory obligations into more formal contractual debt. The extent to which such a policy would truly increase our national indebtedness would only be the extent to which we would have otherwise reneged on the statutory promises embedded in Social Security. The problem with this option is that it does not curtail the unfunded obligations; it merely changes their form. Recognition bonds will have to be either serviced by future generations or paid off by them. Each is a cost.

Creating Transition Mechanisms

For purposes of exposition, the advisory council developed the PSA proposal under the assumption that the costs of making the transition from the current structure of Social Security to the proposed alternative would be paid for by an explicit tax. This tax could take on several forms. It could be a surtax placed on the regular income tax, a supplemental payroll tax, or some completely new tax levied independently of current sources of federal revenues. So that the PSA proponents could fully understand the overall magnitude of the costs of transition, the Social Security actuaries developed two sets of projections in which the transition would be financed through a supplemental payroll tax.

In the first transition scenario, the controlling assumption was that all transition costs would be borne on a pay-go basis. Fairly quickly after the beginning of the transition, the payroll tax to support the non-Medicare portion of the total benefit package would have to increase to roughly 16 percent of payroll from its current level of 12.4 percent. It would gradually taper off over time, but some supplemental tax collections would be required for nearly fifty years. Twenty years into the transition, they would still be nearly 15 percent of covered payroll. Forty years into the transition, payroll taxes would be roughly 1 percentage point higher than those we now bear. Shortly thereafter, they would revert to current rates.

Paying off the transition costs on a pay-go basis would mean that they were completely paid off within the span of a regular working lifetime. Some workers nearing the end of their careers when the plan was implemented would pay only a small portion of the transition costs. Likewise, those entering the workforce near the end of the transition would bear little of the cost. Those workers who were relatively young when the proposal was adopted would have to bear the full brunt of the transition costs throughout their lives. Yet all generations might benefit from this proposal under the right circumstances, with the largest benefits accruing to future workers yet unborn. This raises the question of whether it is fair to hit one generation of workers so much harder with the transition costs than others, or whether these costs might be spread over a broader set of participants in the system.

In an alternative approach to the transition developed by the PSA proponents at the 1994–1996 Advisory Council, Social Security actuaries projected that a payroll tax supplement of 1.52 percent of covered payroll over seventy years would finance the transition. In this case, the underlying assumption was that the government would be willing to borrow in the capital markets to convert a portion of the existing statutory debt created by current Social Security law into more formal debt. The bonds would be used to finance a portion of the transition during the times when the 1.52 percent payroll tax supplement is insufficient to meet pay-as-you-go costs. The designers of the PSA assumed that the government would continue to levy the earmarked tax until all of the transition bonds are redeemed. In this case, the transition would take roughly seventy years, or nearly two full working lifetimes.

If we combined a higher payroll tax with the use of budget surpluses, the level of surplus or explicit additional taxes needed would drop dramatically, and the overall transition time frame would be significantly shortened. For example, assuming the transition tax of 1.5 percentage points, the extra budget surpluses required in the first ten years would average about $40 billion per year in present value to cover in full the pay-go transition costs to a PSA-type plan. The surplus needed over and above the added payroll tax would average about $25 billion per year over the next decade.

Concerns about equity in the Social Security program and about sharing the costs of transition naturally give rise to a question about the potential for sharing some of the burden of the transition from a pay-go system with the current participants in the system who are now receiving benefits. The reason that this question arises is that the benefits that were provided to early participants in the system, including those now retired, were so favorable relative to the taxes these groups paid, as discussed earlier. None of the workers in the baby boom generation or the generation behind it can expect to do as well as their forebears who are now receiving benefits. Under current law, the baby boomer who earned average wages throughout his or her career can expect to get back less than the value of the payroll taxes paid on his or her earnings, accumulated at the interest rates for government bonds. And we know that since current law is unsustainable, the actual situation for the baby boom cohorts will be even worse than current law suggests.

If an explicit marginal payroll tax were used to finance the transition from the pay-go system to a more heavily funded one, individuals now receiving Social Security benefits and grandfathered workers in the current system would not share in paying the transition costs. If those who have received a significantly better deal from the system than younger participants are fully exempted from helping to pay transition costs, it raises an equity issue. One way this might be handled would be to have a one-time or limited series of reductions in the CPI adjustment of benefits. If workers covered under the modified system are required to pay an added payroll tax of 1.5 percent per year, a case could be made that retirees should give up 1.5 percentage points of their COLA increase in the transition year. For people coming onto the rolls in subsequent years, a similar one-time adjustment could be made in their benefits. A one-time adjustment of this sort would carry through in the form of reduced annual benefits for the remainder of their lives. If there is a concern that the reductions in the COLA would jeopardize the low-income elderly, those in the bottom 40 percent of the benefit distribution could be exempted.

Added Funding Will Reduce Returns on Contributions for the Transition Generation

Recently several analyses developed have shown that the transition generation would realize lower rates of return on Social Security contributions if we implement a policy that leads to more funding than is provided in current law. This is not inconsistent with our understanding about the implications of increasing the rate of savings for a macro economy. An increase in the savings rate means a commensurate reduction in the consumption rate in an economy. That means that the immediate standard of living of those doing the saving will decline. Over time, however, our understanding of economic growth is that added saving will lead to improved productivity and ultimately higher levels of output and consumption.

We can apply our general understanding of macroeconomics to the current Social Security reform debate. Many of the reform proposals that would move us from our pay-go system to one that is significantly funded are structured to increase national savings rates as part of the process. The people who do the added saving initially will pay the price of initially reduced consumption. For some of them, the second-order effects of increased productivity will not offset the first-order effect of saving more on their consumption levels. We can devise all manner of fancy models to prove the point, but common sense leads to the same conclusion.

Part of the Social Security debate suggests that there is a way out of our current state without anyone's having to bear added costs. We have looked at this issue carefully and we do not see a "no-cost" solution. That brings us to the question, Who pays? There seems to be some consensus that we do not expect those currently retired or close to retirement to pay very much, if anything, in financing transition costs. That means that the burden will fall on current and future workers. We personally do not think that we should burden a single generation with the whole cost of getting ourselves out of a hole that we have dug over the last sixty to sixty-five years. Mechanisms can be devised to spread out the costs of added savings, and the transition borrowing in the PSA proposal is an example.

There are also ways to defer the bill associated with the moving to a retirement system in this country that is more significantly funded than our current one. We believe that is what pay-go proposals are all about. We do not question the motivations of the people offering that approach, such as Senators Kerrey and Moynihan. Indeed, we admire Senators Kerrey and Moynihan's honesty about what the costs will be to sustain Social Security in its current pay-go form. In the final analysis, however, we oppose their approach because we believe it abandons a fundamental principle that has been part of this country since its founding. That principle is that each generation leaves an estate to its descendants that is larger than the one it inherited. If today's workers are not willing to make an added contribution to savings through Social Security reform, they are going to condemn their children and grandchildren to participation in a system that will continue to be plagued by underfunding and low rates of return. Maybe it is not fair that today's workers themselves have inherited such a system. But that wrong does not make it right for us to pass current, or, more likely, much larger debts on to future generations.

Chapter 22

The Benefits and Risks
Under Alternative Forms of
Retirement Provision

A recurring theme in the discussion over Social Security reform is the "risk" that alternative approaches to reform might pose to workers. Often this discussion tends to focus primarily on the risks that exist in financial markets. For example, Robert Ball and his associates on the 1994–1996 Advisory Council on Social Security wrote of the problems associated with the Personal Security Account proposal: "Perhaps the most disturbing is the increased risk to the individual family. In considerable part, we would be trading a defined-benefit plan with statutory benefits enforceable in the courts for whatever individuals could secure from investment. . . . It is one thing to have retirement income *supplementary* to the Social Security system based on income from investment, such as IRAs and 401(k) plans, but quite another to make the basic system depend on the uncertainties of private investment."[1] The implication of this statement is clear. There are certain guarantees in the current system, certified by the courts, and the alternative would be full of uncertainty. The problem is that the statement is carefully worded to give the wrong impression of how the world works.

Social Security benefits today are indeed benefits defined under the statutes of the Social Security Act. Anyone who does not receive the benefit promised under current law can indeed go to the courts to win the rightful entitlement. The thing that the statement fails to highlight is that the Congress has retained the right to modify the statute defining benefit entitlements any time it feels it should do so. The fact that the system is so badly underfunded for the period from 2010 on means that Congress will

372

undoubtedly change the statute. In the last twenty years or so, Congress has shown a clear willingness to cut benefits when it exerts its authority to change the Social Security Act as it sees fit. For anyone planning retirement around Social Security benefits, that the current system is underfunded poses risks, and so does the fact that Congress adopted Social Security changes in 1977, 1983, and 1993 that reduced benefits for many beneficiaries in one way or another.

The Concept of Risk in Retirement Saving

A problem that workers face is that they cannot make provision for their retirement needs in the last year or two before they retire. The longer the planning horizon in making preparations for retirement, the easier it is for workers to achieve their retirement goals. Most financial planners and retirement plan designers would recommend that workers begin to save for their retirement by their late twenties, or most certainly by their early to mid-thirties. One difficulty workers face in their retirement planning is that there are several contingencies that they cannot accurately predict as they implement their savings plan for retirement. These include accumulating sufficient resources so they can roughly maintain their preretirement standard of living once they quit working. Other contingencies are making provision against a retirement of unknown duration, making provision for increases in the cost of living during the retirement period, and, to the extent that a worker is depending on assets invested in the financial markets, taking precautions against variations in rates of return on savings over time. Finally, given the prospect that Social Security benefits might be adjusted, people must make provisions against political contingencies.

Types of Risk Under Consideration
in Social Security Reform Discussions

The prospect of Social Security benefit reductions means that workers need to be increasingly aware of the other retirement risks that they face. The prospect of benefit reductions means that other saving should be increased to make up for the Social Security cuts. People who are not willing to save more must either take for granted that they will have reduced standards of living in retirement or be willing to commit to a longer work life. As we see it, our current retirement system faces a combination of financial and political risks that cannot be fully escaped. Trade-offs can be made, but the risks cannot be eliminated. Understanding these risks is imperative to figuring out how to deal with them.

Political Risks

In the earlier chapters of our discussion we explored at length the underlying financing structure of our Social Security system. There we showed that the cost of this system was crucially dependent on the relationship between the numbers of retirees and workers in our society, on the one hand, and the relationship between benefit levels and workers' covered wages, on the other. We have shown that the way the program was implemented resulted in a lighter tax burden on early generations of covered workers than if we had provided full retirement benefits to all the elderly at the outset. We have also shown that there were tremendous subsidies for the early generations of beneficiaries.

We believe that the way the program was implemented and the abnormally rich benefits provided to early participants resulted in a larger Social Security system than is politically viable over the long term if it is financed on a pay-as-you-go basis. The people who are arguing today that we have to maintain the current benefit structure of Social Security and roughly its current benefit level are essentially saying that this system is properly sized as an element of our retirement system. We see indications that the program is larger than our society is willing to support. And this realization is at the heart of what we characterize as the political risk associated with the current system.

Economists have observed for years that the tax incentives encouraging home mortgages and employer-sponsored health benefit plans have led to potentially excessive expenditures of our national resources on housing and health care. Similar arguments can be made that the significant subsidization of Social Security benefits during the implementation of the system encouraged it to grow larger than it would have otherwise, and possibly larger than was desirable. While Social Security was relatively redistributional even during its early days, the absolute subsidization of retirement income was much larger for middle- and upper-income workers than it was for those with a career of low earnings.

When economists or insurance theorists consider risks, they generally understand that there are up and down sides to virtually all economic activities. The up side of the evolution of Social Security was that the public demanded more and more of a good thing and the accommodating political process provided it to them. The down side is that the political process overpromised, and now the books have to be rebalanced. The rebalancing is going to be painful for a lot of people, but almost certainly more for some than others.

One should not come to the conclusion that there are no political risks in the recommendations for moving away from our national defined-benefit system to one that is much more dependent on defined-contribution plans. The argument that future Congresses might let workers tap their retirement accumulations before retirement is a legitimate concern. We think it can be managed, but it is still a concern. Another is that it will be difficult in some situations to let the financial markets exert their wiles. Markets not only go up; they also go down. The prospect that we can somehow provide a free floor of protection against down markets and let the investors have all the upside benefits is another false promise. Guarantees of this sort will cost someone money. Not to include that cost in the representation of the system or its reform is misleading.

Financial Market Risks

Gary Burtless at the Brookings Institution provided us with the same historical data series that Bob Ball has used to support his argument that individual accounts are excessively risky.[2] We used this data to replicate Ball's analysis. The results are shown in Figure 22.1. The point that Ball makes about the results shown in the figure is that "variations of this magnitude would represent a serious problem for workers, whose expectations of retirement income could be abruptly undercut."[3]

The picture in Figure 22.1 is misleading in several regards. First of all, the 6 percent contribution rate used in developing the figure bears no relation to what people are contributing to Social Security today. If we wish to show how current workers might fare under a pure defined-contribution system where contributions were invested totally in stock over these hypothetical careers, we should use a different contribution rate. The contribution rate for retirement benefits in the current system is roughly 10 percent of covered payroll. The cost rate of retirement benefits, not including disability, provided under current law for someone retiring in 2030 is currently projected to be more than 15 percent of covered payroll.

In Figure 22.2 we show the variation in benefit levels using the Burtless data but now assuming that the contribution rate would be 15 percent of pay over the working career, not the 6 percent used to derive Figure 22.1. We use 15 percent because it is closer to what would be required to pay a benefit called for under current law for an average worker currently in the

Figure 22.1　Earnings-Replacement Rates of Workers with Forty-Year Careers Who Invest 6 Percent of Pay in the U.S. Stock Market and Retire, 1912–1997

Annuity as percent of earnings near the end of worker's career

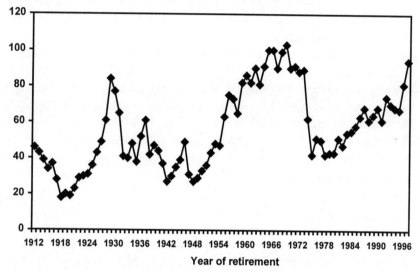

Year of retirement

Source: Calculations by the authors, based on data provided by Gary Burtless at the Brookings Institution, Washington, D.C.

workforce. The bold flat line in Figure 22.2 is the replacement rate provided by current law for workers at the low level of earnings. Workers at higher earning levels will have even lower Social Security replacement rates than shown by the flat line.

The figure presented by Ball adjusted to reflect contributions that are comparable to the projected cost of the existing system if it is to provide benefits in 2030 raises some interesting questions. How important are the absolute benefit levels from two alternative systems? Is it more important that everyone get roughly similar benefits as those retiring before or after, or that they all get a shot at doing better, with the understanding some would do much better than others? Which of the options depicted in Figure 22.2 might workers choose at the beginning of their careers if they were given the choice?

Though Figure 22.2 raises some intriguing questions, it is also misleading. The annuity reflected by the flat line in the figure would be indexed to the consumer price index. The annuities reflected by the variable line would not. Further, the variable line does not take into account how workers might actually invest in a system that included individual accounts. If we look back at Table 21.1 in the last chapter, it is clear that most 401(k) participants reduce their exposure to stocks as they approach retirement age. In addition, the variable line in Figure 22.2 does not take into account administrative expenses related to a system such as the PSA system considered by the 1994–1996 Advisory Council on Social Security. Finally, the line does not take into account the implications of the floor benefit in the PSA proposal that would significantly alleviate the risks implied in Figures 22.1 and 22.2. A host of issues need to be considered in comparing plans. Partial analyses are misleading and cannot be relied on in evaluation of specific proposals.

We have developed our own historical simulations of how workers would have fared if they had been covered under the IA and PSA plans of the 1994–1996 Advisory Council on Social Security. In the simulations, we look at a worker who starts to work at age twenty-two under the two plans.

Figure 22.2   Earnings-Replacement Rates of Workers with Forty-Year Careers Who Invest 15 Percent of Pay in the U.S. Stock Market and Retire, 1912–1997

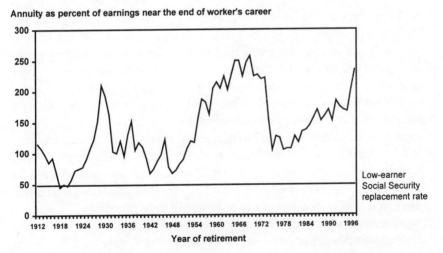

Source: Calculations by the authors based on data provided by Gary Burtless at the Brookings Institution, Washington, D.C.

Figure 22.3   Projected Retirement Benefits Under Specified Social
Security Reforms for Workers Born in 1975

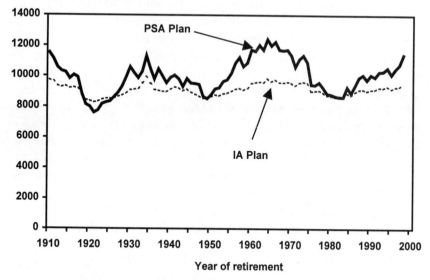

Source: Simulation results developed by Watson Wyatt Worldwide. Historical financial return
data from Bryan Taylor; global financial data at *http://www.globalfindata.com/march1.htm.*

By doing this, we wipe out the issues related to payments of transition benefits. These simulations are based on forty-two-year careers. We use historical stock and bond returns dating back to 1858. The simulations assume that
workers would have diversified their assets between stocks and bonds over
their working career, similarly to the way 401(k) investors invest. Finally,
we assume that workers would have paid 1 percent of their asset balances
per year as a cost associated with administration of the PSA system and
0.1 percent as a cost associated with administration of the IA system.

   The results of our simulations over the same period envisaged in Ball's
presentation for workers at the low level of earnings are shown in Figure
22.3. These results are shown in 1998 dollar levels, rather than as replacement rates. We will come back to a presentation of this type of simulation
with the results presented as replacement rates in Chapter 23. The results
in the figure show that under more realistic sets of simulations than those
used in developing Figures 22.1 and 22.2, the variation in benefit levels
is significantly less. For example, the maximum benefit in Figure 22.1 is
5.72 times the lowest benefit in the series. In Figure 22.3, for the IA plan,

the maximum benefit is 1.20 times the minimum benefit. For the PSA plan in the latter figure, the maximum benefit is 1.64 times the minimum benefit. More realistic simulations of the types of plans that are being proposed result in outcomes significantly different from those which critics of the proposals present.

What If the Trust Fund Invests in Stocks?

A number of people including President Clinton in his 1999 State of the Union address, Henry Aaron and Robert Reischauer,[4] and Bob Ball have advocated retaining the current benefit structure but improving the Social Security system's finances by having the trust fund acquire stocks for a portion of its assets. It is well known that stocks have higher average returns than government bonds. It is also well known that they are riskier. This raises an important question. Can Social Security enjoy the higher returns without bearing the higher risks? Thomas MaCurdy and John Shoven, both Stanford University economists, examined this question in a January 1999 research paper.[5]

The two Stanford economists examined what would have happened in the past if the government had invested part of the trust fund in a diversified portfolio of equities. The question was, Would the trust fund balance have been bigger ten or twenty years later? Not only did they look at the historical sequence of stock market returns, but they also examined what would have happened if the order of these annual returns had been randomly scrambled. The results indicated that although the trust fund was usually enhanced by stock market investment, higher returns were no sure thing. The authors predicted that there was roughly a 20 to 25 percent chance that the inclusion of stocks would worsen the financial balance of the system after ten or even twenty years.

The lesson from their study is a version of economists' favorite saying— "There is no such thing as a free lunch." You cannot enjoy the higher average returns of stocks and the safety of government bonds at the same time. If the trust fund invests in stocks, someone has to bear the risk that they will underperform. Those who bear the risk should almost certainly not be the elderly, so that leaves only one other choice—young workers. Having young workers participate in the stock market is not a bad idea. Our preference for individual accounts is based on a belief that the young should be given a choice regarding the risks that they assume.

Table 22.1   Distribution of Wealth Among the Near-Elderly

Position in the wealth-holding distribution	Retirement Purchasing Power from			
	Personal financial wealth	Social Security wealth	Pension wealth	Total wealth
Bottom 10th	3.4%	93.6%	3.0%	100.0%
1/3 from bottom	18.1	63.4	18.5	100.0
2/3 from bottom	29.9	35.7	34.4	100.0
Top 10th	65.2	10.2	24.6	100.0

Source: James F. Moore and Olivia S. Mitchell, "Projected Retirement Wealth and Savings Adequacy in the Health and Retirement Study," presented at the 1998 Pension Research Council Symposium "Forecasting Retirement Needs and Retirement Wealth," April 27, 1998.

Distribution of Risks in the Context of Social Security Reform

In Chapter 20 we presented a summary of an analysis of the wealth distribution among people on the verge of retirement developed by Olivia Mitchell and James Moore at the Wharton School, University of Pennsylvania. Here we repeat the table from that analysis as Table 22.1. We present it here because we want the reader to think about the distribution across the income or wealth spectrum of different kinds of risk related to Social Security reform.

Recall that Mitchell and Moore were working with data from a sample of people representing the population of the United States between the ages of fifty-one and sixty-one in 1992. The authors had converted pension and future Social Security income into present values so that it could be added together with other forms of wealth. Recall also that we had re-moved the value of owner-occupied housing from the portfolio, because most people do not sell their homes during their retirement period. In essence, Table 22.1 shows the resources that people on the cusp of retirement will have available to finance their day-to-day consumption during their retirement period. It is a good exposition of the uneven distribution of political risk in the current Social Security system.

In Chapter 20 we reviewed the adjustments to the existing system that would be called for under the Kerrey-Moynihan proposal to return Social Security to pay-go financing. We showed there that the adjustment would result in a 25 percent reduction in benefits over the long-term projection period. For the people in the bottom 10 percent with regard to the wealth distribution shown in Table 22.1, a 25 percent reduction in their Social

Security wealth would translate into a 23.4 percent reduction in their total retirement wealth, not including their home if they own one. For people in the top 10 percent with regard to the wealth distribution, a 25 percent reduction in their Social Security wealth would represent a 2.6 percent reduction in their total retirement wealth, again not including their home. Anyone who considers the implications of the kinds of changes in Social Security policy introduced during the session of Congress ending in December 1998 must be aware that the political risks associated with them are highly variable depending on the distribution of income or wealth.

One of the first things that investment advisers counsel investors to do is to diversify their portfolio with the goal of minimizing risk exposure. The problem for workers at the bottom of the wealth distribution scale in Table 22.1 is that they have virtually all of their retirement wealth in one basket. And given the across-the-board benefit reductions incorporated into a number of proposals that have been introduced in Congress over the past couple of years, we believe that it is a highly risky basket. A policy that would diversify the retirement assets at the bottom of the wealth distribution scale would actually enhance the retirement income security of these workers relative to current law. We believe that such workers would be in a significantly more secure position even though diversifying might expose workers with lower earnings to more financial market risk than in the past.

The early motivations for setting up Social Security included the desire to provide the elderly with a secure retirement income base. We are now at a point in the evolution of Social Security where those who depend most significantly on it are the ones rendered the most insecure by proposals to modify the system within its traditional framework. The PSA proposal that Robert Ball has characterized as radical would actually diversify the retirement portfolios of workers at lower earning levels in a more balanced way than his own proposal would.

Some proponents of investing part of the central trust fund in the stock market seem to think that Social Security will somehow be able to take advantage of higher returns without experiencing a commensurate increase in risk. That is no more the case than it is for any other pension plan investing in stocks. The potential for added returns over time will be accompanied by exposure to the downside of the market, and there can be no guarantees. The pursuit of such a policy would entail the need for adjustments to take account of adverse market outcomes. Of course this is true for individual investors as well.

We are convinced that some of the proposals for individual-account reforms of Social Security do not reckon with the risks in the financial markets. For example, Gordon Goodfellow and Sylvester Schieber have simulated a series of individual-account proposals and found that the full movement to individual accounts would pose considerable downside risk for workers at the lower end of the earnings distribution scale. They found that more than one-third would probably receive benefits below those in current law for a fully implemented defined-contribution system. But they also found that benefit reforms can significantly alleviate the problem of financial market risk if partial individual accounts are supported by a floor plan provided through Social Security.[6] In other words, there are ways to offset downside risk while preserving opportunities for upside gains.

One of the risks that we would face if Social Security invested in equities on a pooled basis is that any short-term adjustments implemented because of adverse market conditions would probably have to be implemented across the board. If adverse markets led to benefit cuts, they would probably do so, across the board. If we had individual-account investment, though, that would not be the case. To illustrate this point, we look at the portion of benefits that would be paid out of the individual-account segment of the reformed system and the portion paid out of the residual OASDI system under the advisory council's IA and PSA proposals. The portion of benefits payable out of the individual-account segments under each of these proposals is shown in Table 22.2. For the worker with low lifetime earnings, about 20 percent of his or her benefits under the IA plan would come out of the individual account, once the system had fully matured. Under the PSA plan it would be about 45 percent. Some people look at those percentages and are concerned about the financial market exposure for people close to retirement. But remember, as people get closer and closer to retirement, they tend to sell equities and move into more conservative assets. In Chapter 21 we saw (Table 21.1) that workers in their sixties with low levels of earnings held between 30 and 40 percent of their 401(k) assets in equities. So for a worker with low earnings under the IA plan, we would expect total IA equity holdings to represent only about 6 to 8 percent of the total benefit accrual as the worker neared retirement. Under the PSA plan it would be 15 to 20 percent. These are not tremendous risk exposures for people with a remaining life expectancy of fifteen to twenty years.

For workers represented in Table 22.2 whose earnings are at Social Security's taxable maximum over most of their career, the percentage of their total retirement benefit coming out of the individual account under the IA plan when it matures would still be less than 40 percent. For the PSA plan it would be around 80 percent. At those earning levels, workers approaching retirement age who participate in 401(k) plans still typically

Table 22.2   Portion of Total Social Security Benefits Payable from Personal Accounts for the 1994–1996 Advisory Council's IA and PSA Proposals

Year worker turns 65	Worker's Level of Lifetime Earnings			
	Low	Average	High	Maximum
Percent of benefits coming out of individual accounts				
1995	0.0	0.0	0.0	0.0
2005	1.6	2.2	3.0	3.9
2015	5.0	7.0	8.4	10.4
2025	9.6	13.2	15.9	19.6
2035	15.7	21.7	25.8	28.2
2045	19.9	27.0	31.8	36.9
2055	20.0	27.1	31.9	37.4
2065	20.1	27.2	32.0	37.5
Percent of benefits coming out of Personal Security Accounts				
1995	0.0	0.0	0.0	0.0
2005	0.5	1.5	3.0	3.5
2015	14.7	20.7	24.9	30.7
2025	25.5	36.8	43.9	51.6
2035	37.5	54.2	63.7	71.3
2045	44.3	63.9	73.9	80.8
2055	44.5	64.0	74.1	81.0
2065	44.8	64.2	74.2	81.3

Source: Report of the 1994-1996 Advisory Council on Social Security, vol. 1: *Findings and Recommendations* (Washington, D.C.: Social Security Administration, 1997), pp. 223-226.

have 50 percent of their assets in equities. So workers with higher earnings would have higher risk exposures under the individual-account plans than workers with lower earnings. Most financial analysts would argue that that is a reasonable pattern of risk-sharing. Although 80 percent of total retirement benefits in the PSA plan may seem like a lot to have coming from the market side, we would note that with only half of that in equities, earners at the maximum wage would still have only 40 percent of their benefits exposed to equity variations. For people at relatively high earning levels, this is not an inordinate amount of risk.

Macroeconomic Risks

We can adopt policies in reforming Social Security that either encourage saving or discourage it. If they encourage it, it is almost certain that

Figure 22.4   Growth in Business-Sector Real Capital, Gross Domestic Product, and Labor Supply

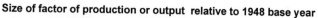
Size of factor of production or output relative to 1948 base year

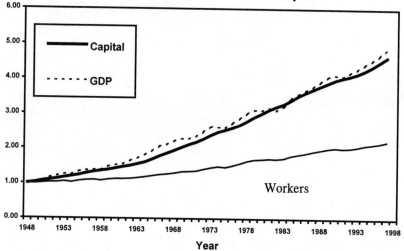

Year

Sources: Bureau of Economic Analysis, U.S. Department of Commerce, *Survey of Current Business* (September 1998), p. 37, and (August 1998), p. 151; and Eva S. Jacobs, ed., *Handbook of U.S. Labor Statistics* (Lanham, Md.: Bernan Press, 1998), p. 10.

such policies will result in growth of the capital stock. As you can see from Figure 22.4, growth in capital stock and growth in total output are closely linked. Increased saving is extremely important as we look to the future. But not all Social Security reforms will encourage additional saving. Policies that increase the payroll tax to support pay-go financing will discourage saving. Such tax increases are converted almost directly into reduced saving by workers and increased consumption by retirees. The inheritance that we leave our children depends critically on how we go about Social Security reform. We must be careful. If we leave them an economy with a larger capacity, we reduce the burden that our retirement programs pose for them. If we leave them with a smaller economy, we increase that burden. In the long run, the heavier the burden that we impose on them, the less likely it is that they are going to be able or willing to pay for the baby boomers' retirement claims.

Henry Aaron, Barry Bosworth, and Gary Burtless at the Brookings Institution in Washington wrote a book several years ago looking at the beneficial effects of added saving in helping us deal with our aging society and pay for Social Security.[7] The authors estimated that a permanent increase in the savings rate equal to 1.5 percent of gross domestic product would result in a 15 percent larger capital stock after fifty years.[8] If we adopt policies that curtail saving, they will depress the growth in the capital base of the economy. If we adopt policies that enhance saving, the capital stock will be larger, future GDP will be higher, future workers will enjoy higher wages, and retirees will benefit from a more secure Social Security system.

Chapter 23

A Proposal for Reform

*N*ow that we have examined the history of Social Security and the difficult choices that it faces for the future, it is time to give you our bottom line—how the system should be changed in order to be successful in the twenty-first century. We will present a specific proposal, which we have named Personal Security Accounts 2000 (*PSA 2000*), thus adopting computer software companies' habit of dating or numbering new versions of their products. Our plan is a clear and close descendant of the PSA plan of the 1994–1996 Advisory Council, but it also contains a number of important new features. We feel that this PSA 2000 plan offers the best combination of equity and efficiency for the participants in the twenty-first-century U.S. economy. We also are proud of the fact that it deals with the financial hangover from the existing program in an honest and straightforward way. The one warning, then, is that you should not expect our plan to offer something for nothing. The current system has a long-term deficit of at least $3 trillion. We aren't going to wave any magic wands or pull any rabbits out of a hat—instead we are going to take a sober look at the problem and offer a program to deal with it.

Guiding Principles

Before presenting an outline of our PSA 2000 proposal, let us enunciate the principles that led us to this plan. We feel that these principles reflect widely held values in this country. Obviously, principles alone will not determine the details of a proposal, but they can offer guidance to both the engineers and the evaluators of proposed solutions. Let us first list the principles that we share regarding the retirement program of Social Security and then elaborate on some of them. They are

Principles for Redesigning Social Security

1. The important "safety net," or progressivity, of the existing Social Security system should be preserved.
2. Any redesign of Social Security should enhance the rate of national savings.
3. The disability and early-survivor insurance programs within OASDI should be preserved.
4. Any reform should offer solvency for the system in the long run, not simply postpone insolvency.
5. Any reform should improve equity for all participants (particularly in its treatment of one- and two-earner couples).
6. We should try to increase economic efficiency by increasing the link between contributions and benefits.
7. The risks borne by individual participants should be diversified and kept at tolerable levels.
8. Administrative costs should be kept to reasonable levels.
9. The reforms should be determined and announced as soon as possible.

We believe that all these goals and principles can be better met through a two-part, or hybrid, defined-benefit/defined-contribution plan in general—and our PSA 2000 plan in particular.

Our first principle stems partially from the fact that we don't want to step back from the single greatest accomplishment of Social Security, namely the relatively low incidence of official poverty among the elderly. As we have discussed in earlier chapters, one of the risks that Social Security insures against is a bad labor market outcome. Bad labor market outcomes can be a result of poor health, a poor economy, or just plain bad luck. We think that it is unseemly for a wealthy society such as ours to force people who have been unsuccessful in their working careers to live out an impoverished old age. The current program offers those with a profile of low lifetime earnings a higher replacement rate than it does to those with above-average lifetime labor earnings. We think that it is important to preserve this general pattern.

Our second principle could be restated like this: we think that more funding is better than less. Just as saving is the only reliable way for a household to get rich, saving is the only reliable way for our country to become wealthier. More wealth for future Americans translates to higher productivity and higher real wages for future workers. The fact that a higher rate of national savings would result in significantly higher real wages within twenty years was effectively argued in 1989 by Henry Aaron, Barry Bosworth, and Gary Burtless.[1] Even with no agreement on the exact magnitudes, there is widespread acceptance that the pay-go Social Security system has depressed personal and national savings. Further, providing for retirement is the most important motive for saving. It is only natural that we try to increase the tendency to save, while restoring the long-run solvency of Social Security. It should be added that we realize that not all the new mandatory funding will result in new savings. Some fraction of the gain in Social Security assets will be offset by reduced savings elsewhere in the economy. However, we believe that half or more of the additional Social Security savings would translate into a higher rate of national savings—and that would be a major accomplishment.

Our third principle, that disability and early-survivor insurance should be preserved, is an outgrowth of our opinion that insuring against these risks is very important and that Social Security is relatively efficient in providing this coverage. The lack of any significant clamor to replace these elements of the system with a private alternative suggests that this type of term insurance should continue to be provided by the Social Security Administration. The long-term finances of our program are sufficiently strong to provide as much for these programs or even somewhat more than is provided through the current payroll tax structure. That is not to say that the disability program in particular shouldn't be studied carefully for inefficiencies. The DI program itself is underfunded by 20 percent over the seventy-five-year projection period used by the actuaries. We believe that it would be totally irresponsible for policymakers to reallocate any additional portion of the payroll tax base to the disability program without a full-blown review of the program's operations.

Our fourth principle was prompted by the 1983 Social Security Amendments. As you will recall from Chapter 13, by no means the least significant contributor to the development of a large seventy-five-year actuarial deficit since 1983 has been the mere passage of time. Even with the optimistic projections of 1983, the reformed system would run large deficits, beginning with the second decade of the twenty-first century. The claim was that the program was balanced for seventy-five years, with the early surpluses financing the later losses. The built-in problem was that with each passing year there was one fewer of the surplus years in the seventy-five-year window—and one more deficit year. What we should now aspire to is not only a system that is balanced over the next seventy-five years, but also one that appears to be workable thereafter. As you will see, our PSA 2000 plan does even better than that.

The fifth principle deals with the equitable treatment of different groups of Social Security participants. Our chief concerns here are the treatment of one-earner and two-earner households and the adequacy of resources available to widows and widowers. While some of the transfers within the existing system are not only defensible but worth preserving, others are not. The large inequities between two-earner couples, one-earner couples, and single individuals should be rethought. Other specific aspects of Social Security rules also seem convoluted and inappropriate. For instance, the cliff vesting of marriages at ten years seems arbitrary. Divorced individuals can claim benefits based on the earnings of their ex-spouse only if they were married for ten years or more. Finally, since poverty is greatest amongst widows, widow and widower benefits should be increased more, by comparison with those for married couples.

The sixth principle is a very important one. There always has been a debate about whether Social Security contributions should be thought of as taxes or as deferred compensation—that is, pension contributions. The current system has a relatively weak link between marginal contributions and marginal benefits and therefore may be viewed by most people as a tax-transfer system rather than a deferred-compensation pension system. For people with covered work histories shorter than ten years and for many whose careers are longer than thirty-five years, there is zero marginal benefit to additional marginal contributions. For secondary earners in two-earner households, the marginal connection between contributions and benefits is small or nil. If the full 15.3 percent payroll tax is viewed as a marginal tax with few or no offsetting marginal benefits,[2] then the distortionary costs of the overall tax system are greatly increased. The total marginal tax rate for someone in the 15 percent federal income tax bracket is more than doubled, and the efficiency costs of the tax system (which go up with the square of the marginal tax rate) more than quadrupled, owing to the payroll tax. If marginal contributions and benefits are closely linked, it can lower the effective marginal tax rate and thereby enhance economic efficiency.

The seventh principle is one of the arguments against a purely privatized system—namely, that such a plan has participants who—some almost certainly unknowingly—take too much risk with their future retirement resources. Sophisticated investors can manage these risks, but many Social Security participants have limited understanding of the stakes. In our view, this concern is greatly reduced or even reversed for a partially privatized plan. A two-tier system where everyone had some individual-account investments would almost certainly prove a stimulus for greatly increasing the level of financial literacy among the general population. At the same time, the tier-one, or floor, benefits provide protection from truly cata-strophic financial results. Both defined-benefit and defined-contribution Social Security programs are risky. The DB plans entail political risks—that is, the government can change the program at any time—and macro-economic and demographic risks. DC plans carry the underlying risks of financial instruments, and we all know that stock and bond returns are highly variable. The optimal thing to do when you have a situation where two different designs face different kinds of risk is to come up with a hy-brid, or "some of each," solution. This follows from the first principles of risk diversification.

The eighth principle, that we should watch administrative costs, is an-other type of efficiency consideration. Social Security will remain the pri-mary retirement program for the majority of Americans. It is important that their contributions not be consumed by high administrative expenses. Any privatization plan or partial privatization plan must attempt to mini-mize the administrative costs of the program. That said, the current pro-gram, which is relatively inexpensively administered, provides very poor information to participants. Annual statements are still not mailed to all participants, and the statements, which are sent out on request, are mis-leading. For instance, the only contributions shown on the statement are the half of payroll taxes attributed to the employee—the other half, those paid by the employer, are simply missing.[3] Most economists agree that the employee bears both halves of the payroll tax, and yet the average partici-pant sees projected benefits and only half the payments to the system. Any private mutual fund or insurance company would be called to account for failing to disclose the cost of the investment fully in its policy or prospec-tus. In reforming the system, we should certainly try to control adminis-trative expenses, but clearly better and more informative communication with participants should also be a goal.

The final principle, namely to do something as soon as possible, stems from a couple of considerations. First, the Social Security trustees them-selves report that the structure of the system is unsustainable after the third decade of the twenty-first century. But the one thing we know is that there is a tremendous advantage in allowing people time to adjust to any changes in the benefit rules. If we didn't know that before President Rea-gan's ill-conceived 1981 Social Security proposals, we should have learned it then. Second, there still is time for the baby boomers to contribute to Social Security's solvency. But, that opportunity is dwindling fast. Finally, the "passage of time" effect keeps bringing the financial problems of the system closer and compounding them. The only way to check the growth of the burden being placed on future generations of workers is to begin making payments on the solution soon.

The PSA 2000 Plan

The two of us have worked on Social Security for fifty years combined. Over that time, we have developed a number of proposals to improve the system. The PSA 2000 proposal represents our latest and best plan for an American Social Security system for the twenty-first century. The general outline of the plan is quite simple. First, the payroll tax would remain unchanged from current legislation. That means that OASDI taxes would continue to be a total of 12.4 percent of annual earnings up to a ceiling amount of $72,600 in 1999. The percentage would stay the same for the next several decades. In the distant future it would be reduced when transition costs were paid off and the residual trust fund for the pay-go-financed flat benefit reached 1.5 years of benefits. In the future, the maximum amount of earnings subject to tax would grow with the general level of wages. All of this, except for the eventual reductions in the payroll tax rates, is exactly as in current legislation.

The benefit side of the program is completely redesigned under our proposal. There would be two parts to Social Security's retirement benefits: (1) a defined-benefit part and (2) a defined-contribution part. In plans such as PSA 2000, these two parts are often referred to as the two tiers of benefits. The first tier would be a flat benefit for all individuals with a full career of thirty-five years or more. The flat benefit amount for single people would be $500 per month in the year 2000. The $500 initial benefit would increase in the future by an amount reflecting the general increase in wage levels. The second tier of benefits results from the participant's accumulation in the defined-contribution part of the plan. The second tier would be financed by a combination of employee contributions and matching contributions from Social Security.

Workers would be required to contribute 2.5 percent of covered pay up to the taxable limit on which payroll taxes are due. Social Security would match the worker's contribution on a one-to-one basis, providing another 2.5 percent of covered earnings. All told, workers would be accumulating 5 percent of their covered earnings in a Personal Security Account. Many people are undoubtedly going to argue that we are proposing an increase in workers' taxes. Under the system that we propose, the account will always be in the worker's name. He or she, while having no discretion about contributing to it while working, will have discretion over how it is invested throughout the working career and redeemed after retirement. We note that in cases where employers offer 401(k) plans with 100 percent matching of employee contributions, participation rates in the plans are typically around 80 percent and are generally somewhat higher for all but the youngest and the lowest-paid employees. We are suggesting putting an offer on the table that most workers would be likely to take up voluntarily anyway.

In retirement, workers would receive the proceeds of these accounts in addition to their tier-one benefit. The government's matching contribution would not come out of thin air. In fact, it is a rebate of the worker's 12.4 percent payroll tax. After paying the 2.5 percent rebates, Social Security would have only a net amount of 9.9 percent of covered pay to finance tier-one benefits and disability and survivors insurance, and to honor the promises of the existing program during the lengthy transition or phase-in period.

The All-Important Details

We have just described the basics of the proposal in a few short paragraphs. Obviously, there are a lot of details to the plan. Here we will cover the most important of them.

1. *Less-than-Full Careers.* A thirty-five-year career is required in order to receive the full flat benefit of tier one ($500 in 2000, indexed for average wage growth thereafter) at the normal retirement age. Those with a minimum-length career (ten years, or forty covered quarters) would receive one-half of the flat tier-one benefit. Those with more than a ten-year covered career would get an extra 2 percent for each extra year, up to a total of 100 percent.

2. *Normal Retirement Age.* To receive the full flat tier-one benefit (or even the reduced benefit resulting from a shorter career), one would have to retire at the normal retirement age. Under the PSA 2000 plan, the normal retirement age increases by two months per year for the years 2000 through 2011 and reaches sixty-seven years in 2011. Thereafter, further increases are indexed to improvements in life expectancies of people at the normal retirement age.

3. *Early and Late Retirements.* As the normal retirement age is gradually advanced, the age of eligibility for early retirement would also be advanced. Eventually, the youngest age for early retirement would reach sixty-five. At that point, the PSA 2000 plan calls for no additional increases in the early retirement age. The adjustments for retiring at ages other than the normal retirement age would remain as in the current law. People retiring before the NRA would face a reduction in tier-one benefits at the rate of five-

ninths of 1 percent per month. People choosing to retire later than the NRA would have their benefits increased by two-thirds of 1 percent per month of delay in the commencement of benefits.

4. *Earnings Test.* Under the current Social Security system, people who are receiving benefits have their benefits reduced if their earnings are above an exempt amount. The reduction is 50 cents for every dollar by which earnings exceed the exempt amount for persons who have not attained Social Security's normal retirement age, and $33\frac{1}{3}$ cents for each dollar for persons who have. This clearly discourages part-time work by Social Security recipients. The PSA 2000 plan completely eliminates the earnings test for beneficiaries who have reached the normal retirement age.

5. *Spousal Benefits.* Spouses would receive the higher of either the tier-one benefit that they would be entitled to receive on the basis of their own earnings history or one-half of the amount of the tier-one benefit of their spouse. Two-earner married couples would be treated as two single people as concerns their tier-one benefits. If both partners had full thirty-five-year careers, they would receive a total of $1,000 per month in tier-one benefits. On the other hand, if one had a thirty-year career (qualifying that person for $450 per month) and one had a twenty-year career (qualification for $350 per month), their total monthly tier-one benefit would be $800. Of course, all these dollar figures will be higher in the future, because the amounts are for the year 2000 and future benefits will be increased to reflect average wage growth. Since the minimum qualifying career (ten years of covered earnings) qualifies a person for one-half of the full tier-one benefit, all two-earner couples (where both have qualifying careers) would receive tier-one benefits (and tier-two benefits, for that matter) based on their own work records. There would be no spousal benefits for the second tier of our system (although the money would be paid out as a joint-survivor annuity rather than a single life annuity). Further, we think that very few couples in the future would qualify for spousal benefits for tier one; the vast majority of married couples would receive benefits based on their own work records.

6. *Widow's Benefits.* Currently many widows and widowers receive two-thirds the amount that the couple received before the spouse's death. The PSA 2000 plan would gradually introduce the following improved program for surviving spouses. The spouse would receive the highest of his or her own tier-one benefit, the deceased spouse's tier-one benefit, or 75 percent of their combined tier-one benefits. The tier-two annuities would be of the joint-survivor type, with the survivor receiving 75 percent of the prior amount.

7. *Divorce.* Tier-two PSA accumulations would be treated like any other

defined-contribution pension plan with regard to dividing the assets in the event of divorce. Personally, we favor community-property rules by which the PSA balances accumulated during a marriage would be divided equally between spouses, independently of which of them worked. Tier-one benefits would be available to divorced spouses only with restrictive rules similar to those of the current program. It is our expectation that the vast majority of adults will earn their own tier-one benefits with a covered work career of at least ten years.

8. *Universal Coverage.* The PSA 2000 plan, like existing Social Security, involves redistribution from those with higher lifetime labor earnings to those with lower lifetime labor earnings. With PSA 2000 the redistribution is transparent. The tier-one benefit is the same for everyone regardless of wage. However, total payroll taxes are higher for those who have more earnings. The well-off pay more for the system than the not-so-well-off. That is the nature of redistribution. However, a fair redistributionary plan means that everyone must participate. Otherwise, groups that are well off opt out, refusing to help fund the transfers to those who are less well off. The bottom line of this discussion is that PSA 2000 features compulsory universal coverage. The new group that is brought into the system is all newly hired state and local government employees.

9. *Annuitization of PSA 2000 Payouts.* Social Security benefits are currently paid out as inflation-indexed life annuities, meaning that once a person starts receiving benefits, he or she gets that amount for the rest of his or her life, with annual increases reflecting price inflation, as measured by the consumer price index. The tier-one PSA 2000 benefits would be paid out in exactly the same manner. At the time of retirement, one-half of the tier-two accumulation would be automatically converted into an inflation-indexed life annuity. This half represents the government's matching contribution to the PSA accounts. There may be a concern that the government would be intruding by requiring the full annuitization of this portion of the benefit in cases where PSA accumulations were quite large. It would be possible to require that annuities meet some minimum level—for example, two times the poverty rate—to assure that beneficiaries would not come back to the government later for means-tested benefits. Individuals would be able to choose the form in which they would like to withdraw the other half of their PSA balance. Social Security could convert it into an indexed life annuity on the same terms as the other half of the assets. Or participants could roll half their PSA balance into an Individual Retirement Account or withdraw the money in any pattern that suited their needs.

10. *Taxation of Benefits.* The payroll tax would continue to be split be-

tween employees and employers. This means that workers would pay tax on half of their OASDI deductions (their half, but not the employers' half). Half the 2.5 percent mandatory contribution to the PSA account would be made with before-tax dollars and half with after-tax dollars. With this system, at the time the money was earned tax would be paid on half of everything contributed to Social Security. During retirement, 50 percent of the payouts from both tier one and tier two would be subject to the personal income tax. This treatment means that the entire PSA 2000 system would be taxed according to consumption tax principles. One way to think about it is that half the contributions are treated like Roth IRAs (where after-tax contributions are withdrawn tax-free in retirement), and half are treated like normal IRAs (where before-tax contributions are taxable upon withdrawal). Taxing half the money going in and half coming out allows people to diversify in accordance with two different tax regimes. It is important to note that just because half the benefits constitute taxable income, it does not mean that all retired people will actually have to pay income taxes on this money. Take, for instance, a married couple that receives $18,000 per year from the two parts of their PSA 2000 plan. Of their PSA payments, $9,000 would be treated as gross taxable income. However, as of 1998, a married couple in which both spouses were over sixty-five was not required to file a federal income tax return unless they had a gross income exceeding $14,200. Therefore, such a couple could have up to $5,200 in other income and still not owe any federal income tax. Only those with larger sources of other income (such as taxable pension distributions, dividends, and interest income) would have to pay income taxes on the $9,000 of taxable PSA distributions.

11. *Investment Choices and Regulation.* The 5 percent tier-two PSA accounts would be funded through payroll deductions (half from the employee and half from Social Security as a rebate of the standard FICA tax). Social Security would offer a limited menu of diversified investment options (indexed stock and bond accounts and one total market account, combining stocks and bonds). It is likely that there would be considerable delays in transferring the money into the intended investment accounts. The government would pay interest on contributions during the delay period. In addition to the standard government-sponsored investment accounts, individuals could choose to place their money with an approved financial service provider such as Schwab, Fidelity, or other such investment managers. All these providers would be required to offer special investment funds for the PSA accounts. The information and service that they provide participants and the administrative costs charged to PSA account holders would be

regulated. The maximum administrative cost would be 1 percent per year. We expect that competition would force many vendors to provide investment products at much lower costs than that. People would be required to invest all their PSA balances with a single approved and regulated vendor. People would be allowed to change vendors on an annual basis. We would favor allowing employers to make direct deposits into the PSA accounts if they so chose, thus bypassing the need for the money to pass through Social Security's hands.

12. *No Early Withdrawals Permitted.* The tier-two Personal Security Account program is an essential part of the new Social Security retirement system. No early withdrawals would be permitted from these accounts for any purpose. That means no hardship withdrawals and no withdrawals for down payments on first homes or for any other reason. The balances could not be used as collateral for loans. They could not even be touched in bankruptcy proceedings. We think that people would accept these restrictions if the rationale for them were explained, namely that the money is intended strictly for provision of retirement income. The one-to-one match also may make the restrictions more acceptable.

13. *The Phase-In.* The new program would be phased in extremely gradually. Current retirees and workers aged fifty-five and older in 2000 would be covered under the existing Social Security system. They would be subject to the accelerated increase in the normal retirement age and the change in the tax treatment of benefits (50 percent would be taxable income under the new program rather than the current 85 percent for those with taxable income above $25,000 [$32,000 for marrieds]). The net change for those fifty-five and over in 2000 would be quite small. The new program would be the only program for those who were under twenty-five in 2000. They would have at least forty years to accumulate assets in their 5 percent PSA accounts until becoming eligible for early retirement at age sixty-five (in 2040 and beyond). Workers who were between age twenty-five and fifty-four in 2000 would get some benefits under the new PSA 2000 plan and some under the existing Social Security rules. The fractions would be different for each age cohort. For instance, someone who was midway between twenty-five and fifty-four, say age forty, in the year 2000, would get half of the full-career tier-one benefit and half of his or her benefits from the existing PIA formula. Someone closer to fifty-four would have a greater proportion of benefits determined the old way, and someone closer to twenty-five would have a greater proportion of benefits determined by the new PSA 2000 plan. It might be possible to devise a somewhat more rapid phase-in, but we have been impressed by the political and economic

importance of changing the rules only very gradually. With our phase-in, the defined-benefit payments from the existing PIA approach would remain essentially unchanged for the first ten years. Then gradually those benefits would be reduced as people began to retire who had some of their benefits determined by the new plan. Benefits under the old plan would be essentially phased out in seventy-five years when the twenty-five-year-olds of 2000 hit the century mark. At that time (or perhaps a little sooner) the 9.9 percent net OASDI taxes would prove more than sufficient to finance the tier-one benefits. A tax cut of approximately 2 to 2.5 percentage points would be feasible. One way to look at it is that this tax cut of 2 to 2.5 percent must be postponed for seventy-five years in order to pay for the extra benefits of the old system (over and above the new system's tier-one benefits). As we said at the beginning of this chapter, our plan is realistic, and that means that it accounts for the costs of transition.

An Analysis of PSA 2000

The new PSA 2000 plan, like the old PIA defined-benefit system, involves risks for participants. However, we have tried to keep these risks to a minimum by designing a two-part system with a very safe floor (tier-one) benefit. Figure 23.1 shows the tier-one benefit for single workers for the year 2000 and the 1999 PIA formula. Both the PIA formula and the $500 flat benefit are indexed for future years to growth in average wages, so their relative shape and position will remain unchanged. The tier-one benefit ($500) is greater than the PIA for people with AIMEs of less than $650. For people with average indexed monthly earnings greater than that amount, there is a gap to be filled by the tier-two-based benefits. You should notice, however, that we have given ourselves a very ambitious goal: to replace the difference between existing benefits and our tier-one benefits with the 5 percent PSA accounts. The goal is ambitious in the sense that we are trying to maintain benefits that the current system promises but cannot deliver. That is the nature of the solvency problem of the current system. Of course, we have more money in total to work with than in the current system, because total payroll deductions are 2.5 percent higher under the PSA 2000 plan.

The gap to make up is much greater for people with higher lifetime earnings. For instance, for someone with an AIME of $1,000, the PIA works out to $612.90 per month, thus leaving a gap of $112.90 (or roughly 18.4 percent of the PIA) for the tier-two benefits to replace. For someone with a much higher AIME of $2,500, PIA under the 1999 formula works out to $1,092.90

Figure 23.1   The 1999 PIA Formula and the PSA 2000 Tier-One Benefit

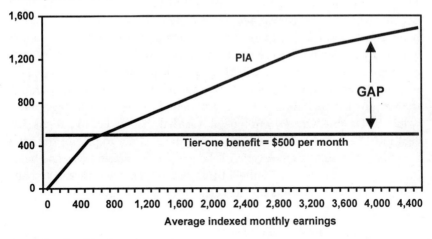

Primary insurance amount in dollars

Source: Developed by the authors.

per month, thus leaving a gap of $592.90 to fill or 54.25 percent. The AIME has increased by a factor of 2.5 in our two examples, but the gap has increased more than fivefold. The bottom line is that low-income people are almost certain to do better with the PSA 2000 plan than with the currently legislated program (because the gap that tier-two needs to replace is relatively small). The situation is somewhat less certain for middle- and higher-income participants.

To estimate how people will ultimately fare with our PSA 2000 plan, we have simulated the returns on the stock and bond investments that will form the PSA portfolios. We have examined the outcome for twenty-three-year-olds in the year 2000 under the proposed PSA 2000 plan as opposed to under current legislation. We have assumed that the normal retirement age will have advanced to sixty-eight by the time this cohort retires (current legislation brings it to sixty-seven by 2027, but we are assuming that it will be sixty-eight by 2045). With only this modest adjustment in the NRA, the current benefit structure could not be maintained for this cohort without significant tax hikes. Nonetheless, that is the comparison we are going to present. Forecasting forty-five years or more into the future is inherently difficult. We think that it would be futile to try to be precise. Still, it makes sense to see how the PSA 2000 plan works under reasonable scenarios.

We assume that inflation will run at a rate of 2 percent between 2000 and 2045, that the average level of wages will grow by 3 percent per year,

and that members of this cohort, who will be gaining in seniority throughout this period, will enjoy increases in earnings of 4 percent per year. We
assume that average life expectancy at age sixty-eight will be 17.5 years
for cohort members. This was approximately the average life expectancy
(averaged over men and women) of sixty-five-year-olds in 1998. We assume
that the average nominal total return on a stock index fund will be 10 percent per year, with a standard deviation of 20 percent. This means that
roughly one-sixth of the time, a stock index fund will experience a total
annual return of −10 percent or worse and that one-sixth of the time it will
enjoy a total annual return of +30 percent or better. At least on an annual
basis, stocks are very risky and are so modeled here. We assume that high-
grade long-term corporate bonds will have an average nominal annual total
return of 6 percent, with a standard deviation of 10 percent. Long-term
Treasury bonds are assumed to yield 5 percent. These bonds are used to
finance the inflation-indexed life annuities during the payout phase for the
tier-two benefits. All these returns are conservative relative to the experience of the 1926–1997 period documented in Ibbotson.[4] Our assumption for
the average yield on stocks over and above inflation (8 percent) contrasts
with the observed premium of 9.7 percent (for the Standard & Poor's 500).
The assumed difference between future corporate bond and stock returns
is also conservative. We have assumed that the difference, on average, will
be 4 percent. The observed difference for the period 1926–1997 was 6.7 percent. We are quite comfortable in making these conservative assumptions.

  With these assumptions about the underlying distributions of stock and
bond returns, we have generated simulated sequences of forty-five years'
worth of returns. The nominal stock returns are chosen from a distribution
with a mean of 10 percent but a standard deviation of 20 percent. Nothing
prevents the computer from choosing several bad outcomes in a row, or
several good ones, for that matter. Our computer simulation also chooses
bond returns and even keeps track of the connection between stock and
bond returns. We have assumed that people allocate half their PSA 2000
accounts to stocks and half to bonds. Further, we have assumed that they
rebalance their portfolios annually to maintain this 50-50 asset allocation.
Finally, we have assumed that all of the tier-two proceeds are converted
into the inflation-indexed life annuities offered by Social Security under
the PSA 2000 plan. We have simulated a thousand separate sequences of
forty-five years of returns with this computer simulation technology. The
results are shown in Figure 23.2.

  The dollar figures in Figure 23.2 are in year 2000 dollars to make them
easier to interpret, even though the actual retirement of this cohort takes

Figure 23.2   Retirement Benefits for a Single Person Retiring
at the Normal Retirement Age in 2045

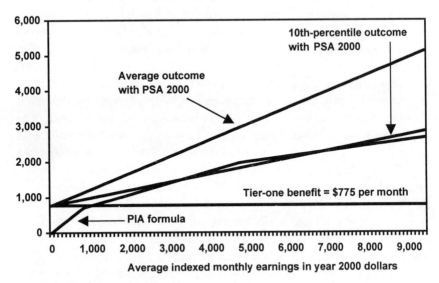

Initial monthly benefit in Year 2000 dollars

Source: Developed by the authors.

place in 2045. The first thing that one notices is that by 2045 both the
PIA formula and our tier-one benefit have become much more generous.
The flat benefit of $500 per month has become $775 per month. The PIA
formula has grown proportionately. All this extra generosity is due to the
assumption that the average level of wages will grow by 1 percent per year
more rapidly than price inflation. If this assumption pans out, then each
year the PIA formula and the flat benefit of the PSA 2000 plan will increase
by 1 percent more than prices. Not surprisingly, after forty-five years this
1 percent per year improvement in the real benefits of the tier-one benefit
(and the PIA formula) compounds to a real 55 percent improvement. We
can't resist saying at this point that the assumption that wages will grow
by at least 1 percent per year faster than prices is significantly more likely
with our PSA 2000 plan than it is if we continue with a unfunded defined-
benefit Social Security system. The reason that the assumption of real wage
growth underlying Figure 23.2 is more likely with PSA 2000 is that our system will lead to significantly higher national savings.

    Figure 23.2 shows that the average retirement income outcome is much
better for this cohort with PSA 2000 than with the current PIA formula. If

financial markets perform as well as the average simulation that we have generated, every member of this cohort (who followed our assumption and invested 50 percent in stocks and 50 percent in bonds) will have more money in retirement than outcomes dependent on current legislation suggest. But it does make sense to be cautious about forecasting future financial returns. The figure also shows what is forecast to happen 10 percent of the time. To be precise, 90 percent of the simulations have outcomes better than (that is, above) the line shown as the tenth-percentile outcome, and 10 percent of the outcomes are worse. Notice that even at the tenth percentile the PSA 2000 benefits are still better than the PIA formula for most people, although it is often quite close. Most important, even at the tenth percentile, the PSA 2000 program gives higher benefits to everyone with an AIME below $3,250—that is, for everyone whose annual indexed earnings are below $39,000. It would have complicated the figure to show more of the information about the distribution of outcomes that we have generated. However, we can report that the PSA 2000 plan generates more retirement income for everyone with annual indexed earnings of less than $21,750 even at the first-percentile outcome, and that the outcome is worse than 99 percent of those generated. Simulations such as this give us confidence that the PSA 2000 plan works for everyone and protects those with low lifetime earnings.

We have also replicated the simulations of historical returns that we adapted from the presentation made by Robert Ball, as reported in Chapter 22. Instead of calling this forecasting or projecting, you might think of it as backcasting. The advantage that this technique has over the kind of simulations done to develop Figure 23.2 is that it shows the real historical patterns of high and low financial markets. It is very seldom that one extremely good year immediately follows one very bad one or vice versa. Good periods and bad tend to occur in cycles, and the backcasting technique captures that phenomenon.

In this case, we actually went further back in history to get stock and bond return results than we did in replicating Ball's presentation. We started the backcasting simulations with returns reported in the U.S. financial markets in 1858. By using real rates of return over a forty-five-year career, we developed the historical results presented here. We assume that our worker, Dan, starts his job at age twenty-three in the year 2000 and works until his normal retirement age of sixty-eight. For his benefit under the PSA, we assume that he invests his PSA balance in accordance with the way in which workers today invest their 401(k) balances, depending on their age and level of earnings. This means that when we assume that

Figure 23.3   Simulated Earnings Replacement for Low-Wage Worker with Forty-Five-Year Career Under PSA 2000 and Under the MB Plan for Workers Aged Twenty-Three in 2000

Percent of final earnings provided at age 68

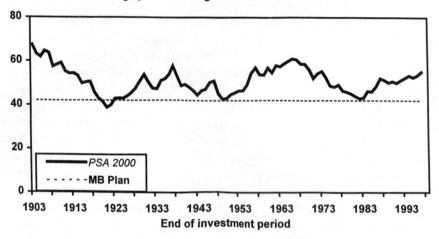

Sources: Simulation results developed by Watson Wyatt Worldwide. Historical financial return data from Bryan Taylor; global financial data at *http://www.globalfindata.com/march1.htm*.

Dan has low earnings, he invests more conservatively than when we simulate a case in which he has high earnings. It also means that when Dan is young, we assume that he invests more aggressively than when he is older. We assume total administrative fees of 100 basis points per year—that is, 1 percent of asset balances—which we believe is considerably higher than actual costs will be.

The results of this simulation for Dan with low earnings are shown in Figure 23.3. The jagged line in the figure uses the real rates of return actually registered in the U.S. financial markets over the series of discrete forty-five-year periods ending in the year shown in the figure. So the first observation shows what Dan's benefit would be if he participated in this plan as assumed and received returns similar to those provided by financial markets between 1858 and 1902, stated in 1998 dollars. The second observation shows the results for the period 1859 to 1903, and so forth. The flat line in the figure represents the benefit that Dan would receive if he participated in Social Security as currently configured but slightly modified in accordance with the provisions laid out in Bob Ball's Maintain Benefits proposal for the 1994–1996 Advisory Council on Social Security. The probability of doing better under PSA 2000 seems to be quite clear from Figure 23.3. Even when the benefit drops below the traditional Social Security benefit, the extent to which it does so is very slight. At the levels of high and maximum earnings, where workers would have the largest share of their benefits exposed to the financial markets because of the relative size of tier-one and tier-two benefits, the picture is essentially the same as that for the worker with low earnings.

There is definitely financial market risk exposure in the PSA 2000 plan as shown by the results displayed in both Figures 23.2 and 23.3. Figure 23.2 suggests that some workers under the PSA 2000 plan might get a benefit below the levels provided in current law. Figure 24.3 shows the potential variation in benefits under the assumption that future rates of return and investment behavior might mirror historical patterns. It also shows that, for some workers, benefits may dip below levels provided under current law. Once again, however, it is good to remember that the structure of benefits under current law cannot be delivered at current tax rates. Indeed, we do not believe that they can be delivered at the same total contribution rates embedded in the PSA 2000 proposal.

In Figure 23.4 we show how workers of the birth cohort that is aged twenty-three in 2000 would have different levels of exposure to the financial markets under the PSA 2000 plan depending on their level of lifetime earnings. This figure closely corresponds to the figures in Chapter 19 showing the framework for analyzing alternative proposals. In those figures, the vertical axis went from pay-as-you-go financing at the bottom to full funding at the top. Figure 24.4 shows the percentage of the benefit that is funded, which is essentially the same thing. In the figures in Chapter 19, the horizontal axis went from a pure defined-benefit plan on the left to a pure defined-contribution plan on the right. The extent to which the two would be mixed under the various approaches to Social Security reform was shown by the position of a particular plan between the two extremes. In Figure 23.4 we show the percentage of the total benefit coming from the defined-contribution portion of the combined tiers of the PSA 2000 plan. If it were zero, that would mean all was coming from the defined-benefit tier. If it were 100 percent, it would be coming completely from the defined-contribution tier.

The figure shows that less than half of the total benefit for the worker with low earnings would be from the defined-contribution tier under our system. For the worker with maximum earnings over virtually a whole career, on the other hand, nearly 85 percent would come from the individual-account tier. We believe that this is a sensible diversification of risk and an optimal plan design from the perspective of retirement accumula-

Figure 23.4   Level of Funding and Source of Benefits Under PSA 2000 for Workers Aged Twenty-Three in 2000, at Different Levels of Lifetime Earnings

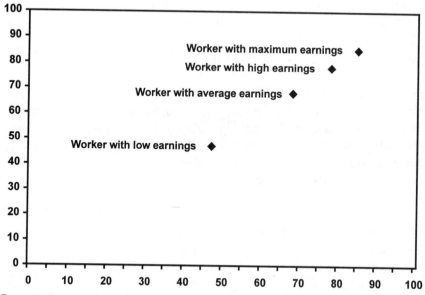

Percent of total benefit that is funded

Percent of total benefit provided through defined-contribution tier in PSA 2000

Source: Developed by the authors.

tion. It is a sensible diversification of risk because it gives all workers a mixture of the defined-benefit and defined-contribution systems. It gives workers with low earnings more of the defined-benefit protection than those with high earnings. Thus it exposes those with higher earnings to much more of the market risk inherent in the second tier of the plan. Those workers who are better off should be better able to handle such risk and to diversify it against other financial assets that they almost certainly have to accumulate for retirement purposes.

We believe that this is an optimal plan design in light of the wide range of considerations reviewed throughout our discussion here. A pure market-based defined-contribution system can be structured to alleviate the downside financial risks of all workers, especially those with low earnings. Thus, some portion of the system should continue to be run on a defined-benefit basis. Given concerns about the government's being able to accumulate wealth to fund that benefit, we believe that the size of the benefit should be kept relatively small and that it should be funded on a pay-go basis. The second-tier benefit is essentially the element of the plan that insures workers against their own myopia regarding the need to save for their retirement from the time they commence their working lives. For this benefit to be an effective means for accumulating retirement assets, it has to be funded. It makes absolutely no sense to finance this part of the benefit for average and high earners through a pay-go plan that puts such unfair burdens on future generations. The biggest accumulation of this component will come at middle and higher earning levels, and it is at those levels that our plan achieves its greatest degree of funding.

The Correspondence Between the Principles and the PSA 2000 Plan

Now that most of the details of the PSA 2000 plan have been presented, it makes sense to refer once again to the principles for redesigning Social Security that we discussed at the outset of the chapter. How does the new proposal match up against the principles for reform? By our assessment, very well, thank you.

Regarding the first principle, preserving the safety net, refer to Figure 23.2. People with below-average lifetime earnings will do very well with the new PSA 2000 plan. The reason that they do so well is that the tier-one benefit is more important for them. We have reduced the defined-benefit portion of the program in a way that strongly favors those with lower incomes. In fact, for those with the lowest incomes, we haven't reduced the DB benefits at all; rather, we have increased them. The total retirement benefits generated by the PSA 2000 are likely to be greater than PIA-based benefits for everyone—but this is particularly true for those with low lifetime incomes.

With regard to the second principle, the PSA 2000 plan promises to significantly enhance national savings. The new 5 percent accounts will generate tremendous wealth, roughly $120 billion in the first year. There are certain to be some offsets, but even a net increase of half that, $60 billion per year, would be a tremendous accomplishment. Mind you, we do not believe the offsets will be this large. People at the lower half of the earnings distribution scale do virtually no saving today, and they cannot reduce their savings with the type of proposal we advocate. In addition, we believe that most workers at higher levels of earnings will not undo the effects of the savings features of the PSA 2000 plan if its features are properly communicated and people realize how they can best take advantage of the opportunities it presents. The additional savings that PSA 2000 would generate would increase future productivity and wages and directly benefit the future generations for which the current program is bound to be a lousy deal.

We will skip over the third principle, except to say that the PSA 2000 program generates enough tax revenue to finance the current program of survivors insurance and a strong, reformed program of disability insurance. The fourth principle is that any new system should offer a permanent fix this time, rather than simply postpone insolvency. The PSA 2000 plan scores well in this dimension. It runs a surplus in the "out years," after the first seventy-five years, so that we have the opposite of the usual "passage of time" effect. As each year passes, a new surplus year would enter the seventy-five-year window and improve the long-run finances of the program. This happens because the PSA 2000 program eventually works off the promises of the old system and then runs significant surpluses each year. As we mentioned earlier, a fairly sizable payroll tax reduction would be feasible, roughly in 2070.

According to our judgment, the PSA 2000 plan scores well in regard to the fifth principle of improving the equity of the system. The equity in discrepancies between singles and one- and two-earner couples is increased, for the benefits of the vast majority of adults will be based on their own work record. The PSA 2000 program is primarily a system based on individuals. A spousal benefit remains for someone who is married and has not been credited with forty quarters of covered employment. The spousal benefit applies only to the tier-one benefit and we think that it would not be applicable in many situations even there. Another dimension of the program in which equity is improved is the treatment of widows and widowers. Widows and widowers now often receive only two-thirds as much from Social Security as they did before their spouses died. As a result, the incidence of poverty is higher among widows than it is for the rest of the elderly population. We have responded to this problem by ensuring that a widow or widower receives at least 75 percent as much as before the death of the spouse.

The PSA 2000 plan also makes a good showing with regard to our sixth principle (improving efficiency by increasing the links between contributions and benefits). There is an absolutely direct connection between contributions and benefits in the tier-two PSA 2000 accounts. In fact, the PSA 2000 plan effectively lowers the OASDI payroll tax from 12.4 percent to 9.9 percent. The 2.5 percent rebate and the 2.5 percent mandatory PSA

2000 contribution cannot properly be called a tax. This money belongs to the PSA participant. He or she directs how the assets are invested. If the participant dies before annuitizing the PSA 2000 tier-two proceeds, then the money passes to the participant's heirs. Participants are required to annuitize only half of their tier-two balances. The 5 percent deposits into the PSA accounts are just like contributions to other defined-contribution pensions. Although they do reduce the take-home pay of workers, they are not a tax, and they do not create a revenue source for the government. One other thing about the second tier of the PSA 2000 plan. Every contribution counts—there is no "high thirty-five rule." If you work part-time, the contributions to your account still result in added benefits during retirement. If you work a very short or a very long career, all contributions to your tier-two PSA account are credited to you. Obviously, the fact that all contributions count helps in linking benefits with the money paid into the system.

We have been very careful regarding the riskiness of the overall system. As mentioned, people with lower incomes will get more of their benefits from tier one, the defined-benefit part of the plan. The investments offered for the defined-contribution part will be regulated with regard to their diversification and customer service and administrative expenses. The government will offer a small menu of cost-efficient portfolios, including a default stock and bond market fund for those who fail to give specific instructions about how to invest their PSA 2000 account money. One of the greatest safety features of all in the plan is that it has not been designed around a rosy set of economic assumptions. Instead, we have consciously erred on the side of conservatism. It should also be noted that the PSA plan is less vulnerable than a PIA-based defined-benefit program to failure of the assumed real wage growth to materialize. In our plan, only the tier-one benefit is tied directly to the evolution of real wages in the economy. All of the initial retirement benefits in a PIA-based approach are tied to the performance of real wages. In Chapters 11 through 13 we reviewed the consequences of the failure of real wages to match assumptions during the 1970s and 1980s.

We have already talked about administrative costs. Several design elements have gone into minimizing them in the PSA 2000 program. We do not see any insurmountable roadblocks to rapid implementation of this plan so that we can begin to tackle Social Security's solvency problem. The IRA and 401(k) markets sprang up rapidly in the 1980s. At least the defined-contribution part of the PSA 2000 plan is similar in structure to these popular pension programs. The PSA plan could be operational by the end of the year 2000. If it were, the outlook for Social Security, for our children and grandchildren, and for the twenty-first century American economy would be significantly enhanced.

The PSA 2000 Plan Works for America

We can summarize our evaluation of the PSA 2000 plan rather briefly. First, it establishes the long-term solvency for the Social Security system. Second, it offers more generous retirement benefits for today's young workers and their children and grandchildren. The PSA 2000 program protects the poor from an impoverished old age better than the existing Social Security system. Although PSA 2000 raises required payroll contributions, it increases personal and national savings and lowers the effective rate of taxation on working. It accomplishes the last feature by allowing people to use 5 percentage points of their payroll deductions to fund their own retirement, thus reducing the reliance on defined benefits funded by younger workers. It manages risk and appropriately diversifies the risks inherent in both defined-benefit and defined-contribution plans. It offers enhanced economic efficiency by perfectly linking contributions and tier-two benefits. In short, it offers a total solution package at the relatively modest cost of a mandatory payroll contribution of an additional 2.5 percent of covered pay.

Now, if we can only get the politicians to play their role and enact the PSA 2000 plan before January 1, 2001, we can start the twenty-first century with a Social Security system designed for the future instead of with the current system, whose failure is already foreseen by Social Security's own trustees.

Chapter 24

It's Your Money We're Talking About

*I*t has always been our view that one cannot understand Social Security's prospects without knowledge of its origins and history. If you have been with us this far, you qualify as one of the more knowledgeable people in the country about Social Security. You have several reasons to participate in the unfolding debate about how to redesign or repair the system so that it can better serve you, your children, and your grandchildren. As a person knowledgeable on this subject, you have an obligation to offer your help in strengthening and modernizing Social Security. This isn't only a social obligation; it is a personal one. Your family's financial health depends on it.

The boxcar numbers you hear about the program—a trillion here and a trillion there—that is your money. When someone claims to be able to fix the program by raising taxes by 2.2 or 2.5 percentage points, remember that you only have 100 percentage points to go around. If you are already retired, raising the payroll tax may seem like a pretty good way to solve Social Security's financial imbalances. Even if you are five or ten years from retirement, it may not seem like that big a deal, especially if your children are out of the nest now and you have a little extra income to spare. But this issue is not just about each of us individually, no matter where we are in the cycle of life—it is about the legacy we leave for our children's children and succeeding generations.

In one of the early chapters we discussed the funding debate that went on between the architects of Social Security, and we described Edwin Witte's concern about the high costs that future generations would incur to support Social Security if the program were not funded. We reported that J. Douglas Brown dismissed Witte's concerns by responding that by then "we will all be dead." Brown was right. But more important, so was Witte.

Time passes, and bills that we run up for our children and grandchildren will ultimately have to be paid. If your children face an extra 2.5 percent tax on their lifetime earnings, that tax will cost them one year's worth of earnings over their working life—that is, the earnings of an extra one of their approximately forty years in the labor market would be handed over to the government. In many cases, asking your children to give the government a larger share of their paycheck means taking food off the table or clothing off the backs of their children. Don't give up a year of your children's economic life casually.

Raising Taxes or Cutting Benefits Will Affect You or Yours

Of course, the leading proposals for Social Security reform probably won't raise taxes in a straightforward way—if the system is refinanced through such an increase. Our political leaders may raise taxes in a hidden way or raise them some forty or fifty years in the future, but politicians seem more than a little nervous about raising workers' taxes right now. So, maybe you should be on the lookout for benefit cuts. These might take the form of raising the retirement age, increasing the income taxes on benefits, adding more years to the calculation of average indexed monthly earnings, or scaling back the inflation indexation of retirement benefits. If our political leaders restore the financial balance of the program through benefit cuts, then they will need to reduce real people's benefits. And here again, we urge you to think about this within a broader context than simply your own situation.

If you are currently retired, you could take the perspective that there is no need to be in any rush to deal with Social Security's financing. After all, the actuaries tell us that there is enough in the trust funds to pay full benefits through 2032. J. Douglas Brown's observation on future higher costs is apropos for almost every retiree getting Social Security benefits today, if we think about the trust fund's being able to last until 2032. Even people retiring at age sixty-two today will be well into their nineties by 2032. For most retirees today, things could work out just fine if we simply left everything alone. If you are a retiree today, though, there is a relatively high probability that you have children, or maybe grandchildren, in the baby boom generation. It is hard for us to imagine that the older people of this society do not share the concerns about the retirement legacy their own children and grandchildren face.

For those in the middle of the baby boom generation, the thought of Social Security's trust fund going bust in 2032 is not so reassuring. They are like the trapper in the canoe who was approaching a waterfall in the movie *To Fly*, as we described him in the opening paragraphs of Chapter 1. The baby boomers have been told about rough water downstream and are looking for a way to get themselves to a safe and secure retirement. Benefit cuts—things like reduced cost-of-living allowances or a gradual increase in the normal retirement age—may not be terribly appealing, but they beat the alternative of an immediate increase in payroll taxes or the collapse of the program during retirement.

For those just setting out in a career, the thought of a little white water may seem invigorating. In the case of Social Security, the thought of a little diet for the COLA or a retirement age that's higher by a few years may even be very appealing. It is easy to think about working until age seventy when age sixty-five is more than forty years away. But we need to be careful here as well. The technical adjustments that have been made to the consumer price index already have our grandmothers on a bit of a diet COLA. If we are not careful, too much diet COLA for grandma can mean that grandma does without meals altogether, instead of just switching from steak to chicken. If we do our Social Security financial rebalancing on the benefit side, we ought to be doing it in ways that enable current and future generations of retirees to lead a dignified life that makes not only them but all of us comfortable. Once again we remind you that back in the 1960s, the venerable television news anchorman, Walter Cronkite, periodically aired a segment on older people eating dog or cat food because they could not afford a regular diet—and the public found that very discomforting. Social Security helped solve that problem to a great extent. We should not assume that future generations of our population would feel any more comfortable if Walter Cronkite's great-granddaughter were reporting a similar situation in 2030 on nightly *Intranet News*—or wherever we get our daily news then. Seeing our elders lead reasonably comfortable lives during their declining years is important to us as well as to them. Let's hope that our children and grandchildren feel the same way when those of us in the baby boom generation actually begin to retire.

Any way you slice this problem that our society faces, Social Security's financial solvency cannot be achieved for the existing pay-go system without serious benefit cuts or tax increases or both. And you know by now that a tax hike of 2.2 or 2.5 percentage points really won't fix the system permanently. It might rebalance it for the seventy-five-year horizon that Social Security fixes on at the time Social Security legislation is passed, but the new arrangement would almost immediately become unbalanced, just as the 1983 one did. The reason is that the out years would still be out of balance, and the mere passage of time brings some of those out-of-balance out years into the seventy-five-year window. Within ten or fifteen years another fix would be required, and we would face yet another round of tax hikes or benefit cuts. The best guess is that it would take an immediate payroll tax increase of between 4.5 and 5 percentage points to make Social Security permanently solvent. Now we are talking about as much as two years' worth of earnings over a lifetime—two years of your children's professional lives. The stakes are high here, and policy proponents are playing with your family's money. So you'll want to pay close attention to this debate.

Watch Out for the Free Ride—It's a Phony Deal

The biggest danger to watch for is the phony solution—the wishful-thinking approach. Any plan that involves a couple of relatively painless benefit cuts and a minuscule tax increase, or one several decades in the future, doesn't have the muscle to solve the problem. Watch closely for the solution that is little more than a shell game. When policymakers were forced to deal with the Medicare Hospital Insurance financing crisis a couple of years ago, they simply moved some of the benefits provided through the payroll-tax-financed HI program over to the Supplemental Health Insurance part of Medicare. Because SMI is financed through general revenues, the demand on the HI trust fund supported by the payroll tax was reduced, but total government expenditures were not. In moving benefits from HI to SMI, policymakers totally ignored the structural problems with the benefits themselves, which will ultimately have to be solved. Some people might think that it is preferable to have the benefits financed out of the income tax rather than the payroll tax, but the fact of the matter is that the middle class in America pays the majority of both taxes. It is not that people at the top or bottom cheat on one or the other of the taxes, it is once again simply the laws of arithmetic at work. Because of its relative numbers the middle class will end up paying the majority of taxes in whatever system we adopt for financing government programs. If we want to control tax burdens, we have to control expenditures. And that brings us back to the balancing problem we face with Social Security.

In addition to keeping an eye out for the phony solution, watch closely for the solution that simply assumes the problem away. Anyone who tells you that our long-term economic or demographic outlook has suddenly gotten a whole lot rosier than we thought it was a couple of years ago and that our new prosperity will solve this problem is pulling your leg. If anyone tells you that growth in wages will make the Social Security financing problem a lot easier to solve, you should remind that person of the story in Chapter 16 about the perpetually rosy assumptions on Medicare financing. Tell the Social Security optimist about the current assumption on projecting Medicare's costs: that future cost escalation will subside just as the baby boomers start making their Medicare claims. Medicare is waiting in the wings to use any economic surplus that might arise if future economic performance outstrips current projections.

The optimist's approach to solving the Social Security financing problem is very risky. It takes the canoe right up to the waterfall, on the assumption the trapper will be strong enough to paddle away against the white-water current. If we adopt such an approach, we are betting our children's and grandchildren's future on a lucky roll of the dice. Keep in mind that proponents of many solutions would roll the dice with the incomes of future generations without consulting them. To revert to the comments of President William Clinton in his address to the college students at Georgetown University in February 1998, some of the potential outcomes would be "horribly unfair" to future generations.[1] Also keep in mind that for most of us, those future generations are going to be our direct blood relatives, our descendants.

Let's Do What's Right

The PSA 2000 plan presented in the previous chapter needs to be carefully scrutinized as well. If we are going to require workers to save an extra 2.5 percent of their covered earnings, we should demand some impressive results in return. The PSA 2000 plan delivers. First, it remedies the insolvency problem rather than simply postponing it. Second, there is every reason to expect it to deliver more resources for our children's retirement than we ourselves will enjoy. Third, by increasing the national savings rate, it will raise the real wages of your children and grandchildren. Rather than leave them with an ever-growing actuarial imbalance, as actuaries are fond of calling Social Security's insolvency problem, the PSA 2000 proposal leaves them with a well-financed program and a more productive economy in which to work and retire. It will empower them, not impoverish them. Fourth, it protects the poor even better than the current system. With the PSA 2000 plan, workers with higher incomes are responsible for most of their own retirement resources, through the second-tier PSA 2000 accounts. The well-off do not get any more defined-benefit promises than the unskilled or unlucky minimum-wage worker. The tier-one benefit provides a strong safety net for everyone. Basically, the PSA 2000 plan solves the Social Security problem once and for all at a considerable, but manageable, cost.

In Chapter 1 we introduced a hypothetical worker named Annette to show how someone embarking on a career today and earning a modest living will be required to make an investment of a half-million dollars in the current Social Security system. As if that is not enough, Social Security actuaries now predict that Annette would have to invest another $125,000 or so to get back the benefits extended by current law. Annette is not some figment of our imaginations. She is everybody's sister, daughter, niece, granddaughter, or friend. Annette could well have been one of the young women sitting in the audience at Georgetown University in February 1998 when President Clinton said: "It's very important you understand this. . . . If you don't do anything, one of two things will happen—either it will go broke and you won't ever get it; or if we wait too long to fix it, the burden on society of taking care of our [the baby boom] generation's Social Security obligations will lower your income and lower your ability to take care of your children to a degree most of us who are your parents think would be horribly wrong and unfair to you and unfair to the future prospects of the United States."[2]

Under the PSA 2000 plan we would ask Annette to put up the added money that some people would advocate having her send to Social Security to maintain the current system essentially the way it is today. For Annette, sending more money to Social Security so we can stay the current policy course would not net retirement benefits any higher than those provided under current law. She would have no assurances that we wouldn't send her another bill a few years down the road. The PSA 2000 plan would not have Annette send any additional money to Social Security. She would put her added contributions under the PSA 2000 plan into an account with her name on it with fund managers that she could vote to fire if they did not manage her money carefully. Not only would we not have Annette send her added contributions to Social Security, but we would have Social Security match the contributions we are asking Annette to make.

In return for letting Annette keep her own additional contributions, along with the federal matching funds, we would ask Annette to essentially stand fully behind the benefit commitments that have been made to her grandparents. We would ask Annette to be the primary backer for the benefit commitments that have been made to her parents. If her parents are over fifty-five in 2001, the only change we would ask of them is a very slight adjustment in their normal retirement age. If they are under age fifty-five in 2001, the changes under PSA 2000 would be modestly more, but they would be phased in very gradually, so Annette's parents would have ample time to adjust their other retirement planning accordingly. The baby boomers and the aged in our society today are going to outvote Annette's generation for the next several years. If Annette's generation and her younger siblings who are not old enough to vote yet are to be treated fairly in this debate, it will be because the older members of society act responsibly toward them. It is our responsibility to do so. If you are reading this, it is your responsibility.

How can you make your voice heard regarding your family's money and Social Security? Let the politicians in Washington know that you understand the magnitude of the Social Security financing problem, and demand that it receive the attention that it deserves. Let your representatives in Congress know that what we need is a program that generates greater savings and investment, rather than one that perpetuates ever-larger transfers from workers to retirees. Express your willingness to save more for your own retirement, if you are still working, or to let your children and grandchildren do so, if you are retired. Express your desire to policymakers that workers be allowed to contribute to their retirement in such a way that they can actually own the added contributions and track them, through Personal Security Accounts. Express your desire—no, your demand—that we restructure the system of dependence on intergenerational transfers that has become so horribly unfair to future generations.

Get Involved

If you feel the way we do, tell your representatives not only that you favor additional saving and investing but that this is real money we are talking about. Tell them that it is your money or the money of other people in your family that they are talking about when they consider changing Social Security. Tell them that the workers who are being asked to contribute hundreds of thousands of dollars to our retirement system should have some control over how at least some of it is invested. Tell them that workers who are already contributing hundreds of thousands of dollars to our retirement system—and being told that they have to either put in more or get back less—should be able to participate. In our system, broken promises are against the law; they should not be merely an excuse to change it.

Proposals that would have the government investing the money for you or your adult children are flawed in ways that you understand. The debate over the government's ability to fund Social Security has gone on now for sixty-five years. That debate has now reached Social Security's normal retirement age without ever prefunding a single generation's benefits to any significant degree. The debate is now old enough to be retired itself. And it ought to be retired, because history has told us time and time again that the matter of funding the promises held out by this program cannot be resolved within the framework of our current contrivances. There is no reason for you to risk having politicians dipping yet again into the trust fund to increase benefits on the eve of some future election. History tells us that that is exactly what would happen if we tried to accomplish the necessary extra saving through a large central trust fund. The history of large public funds elsewhere in this country and around the world indicates that they will not be left as passive investments in index funds. There are too many good causes for governments to pursue. We believe that governments should pursue good causes, but they should do so by raising the taxes from the voting electorate at the time the causes are pursued, not by withdrawing from workers' funds for a secure retirement.

If you are still working or will be working in the future, the alternative to letting the government have yet more of your money with no guarantees is to put your money into your individual personal security account. Under the PSA 2000 plan, you get a one-for-one match from the government; that is actually your money, too, of course. You accept the prohibition on early withdrawals, but you make the decisions about how much risk to take with your money. The PSA 2000 plan treats you like an adult. We assume that you are willing to take the responsibility for your own money and that you don't want to transfer an ever-increasing burden to future generations.

You should write or e-mail your representatives in Washington, D.C. Tell them that you support Social Security reform if it is carried out in an honest and straightforward manner. If you agree with us, tell them that you support the PSA 2000 plan in particular. Tell them that you want action on this sooner rather than later. There are several ways you can contact your elected representatives in Washington.

If you prefer to use e-mail, you can get in touch with the president through the White House web site at *http://www.whitehouse.gov/cgi-bin/ correspondence.* You can contact your senators at *http://www.senate.gov.* You can contact your representative at *http://www.house.gov.* At those sites you can find directories organized by state and by name of the members. After selecting individual members, you can leave them an e-mail message. Also, you can identify the members of the important congressional committees with oversight for Social Security. In the House of Representatives, it is the Ways and Means Committee. In the Senate, it is the Senate Finance Committee. You can get in contact with the Social Security Administration at *http://www.ssa.gov.* A specific selection at the site for the Social Security commissioner includes a brief biography of the commissioner, but no way to send a message. We give a mailing address below.

If you would rather write to your representatives, you can send letters to the president at 1600 Pennsylvania Avenue, N.W., Washington, DC 20500. You can send letters to your state senators to U.S. Senate, Washington, DC 20510. You can send a letter to your representative to U.S. House of Representatives, Washington, DC 20515. Generic letters to majority and minority leaders and to the chairmen of the House Ways and Means Committee and the Senate Finance Committee can be sent to the House or Senate, for which you do not need street addresses. Letters to the Social Security commissioner can be sent to Social Security Administration, 6401 Security Boulevard, Baltimore, MD 21235.

Looking Forward

We cannot erase history and abolish the payroll tax or somehow magically go back and reconsider how we might redo the system from the start. How the Social Security system is changed for the future is extremely important for the nation and for you. At the national level we are talking about literally trillions of dollars. Even for you, however, stakes are easily in the hundreds of thousands. The point is that we are talking about a huge amount of money, no matter how you look at it. The stakes are high for the beneficiary population because the system is such a significant part of many people's retirement portfolios that we have created an undeniable dependency on it. The stakes are even higher for workers. They have to face the prospects of changes in both the financing and the benefit sides of the program. But the stakes are highest of all for the youth of our society today and for children yet to be born.

President Clinton has stated the matter clearly: "If . . . we don't deal with it [Social Security], then it not only affects the generation of the baby boomers and whether they will have enough to live on when they retire; it raises the question of whether they will have enough to live on by unfairly burdening their children and, therefore, unfairly burdening their children's ability to raise their grandchildren. That would be unconscionable."[3] Not only our fictional Annette, but our real children—Jimmy Shoven who is twelve years old and Sean Schieber who is twenty-three—are among the potential victims of the inaction that President Clinton was talking about. We dedicated this book to Jimmy and Sean because they almost certainly have more at stake in securing Social Security's future than we have. If you are willing to help, our children and yours can live in a more prosperous economy, retire in comfort, and pass on a better future to their own children. If we are not careful though, we face the prospect of being the first generation in the United States to leave a national inheritance for our children that is smaller than the one we inherited from our forebears.

Notes

Chapter 1: Social Security

1. *1998 Annual Report of the Board of Trustees of the Federal Old-Age and Survivors Insurance and Disability Insurance Trust Funds* (Washington, D.C.: U.S. Government Printing Office, 1998), pp. 104–105.

2. Ibid., p. 23.

3. President William J. Clinton, speech given at Gaston Hall, Georgetown University, Washington, D.C., February 9, 1998, found at *http://www.ssa.gov/history/clntstmts.html*.

4. Stephen Goss, "Measuring Solvency in the Social Security System," in Olivia S. Mitchell, Robert J. Myers, and Howard Young, eds., *Prospects for Social Security Reform* (Philadelphia: University of Pennsylvania Press, 1999), chap. 2.

5. President William J. Clinton, State of the Union Address, January 27, 1998, found at *http://www.ssa.gov/history/clntstmts.html*.

6. Ibid.

7. Benjamin R. Barber, "Constitutional Rights—Democratic Instrument or Democratic Obstacle," in Robert A. Licht, ed., *The Framers and Fundamental Rights* (Washington, D.C.: AEI Press, 1991), p. 23.

8. Arthur M. Schlesinger, Jr., *The Age of Roosevelt: The Coming of the New Deal* (Boston: Houghton Mifflin, 1959), p. 309.

9. See *http://www.ssa.gov.*

10. Arthur J. Altmeyer, Oral History Collection, Columbia University (1967), p. 199.

11. Wilbur Cohen in a letter to his parents, as quoted in Edward D. Berkowitz, *Mr. Social Security: The Life of Wilbur J. Cohen* (Lawrence: University Press of Kansas, 1995), p. 39.

Chapter 2: The Context for the Passage of the Social Security Act in 1935

1. Abraham Epstein, *Insecurity: A Challenge to America*, 2d rev. ed. (New York: Random House, 1938), p. 25.

2. I. M. Rubinow, *Social Insurance, with Special Reference to American Conditions* (New York: Arno Press, 1916), p. 15.

3. Epstein, *Insecurity*, pp. 26–27.

4. U.S. Bureau of the Census, *Historical Statistics of the United States* (Washington, D.C.: U.S. Government Printing Office, 1975), pp. 139, 465.

5. Ibid., p. 126.

6. Steven A. Sass, *The Promise of Private Pensions, The First Hundred Years* (Cambridge: Harvard University Press, 1997), p. 5.

7. U.S. Bureau of the Census, *Historical Statistics*, p. 14.

8. Committee on Economic Security, *Social Security in America* (Washington, D.C.: U.S. Government Printing Office, 1937), p. 14.

9. William Graebner, *A History of Retirement: The Meaning and Function of an American Institution* (New Haven, Conn.: Yale University Press, 1980), p. 14.

10. Murray W. Latimer, *Industrial Pension Systems in the United States and Canada* (New York: Industrial Relations Counselors, 1933).

11. U.S. Department of Agriculture, *Yearbook* (Washington, D.C.: U.S. Government Printing Office, 1932), pp. 578, 659.

12. *New York Times*, November 22, 1932.

13. U.S. Department of Agriculture, *Fifteenth Census, Agriculture* (Washington, D.C.: U.S. Government Printing Office, 1932), vol. 2, pt. 1, p. 10.

14. U.S. Department of Agriculture, *Yearbook*, 1932, p. 903.

15. Federal Reserve Board, *Eighteenth Annual Report, 1932* (Washington, D.C.: Federal Reserve Board, 1932), p. 125.

16. Testimony of Martin Bodfish, executive manager of the United States Building and Loan League, before the Senate Committee on Banking and Currency, *Hearings on the Home Loan Bank Bill, S. 2959*, pt. 2, p. 258.

17. New York Stock Exchange, *New York Stock Exchange Yearbook, 1932–1933* (New York: New York Stock Exchange), pp. 112–113; and New York Stock Exchange, *New York Stock Exchange Yearbook, 1940* (New York: New York Stock Exchange), pp. 56–57.

18. Social Security Board for the Committee on Economic Security, *Social Security in America* (Washington, D.C.: U.S. Government Printing Office, 1937), p. 146.

19. W. Andrew Achenbaum, *Old Age in the New Land* (Baltimore, Md.: Johns Hopkins University Press, 1978), p. 129.

20. Arnold J. Toynbee in *Survey of International Affairs, 1931* (London: Oxford University Press, 1932), p. 1.

21. Frances Perkins, *The Roosevelt I Knew* (New York: Viking Press, 1946), chap. 13.

22. Ibid., p. 167.

23. Stuart Chase, "The Enemy of Prosperity," *Harper's* (November 1930), pp. 641–648.

24. C. W. Cobb and P. H. Douglas, "A Theory of Production," *American Economic Review Supplement* (March 1928), pp. 139–165.

25. Epstein, *Insecurity*, p. 48.

26. Edward D. Berkowitz, *America's Welfare State: From Roosevelt to Reagan* (Baltimore, Md.: Johns Hopkins University Press, 1991), p. 19.

27. William E. Leuchtenburg, *The FDR Years: On Roosevelt and His Legacy* (New York: Columbia University Press, 1995), pp. 77–80.

28. Perkins, *The Roosevelt I Knew*, p. 279.

29. Jerry R. Cates, *Insuring Inequality: Administrative Leadership in Social Security, 1934–1954* (Ann Arbor: University of Michigan Press, 1983), p. 22.

30. Perkins, *The Roosevelt I Knew*, p. 294.

31. Berkowitz, *America's Welfare State*, p. 23.
32. Arthur M. Schlesinger, Jr., *The Age of Roosevelt*, vol. 3, *The Politics of Upheaval* (Boston: Houghton Mifflin, 1960), p. 325.

Chapter 3: Developing the Social Security Act of 1935

1. Edwin E. Witte, *The Development of the Social Security Act* (Madison: University of Wisconsin Press, 1962), pp. 3-4.
2. Ibid., p. 4.
3. Franklin D. Roosevelt, "Message to Congress Reviewing the Broad Objectives and Accomplishments of the Administration," June 8, 1934.
4. Ibid.
5. Franklin D. Roosevelt, Executive Order No. 6757, June 29, 1934.
6. Roy Lubove, *The Struggle for Social Security, 1900-1935* (Cambridge: Harvard University Press, 1968), pp. 29-30.
7. Jerry R. Cates, *Insuring Inequality: Administrative Leadership in Social Security, 1935-1954* (Ann Arbor: University of Michigan Press, 1983), p. 23.
8. Ibid.
9. Witte, *The Development of the Social Security Act*, pp. 12-13.
10. Theron F. Schlabach, *Edwin E. Witte: Cautious Reformer* (Madison: State Historical Society of Wisconsin, 1969), pp. 220-231.
11. Interview with Arthur J. Altmeyer, Oral History Collection, Columbia University (1967), p. 192.
12. Interview with Barbara Nachtrieb Armstrong, Oral History Collection, Columbia University (1967), pp. 46, 48.
13. Ibid.
14. Barbara Nachtrieb Armstrong, *Insuring the Essentials* (New York: Macmillan, 1932).
15. Frances Perkins, "The Roots of Social Security," speech delivered at Social Security Administration headquarters in Baltimore, Maryland, October 23, 1962, found at *http://www.ssa.gov/history/perkins5.html*.
16. Franklin D. Roosevelt, Address to Advisory Council of the Committee on Economic Security on the Problems of Economic and Social Security, November 14, 1934.
17. Ibid.
18. Ibid.
19. Interview with J. Douglas Brown, Oral History Collection, Columbia University (1966), p. 117.
20. Witte, *The Development of the Social Security Act*, p. 74.
21. Frances Perkins, *The Roosevelt I Knew* (New York: Viking Press, 1946), p. 293.
22. Witte, *The Development of the Social Security Act*, p. 73.
23. Interview with Barbara Nachtrieb Armstrong, Oral History Collection, Columbia University (1965), pp. 204-205.
24. Perkins, *The Roosevelt I Knew*, p. 294.
25. Ibid.
26. Witte, *The Development of the Social Security Act*, pp. 74-75.
27. Ibid.

28. Interview with J. Douglas Brown, Oral History Collection, Columbia University (1966), p. 18.

29. A full-blown discussion of the legislative development of the Social Security Act appears in Witte, *The Development of the Social Security Act*, pp. 75–108.

30. Perkins, "The Roots of Social Security."

31. Arthur J. Altmeyer, *The Formative Years of Social Security* (Madison: University of Wisconsin Press, 1966), p. 3.

32. Letter from Abraham Epstein to William J. Cohen, March 4, 1941, copy in the Library of the Social Security Administration, Washington, D.C., cited in William Haber and William J. Cohen, eds., *Readings in Social Security* (New York: Prentice Hall, 1948), p. 39.

33. Witte, *The Development of the Social Security Act*, p. 83.

34. Ibid., pp. 82–83.

35. Interview with Barbara Nachtrieb Armstrong, Oral History Collection, Columbia University (1965), p. 7.

36. Franklin D. Roosevelt, Presidential Statement at the Signing of the Social Security Act, August 14, 1935.

Chapter 4: Starting Up and Starting Over

1. Arthur J. Altmeyer, *The Formative Years of Social Security* (Madison: University of Wisconsin Press, 1966), p. 44.

2. Frances Perkins, "The Roots of Social Security," a speech delivered at the Social Security Administration Headquarters in Baltimore, Maryland, October 23, 1962, found at *http://www.ssa.gov/history/perkins5.html.*

3. Birchard E. Wyatt and William H. Wandel, *The Social Security Act in Operation* (Washington, D.C.: Graphic Arts Press, 1937), p. 47.

4. Ibid., pp. 48–50.

5. Ibid., pp. 51–63.

6. Arthur J. Altmeyer, *The Formative Years*, pp. 66–67.

7. Ibid., p. 67.

8. Ibid., pp. 45–52.

9. Ibid., p. 53.

10. *Railroad Retirement Board et al. v. Alton R. Co. et al.*, 295 U.S. 330, May 6, 1935.

11. *Helvering v. Davis*, 301 U.S. 619, May 24, 1937.

12. See Roy Lubove, *The Struggle for Social Security, 1900-1935* (Cambridge, Mass: Harvard University Press, 1968), or Jerry R. Cates, *Insuring Inequality: Administrative Leadership in Social Security, 1935-1954* (Ann Arbor: University of Michigan Press, 1983).

13. Abraham Epstein, "Killing Old Age Security with Kindness," *Harper's* (July 1937), p. 182.

14. Ibid., p. 192.

15. Interview with J. Douglas Brown, Oral History Collection, Columbia University (1966), p. 19.

16. Interview with Barbara Nachtrieb Armstrong, Oral History Collection, Columbia University (1965), pp. 234–235.

17. *Senate Report No. 628,* 74th Congress, May 13, 1935, p. 9.

18. Ibid.

19. John T. Flynn, "The Social Security 'Reserve' Swindle," *Harper's* (March 1939), p. 241.

20. Ibid., p. 242.

21. Memorandum from Wilbur J. Cohen to A. J. Altmeyer, Social Security Board Interoffice Communication, "Reserves Vs. Pay-As-You-Go Plan," February 10, 1937.

22. Alfred M. Landon, campaign speech delivered in Milwaukee, Wisconsin, September 27, 1936.

23. Industrial Division, Republican National Committee campaign pamphlet for the 1936 presidential campaign.

24. Arthur J. Altmeyer, *The Formative Years,* pp. 68–69.

25. Senators Arthur Vandenberg and Francis Townsend and Representatives Daniel Reed and Thomas Jenkins, statement quoted in Memorandum from Wilbur J. Cohen to A. J. Altmeyer, Social Security Board Interoffice Communication, "Reserves Vs. Pay-As-You-Go Plan," February 10, 1937.

26. Arthur J. Altmeyer, *The Formative Years,* pp. 88–89.

27. Ibid., pp. 89–90.

28. Letter from Franklin D. Roosevelt to Arthur J. Altmeyer dated April 28, 1938.

29. Theron F. Schlabach, *Edwin E. Witte: Cautious Reformer* (Madison: State Historical Society of Wisconsin, 1969), pp. 163–164.

30. M. A. Linton, "Observations on the Old Age Security Program Embodied in the Social Security Act," box 199, Edwin E. Witte Papers, University of Wisconsin, Madison.

31. Ibid.

32. Schlabach, *Edwin E. Witte,* pp. 168–171.

33. Edwin E. Witte, testimony before the Ways and Means Committee, House of Representatives, March 18, 1939.

34. Edwin E. Witte, handwritten note to W. Rulon Williamson, August 22, 1938, "The Concept of Social Insurance," box 4, Edwin E. Witte Papers, University of Wisconsin, Madison.

35. Martha Derthick, *Policymaking for Social Security* (Washington, D.C.: Brookings Institution, 1979), p. 235, quotes Brown as saying, "Après nous le déluge."

36. Minutes of the Social Security Board meeting, "Discussion of Amendments to Act," February 4, 1937, pp. 26–29, Records of the Social Security Board, Chairman's Files, National Archives, file 013, RG47, box 12.

37. Robert J. Myers, "History of Replacement Rates for Various Amendments to the Social Security Act," Memorandum No. 2 (Washington, D.C.: National Commission on Social Security Reform, 1982), p. 3.

38. *Senate Report No. 628,* 74th Congress, May 13, 1935, p. 9 and *Senate Report No. 734,* 76th Cong., 1st sess., p. 17.

39. Henry Morgenthau, Jr., secretary of Treasury, statement before the Ways and Means Committee of the House of Representatives, March 24, 1939.

40. Memorandum from Ewan Clague, Acting Director, Bureau of Research and Statistics, to Arthur J. Altmeyer, "Old-Age Insurance," July 1, 1937, Records of the Social Security Board, National Archives, file 011, RG47, box 3.

41. Memorandum from Louis Resnick, director, Information Service, to Frank Bane, executive director, July 26, 1937, Records of the Social Security Board, National Archives, file 011, RG47, box 3.

42. Memorandum from W. Rulon Williamson, chief actuary, to Arthur J. Altmeyer, et al., "Social Security in the United States—the Old-Age Benefits Provisions as Insurance," October 28, 1937, Records of the Social Security Board, Records of the Office of the Commissioner, chairman's file, National Archives, file 700, RG47, box 96.

43. J. Douglas Brown, statement before the Senate Finance Committee, June 13, 1939, pp. 153–154.

44. Abraham Epstein, secretary, American Association for Social Security, Editorial, "1939 Marks Association's Greatest Victories," *Social Security* (September–October, 1939), p. 3.

45. Edwin E. Witte, "Social Security—1940 Model," *American Labor Legislation Review* (September 1939), p. 105.

Chapter 5: To Fund or Not to Fund?

1. *Senate Report No. 628*, 74th Congress, May 13, 1935, p. 9.

2. Arthur J. Altmeyer, *The Formative Years of Social Security* (Madison: University of Wisconsin Press, 1966), p. 89.

3. Interview with Arthur J. Altmeyer, Oral History Collection, Columbia University (1967).

4. Arthur Altmeyer, chairman's file, file 705, box 98, Records of the Social Security Board, National Archives, pp. 4, 14.

5. Arthur H. Vandenberg, "The $47,000,000,000 Blight," *Saturday Evening Post* (April 24, 1937), p. 1.

6. Ibid.

7. An article by J. H. Van Deventer, "Social Security in Frogdom," source unknown, sent by M. A. Linton to Arthur Altmeyer, December 2, 1937.

8. Letter from A. J. Altmeyer to M. A. Linton, December 4, 1937.

Chapter 6: Unresolved Issues

1. M. Albert Linton, "Observations on the Old Age Security Program Embodied in the Social Security Act," November 1937, box 199, Edwin E. Witte Papers, University of Wisconsin, Madison.

2. Robert J. Myers, Memorandum to Wilbur J. Cohen, "Relative 'Bargains' Under the 1939 Act and Under H.R. 2893," February 23, 1949 (Madison: State Historical Society of Wisconsin), Arthur J. Altmeyer papers, box 12, folder 4.

3. Arthur J. Altmeyer, *The Formative Years of Social Security* (Madison: University of Wisconsin Press, 1966), pp. 122–123.

4. *New York Times*, September 12, 1940, p. 14.

5. Franklin D. Roosevelt, as quoted in Altmeyer, *The Formative Years*, p. 126.

6. Ibid.

7. Senator Sheridan Downey, *Congressional Record*, 76th Cong., 3rd sess., 1940, 86, pt. 14: A1423.

8. Arthur J. Altmeyer, Memorandum to the President, July 5, 1939 (Madison: State Historical Society of Wisconsin), Arthur J. Altmeyer papers, box 2.

9. Draft double-decker plan as transmitted by Ida C. Merriam and attached to a memorandum to Arthur J. Altmeyer, "Double-Decker Plan—Tentative Specifications and Cost Estimates" (Washington, D.C.: Social Security Board, March 23, 1949), p. 3.

10. Ibid., p. 4.

11. Ibid., p. 6.

12. Carl T. Curtis, "Additional Minority Views," *Social Security Act Amendments of 1949*, Report No. 1300 (Washington, D.C.: U.S. House of Representatives, 1949), p. 176.

13. Altmeyer, *The Formative Years of Social Security*, pp. 125–126.

14. Arthur J. Altmeyer, press conference transcript, August 7, 1939, p. 17.

15. Henry Morgenthau, Jr., *Hearings on Social Security*, Committee on Ways and Means, House of Representatives, February–April 1939, 76th Congress, p. 2113.

16. Altmeyer, *The Formative Years of Social Security*, pp. 137–161.

17. *First Annual Report of the Board of Trustees of the Old-Age and Survivors Insurance Trust Fund* (Washington, D.C.: Social Security Board of Trustees, January 3, 1941).

18. Letter from the Board of Trustees of the Old-Age and Survivors Insurance Trust Fund (Washington, D.C.: Social Security Board of Trustees, April 4, 1950), pp. 6, 12.

19. Arthur H. Vandenberg, "Statement on Prospective Increases in Social Security Taxes," *Congressional Record* (September 14, 1943), p. 7529.

20. Letter from Senator Arthur H. Vandenberg to Arthur J. Altmeyer, November 14, 1944.

21. Franklin D. Roosevelt, letter to the Honorable Walter F. George, chairman, Senate Finance Committee, and the Honorable Robert L. Doughton, chairman, House Ways and Means Committee, October 3, 1942.

22. Franklin D. Roosevelt, statement accompanying the signing of H.R. 5564, "An Act to Fix the Tax Under the Federal Insurance Contributions Act, on Employer and Employees for Calendar Year 1945," December 16, 1944.

23. Edwin E. Witte, "The 'Bug-A-Boo' of 'The Welfare State,'" address at the town hall of Los Angeles, July 25, 1949, National Archives, RG47, MLR 6, box 27, Records of the Office of the Commissioner.

24. Edwin E. Witte, "Social Security: A Wild Dream or a Practical Plan?" in Robert J. Lampman, ed., *Social Security Perspectives: Essays by Edwin E. Witte* (Madison: University of Wisconsin Press, 1962), p. 10.

25. Edwin E. Witte, "Social Security—1948" in Lampman, ed., *Social Security Perspectives*, p. 35.

26. I. S. Falk, "Questions and Answers on Financing of Old-Age and Survivors Insurance," memorandum to O. C. Pogge, director, Bureau of Old-Age and Survivors Insurance, February 9, 1945, p. 16.

27. Letter with attachment from Arthur J. Altmeyer to Senator Robert F. Wagner, July 5, 1940.

28. Letter with attachment from Arthur J. Altmeyer to President Franklin D. Roosevelt, December 4, 1942.

29. Ibid.

426 Notes to Pages 89–104

30. Altmeyer, *The Formative Years of Social Security*, pp. 169–170.

31. Edward D. Berkowitz, *America's Welfare State: From Roosevelt to Reagan* (Baltimore: Johns Hopkins University Press, 1991), pp. 57–61.

32. Wilbur J. Cohen and Robert J. Myers, "Social Security Act Amendments of 1950: A Summary and Legislative History," *Social Security Bulletin* (October 1950), p. 1.

33. J. Douglas Brown, quoted in Berkowitz, *America's Welfare State*, p. 64.

34. Memorandum from O. C. Pogge, director of the Bureau of Old-Age and Survivors Insurance, to all bureau employees, July 27, 1950.

35. Ibid.

Chapter 7: A Deal That Couldn't Be Beat

1. Dean R. Leimer, "Cohort-Specific Measures of Lifetime Net Social Security Transfers," ORS Working Paper Series, No. 59 (Washington, D.C.: Social Security Administration, February 1994).

2. See Gordon P. Goodfellow and Sylvester J. Schieber, "Investment of Assets in Self-Directed Retirement Plans," in Olivia S. Mitchell and Marc M. Twinney, eds., *Positioning Pensions for the Twenty-First Century* (Philadelphia: Pension Research Council and University of Pennsylvania Press, 1997), pp. 67–90; and Robert C. Clark, Gordon P. Goodfellow, Sylvester J. Schieber, and Drew Warwick, "Making the Most of 401(k) Plans: Who's Choosing What and Why?" in Brett Hammond, Olivia S. Mitchell, and Anna Rappaport, *Forecasting Retirement Needs and Retirement Wealth* (Philadelphia: Pension Research Council and University of Pennsylvania Press, forthcoming).

3. For workers who were sixty-five in 1940, we considered only their wages and contributions for the years when they were sixty-two to sixty-four, because the payroll taxes were collected only from 1937 onward. For those who were sixty-five in 1941, we considered their wages for four years when they were ages sixty-one to sixty-four, and so forth. Workers who turned sixty-five in 1980 had been age twenty-two in 1937 and would have had forty-three years of contributions to the system, according to our calculations. For each subsequent cohort of workers, we assumed that they started working at twenty-two, and so all cohorts retiring after 1980 were assumed to have had forty-three years of covered employment.

4. This program can be found at *http://www.ssa.gov/OACT.*

5. In the early years of the Social Security program, retirement benefits were not indexed on a regular basis. Therefore, a monthly benefit for the cohorts that reached age sixty-five from 1940 to 1970 was calculated for each month from initial entitlement through December 1974. After that time, the monthly benefits were adjusted according to the regular annual cost-of-living adjustment. For the cohorts that reached age sixty-five in 1975 and after, only an initial monthly benefit was calculated using the program mentioned above. Subsequent monthly benefits were adjusted to reflect the regular cost-of-living adjustment. The annual cost-of-living adjustment following historical values through December 1997 and projected values for the CPI in the *1998 Social Security Trustee Report*, table II.D1, pp. 57–58.

6. In order to calculate the present value of the lifetime stream of annual benefits, we used mortality tables provided by the Social Security Administration for cohorts born in 1875 and then for every fifth year from 1920 to 1995. Mortality tables for the

cohorts born in 1880 to 1915 were constructed assuming a linear change in mortality from 1875 to 1920. The interest rate used to discount future benefits to the age of retirement for each cohort was the three-year average of the bond rates for the three years just before retirement.

7. In order to do the research behind this book, we used every source available, including the web site of the Social Security Administration at *http://www.ssa.gov.* There we were able to benefit from the work of the Social Security historian who has put many useful documents on the web. In mid-1998 there was a section of the site which covered "myths" about Social Security and devoted considerable coverage to Charles Ponzi and the "myth" that Social Security operated like one of his notorious schemes. The entry argued that there was no similarity between a responsible pay-go system such as Social Security and a chain letter or Ponzi scheme. It also contained a very clear presentation on Ponzi and his schemes, from which this discussion is drawn. As we expressed interest in the entry, Social Security officials ordered their historian to remove it from the web site. Apparently, they think the less said about Ponzi and Social Security the better.

8. Paul Samuelson, "An Exact Consumption-Loan Model of Interest with or Without the Social Contrivance of Money," *Journal of Political Economy* (December 1958), pp. 467–482.

9. Paul A. Samuelson, "Social Security," *Newsweek* (February 12, 1967), p. 88.

Chapter 8: The Inside Movers and Shakers

1. Martha Derthick, *Policymaking for Social Security* (Washington, D.C.: Brookings Institution, 1979), p. 235.

2. Jerry R. Cates, *Insuring Inequality: Administrative Leadership in Social Security, 1935–1954* (Ann Arbor: University of Michigan Press, 1983).

3. Charles Schottland, who served as commissioner of Social Security from 1954 to 1958, makes it clear that he was preoccupied with matters other than OASI and that Bob Ball was a strong and able administrator, philosopher, and exponent of the program. While Ball was the number-two person in the operation, Schottland was obviously a stronger, more dominating character than his immediate boss. Schottland also indicates that relations were smooth between him and the bureau because he left it pretty much alone, with Ball in charge. Schottland, Oral History Collection, Columbia University (1967), pp. 42, 78, 82, and 125.

4. Derthick, *Policymaking for Social Security,* p. 19.

5. Arthur J. Altmeyer, *The Formative Years of Social Security* (Madison: University of Wisconsin Press, 1966), pp. 142–143.

6. Ibid., p. 146.

7. Ibid., pp. 144–149.

8. Edward D. Berkowitz, *America's Welfare State: From Roosevelt to Reagan* (Baltimore: Johns Hopkins University Press, 1991), p. 164.

9. Robert J. Myers, Oral History Collection, Columbia University (1996), p. 23.

10. Berkowitz, *America's Welfare State,* p. 167.

11. Derthick, *Policymaking for Social Security,* p. 115.

12. Interview with Wilbur J. Cohen by David G. McComb for the Lyndon Baines

Johnson Library (1968), as quoted in Martha Derthick, *Policymaking for Social Security*, p. 26.

13. Robert J. Myers, *Expansionism in Social Insurance* (London: Institute of Economic Affairs, 1970), p. 29.

14. A. Haeworth Robertson, *The Coming Revolution in Social Security* (Reston, Va: Reston Publishing Company, 1981), and *The Big Lie: What Every Baby Boomer Should Know About Social Security and Medicare* (Washington, D.C.: Retirement Policy Institute, 1997).

15. Robert J. Myers, "Position Statement by Robert J. Myers," *Transactions of the Society of Actuaries* (Chicago: Society of Actuaries, 1970), p. D313.

16. Myers, *Expansionism in Social Insurance*, p. 19.

17. Ibid., pp. 19–20.

18. Robert M. Ball, Oral History Collection, Columbia University (1987), pp. 6–8.

19. Ibid., pp. 9–10.

20. Ibid., p. 11.

21. Ibid., p. 14.

22. Ibid., p. 15.

23. Ibid.

24. Robert M. Ball, with Thomas N. Bethell, *Straight Talk About Social Security* (New York: A Century Foundation/Twentieth Century Fund, 1998).

Chapter 9: The Outside Movers, Shakers, and Takers

1. Martha Derthick, *Policymaking for Social Security* (Washington, D.C.: Brookings Institution, 1979), p. 110.

2. Ibid., p. 111.

3. Ibid., pp. 114–115.

4. *Inland Steel Company v. United Steel Workers of America* (CIO), 77 NLRB 4 (1948). The decision was based on two premises. The first was that wages as defined in the Labor-Management Relations Act of 1947 included such things as pensions and insurance benefits. The second was that the detailed provisions of pension plans come within the purview of "conditions of employment" and constitute an appropriate subject for collective bargaining.

5. Birchard E. Wyatt, "Private Group Retirement Plans," Ph.D. dissertation, Columbia University, 1936.

6. Steven A. Sass, *The Promise of Private Pensions: The First Hundred Years* (Cambridge: Harvard University Press, 1997), p. 158.

7. J. K. Lasser and Walter Roos, "You Are Richer Than You Think," *Nation's Business* (October 1951), p. 25.

8. Ibid., p. 84.

9. Marion B. Folsom, Oral History Collection, Columbia University (1970).

10. Ibid., pp. 50–51.

11. C. E. Wilson, in "Economic Factors of Collective Bargaining," a speech before the Chicago Executives Club, excerpted in Neil W. Chamberlain, *Sourcebook on Labor* (New York: McGraw-Hill, 1958), pp. 1000–1001.

12. Ibid., p. 61.

13. Arthur H. Vandenberg, "Reserves Under Federal Old-Age Benefit Plan–Social Security Act," hearing before the Senate Committee on Finance, 75th Cong., 1st sess. (Washington, D.C.: U.S.Government Printing Office, 1937), p. 22.

14. Derthick, *Policymaking for Social Security*, pp. 89–90.

15. Interview with Roswell B. Perkins, Oral History Collection, Columbia University (1968), pp. 139–141.

16. Derthick, *Policymaking for Social Security*, pp. 94–95.

17. Marion B. Folsom, Oral History Collection, Columbia University (1965–1968), pp. 116–117.

18. Joseph A. Pechman, Henry J. Aaron, and Michael K. Taussig, *Social Security: Perspectives for Reform* (Washington, D.C.: Brookings Institution, 1968).

19. See, for example, Martin Feldstein, "Social Security, Induced Retirement, and Aggregate Capital Accumulation," *Journal of Political Economy* (September–October, 1974), pp. 905–926.

20. Lawrence Thompson, "An Analysis of the Factors Currently Determining Benefit-Level Adjustments in the Social Security Retirement Program," Technical Analysis Paper No. 1, Office of Income Security Policy, Office of the Assistant Secretary for Planning and Evaluation, Department of Health, Education, and Welfare, September 1974.

21. Edward D. Berkowitz, *Mr. Social Security: The Life of Wilbur J. Cohen* (Lawrence: University Press of Kansas, 1995), p. 292.

22. Ibid., p. 294.

23. Robert J. Myers, "The Role of Actuaries and Economists in Cost Analyses and Financing Aspects of Social Security Program," *Record* (Washington, D.C.: Society of Actuaries, 1976), vol. 2, no. 1, p. 83.

24. Ibid., p. 95.

25. A. Haeworth Robertson, *The Big Lie: What Every Baby Boomer Should Know About Social Security and Medicare* (Washington, D.C.: Retirement Policy Institute, 1997), p. xi.

26. Derthick, *Policymaking for Social Security*, p. 235, quoting Brown as saying "Après nous le déluge."

27. Ibid., p. 67.

Chapter 10: The End of the Beginning

1. Robert M. Ball, "Policy Issues in Social Security," *Social Security Bulletin* (June 1966), vol. 29, pp. 3–9.

2. Ibid., pp. 5–7.

3. Ibid., p. 8.

4. Martha Derthick, *Policymaking for Social Security* (Washington, D.C.: Brookings Institution, 1979), p. 342.

5. Ball, "Policy Issues in Social Security," p. 6.

6. Ibid., p. 8.

7. Robert J. Myers, *Expansionism in Social Insurance* (London: Institute of Economic Affairs, 1970).

8. For example, see J. Douglas Brown, "The American Philosophy of Social Insurance," Sidney Hillman Memorial Lecture delivered at the University of Wisconsin,

November 18, 1955. Part of this lecture was also delivered at Social Security Administration Headquarters in Baltimore, Maryland, November 7, 1957. Text of the speech can be found at *http://www.ssa.gov.*

9. J. Douglas Brown, Oral History Collection, Columbia University, 1966, p. 41.

10. Ibid., 61.

11. Edward D. Berkowitz, *Mr. Social Security: The Life of Wilbur J. Cohen* (Lawrence: University Press of Kansas, 1995), pp. 249–250.

12. Ibid., p. 250.

13. Ibid., p. 259.

14. Derthick, *Policymaking for Social Security*, p. 345; and *Social Security Bulletin, Annual Statistical Supplement, 1996*, p. 34.

15. Robert J. Myers, *Expansionism in Social Insurance*, pp. 12–20.

16. Robert J. Myers, resignation letter to Robert Finch, *Congressional Record* (June 3, 1970), p. 18059.

17. 1971 Advisory Council on Social Security, *Reports on the Old-Age, Survivors, and Disability Insurance and Medicare Programs* (Washington, D.C.: Social Security Administration, 1971), pp. 7, 13.

18. Ibid., p. 77.

19. Ibid., p. 85.

20. Ibid.

21. Joseph A. Pechman, Henry J. Aaron, and Michael K. Taussig, *Social Security: Perspectives for Reform* (Washington, D.C.: Brookings Institution, 1968), p. 152.

22. Ibid., pp. 157–158.

23. Robert M. Ball, "Social Security Amendments of 1971: Summary and Legislative History," *Social Security Bulletin* (March 1973), p. 12.

24. Robert M. Ball, Oral History Collection, Columbia University (1987), p. 16.

25. John Byrnes, *Congressional Record* (July 31, 1958), p. 15746.

26. John Byrnes, *Congressional Record* (June 30, 1972), p. 23733.

27. Derthick, *Policymaking for Social Security*, p. 346.

28. Wilbur J. Cohen, quoted in Berkowitz, *Mr. Social Security*, p. 294.

Chapter 11: A Tale of Good Intentions Gone Bad

1. Paul Samuelson, "Social Security," *Newsweek* (February 12, 1967), reprinted in *The Samuelson Sampler* (Glen Ridge, N.J.: Thomas Horton, 1973), pp. 146–148.

2. Ibid.

3. Joseph A. Pechman, "Editor's Preface," *Economics for Policymaking: Selected Essays of Arthur M. Okun*, Joseph A. Pechman, ed. (Cambridge: MIT Press, 1983), p. viii.

4. Lawrence Thompson, "An Analysis of the Factors Currently Determining Benefit Level Adjustments in the Social Security Retirement Program," Technical Analysis Paper No. 1, Office of Income Security Policy, Office of the Assistant Secretary for Planning and Evaluation, Department of Health, Education, and Welfare, September 1974.

5. Ibid.

6. Memorandum from William Robinson to James Schlesinger, Director Bureau of the Budget, Executive Office of the President, and accompanying "Staff Paper on the Implications of Future Changes in Benefit Levels of Social Security," April 29, 1970.

7. Ibid., p. 1 of the staff paper.

8. Ibid., p. 10.

9. 1971 Advisory Council on Social Security, *Reports on the Old-Age, Survivors, and Disability Insurance and Medicare Programs* (Washington, D.C.: Social Security Administration, 1971), p. 56.

10. Thompson, "An Analysis of the Factors."

11. A. Haeworth Robertson, "Financial Status of Social Security Program After the Social Security Amendments of 1977," *Social Security Bulletin* (March 1978), p. 21.

12. Ibid.

13. John Snee and Mary Ross, "Social Security Amendments of 1977: Legislative History and Summary of Provisions," *Social Security Bulletin* (March 1978), pp. 3-20.

14. Ibid.

15. W. Andrew Achenbaum, *Social Security: Visions and Revisions* (Cambridge University Press, New York, 1986), p. 65.

16. Ibid.

17. Ibid.

18. Snee and Ross, "Social Security Amendments of 1977," pp. 3-20.

19. Ibid.

20. Ibid.

21. Ibid.

22. Ibid.

23. Ibid.

24. Ibid.

25. The actual amount in 1987 turned out to be $6,263.40.

26. Snee and Ross, "Social Security Amendments of 1977," pp. 3-20.

27. From table 5 in Robertson, "Financial Status of Social Security Program," p. 27.

28. Snee and Ross, "Social Security Amendments of 1977," pp. 3-20.

29. Office of the White House press secretary, "Remarks of the President on Signing H.R. 9346, a Bill to Amend the Social Security Act and the Internal Revenue Code of 1954," Indian Treaty Room, December 20, 1977.

30. Statement of Don I. Wortman, acting commissioner of Social Security, *Social Security Bulletin* (March 1978), p. 4.

31. "Social Security Commissioner Calls Improvements in Benefits Unlikely," *New York Times*, July 17, 1979, p. 10. This material also appears in W. Andrew Achenbaum, *Social Security: Visions and Revisions* (New York: Cambridge University Press, 1986), p. 69.

Chapter 12: The Continued Deterioration of the System and the Big Fix

1. W. Andrew Achenbaum, *Social Security: Visions and Revisions* (New York: Cambridge University Press, 1986), p. 75.

2. HHS News, U.S. Department of Health and Human Services, "Statement of HHS Secretary Richard S. Schweiker," released Tuesday, May 12, 1981.

3. Paul Light, *Still Artful Work: The Continuing Politics of Social Security Reform*, 2d edition (New York: McGraw-Hill, 1995), pp. 114-115.

4. Achenbaum, *Social Security*, p. 79.

5. HHS News, U.S. Department of Health and Human Services, Statement of HHS Secretary Richard S. Schweiker, released Tuesday, May 12, 1981.

6. Senator Moynihan, quoted in the *1981 Congressional Quarterly Almanac*, p. 284.

7. Senator Armstrong, quoted in the *1981 Congressional Quarterly Almanac*, p. 118.

8. Speaker O'Neill, quoted in "Senate Rejects Reagan Bid to Trim Social Security," *New York Times*, May 21, 1981, p. B14.

9. Speaker O'Neill quoted in *Newsweek* (January 24, 1983), p. 20. The original quotation by O'Neill was from May 1981.

10. Charles M. Brain, *Social Security at the Crossroads: Public Opinion and Public Policy* (New York: Garland Publishing, 1991), p. 81.

11. Paul Light, *Artful Work: The Politics of Social Security Reform* (New York: McGraw-Hill, 1985), p. 120.

12. Ibid.

13. *Newsweek* (January 24, 1983).

14. Brain, *Social Security at the Crossroads*, p. 82.

15. Ibid.

16. Achenbaum, *Social Security*, p. 81.

17. Robert Myers, National Commission on Social Security Reform, "Actuarial Cost Estimates for OASDI and HI and for Various Possible Changes in OASDI and Historical Data for OASDI and HI," November 1982 memo.

18. Ibid.

19. Achenbaum, *Social Security*, p. 84.

20. Ibid.

21. Robert Dole, "Reagan's Faithful Allies," *New York Times*, January 3, 1983, p. 14.

22. Daniel Patrick Moynihan, "More Than Social Security Was at Stake," *Washington Post*, January 18, 1983, p. A17.

23. Achenbaum, *Social Security*, p. 86.

24. Ibid.

25. Ibid., p. 89.

26. Ibid.

27. "Pension Changes Signed into Law," *New York Times*, April 21, 1983, p. A1.

Chapter 14: Fundamental Questions

1. Social Security Administration, *Income of the Population 66 or Older, 1996* (Washington, D.C.: Social Security Administration, 1998).

2. http://www.americansdiscuss.org/poll_data/policyrpt.html.

3. Robert M. Ball, with Thomas N. Bethell, *Straight Talk About Social Security* (New York: Century Foundation Press, 1998), p. 2.

4. See, for example, Ronald Lee and Shripad Tuljapurkar, "Stochastic Forecasts for Social Security," and the "Comment" on their paper, by Sylvester J. Schieber in David A. Wise, ed., *Frontiers in the Economics of Aging* (Chicago: University of Chicago Press, 1998).

5. For a critical discussion of this issue see appendix C, "Mortality Assumptions of the SSA Actuaries," in *Reports of the Technical Panel on Assumptions and Methods:*

Report of the 1994-1995 Advisory Council on Social Security (Washington, D.C.: Social Security Administration, 1996), vol. 2, pp. 251-262.

6. Ibid., p. 156.

7. Robert J. Myers and Bruce D. Schobel, "A Money's-Worth Analysis of Social Security Retirement Benefits," *Transactions* (Society of Actuaries, 1983), pp. 542-543.

8. Stephen C. Goss and Orlo R. Nichols, "OASDI Money's Worth Analysis for Hypothetical Cohorts—INFORMATION" (Office of the Actuary, Social Security Administration internal memorandum, March 1, 1993), p. 4.

9. Eugene Rogot, Paul D. Sorlie, and Norman J. Johnson, "Life Expectancy by Employment Status, Income, and Education in the National Longitudinal Mortality Study," *Public Health Reports* (July–August 1992), p. 459.

10. William W. Beach and Gareth G. Davis, *Social Security's Rate of Return* (Washington, D.C.: Heritage Foundation, 1998), p. 2.

11. Paul L. Menchik, "Economic Status as a Determinant of Mortality Among Black and White Older Men: Does Poverty Kill?" *Population Studies* 47 (1993), pp. 427-436.

12. William W. Beach and Gareth G. Davis, *Social Security's Rate of Return* (Washington, D.C.: Heritage Foundation, 1998).

13. Robert J. Myers, "A Glaring Error: Why One Study of Social Security Misstates Returns," *Actuary* (September 1998), p. 5.

14. Martha Derthick, *Policymaking for Social Security* (Washington, D.C.: Brookings Institution, 1979), p. 19.

Chapter 15: The Iron Rules of Arithmetic Assert Themselves

1. James P. Smith and Barry Edmonston, eds., *The New Americans* (Washington, D.C.: National Academy Press, 1977, p. 3.

2. Paul A. Samuelson, "Social Security," *Newsweek* (February 12, 1967), p. 88.

3. John Geanakoplos, Olivia S. Mitchell, and Stephen P. Zeldes, "Would a Privatized Social Security System Really Pay a Higher Rate of Return?" paper presented at a conference on Social Security reform sponsored by the National Academy of Social Insurance, Washington, D.C., January 1998.

Chapter 16: Social Security in the Bigger Picture

1. Robert M. Ball, "Panel on Formulating a Deficit Reduction Package: What Is the Role of Social Security?" in Henry J. Aaron, ed., *Social Security and the Budget* (Washington, D.C.: National Academy of Social Insurance, 1988), p. 123.

2. Ibid., 124.

3. *Historical Tables, Budget of the United States Government, Fiscal Year 1999* (Washington, D.C.: U.S. Government Printing Office, 1998), pp. 121-130, 212-248.

4. Bipartisan Commission on Entitlement and Tax Reform, *Interim Report to the President* (Washington, D.C.: Bipartisan Commission, August 1994), p. 6.

5. Congressional Budget Office, *Long-Term Budgetary Pressures and Policy Options* (Washington, D.C.: Congressional Budget Office, May 1998), pp. 20-21.

6. Robert M. Ball, with Thomas N. Bethell, *Straight Talk About Social Security* (New York: Century Foundation Press, 1998), p. 3.

7. Congressional Budget Office, *Long-Term Budgetary Pressures and Policy Options*, p. 6.

8. *1998 Annual Report of the Board of Trustees of the Federal Old-Age and Survivors Insurance and Disability Insurance Trust Funds*, p. 187.

9. Henry Aaron, "Is a Crisis Really Coming?" *Newsweek* (December 9, 1996), p. 31.

10. Roland D. McDevitt and Sylvester J. Schieber, *From Baby Boom to Elder Boom: Providing Health Care for an Aging Population* (Washington, D.C.: Watson Wyatt Worldwide, 1996).

11. McDevitt and Schieber, *From Baby Boom to Elder Boom.*

12. Congressional Budget Office, *Long-Term Budgetary Pressures and Policy Options*, p. xix.

13. Ibid.

14. *The 1996 Annual Report of the Board of Trustees of the Federal Hospital Insurance Trust Fund*, p. 8.

15. Ibid., p. 12.

16. Congressional Budget Office, *Long-Term Budgetary Pressures and Policy Options*, p. xx.

Chapter 17: Heathens in the Temple

1. Martha Derthick, *Policymaking for Social Security* (Washington, D.C.: Brookings Institution, 1979), p. 100.

2. Ibid.

3. *Report of the 1994-1996 Advisory Council on Social Security*, vol. 1, *Findings and Recommendations* (Washington, D.C.: Social Security Administration, 1997), p. 2.

4. *Report of the 1994-1996 Advisory Council on Social Security*, vol. 2, *Reports of the Technical Panel on Assumptions and Methods and the Technical Panel on Trends and Issues in Retirement Savings* (Washington, D.C.: Social Security Administration, 1996), p. 7.

5. Ibid., p. 8

6. Barry P. Bosworth, "Fund Accumulation: How Much? How Managed?" in Peter A. Diamond, David C. Lindeman, and Howard Young, eds., *Social Security: What Role for the Future?* (Washington, D.C.: National Academy of Social Insurance, 1996), pp. 111-113.

7. Final minutes of the meeting of the 1994-1996 Advisory Council on Social Security held on February 10-11, 1995, Washington, D.C., p. 2.

8. Transcript of the meeting of the 1994-1996 Advisory Council on Social Security held on February 10-11, 1995, Washington, D.C., p. 180.

9. Ibid., p. 181.

10. Ibid., p. 190.

11. Ibid., p. 245.

12. Ibid., pp. 250-251.

13. Ibid., pp. 256-257.

14. Ibid., p. 259.

15. Ibid., p. 264.

16. Ibid., p. 269.

17. Ibid., pp. 270-271.

18. Ibid., p. 219.

19. Transcript of the meeting of the 1994-1996 Advisory Council on Social Security held on March 10, 1995, Washington, D.C., pp. 212-213.

20. Ibid., p. 248.

21. Ibid., p. 252.

22. Ibid., p. 223.

23. Ibid., p. 227.

24. Ibid., p. 229.

25. Ibid., p. 234.

26. Transcript of the meeting of the 1994-1996 Advisory Council on Social Security held on February 10-11, 1995, Washington, D.C., pp. 154-155.

27. "Illustrative Plan to Restore Long-Range Solvency," attachment A to the final minutes of the meeting of the 1994-1996 Advisory Council on Social Security held on April 21-22, 1995, Washington, D.C.

28. Transcript of the meeting of the 1994-1996 Advisory Council on Social Security held on February 10-11, 1995, Washington, D.C., pp. 154-155.

29. Sylvester J. Schieber, "Retirement Income Adequacy at Risk: Baby Boomers' Prospects in the New Millennium," in Sylvester J. Schieber and John B. Shoven, eds., *Public Policy Toward Pensions* (Cambridge, Mass.: MIT Press, 1997), pp. 267-312.

30. Transcript of the meeting of the 1994-1996 Advisory Council on Social Security held on April 11, 1995, Washington, D.C., pp. 79-81.

31. Ibid., p. 81.

32. Ibid., p. 88.

33. Ibid., pp. 88-89.

34. Ibid., p. 117.

35. Ibid., p. 125.

36. Ibid., p. 91.

37. Ibid., p. 111.

38. Ibid., p. 155.

39. Ibid., p. 156.

40. Ibid., p. 100.

41. Ibid., p. 214.

42. Transcript of the meeting of the 1994-1996 Advisory Council on Social Security held on June 2, 1995, Washington, D.C., p. 26.

43. Transcript of the meeting of the 1994-1996 Advisory Council on Social Security held on July 27-28, 1995, Washington, D.C., p. 73.

44. Ibid.

45. Ibid., p. 74.

46. Ibid., p. 356.

47. Ibid., p. 364.

48. Ibid., p. 366.

49. Ibid., p. 377.

50. Ibid., p. 384.

51. Ibid., p. 387.

52. Ibid., p. 388.

53. Ibid., p. 388.
54. Ibid., p. 389.
55. Ibid., p. 402.
56. Transcript of the meeting of the 1994-1996 Advisory Council on Social Security held on August 31, 1995, Washington, D.C., p. 143.
57. Ibid., pp. 172-173.
58. Ibid., p. 173.
59. Ibid., pp. 188-189.
60. Transcript of the meeting of the 1994-1996 Advisory Council on Social Security held on December 14, 1995, Washington, D.C., p. 108.
61. Ibid., pp. 108-109.
62. Ibid., p. 109.
63. Ibid., p. 149.
64. Ibid., pp. 149-150.
65. Ibid., pp. 155-156.
66. Ibid., p. 177.
67. *Report of the 1994-1996 Advisory Council on Social Security*, vol. 1, *Findings and Recommendations*.

Chapter 18: Social Security Today and Marginal Proposals for Reform

1. There would be a difference of substance if the age of early retirement, or earliest eligibility age (EEA), were advanced along with the age of normal retirement. A few proposals have this feature, although most do not.
2. As an analogy, consider a course that has forty homework assignments, each individually graded. If the teacher changes from taking the average of your best thirty-five scores to taking the average of your best thirty-eight or even forty, what happens to your average grade? Obviously, it goes down.

Chapter 19: A Framework for Understanding the Options for Social Security Reform

1. E. Bos, M. T. Vu, E. Massiah, and R. Bulatao, *World Population Projections, 1994-95*, published for the International Bank for Reconstruction and Development, World Bank (Baltimore, Md.: Johns Hopkins University Press, 1994).
2. Readers interested in the details of the challenges these systems are facing should see Peter Peterson, *The Gray Dawn* (New York: Random House/Times Books, 1999).
3. See *http://ns.hm-treasury.gov.uk/pub/html/docs/misc/pensions.html.*
4. A full discussion of the changes to the Canadian Pension Plan can be found at *http://www.hrdc-drhc.gc.ca/isp/cpp/cpplcqa.html.*
5. A full discussion of the changes to the Swedish state retirement system can be found at *http://www.pension.gov.se/in%20English/summary.html.*
6. See *http://ns.hm-treasury.gov.uk/pub/html/docs/misc/pensions.html.*
7. Ibid.

8. Ibid.

9. See, for example, Peter Diamond and Salvador Valdes-Preito, "Social Security Reforms," in Barry P. Bosworth, Rudiger Dornbusch, and Raul Laban, eds., *The Chilean Economy: Policy Lessons and Challenges* (Washington, D.C.: Brookings Institution, 1995), and Dimitri Vittas, "Strengths and Weaknesses of the Chilean Pension Reform," mimeograph, Financial Sector, Development Department of the World Bank, May 1995.

10. All capital market and asset numbers taken from Vittas, "Strengths and Weaknesses."

11. Susan Ryan: "Quality of Life as It Relates to Australia's Aging Population, or Living to 100 in a Civilized Society," speech given to the Association of Superannuation Funds of Australia, Newcastle, Australia, 1997.

12. *Report of the 1994-1996 Advisory Council on Social Security*, vol. 1 *Findings and Recommendations* (Washington, D.C.: Social Security Administration, 1997), pp. 25-27.

13. Ibid., p. 25.

14. Ibid.

15. Alan Greenspan, testimony before the Senate Budget Committee Task Force on Social Security, November 20, 1997.

16. *Report of the 1994-1996 Advisory Council on Social Security*, pp. 28-29.

17. Ibid.

18. National Commission on Retirement Policy, "The 21st Century Retirement Security Plan" (Washington, D.C.: Center for Strategic and International Studies, May 19, 1998).

19. Ibid., pp. 30-33.

20. Peter J. Ferrara, *Social Security: The Inherent Contradiction* (San Francisco: Cato Institute, 1980), especially chap. 11.

21. John Geanakoplos, Olivia S. Mitchell, and Stephen P. Zeldes, "Would a Privatized Social Security System Really Pay a Higher Rate of Return?" paper presented at a conference on Social Security reform sponsored by the National Academy of Social Insurance, Washington, D.C., January 1998.

22. Martin Feldstein and Andrew Samwick, "The Transition Path in Privatizing Social Security," in Martin Feldstein, ed., *Privatizing Social Security* (Chicago: University of Chicago Press, 1998), pp. 215-260.

23. Ibid., p. 218.

24. Ibid., pp. 247-250.

25. Ibid., pp. 241-242.

Chapter 20: The Return to Pay-Go Financing

1. Arthur H. Vandenberg, "The $47,000,000,000 Blight," *Saturday Evening Post* (April 24, 1937), pp. 5-7.

2. Arthur J. Altmeyer, chairman, Social Security Board, letter to Senator Arthur H. Vandenberg of August 27, 1943, *Congressional Record* (September 4, 1943).

3. Transcript of the meeting of the 1994-1996 Advisory Council on Social Security held on February 10-11, 1995, Washington, D.C., p. 190.

4. Ibid., p. 248.

5. Senator J. Robert Kerrey, C-SPAN2 tape of Senate Finance Committee Hearing on Retirement Income Policy, August 1998.

6. *1998 Annual Report of the Board of Trustees of the Federal Old-Age and Survivors Insurance and Disability Insurance Trust Funds*, p. 177.

7. Ibid.

8. Ibid. Calculations from raw numbers were developed by the authors.

9. Sylvester J. Schieber, "Retirement Income Adequacy at Risk," in Sylvester J. Schieber and John B. Shoven, eds., *Public Policy Toward Pensions* (Cambridge, Mass.: MIT Press, 1997), pp. 267–312.

10. Ibid.

11. James F. Moore and Olivia S. Mitchell, "Projected Retirement Wealth and Savings Adequacy in the Health and Retirement Study," paper presented at the 1998 Pension Research Council Symposium "Forecasting Retirement Needs and Retirement Wealth," April 27, 1998.

12. This can be found on Senator Moynihan's Internet web page at *http://www.senate.gov/~moynihan/jfkspch.html*.

13. Office of the Actuary, Social Security Administration.

Chapter 21: Wanting to Fund Is Not Enough

1. Transcript of the meeting of the 1994–1996 Advisory Council on Social Security held on February 10–11, 1995, Washington, D.C., pp. 269–270.

2. Thomas E. MaCurdy and John B. Shoven, "Stocks, Bonds, and Pension Wealth," in David A. Wise, ed., *Topics in the Economics of Aging* (Chicago: University of Chicago Press, 1992), pp. 61–75.

3. Roberta Romano, "Public Pension Fund Activism in Corporate Governance Reconsidered," *Columbia Law Review* (May 1993), pp. 795–853.

4. Ibid., pp. 798–799.

5. Ibid., pp. 801–810.

6. World Bank, *Averting the Old Age Crisis* (Oxford: Oxford University Press, 1994), p. 94.

7. Anil Netto, "Malaysia: Workers Unhappy over Management of Pension Fund," Inter Press Service, June 24, 1998.

8. Mukul G. Asher, "Investment Policies and Performance of Provident Funds in Southeast Asia," a paper prepared for the Economic Development Institute of the World Bank Workshop on Pension System Reform, Governance, and Fund Management, Yangzou City, Jiangsu Province, China, January 13–15, 1998.

9. World Bank, *Averting the Old Age Crisis*, p. 127.

10. Transcript of the meeting of the 1994–1996 Advisory Council on Social Security held on March 10–11, 1995, Washington, D.C., pp. 261–262.

11. Transcript of the meeting of the 1994–1996 Advisory Council on Social Security held on December 14, 1995, Washington, D.C., pp. 44–45.

12. Bruce Kelly, "CPP Readies for Equities: Rules for Canada's Social Security System Are Changing," *Pensions & Investments* (November 16, 1998), p. 16.

13. Robert M. Ball, with Thomas N. Bethell, *Straight Talk About Social Security* (New York: Century Foundation Press, 1998), p. 41.

14. Dean R. Leimer, "Cohort-Specific Measures of Lifetime Net Social Security

Transfers," ORS Working Paper Series, No. 59 (Washington, D.C.: Social Security Administration, February 1994).

15. Stephen C. Goss and Orlo R. Nichols, "OASDI Money's Worth Analysis for Hypothetical Cohorts—INFORMATION" (Office of the Actuary, Social Security Administration internal memorandum, March 1, 1993), p. 5.

16. Ibid., p. 72.

17. U.S. Department of Labor, Pension and Welfare Benefits Administration, *Private Pension Plan Bulletin* (Washington, D.C.: U.S. Department of Labor, spring 1998), No. 7.

18. Ibid.

19. Robert M. Ball, with Thomas N. Bethell, *Straight Talk About Social Security*, p. 43.

20. *Evaluating Issues in Privatizing Social Security*, report of the Panel on Privatization of Social Security (Washington, D.C.: National Academy of Social Insurance, November 1998), footnote 24.

21. Peter A. Diamond, "Social Security Reform in Chile: An Economist's Perspective," in Peter A. Diamond, David C. Lindeman, and Howard Young, eds., *Social Security: What Role for the Future?* (Washington, D.C.: National Academy of Social Insurance, 1996), p. 217.

22. Sylvester J. Schieber and John B. Shoven, "Administering a Cost-Effective National Program of Personal Security Accounts," paper presented at a conference of the National Bureau of Economic Research, Cambridge, Massachusetts, December 4, 1998.

23. HR Investment Consultants, *401(k) Provider Directory* (Baltimore, Md.: HR Investment Consultants, 1997).

24. Robert M. Ball, with Thomas N. Bethell, *Straight Talk About Social Security*, p. 47.

25. Social Security Advisory Board, *How SSA's Disability Programs Can Be Improved* (Washington, D.C.: Social Security Advisory Board, 1998).

26. Ibid., p. 45.

27. See Robert M. Ball, Edith U. Fierst, Gloria T. Johnson, Thomas W. Jones, George Kourpias, and Gerald M. Shea, "Social Security for the 21st Century: A Strategy to Maintain Benefits and Strengthen America's Family Protection Plan," *Report of the 1994–1996 Advisory Council on Social Security*, vol. 1: *Findings and Recommendations* (Washington, D.C.: Social Security Administration, 1997), p. 71.

28. Peter J. Ferrara and Michael Tanner, *A New Deal for Social Security* (Washington, D.C.: Cato Institute, 1998), pp. 184–194.

Chapter 22: The Benefits and Risks Under Alternative Forms
of Retirement Provision

1. See Robert M. Ball, Edith U. Fierst, Gloria T. Johnson, Thomas W. Jones, George Kourpias, and Gerald M. Shea, "Social Security for the 21st Century: A Strategy to Maintain Benefits and Strengthen America's Family Protection Plan," *Report of the 1994–1996 Advisory Council on Social Security*, vol. 1: *Findings and Recommendations* (Washington, D.C.: Social Security Administration, 1997), p. 69.

2. Robert M. Ball, with Thomas N. Bethell, *Straight Talk About Social Security* (New York: Century Foundation Press, 1998), p. 43.

3. Ibid., p. 45.

4. Henry J. Aaron and Robert D. Reischauer, *Countdown to Reform: The Great Social Security Debate* (New York: Century Foundation Press, 1998).

5. Thomas E. MaCurdy and John B. Shoven, "Asset Allocation and Risk Allocation: Can Social Security Improve Its Future Solvency Problem by Investing in Private Securities?" (Cambridge, Mass.: NBER Working Paper, 1999).

6. Gordon P. Goodfellow and Sylvester J. Schieber, "Simulating Benefit Levels Under Alternative Social Security Reform Approaches," in Olivia S. Mitchell, Robert J. Myers, and Howard Young, eds., *Prospects for Social Security Reform* (Philadelphia: University of Pennsylvania Press, 1999).

7. Henry J. Aaron, Barry P. Bosworth, and Gary Burtless, *Can America Afford to Grow Old? Paying for Social Security* (Washington, D.C.: Brookings Institution, 1989).

8. Ibid., p. 62.

Chapter 23: A Proposal for Reform

1. Henry J. Aaron, Barry P. Bosworth and Gary Burtless, *Can America Afford To Grow Old? Paying for Social Security* (Washington, D.C.: Brookings Institution, 1989).

2. Because one is either eligible for Medicare benefits or not, there is zero marginal benefit from additional payments of the Medicare portion of the payroll tax.

3. The distinction between employer and employee contributions is overblown, any way you look at it. In terms of who sends the money to the Treasury, all the checks come from employers. For the non-self-employed, the distinction is whether or not the payroll tax deduction shows up on the weekly or monthly paycheck (or on the annual W-2 form). Only half the money actually sent to the Treasury for OASDHI is shown on these forms; the other half is hidden from workers. Its being hidden wouldn't make any difference whatsoever if the personal income tax didn't treat the "employer" and the employee contribution differently. The employee half (the half that shows up on the paycheck stub and the W-2 form) is subject to personal income taxation, whereas the "employer" half is not.

4. Ibbotson Associates, *Stocks, Bonds, Bills and Inflation: 1998 Yearbook, Market Results for 1926-1997* (Chicago: Ibbotson Associates, 1998).

Chapter 24: It's Your Money We're Talking About

1. President William J. Clinton, speech given at Gaston Hall, Georgetown University, Washington, D.C., February 9, 1998, at *http://www.ssa.gov/history/clntstmts.html*.

2. Ibid.

3. Ibid.

Index